INTRIGUE

ALLAN HEPBURN

Intrigue

ESPIONAGE AND CULTURE

YALE UNIVERSITY PRESS   NEW HAVEN & LONDON

Set in FontShop Scala and Scala Sans by Duke & Company, Devon, Pennsylvania.

Printed in the United States of America.

Library of Congress Cataloging-in-Publication Data
Hepburn, Allan.
Intrigue : espionage and culture / Allan Hepburn.
p. cm.
Includes bibliographical references and index.
ISBN 0-300-10498-7 (alk. paper)
1. Spy stories, English—History and criticism. 2. American fiction—20th century—
History and criticism. 3. English fiction—20th century—History and criticism.
4. Spy stories, American—History and criticism. 5. Espionage, American—History—
20th century. 6. Espionage, British—History—20th century. 7. Spy films—History
and criticism. 8. Espionage in literature. 9. Spies in literature. I. Title.
PR888.S65H47 2004
823'.087209091—dc22
2004015680

A catalogue record for this book is available from the British Library.

The paper in this book meets the guidelines for permanence and durability of the Committee on Production Guidelines for Book Longevity of the Council on Library Resources.

10 9 8 7 6 5 4 3 2 1

This book is dedicated to the memory of my mother,
Audrey Hepburn, 1932–2002

CONTENTS

ACKNOWLEDGMENTS

MANY PEOPLE have supported the writing of this book. I have benefited immeasurably from the wisdom of colleagues at the University of Toronto and McGill University. At Toronto, Lora Carney, Caryl Clark, Brian Greenspan, Franca Iacovetta, Garry Leonard, Jill Matus, Andrew Patenall, Arthur Sheps, and Jude Seaboyer made teaching a daily pleasure. Members of WIPE (Works in Progress in English), especially Alan Buell, Brian Corman, Linda Hutcheon, and Heather Jackson, shared their interpretive finesse. Wesley Wark invited me to talk about espionage for a radio documentary broadcast on CJRT in Toronto. At McGill, Maggie Kilgour, a dauntless chair, welcomed me into the English Department. Brian Trehearne's distinction between ghosts of the dead and ghosts of the living altered my ideas about Conrad. Berkeley Kaite found research money when it was needed. Trevor Ponech graciously volunteered to read chapters. Leanore Lieblein reminded me of the intelligence-gatherers in Jonson's *Volpone*.

Several chapters were given in various venues as works-in-progress. I aired ideas about romance in *Democracy* at the Narrative Conference in Evanston in April 1998. A talk on *The Third Man* was given at the Narrative Conference in Atlanta in April 2000. I presented ideas about *The Heat of the Day* at "The Space Between" in London, Ontario, in May 2000. I dress-rehearsed the chapter on *Under Western Eyes* in ten minutes flat at the MLA in Chicago in December 1999. Other versions of that chapter were presented at the University of Western Ontario in March 1999 and at McGill University in February 2000. I addressed the Senior Alumni Association at the University of Toronto at Scarborough on the subject of collaboration in *Casablanca* and *Notorious* in April 2000. Will Straw invited me to talk about disappearances in *Sabbatical* for the "Traces" colloquium series at McGill in January 2002. I thank these organizations and people for their input, freely given.

Friends offered wit, glamour, gallantry, and unbridled opinions while I busied myself writing. Terry Brand sustained me with *sprezzatura* and nights on the town. Michael Ciciretto helped with references to 1950s and 1960s television, about which he knows everything. Maria DiBattista taught me to think *humanly* about narrative. Ann Gaylin sophisticated ideas. Audrey Hepburn, my mother, and Rachel Hepburn, my sister, lent moral support; I wish my mother had lived to see the completion of this project, and longer still. Lee Jacobson urged subtlety in my arguments. Mark Kingwell set a paradigm for thoughtful elegance. Gus Matute-Bello proved that $1 = 0$. Barbara Morris refreshed me with fishcakes and *conversazione*. Karen Mulhallen served chartreuse on the rocks in her enchanted garden on the last sunny sad day I spent in Toronto before I moved to Montreal. Barbara Shankland and Norman Ingram gave me the keys to *la belle province. Gil-Olivier Raynal m'a appris la vraie définition de la modestie—l'art de se faire complimenter deux fois—ainsi que l'histoire des chiffres. Gilles Beaudry m'a encouragé autant par sa précision cartésienne, sa patience, et son amour, que par les chansons qu'il a inventées et m'a chantées au téléphone.*

Five peerless researchers made writing this book easier. Brendan Robert, Jeremy Derksen, Lukas Lhotsky, Deena Yanofsky, and Liisa Stephenson deserve my warmest thanks. I have taught three courses on spy fiction: once at the University of Toronto in 1997 and twice at McGill in 2000 and in 2003. Students kindly indulged my ideas about accents, sewers, surveillance, leaks, codes, ghosts, death, and masculinity.

At Yale University Press, three anonymous reviewers thoughtfully advised me on ways to improve the manuscript. Lara Heimert, Heidi Downey, and Eliza Childs escorted this work through the press with tact and keen-eyed skill.

From 1990 to 1992, the Social Sciences and Humanities Research

Council of Canada generously funded a postdoctoral project called "Surveillance, Paranoia, and the Contemporary American Novel," out of which the present book, much changed, has grown.

INTRODUCTION

THIS BOOK deals with espionage narratives produced between 1900 and 2000. During the twentieth century, a period of formalized and unprecedented spying, cultural fantasies and deformations of history created a representational legacy of treachery, doubleness, and paranoia.

In literary representations, spies recall dissonance at the heart of ideological certainty. Throughout this book, I question whether identities associated with spying—recruits, moles, femmes fatales, double agents, leaks—come into being as historical phenomena or whether they exist prior to history and merely find expression within a culture of espionage. A spy may be born, not made: endowed with a desire to know, the spy extends innate human curiosity to realms of political intrigue. More likely, espionage creates identities; identities are historically contingent, not essential categories. Character gets inflected in spy narratives through social interaction and specific circumstances. Treason arises from one or more factors: "ideology, financial problems, disgruntlement on the job, the heady perfume of a double life, the power of being the keeper of secrets, the attention bestowed on an anxious agent by his handlers . . . , twists of childhood or biology" (Goode 1). The spy's identity is contingent, too, on violence as a cause for social change. The spies and anarchists in Joseph Conrad's 1907 novel *The Secret Agent* would be nothing without their dynamite and nitroglycerine. Knowing that his identity is historically contingent, the spy plays up the theatricality of his role and the pliancy of his affiliations.

Spies flicker and vanish through the pages of novels by Erskine Childers, Joseph Conrad, John Buchan, Graham Greene, Len Deighton, Ian Fleming, Ken Follett, Somerset Maugham, Elizabeth Bowen, John le Carré, and numerous other writers. Spies also have a ubiquitous presence in cinema. Such films as *Spione* (1928), *The Lady Vanishes* (1938), *The Ministry of Fear* (1944), *Notorious* (1946), *Diamonds Are Forever* (1971), *The Day of the Jackal* (1973), *Three Days of the Condor* (1975), *No Way Out* (1987), *La Femme Nikita* (1990), and *Spy Games* (2002), to cite a handful of examples, all represent secret agents. In a medium seldom analyzed for its relation to paranoid fantasies, television spies had a heyday in the 1960s and 1970s as Cold Warriors. *The Avengers, Rocky and Bullwinkle, Mission: Impossible, Get Smart, The Man From U.N.C.L.E.*, and *The Six Million Dollar Man* feature a gamut of friendly and not-so-friendly agents. In all of these media, spies tend to be male, but they are not exclusively so. They traffic in secrets. Fearing for their lives, they turn tail and run in the face of danger. Or they chase others. Spies work for acronymic intelligence organizations such as MI6 or the CIA or the KGB. Recruited into these organizations, spies challenge narrow definitions of political agency. Ideology produces spies, but spies, like most people, temper ideology with private motives. Intrigue occurs where psychological and ideological commitments overlap and mask each other. The spy embodies ambiguous allegiances, some declared, some concealed. The spy therefore stands as a cipher for conflicts waged among national, international, familial, human, humanitarian, ethical, and romantic identities. A marionette in the theater of competing interests, the spy improvises roles by drawing on one or more of these identities at any given time. Acting a part, the twentieth-century fictional spy tells us that authenticity may be irrelevant to commitment or character. Indeed, a spy's identity is often an illusion.

Oriented towards theories of psychoanalysis, trauma, gender, narratology, and the representation of death, this book examines codes and conducts of behavior in intrigue narratives. In my choice of examples, I migrate between literary and mass-market fiction. I do not offer an introduction to espionage literature since others have done so with expertise (Gardner 70–80; C. Bloom 1–11). Nor do I describe how espionage agencies evolve, since many studies already convey the minute details and broad history of twentieth-century security. Instead, this study elaborates cultural and literary contexts in which to interpret clandestine plots. When I refer to espionage narratives, my chief object of investigation is the spy as a locus for cultural fantasies. "Culture," for my purposes, means the nexus of narratives, institutions, practices, values, spaces, habits, and customs that shape human activities in material and symbolic forms. "Intrigue," as a cultural formation, refers to twentieth-century reinforcement of spying as an activity through novels and films, as well as through laws, secret defense services, defections, the digging of tunnels, the building of walls, the evolution of technology, and so forth. Although I focus on literary examples, I wish to imply that historical events, such as the defection of Kim Philby or the construction of the Berlin Wall, contribute to the culture of intrigue. The spy, then, is a symptomatic manifestation of ideologies that play out as historical events and as representations in fiction and film. I interpret espionage narratives in order to access some of the dimensions of the culture of intrigue, broadly conceived.

In some of the novels that I discuss, such as *The Third Man,* spies are incidental or merge with policemen; in other works, such as *The Man Who Came in From the Cold,* clandestine activities are central to the plot and contribute to narratives that withhold information, advance clues or hunches, collude with certain characters but not with others. Some spy novels are set in the past, as if to provide a genealogy of espionage. For example, Ken Follett's *The Man From St. Petersburg,* published in 1983, takes place in the summer of 1914. Historical distance allows readers to see the advantages of living safely in the present since dangers in the past have been eradicated. Most of the narratives that I examine, however, are located in roughly contemporary time and therefore promote a conception of the thriller as a commentary on politics. As the expression of wish fulfillment, narratives of intrigue allow readers to engage their political imaginaries, to speculate on the nature of statehood and citizenship. As documents of recruitment and survival, spy narratives allegorize civic responsibility by figuring competing loyalties to one's country, one's family, or oneself.

In part 1 of this book, I discuss the aesthetics of spy narratives. The initial trauma in narratives of intrigue may be the shocked recognition that the body cannot be relinquished. Whatever invisibility a spy may have or may desire, he can never disappear entirely. He is spectral, but he is not dead. Spies express ambivalence about whether death prowls the world or lurks in the body. Fear of death and fear of being caught motivate spies' actions. Yet no adequate definition of fear as an aesthetic effect exists, especially when aesthetic effects have a political valence. Fear has its own proprieties and consequences. I define the cathartic implications of fear and thrills, which bring various individuals—readers, deviants, spies— into line with dominant ideology. The thrill, a bodily event, destabilizes individuals and frequently results in conformity with, not revolt against, the state. In the thrill, catharsis is neither ideologically neutral nor aesthetically pure. Spy thrillers imply that political commitments are ambiguous, in that spies rarely adhere to a single ideology. They manipulate social and political codes to their advantage, and their bodies are made to signify, in encoded fashion, split allegiances. I therefore turn to the problem of encryption in texts of intrigue. Espionage plots provide rules for their decipherment, a user's guide as it were, to help the fit reader read aright. Figured as games or puzzles, espionage narratives blur meaningful details with meaningless details. Interpretation requires vigilant separation of truth from lies. I conclude that reading, as a hermeneutical exercise, leads to a discovery of mortality within encrypted texts.

In part 2, I investigate the representation of spies' bodies in British and Irish novels. Conrad's obsession with ghosts is given extra heft in *Under Western Eyes,* a novel about unwanted recruitment into a spying mission, because the protagonist Razumov is, literally, a bastard. Abandoned to the state, Razumov works for the police in Russia against his will. Ghostliness represents an evacuation of corporeality and responsibilities in *Under Western Eyes.* Preoccupation with ghosts and death runs through many spy novels as a way of figuring the insoluble riddle of commitment. A chapter on Graham Greene's *The Third Man* evaluates the imperiled body of an underground racketeer. Greene's novella concludes with a chase through the sewers of Vienna. Fantasies of dread and pursuit concern culpability and the desire to be caught, whether those fantasies are rooted in political guilt or personal terror. Although chases embody the flight towards or flight from commitment, not all spy fiction treats commitment as a physical event. In Elizabeth Bowen's *The Heat of the Day,* a woman is implicated in a love affair with a spy. She is recruited via her sentiments, not via her rational beliefs, which indicates that commitment need not mean choosing sides consciously. Memory and haunting reinforce the espionage paradigm of pasts that rear up to afflict those who have collaborated, knowingly or unknowingly. Because loved, a spy is not necessarily reliable. The spy's body may be cherished as a body without being cherished for the political beliefs that the spy harbors. Spies' bodies signify differently in other narratives. In John le Carré's *The Spy Who Came in From the Cold*, an aging, dissolute agent is sacrificed to East versus West politics. In this novel, walls signify obstacles to understanding in both political and personal domains; the wall, an absolute impasse, prevents ideologies from blending with each other. A chapter on John Banville's *The Untouchable* relates the gay spy's body to the history of the Cambridge spies and concepts of masculinity. Although the gay spy is accused of leaking information and being unfirm in his alliances, he exposes the ideological biases of heterosexual spies, who often let passion lead them into disclosure of secrets even while they maintain a rigid denial of pleasure.

In part 3, I turn to the cross-fertilization of American romance with spy narratives. In John Barth's *Sabbatical*, the spy disappears and his body is never recovered. The motif of disappearance dominates spy literature and becomes, in this case, a trope for absentee, mystical authority associated with the CIA. Finally, in a chapter on Joan Didion's *Democracy*, I resume a consideration of space, inaugurated in my discussions of sewers in *The Third Man* and walls in *The Spy Who Came in From the Cold*, by interpreting travel as a sign of vacillation. In *Democracy*, a CIA agent named Jack Lovett glides in and out of the representational frame of the novel. The spy, by definition, eludes representation. As a skeptical postmodern romance, *Democracy* reveals that action is based on illusion, not conviction, on romance conventions, not politics per se.

PART ONE ON BEING THRILLED

CHAPTER ONE

Spies

THE SPY'S BODY

A body floats in the Mediterranean Sea in the opening chapter of Robert Ludlum's 1980 spy thriller *The Bourne Identity*. Although the man—for the body is male—appears "fully drowned, passed from this world" (10), he is still alive. The man clings to a piece of debris until fishermen pull him out of the water. He is unconscious, with bullets lodged in his chest, legs, and stomach. Another and more dangerous bullet in his head has caused him to lose his memory. The fishermen expect the wounded man to become "a corpse" (11) before he reaches a doctor. Saved by some tricky surgical intervention, the amnesiac turns out to be a CIA agent who has been working undercover for three years. The agent, because he has lost his memory, does not understand what he does, why he knows what he knows, or who he is. *"What's left when your memory's gone? And your identity"* (204), he wonders. He deduces his mission through partial clues. While pretending to be a killer, the agent is actually trying to flush out a notorious assassin named Carlos. Pursued from Marseilles to Zurich to Paris and, in the final pages of the novel, to New York, the agent acts from instinct, rather than knowledge. Suspecting a doublecross, some of his operators at the CIA turn against him because they do not know he has lost his memory. Ludlum's narrative thus positions the agent as a political subject who does not understand the reasons that animate his political

3

subjectivity. *The Bourne Identity*, as a narrative of intrigue, represents the relation of character to action as a puzzle. Intrigue means the underhanded machinations of the state, though it refers equally—in Ludlum's thriller and in spy fiction generally—to the fundamental obscurity of identity in relation to convictions, belonging, citizenship, and agency.

The agent in Ludlum's novel has several aliases, including Washburn, Chamford, Jason Bourne, Cain, and Delta. His real name is David Webb. His surname alludes to the multiple interconnected identities that combine in one character—killer and husband, spy and teacher—as well as the conspiracy masterminded by the CIA that covers the entire globe and connects seemingly disparate events. If we call this character "Bourne," as the title of the novel urges us to do, we cannot lose sight of the way that "Bourne" harnesses together multiple identities that have been adopted and discarded. Through a debriefing at the end of the novel, we learn that David Webb worked as a "foreign service officer, a specialist in Far Eastern affairs" (532). We also learn that his Thai wife and two children were strafed by a "stray aircraft" (532) in Cambodia during the Vietnam War. Their deaths cause Webb to head for Saigon and train as a tactical murderer. Further deaths vindicate the deaths in his family, according to Webb's logic. Acquiring his first code name, David Webb becomes "Delta" (532) in an operation called Medusa, a unit of mercenaries responsible for assassinations and brutal missions in the Vietnam jungle. On March 25, 1968, Delta, on a mission in the Tam Quan sector, kills a traitor within the Medusa unit. That traitor's name is Jason Bourne. Several years later, David "Delta" Webb, created as an undercover agent by the CIA, assumes "'the name of the man he had killed in Tam Quan'" (533), which is to say that he puts himself in the place of death by naming himself after someone he executed: Jason Bourne. He incarnates death and he acts as the agent of death. Webb, turned Delta, turned Bourne, acquires the name Cain for the CIA operation, an identity intended to wipe out Webb and Delta and replace them with the encoded, recessive identity of a dead man. On one hand, the resuscitated Jason Bourne "'was never real'" (367). On the other hand, he is "'a functioning microcosm of us all'" (535). He blends other identities within himself. Formed by agonistic forces, Bourne combats underworld assassins, the CIA, and his own partly erased past. His multiple names indicate that no single representation of a straightforward self exists and that political identity is a code for conflicted allegiances.

Ludlum's novel can be taken as representative of spy fiction. *The Bourne Identity* defines political subjectivity as a mysterious, if thrilling, set of contradictions—mysterious principally to the agent who lives out the consequences of those contradictions. While exploiting espionage tropes of recruitment, codes, thrills, chases, fear, bodily durability, violence, enmity, darkness, and disappearance, *The Bourne Identity* suggests that every corpse has a position in history. As with another body found floating off the coast of Portugal during World War II, a body planted with false papers meant to find their way to the German embassy in Lisbon (293), Bourne's body bears plural meanings, none of which cancels or preempts others. He may be a rogue agent. He may have recidivist tendencies to murder after he leaves Vietnam. He may be a particularly effective and loyal CIA agent. The interest of this thriller resides not so much in the determinants of Bourne's character, but in the conditions that make political identity narratable, which is to say "the instances of disequilibrium, suspense, and general insufficiency from which a given narrative appears to arise" (Miller, *Narrative* ix). Bourne himself narrates his life in several fashions (332). He ultimately pens "a confession" (501) to explain his actions. Narratability in *The Bourne Identity* depends on finding a way to describe the out-of-joint relation of individual to state. Disequilibrium in the political order brings Bourne into being as a narratable entity. By breaking laws, Bourne enters into representation. He is guilty of assassination presumably for a just cause. Although he is recruited into murderousness to avenge the deaths of his wife and children, the CIA channels that murderousness for the good of the state. Ironically, his alienation from the state makes him an upholder of the state. Bourne moves "'beyond the laws'" (327) in order to trap law-breaking Carlos.

In this sense, novels of intrigue involving spies provide speculations on the duties of citizenship. Certain unjust acts, if undertaken rationally to combat other unjust acts, are not judged by universal laws but according to the contexts in which they transpire. One of the duties of citizenship is the testing of laws to prove their worthiness or unworthiness, their contextual or universal applicability. Not all laws are just for all citizens; not all citizens, certainly, perceive all laws to be just. Spy novels worry about the disequilibrium of justice for individuals over and against justice for a polity. Should a citizen remain faithful to a political regime that denies liberties to its citizens? Spies are emblems of doubt insofar as they live at a distance from conviction and keep testing allegiances. Lukács in *The Theory of the Novel* sees characters take form in the "gap" or "chasm" (78) between the inner world (of soul-making, of feeling, of desire) and the outer world (of conflict, of structure, of society). Secret agents thrive in that gap, which stands, at least in espionage literature, for the distance between conviction and responsibility.

Lukács theorizes that the novel as a genre expresses difference from dominant ideology on the grounds that novels represent the nonconformity of individuals within regimes of social reality. In *The Theory of the Novel,* Lukács, speaking of *Wilhelm Meister,* claims that "a reconciliation between interiority and reality, although problematic, is nevertheless possible" (132). An "incommensurability" (Lukács 97) between interior worlds and external worlds drives novels. Yet characters are not invariably antithetical in their predispositions towards ideology. Inner worlds sometimes extend or confirm outer worlds, even if a character appears at odds with external reality. Although agents sometimes act as renegades within the bureaucracies for which they work, they do not view their actions as inevitably incommensurate with external worlds. Conflicts arise, but dominant ideology asserts itself in the end. In the case of *The Bourne Identity,* the outer world is a morass of financial intrigue and globalized money. The novel is rife with references to capital and its international migrations. Bourne transfers funds from a Swiss bank to untraceable accounts. He crashes a conference of economists in Zurich. He aims to "undercut [Carlos's] prices" for assassinations (428), as if murder were a purely lucrative enterprise without other ramifications. Throughout the novel, the narrator gives a precise accounting of Bourne's tips and payments: how much for a couturier dress, how much for a taxi, how much for a telephone call. Michael Denning claims that spies function as cryptocapitalists: "the intelligence community serves as a shadowy figure for the social world of late capitalism where the opacities that surround human agency are cut through by projecting an essentially marginal figure, the secret agent" (29). Analogies between capitalists and spies are proven by Bourne's financial savvy, including his supposed embezzlement of CIA funds. Moreover, the number of his Swiss bank account is implanted under his skin on a microchip: "ZERO-SEVEN-SEVENTEEN-TWELVE-ZERO-FOURTEEN-TWENTY-SIX-ZERO" (19). He is literally written into capitalist ideology as a code for an account. The same handwritten numbers serve as Bourne's "signature" (19). His bank account, subcutaneous and ciphered, confirms his identity when he cannot do so otherwise because of memory loss. Yet Bourne, as an agent, transcends the spy's capitalistic function as defined by Denning. Money does not motivate him. Rather, Bourne incarnates the ways that individuals are recruited into ideology and deploy violence in order to serve personal motives as well as the common good.

The CIA recruits Bourne because of his antipathy for the government. Notwithstanding his career as a foreign service officer and soldier, Bourne feels alienated from his government and its foreign policy: "'He hated that war [in Vietnam], hated everybody in it'" (325). Hatred prompts physical violence, even though the object of his rage is not always precise. He lashes out reflexively, not rationally. Many men in *The Bourne Identity* erupt in anger or frustration because of the way things are done. The eyes of an outraged French general widen with "uncompromising abhorrence" (355). Hatred animates Alfred Gillette, a "vindictive" (227) mole whose "resent-[ment]" (302) goads him into selling secrets to enemies of the CIA. Conklin, a Vietnam veteran, is a "coiled spring of anger" (322). The jaw muscles of Brigadier General Crawford "puls[e] in anger" (323). Bourne, "swept by feelings of anger and futility" (352), hates men who wage war. Like other characters, Bourne is recruited into spying because he cannot contain his hostility. His vendetta originates in personal feelings—grief and rage over the death of his family—yet his actions, especially taking out underworld assassins, protect others.

Anger in itself does not tip the balance of power in the novel. In fact, anger might be read as a symptom of democracy in that the imperfect workings of the state (in this case, the United States) alienate individuals. As a post-Watergate novel, *The Bourne Identity* detects corruption within the branches of the government. Whereas Marie St. Jacques harshly assesses "mindless, stupid men" (514) at the CIA, General Brigadier Crawford opines tolerantly that the CIA is filled with "'flawed but decent'" (507) individuals. Both assessments may prove true in that a citizen can be both stupid and decent at the same time. The more urgent question posed by *The Bourne Identity*, however, touches on espionage intelligence and its justifiability as a mechanism of state security. Liberal theories, including John Rawls's, emphasize consensus and reasonableness as necessary elements in the definition of democracy. Rawls describes an overlapping consensus within a pluralist polity that, "despite its deep divisions, [might] achieve stability and social unity by the public recognition of a reasonable political conception of justice" (423). Rawls connects such consensus to an "idea of free public reason" (442). Of course spies do not work only within the parameters of liberal democracy. Nor does espionage function according to consensus or reasonableness founded in public debate. Spies work alone and outside the law. Spying therefore appears to position the putative good of the public ahead of justice. The anger expressed by CIA agents and army officers in *The Bourne Identity* might be attributed to discrepancies between the just and the good. Bourne acts independently, as if his judgments require no validation by the state that he serves. In common with other spy thrillers, *The Bourne Identity* renders anger and its manifestations in violence—shoot-outs, deaths, broken limbs—as an alternative style of democracy, namely, a democracy that avows antagonism as a form of dissent. Chantal Mouffe argues that "far from jeopardizing democracy, agonistic confrontation is in fact its very condition of possibility" (92). Mouffe considers antagonism and violence as constitutive of democracy and catalytic in the process of shaping politics according to felt public needs. Democracies must change over time to reflect changes in the citizenry, and hostility is one way to promote change. Narratives of intrigue, through their representation of angered recruitment and lethal violence, typically speculate on what constitutes an individual's belonging to a political order. An American, Jason Bourne affirms his loathing for America. Bourne's flashpoint irritability may be interpreted as his dissent that finds no other medium for expression. Violent action registers Bourne's clashes with the state and its apparatuses. The instances of violence in *The Bourne Identity* bespeak anterior instances of injustice—such as the random killing of Bourne's civilian wife and children, the war in Vietnam, and the murky machinations of an espionage outfit that functions beyond public cognizance. If narrative arises because of disequilibrium or insufficiency, spy narratives arise from a disequilibrium between the individual and the regime within whose ideology the spy lives and from which he dissents.

Anger produces bodily effects, such as pulsing jaw muscles and widened eyes, as well as more dangerous consequences, such as gunfights and chases. Like most spy novels, *The Bourne Identity* demonstrates that clandestine agency requires a body. If, as I have suggested, the spy emblematizes disagreement with ideology, that disagreement can be measured by harm inflicted on the spy's person. After being pulled from the sea, Bourne recuperates for months at a doctor's house. Once he is back in commission, he gets mixed up in a series of fights that involve different degrees of violence. A goon smashes Bourne's left hand with a pistol. During a subsequent gunfight, Bourne tears apart scarcely healed muscles and tissue. Injured again, he limps and grimaces in pain. In another skirmish, he takes a bullet in the shoulder and another grazes his head: "areas of his body had frozen. Although the penetration in his shoulder and the graze at his temple were real and painful, neither was serious enough to immobilize him" (104). Still mobile despite these wounds, he gets caught in other battles. A piece of steel gashes his neck: "blood erupted" (122). In Paris, a beggar shoots at Bourne and narrowly misses (411). In New York, a marksman, aiming at Bourne, kills a taxi driver by mistake (504). In a hand-to-hand fight with Carlos, the renegade killer fires his gun repeatedly at Bourne: "hot needles slicing across his neck, piercing his legs, cutting up to his waist" (528). In all of these grim encounters, the spy's body —invincible, resourceful—enters into a signifying process that is political. Bourne calls blood pouring from a wound "a warning" (525). He means that he has little time to finish fighting Carlos. But we can interpret the "warning" as the proximity of Bourne to the sources of corruption (Carlos and the CIA) that have placed him in such a precarious position. His operators leave him more or less unprotected. Political exigency is felt as bodily pain—a different kind of warning, whether to desist or to persevere. The warning might be read as the moment when the spy realizes his body is not indomitable, nor are the interests that he represents. To annihilate the spy entails the annihilation of his politics. Pain brings the spy's body into being at the moment that pain threatens to eradicate that body once and for all.

The spy's body is thus a site of contradictions. Visible to narrative, the spy should, by all accounts, remain invisible. Bourne claims that his "entire strategy was based on darkness" (504). On numerous occasions, he imagines that he can just "disappear, and not look back," as he tells Marie St. Jacques (198). Bourne's name appears on a list of Medusa mercenaries who "'vanished without a trace'" (243). He vows to "find a way to disappear" (270). Marie accuses him of wanting to flee to spare her harm: "'You will heroically disappear'" (333), she says balefully. No photographs of Bourne circulate in the press, despite his international reputation as an assassin. His enemies wonder what he looks like (113). This anonymity keeps him alive, since a target without a recognizable face or physique is not much of a target. Lacking a definite physical profile, he has, in a sense, already vanished. To enhance his anonymity, he has cosmetic surgery that alters his appearance. Weirdly, because he has adopted the identity of a dead Australian narcotics dealer and mercenary (the original Bourne), Bourne possesses a body that is never entirely his own. When he wonders how to decipher his identity after losing his memory, he has to factor in the problem of having lost his body as well, in a manner of speaking. The body and the death of the original Jason Bourne ghost the body and the actions of the second Jason Bourne. Death twins the spy's body, making that body spectral. By an opposite momentum, fights and violent acts require Bourne to have a body. Violence produces him as a political subject. Bourne's identity resides in tension between shadowiness and visibility, anonymity and recognition. Bourne tries to shed his body, just as he tries to shed his identity. Indeed, the narrative plays up the fantastic side of disappearance and invisibility when Bourne's unmistakable, unique fingerprints are found on a glass at a murder site in New York while the reader knows that Bourne is still in Paris (324). In fact, the actual murderer has planted the fingerprints. Never having been in New York, Bourne leaves traces of his physical presence, even if falsely planted. The body dissociates from itself, leaving vestiges to indicate its passing. If identity is housed in the body, and if that body shirks its identity by going undercover or by disappearing into darkness, the body is also required as a political effect, as *The Bourne Identity* intimates. There is no political identity without a body, just as, conversely, there is no body without a political identity. The numbers implanted on a microchip in Bourne's hip suggest that the spy's identity is always a riddle that, once solved, will prove that the body is not itself, but rather the container of other selves. Like other spy thrillers, *The Bourne Identity* makes the narration of the body meaningful within a political paradigm.

A POCKET GUIDE TO ESPIONAGE

The Bourne Identity does not originate tropes of hatred, disappearance, and recruitment. They belong to the thriller genre from its inception and migrate into British, Irish, and American spy narratives over the course of the twentieth century.[1] As a genre distinct from detective fiction and realist novels, spy narratives come into their own in the first decade of the twentieth century in works by William Le Queux, Erskine Childers,

E. Phillips Oppenheim, and Joseph Conrad. These political writers address Edwardian unease about national security (Stafford, "Spies" 494–502; Stafford, *Silent Game* 8–13; Trotter, "Politics" 30–54; Hiley 55–59). Fearing the end of the empire and the encroachment of foreigners into the United Kingdom, Edwardians suffered from xenophobic paranoia (Hynes, *Edwardian* 33–34). The Home Office, having started an unofficial register of aliens living in the United Kingdom in the first decade of the twentieth century, listed 28,300 people as nonnationals (French 360). The Official Secrets Act of 1910, ostensibly meant to suppress leaks of naval and military information, actually facilitated prosecution of spies on "scanty" evidence (French 361). The origins of MI5 and MI6, the agencies responsible for domestic and international security in England, can be traced to the formation of a secret service in 1909. The policing of boundaries became a means of calculating differences between natives and aliens. By traversing borders, the spy paradoxically challenges frontier mentality and reinforces nationalist interests by keeping boundaries intact.

Intrigue plots create and manage crises of belonging. In effect, a spy belongs nowhere. In Edwardian fiction, crises are instigated outside British national borders by French, German, Japanese, Russian, or Eastern European characters, or from within by anarchists, suffragettes, communists, revolutionaries, or terrorists. Invasion tales published by William Le Queux predict attacks by French militia (in the 1894 novel *The Great War in England in 1897*) and by German forces (in the 1909 novel *Spies of the Kaiser*). Le Queux varies the enemy according to shifting alliances and animosities: now French, now German. Threat from without also animates Erskine Childers's 1903 novel *The Riddle of the Sands,* in which two duffers named Carruthers and Davies, cruising in the North Sea among the Frisian Islands, uncover a plot fostered by Herr Dollmann, a British navy officer gone bad. Although British, Dollmann adopts a German moniker and worldview, a disguise of foreignness that masks his hostility for the United Kingdom. The foreign invader thus externalizes the pressures of conforming to a strict ideology that citizens may or may not be able to uphold.

The Edwardian thriller creates ways of representing the spy's body that carry through the twentieth century. Fear of invasion from *without* in Childers's novel masks dangerous doubleness *within* the body politic and within the body itself. Paranoia concerning allegiance and commitment appears on the body as a telltale sign. Carruthers and Davies read bodies for clues about motive and allegiance. They scrutinize tics, gestures, scars, and accents that belie treachery in their foes. Not fully in charge of its desires and convictions, the spy's body announces various kinds of treachery. Davies observes a weal on villainous von Brüning's forehead that indicates he has been up to mischief (Childers 209), and von Brüning himself keenly watches Carruthers and Davies for slipups in their alibi (Childers 208–11). Both sides suspect that the other is hatching plots, and the way to uncover those plots is through a scrupulous monitoring of the body. By contrast to the dubious performance of German spies, Davies "was convincing, because he was himself" (Childers 134). According to the laws of spy narratives, the subject has no control over physical manifestations of identity. The spy's body registers national identities in physical characteristics, voice, and gestures. Vigilant Davies notices a twang of nonnative German in Fräulein Dollmann's voice: "By her voice, when she spoke, I knew that she must have talked German habitually from childhood; diction and accent were faultless, at least to my English ear; but the native constitutional ring was wanting" (Childers 157). Her voice belies her inauthenticity. A "native" ring prohibits even the fully bilingual foreigner from passing as a real German. Although English, Carruthers gibbers like a gibbon in German and licenses himself to judge others' Teutonic credentials. Fräulein Dollmann, her suspicious accent having been detected, may well be an Englishwoman gone over to the enemies' camp, as her father has.

Spies tend to speak several languages. James Bond gets by nicely in French and German. Charles Latimer in Eric Ambler's *A Coffin for Dimitrios* speaks modern Greek but not, he specifies ruefully, Bulgarian. Dimitrios's accent betrays him; he "was aware of the ugliness of his voice and tried to conceal it. He failed" (Ambler 249). In *The Bourne Identity*, Bourne speaks English, French, and smatterings of unspecified Asian languages, but not Russian. Bourne, from time to time, has to "'rough up [his] French. Mispronounce a few words'" (Ludlum 164). Roughed up, the voice cannot always be interpreted as a reliable indicator of nationality. Bourne adopts a double disguise for his voice. Despite being an American who speaks flawless French, he pretends to be an American with an imperfect command of foreign mores and subtleties. In many spy novels, including *The Riddle of the Sands, A Coffin for Dimitrios,* and *The Bourne Identity,* facility with language taps into a semiotics of duplicity: if the voice signifies authenticity, then the spy, speaking a foreign tongue, is never just himself, but an unrecognizable alien lodged within a recognizable body.

Disguise extends to profession as well. The polyglot spy often teaches to enhance his cover as an ordinary person. In *The Bourne Identity,* David Webb, prior to becoming Jason Bourne, teaches at a "'small college in New Hampshire'" (Ludlum 533). Latimer in *A Coffin for Dimitrios* is "a lecturer in political economy at a minor English university" (Ambler 4) before he takes up writing detective novels. Once he achieves success as a novelist, Latimer quits his university job and does some amateur detection into the identity of Dimitrios. Even in the midst of his haphazard investigation, he retains his scholarly habits of defensiveness: "He had come to regard Dimitrios as his own property, a problem as academic as that of the authorship of an anonymous sixteenth century lyric" (Ambler 109). In John le Carré's novels, George Smiley, drawn from "dubious retirement" (*Smiley's People* 11) to solve counterespionage plots, has a scholar's manner. A spymaster with a mind for puzzles, Smiley seems "to have come into the world fully educated at the age of eighteen. Obscurity was his nature, as well as his profession" (le Carré, *A Murder of Quality* 222). As a manifestation of his obscurity, he reads philology and eighteenth-century German poetry. In John Banville's *The Untouchable,* the spy Victor Maskell is a world-renowned expert in the paintings of Nicolas Poussin, director of an art institute, and a teacher. Spies spend a lot of time in libraries or surrounded by books. In the film *Three Days of the Condor,* Robert Redford plays a character who works among books at an unassuming historical institute in Manhattan, a cover paid for by the CIA. In John Barth's *Sabbatical,* Professor Susan Seckler, sister-in-law of a spy and wife of a former spy, teaches English literature. Scholarly spies or spy-handlers recapitulate the Cartesian separation of brain and brawn. Thoughtful and shambling, they compensate for their lack of athleticism with superior tactical maneuvering. From behind the scenes, smart spies handle spies working in the field.

Whether cruising in the North Sea or teaching at a prep school, the spy allegorizes political crosscurrents and acts of commitment that otherwise remain incomprehensible or unrepresentable. The spy's appeal is his ambiguity, his articulation of doubts, violence, and mixed motives. The spy's body—a vessel, a valise, a vault—contains hidden allegiances and predispositions. Disguised as a meek professor or ordinary bloke, the spy conceals his corporeality because it is a liability to his mission as an agent. His body may be imperfect, but he must lug it with him wherever he goes. As Peter Brooks points out in *Body Work,* the Cartesian dualism of a thinking entity distinct from a corporeal entity "creates a body that is no longer 'in' language but rather the object of discourse" (5). Language and physicality oppose each other. As an agent of secrets, the spy dwells in the cleavage between rationality and corporeality. Typically, the spy represses desires that issue from the body, including sexual desires and the desire to commit to a single purpose. The spy's body expresses a dialectic of mind over body, in which the body executes orders issued from the brain, command post of the human organism. Pursued and tortured, the body actualizes agency, while the mind, by contrast, becomes the domain of an unimaginable, uncertain freedom. The spy's body is phantasmatic, more imagined than real in terms of the desires that animate it.

Brooks argues that the body generates narrative: "modern narratives appear to produce a semioticization of the body which is matched by a somatization of story" (xii). Bodies, in other words, give rise to stories and signification. It is, at the same time, very hard to conceive of a story without a body. In extension of this principle, narratives of intrigue represent the spy's body in unusual ways by comparison with other narratives or generic types. Semiotics of the spy's body include his idiosyncratic relation to libidinal energies. The spy frequently resists pleasure or separates it from his clandestine activities. Or, as in the allegations leveled at Mata Hari and Christine Keeler, sex is deemed useful as a means to obtain information. The spy, subject to sexual predation by "fem-bots" in the Austin Powers movie *The Spy Who Shagged Me* or the allurements of duplicitous women in any of Ian Fleming's novels, relaxes too much when confronted with sexual opportunity, in part because sex is bracketed off from duty in the minds of men. Bond has to learn over and over again that women can be agents too, because his conception of masculinity forbids such a recognition. Bond is never depleted by sex, nor is he impressed *enough* by the voluptuous women who offer themselves to him, since they regularly turn out to be duplicitous.[2]

Reading sex and romance in spy narratives allows us to see how the male spy's body figures as invulnerable to sentiment, including the sentiments of effeminacy, happiness, sadness, or charm. Love is a weakness for the male spy; sex, a betrayal. Love or sex figures as a pause in the momentum of intrigue narratives, a reward for punishments inflicted on the

male body. The spy does not typically seek romance, although it arises
with great frequency as a compensation for the spy's disconnectedness
from communities and social orders. Being out in the cold leads to a desire to come in from the cold. With great frequency, romance contributes
to the downfall of the spy: in *Under Western Eyes*, in *The Heat of the Day*,
in *The Spy Who Came in From the Cold*, and other narratives. In *The Bourne
Identity*, sex and love are incidental to Bourne's quest to find out who he
is. Pursued by killers, Bourne initially uses Marie St. Jacques, a French-
Canadian economist, as a body shield. Pursued by killers, he propels St.
Jacques through a dark auditorium. Although terrified at first by her ab-
ductor, St. Jacques falls in love with Bourne when she sees latent generosity in his eyes. On the day that he threatens to kill her if she disobeys
his orders, he also saves her from being raped and murdered, a double
crime that she subsequently puts from her mind with alarming efficiency.
Thereafter she refuses to leave him. Within a matter of days, the two refer
to each other as "'darling'" and declare with feeling, "'I love you'" (Ludlum
394). Bourne seems to fall in love because of inexperience. As an amnesiac,
he cannot connect St. Jacques with any other woman: "He had no memory
of a woman and, perhaps because he had none she was everything he
could imagine; everything and much, much more. She repelled the darkness for him. She stopped the pain" (145). No longer a body shield protecting Bourne from bullets, St. Jacques becomes a metaphorical shield protecting Bourne from emotional and remembered pain. While they nestle
together, she carefully avoids rubbing or knocking against the wound in
his shoulder. Touching as this circumspect and very male-centered version
of eros might be, it should not occlude the strange relationship between
wounds, masculinity, and libido. The male spy has sex not because it interests him, but because it proves that his wounds cannot interfere with his
mobility. St. Jacques's lust is a mirror of Bourne's; she expresses desire to
reward him for having saved her. St. Jacques is still with Bourne at the
end of the novel, which differentiates this narrative from other spy stories.
Usually closure in spy novels occurs with the death of the spy, the death
of the woman who accompanies him, or their irreparable separation. The
male spy therefore steels himself against romance or any emotional entanglement to avoid compromising his political duty.

The spy enhances his masculinity and invincibility with technology.
Bourne constantly places phone calls from shifting locations. Long-distance

technology supplements his senses. Technology makes human eyes, ears, and limbs more powerful by leaving an impression of the spy's ubiquity. The most common technology in spy novels is the gun, so often represented and so typically the expression of violence that its irreality as a symbolic marker almost goes unnoticed. Bourne relies on various guns—instruments that inflict destruction while maintaining distance—to preserve his invisibility. As with Almásy who flies his plane over the North African desert to reconnoiter the terrain in Michael Ondaatje's *The English Patient*, or the Russian diplomat who smuggles a camera into the "War Room" in *Dr. Strangelove* to photograph the "Big Board" that tracks American bombers and Russian targets, the spy uses gadgets to further his ends. Guns and telephones, photographs and missiles extend the physical capacities of the human body. Certain gadgets are proximate to the body, whereas others replace body parts. In the popular television series *Get Smart* (1965–70), a spoof of James Bond-style machismo, American spy Maxwell Smart, also known as Agent 86, keeps a telephone in his shoe. In *Dr. Strangelove*, Slim Pickens, playing an Air Force pilot, straddles a missile as if it were a bull at a rodeo and, whooping with misplaced Wild West glee, plummets to certain death. Cold War tensions end with giddy annihilation brought about by sophisticated technology. Gadgetry that grants extrasensory perception or enhanced abilities—telephoto lenses, infrared cameras, lariats, grapple hooks, miniature pistols, exploding pens, video equipment, satellites, fast cars, Batmobiles, bionic legs—makes the spy seem less vulnerable to enemy intrusions.

A trajectory of bodily mechanization can be traced through twentieth-century spy narratives. In John Buchan's influential 1915 thriller *The Thirty-Nine Steps*, Richard Hannay pits his cunning against airplanes, automobiles, and chemicals. He depends on disguises and his discerning IQ to defeat German spies who threaten to invade England. Shrewdness of observation gets him out of his worst scrapes. Hannay lays claim to "a good memory and reasonable powers of observation" (Buchan, *Thirty-Nine Steps* 107). In *Mr. Standfast*, a sequel to *The Thirty-Nine Steps* set in the last months of World War I, Hannay, again the wily protagonist, relies heavily on technology instead of his legs and his wits. He squeezes into a light aircraft to evade enemies: "The engine started and the mechanics stood clear. As we taxied over the turf I looked back and saw several figures running in our direction. The next second we had left the bumpy earth for the smooth highroad of the air" (Buchan, *Mr. Standfast* 133). Instead of being the target exposed to enemy airplanes as in *The Thirty-Nine Steps,* Hannay maximizes his speed via machinery in *Mr. Standfast*. He adapts technology for inimical purposes without losing sight of the benefits of intelligence. He mixes technical know-how with abstract reasoning. Intellectual prowess, coupled with athletic skill and bravery, makes him a war hero. Action and reflection in combination become a fallback position for all subsequent spies. Although James Bond might be rigged out with every necessity for saving his life (scientific Q keeps inventing cunning and sometimes useless gadgets to help Bond crack conspiracies), he always depends, like Hannay, on his native intelligence to outsmart pursuers, aided and abetted by his endless stock of machines and gizmos.

Technology increasingly invades the agent's body during the twentieth century. *The Six Million Dollar Man* (1974–78), a television series about a pilot whose aircraft crashes and who requires inordinate, innovative surgery to make him whole again ("we can rebuild him, we have the technology," says the lead-in voice-over to the show), treats the male body as mechanistic and human in nearly equal parts. Colonel Steve Austin has a telephoto eye that can zoom in on tiny targets. He runs at unearthly speeds; the opening credits suggest velocity by, paradoxically, showing the bionic man sprinting in slow motion. Swiftness and precision make him superhuman. He brags about the cost of the American military complex by pinpointing the cost of his restructuring: six million dollars for one partially robotic man. In the film version of *The Bourne Identity* (2002), Jason Bourne, played by Matt Damon, costs thirty million CIA dollars to perfect.[3] The spy's body is an investment. As technology encroaches on the body, as microchips are implanted in brains and vision is enhanced with computers, the spy is pushed to new limits of inhumanity, of struggles that have nothing to do with ideology and everything to do with gamesmanship. In scenarios where the spy is technologized, his body belongs to the state and is manipulated like a pawn in a game that proves the arbitrariness of ideology.

Technology sometimes postpones death and sometimes enables it. As in *The Bourne Identity,* the spy incarnates death and inflicts death on others. Indeed, spy fiction exaggerates the representation of danger that ends in death. Neither technology nor backup teams can save the spy. Death is the outcome of exposure to danger, the spy's willingness to risk violent encounters. Whereas nineteenth-century realist novels treat character as the sum of experience, twentieth-century spy fiction represents experience as an assault on character. The spy sacrifices himself to abstract institutions and ideals. As Magnus Pym says about espionage training in le Carré's *A Perfect Spy*, "violence is not only of the body. It is the ravishment that must be done to truth, friendship, and, if need be, honour in the interest of Mother England" (534). Often the conclusion of spy narratives is punitive insofar as the rebellious or independent individual dies or suffers physical torment. Independence gets brought into line with systems of power. The protagonists of novels that I discuss in this book fare badly: Razumov is deafened and mutilated; Harry Lime dies in a sewer; Leamas is shot to death at the Berlin Wall; Robert Kelway falls or leaps to his death from a London rooftop; Victor Maskell, suffering from cancer, approaches death; Manfred is dead or missing; and Jack Lovett dies of a heart attack in a Jakarta swimming pool. The body count in these and other spy narratives intimates the sacrificial logic of espionage. Although spies dodge death as long as they can, death is a likely outcome of their line of work. Death serves as an alternative to complicated allegiances, often the only way out of impossible situations. In the psychological register of these narratives, death is the most closely held secret that spies carry.

INTRIGUE

Espionage is not strictly a novelistic phenomenon, nor a twentieth-century one.[4] Literature and spying have a long intertwined lineage. In the Bible, King David maintains power by a system of emissaries whom his enemies call spies (2 Samuel 10:2–4), and David's own son Absalom establishes a network of spies to usurp his father (2 Samuel 15:10). In *The Iliad*, Odysseus sneaks around Troy and seizes the spy Dolon from whom he extorts information about a bivouac. Odysseus then kills his informer on the assumption that, set free, Dolon would come back "either to spy on us once more, or to fight strongly with us" (Homer 230). In Shakespeare's *Hamlet*, Rosencrantz and Guildenstern spy on their friend, the Danish prince. In Ben Jonson's *Volpone*, the Englishman Sir Politic Would-Be, traveling in Venice, loves "to note and to observe . . . and know the ebbs / And flows of state" (26), which is to say that he spies. Spies become novelistic creatures in the nineteenth century. Casual spying in domestic circumstances binds characters to each other in the Victorian novel. In Sheridan Le Fanu's *Uncle Silas*, for example, Maud peeks through grilled windows and jumps back "in an extremity of horror" (384) or "in a panic" (404) every time the door to her room opens because she knows that her movements are being watched. As in *Harriet the Spy,* espionage is stock-in-trade for children's literature. Harry Potter in J. K. Rowling's children's series is a grade-A snoop but not an A-grade student. In *Harry Potter and the Prisoner of Azkaban,* Dumbledore, head of Harry's school, keeps a network of "useful spies" (152). Harry's enemies try to check his curiosity, as when Barty Crouch in *Harry Potter and the Goblet of Fire* spies on Harry using a magic map, just as Harry himself has spied on Crouch earlier (599). These examples suggest a distinction between politically motivated spying (in Homer and Ludlum) and domestic surveillance (in Le Fanu and Rowling). State secrets motivate the former, curiosity the latter.

Narratives of intrigue are plotted to satisfy the desire to know as that desire relates to ethics and politics. " 'I've got to know!' " (198) shouts Jason in *The Bourne Identity* about information pertinent to who he is. In narratives of intrigue, deficiencies in knowledge pass from spy to reader. Occasionally the reader knows more than the spy does, whether through supplementary briefings or through exposition that excludes the spy. At several points in Ludlum's novel, the narrative breaks away from Bourne to supply background information or to narrate events that happen at the Pentagon or at a safe house in Manhattan. While on the run, Bourne is not privy to a conference that occurs among four CIA personnel and a congressman, whose "opinion [does] not count" (227) because he is a civilian. The congressman poses basic questions about the operation involving Bourne. As a naive interrogator, the congressman acts as a dummy for the reader. Using a model of briefing and debriefing, the narrative of this conference furnishes the reader with more information than Bourne himself possesses. Each person discredits or validates the information advanced by others: " 'We've simply received all information as bona fide data, stored and accepted as valid' " (233). Not all of those data are true however. Each character at the meeting has information that he does not share with his peers. One person, in fact, is a mole whose business is to collect information and sell it. When the briefing mode returns in *The Bourne Identity* (322–27; 531–35), the reader is again subjected to a combination of truth and lies. The briefing mode that disseminates disinformation therefore requires the reader to read ideologically through a series of hunches and skeptical deductions.

A theory of intrigue implies the production of a text as an ideological event through an act of critical interpretation. That production occurs as an interaction between the reader and the text. As Pierre Macherey argues in *A Theory of Literary Production,* "the book is not the extension of a meaning; it is generated from the incompatibility of several meanings, the strongest bond by which it is attached to reality, in a tense and ever-renewed confrontation" (80). Arguing for a nonmimetic idea of representation, Macherey claims that literary discourse, as a contestation of language, creates a set of relations that interact with ideology: "an illusion that has been *set to work* becomes more than just an illusion, more than a mere deception. It is an illusion *interrupted, released,* completely transformed" (62). Macherey interprets fiction as constitutive of ideology, even as it reworks the determinants of ideology. Spy fiction, incorporating confrontation as it does, invites a sharper definition of the process of ideological transformation than Macherey gives. The illusion that a narrative of intrigue generates—an illusion sustained by an elaborate set of hypotheses concerning recruitment, agency, masculinity, technology, conspiracy, and other factors—intervenes in the reader's conception of violence, justice, and duty. Acting without complete knowledge, spies represent disturbances in ideology, as emblems of doubt and doublecrosses. The reader, susceptible to briefings and disinformation, deciphers the ideological importance of spies' actions, notwithstanding the unreliability of agents. Furthermore, ideology is not hidden but foregrounded in narratives of intrigue. The reader's experience of spy narratives might, in fact, not interrupt political belief and bring about transformation but confirm certain convictions, namely, that the spy, although working independently, acts in the interests of the public or the state.

The term "ideology," as I use it here, refers to ideas and tacit beliefs that result in actions and attitudes. Ideology also means lived relations to reality that socially constituted subjects experience: "Ideology offers the social subject not a set of narrowly 'political' ideas but a fundamental framework of assumptions that defines the parameters of the real and of the self" (Kavanaugh 310). These assumptions downplay contradictions and permit degrees of individual dissent. Ideology shapes the unconscious and affects interactions with others. The embodiment of ideology in artworks often inspires critics to isolate instances of subversion as especially valuable. The more subversive a text, the more value the text is accorded by critics. Marxist critique of literature emphasizes the *"distantiation"* (Althusser 222) of art from life. According to many Marxists, good art "challenges" (Eagleton 17) the ideological assumptions of its time. By contrast, naive art is said to reproduce ideologies without questioning them. Sussing out oppositional strategies in narrative often blinds critics to conservative convictions that those narratives express, namely, that subversion, whether embodied in terrorists or rogue agents, is eliminated from political representation as too dangerous. Intrigue narratives invent ideological alternatives, but those alternatives are not de facto revolutionary or subversive. Metaphors of "fragility" (Lukács 75), "transparency" (Easthope 10–12), "phantoms" (Marx and Engels 42), or "illusion" (Macherey 62) underlie Marxist definitions of ideology, as if the contradictory principles and ideas by which everyone lives were always invisible or ungraspable. Ideology is not necessarily illusory to readers, although it often is to characters within spy narratives, in part because spies allow personal motives to influence their commitments and actions. As Macherey claims, a work of criticism says what the literary work "does not and could not say" (77) overtly. I do not mean that the value of intrigue narratives resides in their repressiveness or their reinforcement of ideology. I mean, rather, that the critical tendency to read texts for subversion prevents critics from seeing encoded messages of repression and conservatism, masculinity and sexuality, dread and commitment. Dismissing spy fiction as formulaic, for example, is one way of ignoring ideological content.

Many studies of spy fiction emphasize its conventions (Cawelti, *Adventure* 5–36; Sauerberg 19–22). Mass culture critique tends to foreclose on representational variants by appealing to the criterion of sameness. "There are but a very limited number of plots and problems which are repeated over and over again in successful movies and short stories," claims Leo Lowenthal (134). I do not dispute that spy narratives rehearse certain patterns and motifs. But such structuralist and formalist interpretations of intrigue narratives should not preempt ideological criticism. The repetition of tropes in espionage narratives does not diminish the pleasure derived from those narratives. Repetition is not an obstacle to pleasure, as anyone who watches television or listens to pop music knows. The pleasure of ignorance for the reader of spy thrillers is one way that ideology asserts itself. Enjoyment is "not an immediate spontaneous state" (Žižek 114). "Enjoy!" is a cultural imperative. To enjoy formulae in spy fiction is to engage in the making of political subjectivity, which need not be a conscious activity. John Cawelti suggests that "formulas resolve tensions and ambiguities resulting from the conflicting interests of different groups within the culture," and "formulas enable the audience to explore in fantasy the boundary between the permitted and the forbidden" (36). While applying formulae, narratives of intrigue open up an array of psychological insights that might not be available through the discourses of political science or official history. Recurrent tropes in spy fiction acquire new meanings when located in different narratives, since variations in representation bring variations in signification. The problem of intrigue narratives is not one of formulaic repetition, but of interpreting repetition as a clue to ideologically sensitive material.

As I have already suggested, narratives of intrigue pose riddles of political identity. These riddles are often represented as a spy's lack of knowledge or a deficiency in a spy's agency. Spy fiction speculates on the meaning of action in different scenarios. Repeatedly, intrigue narratives try to determine whether action can be categorized as authentic or inauthentic. The term "secret agent" designates both a character and the actions undertaken by that character, in the sense that the word "agent," like the word "agenda" and the word "action," derives from the Latin infinitive *agere,* meaning "to act" or "to do." As a *bearer* and *perpetrator* of secrets, the agent devises covert plots from secrets—bomb blast, ambush, assassination, abduction, murder, coup d'état, information leak, treason. If a spy is not genuine in his motives or commitments, his actions may not express authenticity. Pretending to be an ex-spy on the dole during the Cold War, like Leamas in *The Spy Who Came in From the Cold,* mitigates the force of his recruitment by communist agents. If, like Charlie in le Carré's *The Little Drummer Girl,* the agent sleeps with a Palestinian playboy in order to locate his terrorist brother, that pretext alters the nature of sexual passion. She counterfeits ecstasy to obtain vital information. An action undertaken with disguises, pseudonyms, and false motives is an action nonetheless. "Terror is theatre," Charlie concludes about her manipulation of men in exchange for information in *The Little Drummer Girl* (494).

In this regard, narratives of intrigue modify Aristotle's definition of action as the outward expression of character. Aristotle argues that action in drama does not, first and foremost, represent character: "character comes in as subsidiary to action" (53). Action bespeaks character. As a character claims in John le Carré's *Call for the Dead,* " 'Thought alone was valueless. You must act for thought to become effective'" (90). In spy fiction, action does not necessarily change or betray character. Spy fiction repeatedly challenges the idea that action determines character since actions are undertaken not because of personal conviction but because of necessity. Character remains apart from the execution of specific deeds. In *Under Western Eyes* and *The Heat of the Day*, character detaches itself from action. The spy is not the totality of what he does. Character overrules conduct the way a whole exceeds the sum of its parts.

False action compounds epistemological crises in spy narratives. Recruited into ideology, the reader, like the spy, possesses imperfect information about plots, counterplots, and laws that circumscribe subjectivity. Secret agents are out of touch with their operators. They are figures who *do not know* or do not know *enough*. Through their ignorance, they challenge epistemology. One never possesses enough knowledge, yet one is forced to act nevertheless. If one acts without understanding the relation of that action to a fully developed plot, ignorance does not nullify the action. Intrigue narratives, as allegories of ideology, incorporate not knowing into the representation of the secret agent. Cawelti and Rosenberg in *The Spy Story* emphasize the spy's lack of control over domains of knowledge: "The clandestine participant must remember the attitudes, perceptions, and words characteristic of both the clandestine world and the world outside, and he must manipulate both consciousnesses effectively enough to shift back and forth between them with ease" (17). The spy's performance turns anxious when he loses sight of his allegiances or forgets the rules of the game, when the unconscious threatens to overwhelm conscious control. What he does not know about himself, or about the plot in which he has been implicated, will result in rash action. Out of anger or miscalculation, Richard Hannay, James Bond, and Jason Bourne sometimes make stupid moves that jeopardize their safety. Ignorance motivates their decisions.

Ignorance metastasizes to readers. Uncertain of what is about to come, readers express their ignorance as fear. Suspense, and the thrills that it elicits, define the reader's apprehension vis-à-vis ideology. Like the spy, the reader of suspense narratives never possesses enough information. In moments of dread, recruitment happens, for readers as for novelistic characters. Narratives of intrigue play up and play on the fears of individuals who are at a loss about their place in the social order. Fear is useful, indeed indispensable, in the making of political subjects.

CHAPTER TWO

Thrills

FEAR AND CATHARSIS AS IDEOLOGICAL EFFECTS

I wanted to find one law to cover all of living, I found fear.

Anne Carson, *Plainwater* (204)

My fear is *free* and manifests my freedom; I have put all my
freedom into my fear, and I have chosen myself as fearful in this
or that circumstance.

Jean-Paul Sartre, *Being and Nothingness* (574)

FEAR

Spy narratives rely on thrills, those tremors of almost-out-of-body atten-
tiveness that seize a reader or action film spectator at moments of crisis,
as when the villain and pursuer race through the sewers of Vienna in *The
Third Man,* as when the double agent, gun in hand, tracks his antagonist
through a greenhouse and confronts him with a lifetime of betrayals in
The Untouchable. Speaking of the many risks he took as a communist sym-
pathizer and seller of secrets, Victor Maskell, septuagenarian narrator of
The Untouchable, acknowledges the pleasures of being caught: "What a
risk I took—my God, when I think of it, the damage they could have
wrought! But then, it was precisely in the danger of it that the pleasure
lay" (310). Although his heart pounds and his blood leaps through his
veins at the thought of public exposure, Maskell sees the erotic charge
that danger bears, at least for him: "Wanting to be caught. To be set upon.
To be manhandled" (6). He's talking about both the pleasures of prowling
public toilets for quick sex and the terror of having his cover as a trusted
British administrator blown. Political danger overlaps with sexual danger
in his mind. The secret agent avows what political scientists and psychoanalysts do not, that the twentieth-century political subject is also a sexual

subject and that self-interest is indissociable from civic allegiances. Rippling across flesh, thrill arises when the edges of politics and sexuality rub together.

The thrill unites numerous, dissimilar components. Hazard, fear, pain, eros, aggression, cravenness, bodiliness, athleticism, and subjugation meet in the instant when the thrill happens. It shakes the mind and the body together. Like the classic Burkean definition of the sublime in which awe and terror conjoin, unlikely emotions combine in the thrill. The shocked individual is also an awed individual. In an attempt to redraw political boundaries—to create a definition of citizenship that might include foreigners, defectors, refugees, dissidents, Jews, homosexuals, traitors—the spy thriller postulates absolute, unswerving allegiance to country or ideology, an allegiance that few citizens of the twentieth-century world could endorse. The thrill, therefore, speaks to moments of conscious or unconscious discrepancy between individual and state. Razumov, in *Under Western Eyes,* thinks that "'Perhaps life is just that. . . . A dream and a fear'" (316). The verbless sentence is ambiguous. Perhaps the dream expresses fear. Fear clouds judgment the way a dream clouds reality. Or perhaps Razumov means that dreams oppose fears, and that human life oscillates between poles of happiness and terror, ideals and paralysis. The thrill, uniting alarm and pleasure-in-alarm, points to the social and political utility of fear in the making of subjects. Fear dissolves reason and loyalties in order to allow recruitment to take place.

Thrills in espionage narratives can trace an ancestry in nineteenth-century detective and sensation fiction (such as *Lady Audley's Secret* and *Uncle Silas*) and late Victorian adventure tales (such as *Treasure Island* and *Moonfleet*). Spy narratives differ from their antecedents insofar as the espionage thriller inculcates the impossibility of truth and commitment within ideology. Spies deal with betrayal and doublecrosses the way detectives deal with motives and crimes, as objects for examination and analysis. Yet spy fiction is not the same as detective fiction. Spy fiction is about codes; detective fiction is about clues. Extrapolating from that observation, we can generalize that spy fiction is about hermeneusis (codes, typically numbers or words, require decipherment as allegory) and detective fiction is about exegesis (clues, typically objects and instruments, require literal reading in a linear order as realism). Detective fiction assumes guilt within the context of a home or family; espionage fiction assumes guilt within the context of statecraft and diplomacy. In detective fiction, death is requisite. There can be no detection without a corpse. In spy narratives, the corpse does not have a priori inevitability. Cadavers may pile up, but they are incidental to narratives of intrigue. In detective fiction, the culpable character runs away and is caught; the point of view is usually, though not always, on the side of the law, embodied in the detective who pursues. By contrast, the honest and often unsuspecting character in espionage fiction runs away after being embroiled in a plot that he does not understand; villains chase him to indicate that the plot extends even to those characters who are not in the know.

The thrill felt in the chase transmits electrically from character to reader. To speak of the thrill is to address the imperilment of character and the aesthetic engagement of reader in the same breath. The thrill, a shudder tripping along the body, forfeits ratiocination for intuition. Fear erases the possibility of rational thinking. For example, Winston Smith, in George Orwell's *Nineteen Eighty-Four,* goes to the "flicks" (11) to see a propaganda film. In that film a helicopter pursues a man trying to escape by swimming. Snipers shoot at the man until he dies. The helicopter then bombs a lifeboat filled with children and a middle-aged woman who shields her child from danger. Having legitimated one murder in the name of the state, the shooters in the helicopter proceed to large-scale extermination. Winston, as witness to this outrage in cinematic form, registers violence as traumatic shock. As he narrates the events of the film, he loses his syntax, his punctuation, his capitalization, his ability to keep fear at bay. The sequence ends with Winston describing the audience's reaction, which contrasts with his own. The headlong frenzy of the prose mimics panic: "then the helicopter planted a 20 kilo bomb in among them terrific flash and the boat went all to matchwood. Then there was a wonderful shot of a childs arm going up up up right up into the air a helicopter with a camera in its nose must have followed it up and there was a lot of applause from the party seats but a woman down in the prole part of the house suddenly started kicking up a fuss and shouting they didnt oughter of showed it not in front of the kids they didnt it aint right not in front of kids it aint until the police turned her turned her out i don't suppose anything happened to her nobody cares" (11). Fear propels loss of orthographic control. Winston slips from I to i in his self-definition and incorporates the voice of the prole woman into his own. He drops apostrophes and periods.

When the proles laugh, Winston cringes. His reaction is determined by his class differences from the proles, but also by his stance towards horror, which makes his body contract. The scene defines a moment of ideological transmission, in which the dominant aesthetic is fear. Winston realizes that arbitrary measures of justice—shooting a man, bombing a lifeboat —are within the realm of the imaginable in a totalitarian state. Fear defines Winston's political subjectivity as a limit that he himself does not set and that he cannot transgress. Personalizing this external limit, he lives in and through fear. Yet, as Brian Massumi wonders, "If we are in collective complicity with fear, does that mean that fear no longer sets social boundaries, but transcends them? If so, how does domination function without set boundaries?" (ix). Thinking of Winston's out-of-body panic, we could answer Massumi's questions rudimentarily by saying that, in the spy novel, political domination continues through aesthetic representation, where thrills triumph over rationality.

As in the case of Winston at the movies, the thrill is often, though need not be, scopic. In the film *Terminator 2: Judgment Day* (1992), a liquid metal "terminator"—a cyborg from the future who chases a vulnerable child living under the protection of a good "terminator"—speeds after moving vehicles. He moves so fast that he appears to be here, there, everywhere. Blasted to smithereens, the bad terminator regroups by drawing the disassembled molecules of his metallic body back together. Indefatigable, he continues to plot and pursue. In my opinion, this evil robotic terminator is a stand-in for the thrilled viewer. Shattered by the experience of extreme danger, rendered visually in *Terminator 2* as the disintegration of a humanoid body, the viewer re-collects himself Humpty Dumpty-like. Thrill demonstrates what violence can be delivered against the human body, what pain or sudden death awaits the unsuspecting, what punishment gets meted out to traitors. The fight-or-flight aesthetic of the thrill combines physiological seizure and pleasure in terror. Thus the thrill is directed towards an audience and is motivated by a desire to convert an audience.[1] The audience seeks thrills willingly and uses "thrillingness" as a criterion for the aesthetic success or failure of a representation of action. *I was thrilled to death*. Beside himself with fear, the viewer can transform back to something resembling human wholeness, even though such wholeness is destined to be lost again in the next fearsome assault.

The unafraid body may be a specter, a projection in language of a unity that allows the subject to disperse bothersome anxieties. The unscared witness identifies his fears and thereby conquers them: he is in his perfect, unshaken mind. Julia Kristeva claims that fear seeks an object, a "*hieroglyph that condenses all fears*, from unnamable to namable" (33). This object can be a representation, either a novel or a film. Kristeva's insight, however, points to the separation of fear and language; fear is the domain of feeling that lies beyond language and establishes a frontier for language. The positing of an object that condenses fears is only a translation, a rendering visible of an intangible, unconscious state. In this positing of an object, fear releases its grip on the mind. The cinemagoer, seeing terrors visibly set forth in an action thriller, does not invariably master those fears after having witnessed them. More profoundly, fear tells us that something that we thought we had mastered through reason, repetition, or habit escapes our control; we remain at its mercy. We have not aligned our public selves with our unconscious, which is the name we give to all those things that we do not know, but suspect, about ourselves. The thrill manifests the unconscious in a flash—the *jouissance* brought on by the cresting of a roller-coaster just before it careens downward and proves that human bodies are alienable possessions.

Terror tosses us beyond language. The body, inadequately containing terror, breaks out in nonlinguistic shrieks. We scream when scared because we can express in no words that we know the feeling that inhabits us at the moment of fear. Gothic novels, sensation fiction, opera, melodrama, and horror films rely on the scream as the last resort of the endangered, fearful body. Terrors may be in the world or they may be within ourselves. If we assume they are within ourselves, they could be estranged wishes, thoughts, or feelings that we cannot represent or even acknowledge. They are fantasies that return to terrify us. Although we hypothesize fear in relation to external objects, that relation may reveal a gap of difference in ourselves, namely the gap between what we think we are and what we want. Lack terrifies us because it suggests our culpability within a social order where we are presumed to know, where we are presumed to be already guilty. Conversely, the very magnitude of our desire throws us into a fearful tizzy. "We are too much for ourselves," writes Adam Phillips in *Terrors and Experts;* "we are, in a sense, terrorized by an excess of feeling, by an impossibility of desire" (xii). The scream enshrines terror in sound as the sign of excess. It begins to translate terror into intelligibility without having any words that adequately bear the meaning of fear. The terrified scream signifies distress without specifying the nature or kind of distress. As in bungee jumping, roller-coaster rides, and white-water rafting, thrill is an "experience [that] cannot adequately translate into signs, metonyms, or paradigms" (Anderson 18). The postmodern search for supererogatory terror—at movies or at paint-ball parks—may accustom us to terrors that we cannot quite imagine without some prompting, but that we are nevertheless happy to conquer once we know they are possibilities. Similarly, the scream of the thrilled reader or the panicked character within a narrative begins to alleviate terror by rendering vocal the body and the menaces that assault the body. If "pain . . . can be translated, like a language" (Phillips 4), then we have the wherewithal to understand the sources and manifestations of terror. At the cusp of articulation, the scream punctures fear and smuggles terror, a hostage, into the quasi-language of human voice. The scream is Esperanto for "I want and I fear."

Readers learn through the body and the senses. Reader-response and reception theorists imagine that we readers are "transposed to a realm outside our bodily existence" (Iser 312). On the contrary, espionage fiction works its effects through the body, by putting the body in jeopardy while the mind takes a holiday. The aesthetic of espionage narrative requires that we acknowledge our identification with the fugitive or the agent who hovers on the borders of legality and who, therefore, best expresses the reader's uncertainty about living inside and outside the law at the same time. Suffering from "spyonnoia," as one psychiatrist calls the compulsion to survey and denounce others in the 1950s, the reader offloads fears onto others: "we want to spy on others in order to accuse them and thus rid ourselves of our fear of them" (Meerloo 45). Similarly, readers tail spies and traitors through novels in order to learn how to negotiate otherwise inexpressible states of panic. Novels habituate readers to social, psychological, and political fears. Fear inoculates the reader by delivering small doses of terror through representations.

Within narratives of intrigue in particular, fear complicates knowledge. The fearful states suffered by secret agents are sometimes felt more acutely by the reader who has, through ironic insight, greater knowledge of the whereabouts of a secret agent's antagonists. The reader of Joseph Conrad's *The Secret Agent* knows that Verloc works for both revolutionaries and the British government, yet Verloc's wife Winnie does not know this. A surprising number of spy novels are written in the first person to emphasize the limits of knowledge. Because of first-person limitations, what one learns in spy narratives is not necessarily beneficial. Information may not be reliable. Knowing that details are imparted to dupe intelligence-gatherers, the reader feels equally susceptible to being misinformed. For instance, the reader of *Sabbatical*, John Barth's CIA romance, is informed (or misinformed) by a pair of know-it-all first-person narrators who apostrophize the reader directly: "Incidentally, reader, there was no suicide clause in his life-insurance policies" (109). *Incidentally*, reader, we know this, but you do not, the narrators imply. *Incidentally*, what you don't know can be used against you. *Incidentally*, we control the flow of information in this narrative, and we're only going to tell you a few tidbits. Such asides, which are really information leaks, clarify the liabilities of readers' dependence on the narrator. Through no fault of her or his own, the reader is guilty of *not knowing enough information*. Like the agent, the reader sifts through misinformation and erroneous programming. Barth's reader retaliates by being nominally included in a rhetoric of doubt: "are we really to believe [this]?" (*Sabbatical* 355). The reader gets a thrill from the conflict between knowledgeable detachment from narrative and emotional engagement in narrative. But the point of spy fiction is that the reader never knows enough either in the epistemological sense of accumulating and structuring information, despite the difficulties of receiving true information, or in the sense of performing ideological positions that the reader may not even be able to articulate.

Spy fiction in the twentieth century addresses the complex sense of alienation and engagement that citizens feel towards political questions, such as "is my family more important than my country?" or "do I transmit ideology or do I make ideology through every action that I perform?" or "do I know more than I can articulate?" What any person does *not* know may hurt him, contrary to the adage. Lacking knowledge, characters get recruited to work for clandestine agencies. Some characters allow themselves to be recruited out of sheer ennui. They practice indifference to the complexities of political plots that envelop them. In *The Thirty-Nine Steps*, Richard Hannay feels "liverish" in London, as if he has "'got into the wrong ditch'" (Buchan 7). His own boredom disgusts him. Similarly, Miss Froy, an innocuous gray-haired lady with a pince-nez who works as a British spy in Alfred Hitchcock's *The Lady Vanishes*, confides in a bored young couple. The couple do not immediately grasp the ramifications of bearing a coded message to the Foreign Office. They undertake the assignment willingly, in part to help the little old lady and in part to break the spell of boredom they feel while riding a train. Razumov, the spy in *Under Western Eyes,* gets recruited because he wants to prove his allegiance to the autocratic state and to win a silver university medal. Lyle Wynant in Don DeLillo's *Players* is so bored with his job on the New York Stock Exchange that he allows himself to be recruited to help terrorists bomb the Exchange, the source of "invisible power" (107), because it will give him something to do; it will make him slightly less ordinary or maybe less part of "the pattern of repression" (34). Boredom arises out of lack of adventure, which enlistment into a terrorist plot will resolve. Intrigue counteracts the ordinariness of selling stocks or idling about London.

By a psychological fillip, the very ordinariness that gives rise to boredom converts into the perfect pretext for espionage. Ordinariness of behavior, look, accent, or career disguises the spy. No one can tell by looking at her that Miss Froy is a spy. The same is true for Razumov, for Smiley in John le Carré's novels, and for Robert in *The Heat of the Day.* Ordinariness cuts two ways. First, ordinariness preserves the spy's secret mission. Second, ordinary people bear political meaning that they cannot define in language. Like the spy in the film *No Way Out*—a Russian infiltrator who has worked so long for the U.S. navy that he forgets his mother tongue—the least likely suspect turns out to be an agent. The mole's adherence to Soviet Russia lasts long after his native language disappears, which literalizes the relation most people have to ideology. It is a belief structure that supersedes individual knowing and language. In *No Way Out,* the thrilling reversal of knowledge, the unmasking of a Russian working as a CIA liaison officer, calls into question the integrity of information in spy narratives. Moles and leaks reinforce suspicion. The exciting disclosure that the ordinary citizen spies on friends and neighbors creates the possibility that all ordinary citizens are, to some degree, agents of ideology, not just its transmitters. They act out and fashion ideology.

The thrill in espionage narrative is an Althusserian moment of "Hey, you there!" interpellation (Althusser 174). Interpellation, as Althusser defines it, assumes guilt as the core of subjectivity. The hailed subject turns around in the street because he knows—fundamentally, psychologically—that the police recognize his guilt. According to Judith Butler, this

moment of hailing supplies (at least) two constitutive ingredients of subjectivity: it recognizes, and invokes, the body of the subject; it is an oral, not
written, event. The hailing echoes over time and modifies the body and
its performative possibilities. The subject learns to perform according to
the demands of ideology. As Butler writes in *Excitable Speech*, "The way
in which that interpellative call continues to call, to take form in a bodily
stylistics that, in turn, performs its own social magic constitutes the tacit
and corporeal operation of performativity" (153). By performativity, Butler
means that psychic events and phantasms of the unconscious inscribe
themselves on the body; the body encloses and structures interior life. On
the surface of the body, words, acts, gestures, and desires flicker. In their
flickering, they intimate principles of identity. These are, however, codes.
They might constitute a discourse, a repertory of behavior, but they are
not identity itself. They translate or perform identity, as Butler claims in
Gender Trouble: "Such acts, gestures, enactments, generally construed, are
performative in the sense that the essence of identity that they otherwise
purport to express are *fabrications* manufactured and sustained through
corporeal signs and other discursive means" (173). Performative moments
register what is not there and what is not spoken, as well as what is there
and what is spoken. These performances invite the question of whether
an essence of identity exists at all. Just as the secret agent has no perfectly
coherent commitment to one side or another, performative gestures imply
that identity is phantasmatic. The performative accommodates the unconscious as best it can, since the unconscious, by its very nature, can never
be fully known or accommodated. Freud's term *das Unbewußte* translates
as "the unknown," and homes in on the relation of identity to knowledge
that the translated term "unconscious" does not (Meltzer 149). Not knowing, according to Freud, is foundational to identity. Words can partly translate the unknown, though the unknown motivations for action or character
can never be exhausted. A shudder, expressing the unknown in a ripple
of fear, performs the unconscious, which is to say that fear is a performance
of fear. The unknown generates meaning that may never be decoded and
that manifests itself on the surface of the body as an enigma. The applicability of this psychoanalytic model to espionage might be obvious: the languages and performances of identity are coded and ideologically freighted.
Interpellation generates more than guilty subjectivity. Once hailed, the
body of the subject enters ideology, begins to perform its ideological role.

The address invokes the body and causes it to posture within the field of action. Thrill is the moment when the unconscious, or the unknown, bursts forth in the body, when what has been secret comes to light in a gesture or a code.

Although an initial reaction to "Hey, you there!" may be fear generated by guilt, another answer to the policeman's interpellative call is, "Who me? I didn't do anything, officer." Such an answer opens a chasm between identity and action. *You can judge me by what actions I commit, not by my innate traits of character.* The hailed subject disclaims culpability. *You can see for yourself that I'm innocent.* Like Lee Harvey Oswald's confrontation with a policeman after the assassination of JFK in Don DeLillo's *Libra,* the citizen just happens to be walking down the street and denies his guilt when there is no proof that he has done anything wrong. The imputation of guilt does not disperse, however, just because guilt is denied. In the contest between committed action and the potential to perpetrate actions in the future, thrill happens. The subject, after all, may be guilty at any time in the future. Political subjectivity is always in part premised on actions that have yet to occur and the vigilance required to bring such events about or to prevent such events from happening. Futurity is part of a plot, since a plot depends on an evolving sequence of causally linked events stretching through time.

Guilt and discovery of criminal action have everything to do with timeliness and with the assertion of innocence until culpability is established. In common law, a subject is not guilty unless proven guilty, although he may be convoked before a judge to attest to his actions. Legal deliberation does not figure in Althusser's interpellative moment. Danger derives from the hailed subject's lack of immediate legal recourse. Like the hailed subject in the street, the spy may not know the reasons for his involvement in a plot. Especially in spy narratives, plots predate and predetermine behavior. The citizen need only be called to participate in a preexistent plot. Ideology is there, even if "transparent," a mechanism to "transport the reader smoothly to the meaning [of discourse and narrative] without drawing attention to itself" (Easthope 112). Althusser casts the interpellative moment in terms of espionage recruitment: "ideology 'acts' or 'functions' in such a way that it 'recruits' subjects among the individuals (it recruits them all), or 'transforms' the individuals into subjects (it transforms them all)" (Althusser 174). At the moment of interpellation, the hailed subject might become an agent of the law, not just the subject of the law. Recruitment tweaks the subject's will to power. Although most interpretations of interpellation dwell on subjugation as constitutive of identity, interpellation "recruits" agents as well on behalf of the law. Interpellation causes a thrill because it promises the subject protection by virtue of having a position located above the law or empowered by the law.

Secret agents work inside and outside hierarchical structures at the same time. The bureaucratic and hierarchical structures of spy narratives diffuse authority: Agent 007 reports to M in James Bond novels; Verloc reports to the Assistant Commissioner in *The Secret Agent;* Davis reports to Castle who reports to Daintry who reports to Tomlinson in *The Human Factor;* Charlie's female agents report to the invisible but omnipotent Charlie in the 1970s TV series *Charlie's Angels.* There are several implications to these hierarchies. Because authority is dispersed throughout the hierarchy, no one controls all details of intelligence. The agent never sees the full picture. His actions are therefore deniable. Nevertheless, he must react as if he understands the immediate effect of his actions while trusting that their long-term consequences contribute to the overall plot. At any point in the chain of command, a leak might occur. An agent might sell secrets as a means of disrupting a preformed plot. As the result of a leak or a personal resentment against a hierarchical bureaucracy, an ambiguity of allegiance might arise. The uncertainties of hierarchical authority are present also in Althusser's model of interpellation. Thrill springs from ambiguity implicit in the moment when the hailed subject realizes that he can run or respond, enact guilt or perform innocence. Whereas espionage narratives assume that a subject is an agent of some sort, the narrative does not have to announce for whom the agent works. Therein lies the thrill.

To be thrilled is to sense alien presence. To satiate an audience's desire for titillation, new varieties of violence and diabolical enemies must be produced. Steffan Hantke remarks that "contemporary conspiratorial theories have brought the object of fear home, placing 'the Other' in our midst as a danger that needs to be combated with steadily increasing budgets for surveillance" (221) and legitimating the paranoid use of excessive violence to fend off enemies within. Fredric Jameson sees otherness as a problem of class-based fear of "proletarianization, of slipping down the ladder" (*Postmodernism* 286). Separation by class allows the stigmatization of otherness along class lines. Jameson concludes that hypothesizing otherness blinds contemporary audiences to evil: "we really [should not] require our flesh to creep before reaching a sober and political decision as to the people and forces who are collectively 'evil' in our contemporary world" (*Postmodernism* 290). Jameson raises several issues at the same time. Fear, which underlies the aesthetic of thrills, inures culture-imbibers to the prospects of failure. Thrill depends not just on the retreat into bourgeois security—*I'm glad I'm not put at risk!* Thrill depends on becoming the other, of passing into the role of the stigmatized outcast, alien, or terrorist.

And yet seeing ourselves as alien hardly explains why things that frighten us frighten us more intensely when we know they are about to occur. Watching a suspense film a second time induces terror not of the unknown but of the known. Anticipating the moment of terror, when the nerves tauten and the eyes widen, does not allay fear. Expectation may enhance terror because we know what to watch for. Espionage, as a narrative genre, promises to conquer otherness. Narratives of intrigue keep this promise by relying on the repetition of conventions and characters. "Under the guise of a machine that produces information," writes Umberto Eco about James Bond narratives, "the criminal novel produces redundancy; pretending to rouse the reader, it in fact reconfirms him in a sort of imaginative laziness and creates escape by narrating, not the Unknown, but the Already Known" (160). Seeing Bond drugged, slugged, and endangered does not prevent viewers from wanting to see him drugged, slugged, and endangered again. Ideology confirms itself in repetition. The *frisson* brought on by imperilment reinforces ideology in spy narratives rather than destabilizing belief systems. What we see on screen or read in a novel is a version of our worst fears. What we see or read is what we had repressed because it was scary. It comes back to haunt us because it was inadequately dealt with in the first instance.

In the case of the propaganda film in *Nineteen Eighty-Four,* at which the proles laugh, the audience is, with the exception of Winston, not sufficiently afraid, in the sense that fear has not yet spilled over into rebellion. This insufficiency should not obviate the fact that fear is an instrument of control brought to bear through police tactics. Fear can be used to erase history and replace it with made-up versions of past events. Important as fear as a political weapon may be, my concern here is with the instrumentality of fear in representation. Plato strongly advises, though not without irony, that the telling of stories riles the citizens of a polity, and therefore story-telling cannot be permitted lest it disturb the balance of power within a republic (Plato 18–25). Spy fiction, at bottom, tends to prove that political power cannot be modified or overturned. Razumov, for instance, in *Under Western Eyes*, does not do anything revolutionary; he works for the Russian secret police and consolidates their authority when he infiltrates a revolutionary cell in Geneva. The aesthetic problem of the spy thriller is that ideological difference cannot be seen in the body. In *The Spy Who Came in From the Cold*, the good guys blend with the bad guys: Leamas acts as a disaffected ex-agent who wants to sell secrets to the communists, although this performance of a doublecross is scripted in London in order to keep an East German double agent in operation, which amounts to a double doublecross. In the same novel, Mundt and Fiedler play a complex game of cat-and-mouse, in which one or the other of them spies for the British. Fear derives from the impossibility of discerning who embodies which ideology. Fear, in other words, reflects a reader's alarm about harboring ideological convictions that he didn't even know he had. Spy narratives work to exorcise such fears and self-doubts and to impose regularity of belief. Such narratives purge pity and fear in cathartic release. After deliberately antagonizing the audience's sense of right and wrong, after heightening suspense through a narrow escape (the darkened streets of Berlin in *The Spy Who Came in From the Cold*) or a chase (through the sewers of Vienna in *The Third Man*), the spy thriller jettisons threatening elements, whether racketeers, double agents, traitors, or misguided spies. Leamas, tainted by ambiguity, cannot return to his former life as a British agent once he has gone into the cold zone of communism. The object of fear in spy fiction is often the spy himself or herself, since the spy is almost always the least ideologically assured and most untrustworthy character.

STORYBOARDS: FIVE VARIATIONS ON THE CHASE SCENE
Scene #1. Fear disorients you. You are running through the snow. Your fur coat, your purse fall off you in pieces. You wear a fur-tipped sweater set. It's 1938, November, Savoy, woods, a bend in the road. After seeing your husband knifed to death by fascists, you jump from your car. You stumble. Trees loom up. You run, but not very fast, not very far.

Killers chase you. They shoot at you. You shriek with fear. You stagger. Marcello, the conformist, listens, inside his car. Sheltered and cowardly, he does not help. You scream at him. Once. Piercingly. As if you would shatter glass with your cry of anguish and terror. You bang the glass of the car window with your open palm.

Fear numbs every corpuscle in your body. After your single scream, your tongue locks to the roof of your fear-stricken mouth. Terror paralyses you, then makes you run. There is no plausible end to this ambush except death. All chases incorporate the possibility of being run to ground. Anonymous enemies have ambushed your car on this snowy, curving road. You are crocheted into a conspiracy, an intrigue that has nothing to do with you. Assassins have killed the professor, your husband, because of his beliefs. You fall. You get up.

Your name is Anna. You are a predatory lesbian.

You are running for your life through Bernardo Bertolucci's *The Conformist*.

Handheld camera work conveys your nausea.

In Alberto Moravia's novel from which Bertolucci's screenplay is drawn, your name is Lina and you die in a sentence, heroically trying to save your husband, antifascist Professor Quadri: "'she threw herself onto her husband to protect him and took two slugs for him. He ran away into the woods'" (Moravia 283). You die swiftly in the novel because there are so few words to describe terror.

Cinema would be nothing without chase scenes. In the film, you run unendingly through the woods but you get nowhere. You die by images, slowly.

The killers shoot you ultimately.

From *The Conformist*, we learn lessons in fear. Fear spreads. Fear paralyses. Fear drags the body beyond its natural limits. Fear screams; it has no language but the shriek, the shout, the reverberant cry.

*

Scene #2. You dream about wolves. They are not ordinary creatures. You dream about white wolves with bushy, flicking tails. The wolves sit in trees.

You must imagine that trees would be one of the few places where you could escape from hungry, menacing wolves: high up among the branches. Yet that's where the wolves sit. They prick up their ears. They look at you.

You yell, then awake from this dream *"in great terror"* (Freud, *Infantile Neurosis* 29).

You narrate this dream to your psychoanalyst, Sigmund Freud. He concludes you suffer from castration anxiety. Written down in a dossier, your fear finds a language of sorts: "any practice of speech, inasmuch as it involves writing, is a language of fear" (Kristeva 38).

You suffer from fear of being chased and eaten. You suffer from guilt over this fear. You fantasize being incorporated into the wolf's body as an escape from fear. Once eaten, you will know what you feared. You want to be eaten alive, the way children, thinking of big bad wolves in grannies' clothing, thrill to the possibility of being consumed.

Why do so many children's games include chases, such as tag, or hide-and-seek, or kick-the-can, or fox-and-goose? You hide. Then you run. Then you hide.

Fear camouflages aggression. Since you are dreaming about these wolves, they project your wish to violate, to gorge on flesh.

You lie in bed without moving. The wolves watch without moving. You will never be seduced. That is your secret tragedy. No one, nothing, moves.

Fear renders you passive. That is easy to see. But can it also render you aggressive, the wolfish predator?

*

Scene #3. You have stolen money from your father. You wear bad clothes and have a boyfriend with a motorcycle. It is the 1990s. It is Washington, D.C.

You are too self-absorbed to realize that your father is a CIA agent masquerading to his family as a computer salesman.

An Arab terrorist kidnaps you when your mother and father disappear to a key off Florida. They, too, have been abducted but for a different reason, namely, to declare to the world that the terrorist has nuclear weapons in his possession and that he will use them against the United States.

You are held hostage in a skyscraper under construction in Miami.

You steal a key from the Arab terrorist, not just any key, but the key that when turned in a timing device will set off a nuclear explosion in Miami.

You flee. The terrorist chases you. He splatters walls with bullets.

You flee up a stairwell. The terrorist follows right behind shooting as he goes.

You flee up a yellow construction crane, to its very tip. The terrorist chases you, inch by unfazed inch.

You scream, "Don't come any closer." But he does.

The terrorist calls you "child," and you call him "wacko." It slips out.

You loop the key around your neck.

You slip from the construction crane. But you save yourself with a single inspired clutch of a hand. You dangle like an acrobat over Miami.

Your father, Arnold Schwarzenegger (none other), flies up in a Hawker-Harrier jet and hovers below you. You are shocked to see him. You say, quizzically, "Daddy?" You overact, but that's okay. You didn't know your father was a daredevil. You didn't know he was a spy.

You have foolishly stolen money from his wallet. Your father knows you have stolen his money because he was spying on you with a concealed camera. You have not only been bad, you have been caught. Yet theft pays. You've wisely stolen the key to the timing device.

You hang over the nose cone of your daddy's jet. You slip.

You fall onto the jet. And still the Arab terrorist chases you. Nothing shakes him from your trail.

You are Dana, the teenager in *True Lies*. Your function in the plot is to be pursued.

*

Scene #4. You are a secret agent named Karl. You approach a checkpoint between East and West Berlin. It is 1963 or so. You have been working in East Germany on a mission. You have been out in the cold. Metaphorically. You act as if you are calm. You push a bicycle. You are nine hours late. You are frightened.

You have made a grievous error. You have an East German mistress named Elvira. You know that she is married. You show her to your fellow agent Leamas at a dinner. You tell Elvira everything: passwords, routes, letter drops, safe houses. For an agent, you have been one hell of a blabbermouth. You love Elvira, but why? Her name alone should have been a clue.

You approach document check. You get through. Then you approach customs. You get through. You have to pass the last East German sentry.

You do not know that Leamas, who is calling himself Thomas for the nonce, waits for you just inside the West German border. You don't know that Leamas has been there, in the cold, for hours. You don't know that Elvira has already driven off. All things considered, you don't know very much. You are an agent trying to get back to the west in *The Spy Who Came in From the Cold*. You will be the first fatality of the book. An instructive casualty.

You suddenly sense danger. You pedal your bicycle furiously towards the border. Fear spurs you on. The East German sentry shoots you once, twice.

The chase lasts a few seconds. You got spooked. You couldn't possibly have known what awaited you on the other side of the wall.

*

Scene #5. You work in the Foreign Office handling African communiqués. Your name is Castle, Maurice Castle. You are the hunted man in Graham Greene's *The Human Factor*. You are the leak in section 6 of the Foreign Office. You send coded messages to Russian agents named Boris and Ivan using novels as your code books. You don't trust your Russian contacts. You realize, belatedly, how little you have been trusted "even by those who had the most reason to trust" (284). You indirectly cause the death of your subordinate Davis. You have learned over the years not to run. Hurrying causes mistakes. You transmute fear into method. In turn, you have been detected in your crime through patient ploys plotted by your bosses. There is no need to run. This is not a footrace. When you know you have been found out, you wait in your house for someone to come. You do not dash. You wait. You defect. You do not die. You suffer a worse fate than death, which is to live through the discomforts of a Moscow winter. You wonder if you will ever see your wife Sarah again. Sarah is black and from South Africa. You have sold secrets to the Russians because you thought you were "'helping Sarah's people'" (339). You are not a communist (160). You discover, too late, that you have been doubly fooled, for the information you sold was used to authenticate reports from a Russian posing as a British-run spy. Your information did nothing to help Sarah's people. You wait in Moscow, but nothing happens. Fear of your absolute irrelevance yawns before you. Your secrets and lies have all been for naught. You have lived a life that was neither conscious nor political enough.

Defection is another version of the chase, one that does not involve sprinting.

CHASE

The thrill manifests itself in chases. It is almost impossible to identify a spy novel or film that does not include at least one chase scene. *The Day of the Jackal* contains a long section called "Anatomy of a Manhunt." Graham Greene divides *The Confidential Agent* into "The Hunted," "The Hunter," "The Last Shot," and "The End." The chase can take a slower, more methodical pace. Harrison shadows Robert Kelway throughout *The Heat of the Day* without ever provoking a face-to-face confrontation. Chases are not confined to land. Carruthers and Davies, the yachtsmen in *The Riddle of the Sands,* pursue Dollmann around the North Sea, across treacherous shoals and through lashing storms. Chases often involve transgressing boundaries: leaping barriers, sloshing through sewers, climbing walls, rushing down stairwells. The chase implies self-control and self-vigilance: one needs a steady hand to shoot at one's pursuers and steady convictions to avoid being frightened out of one's wits. Pursuit is always about control of information; those who chase you want what you have. Sometimes the only thing that you have left to offer is your life. Chases, inspiring terror and bred from terror, are akin to death because they exhibit the vulnerability of the body to physical limitations and violence. The guy on the lam can run only so fast.

In le Carré's *Tinker Tailor Soldier Spy,* a schoolboy named Roach stumbles upon a retired agent loading bullets into a gun. Roach runs:

> Roach had blundered wildly to the brow. He was running
> between the hummocks, making for the drive, but running
> slower than he had ever run before; running through sand
> and deep water and dragging grass, gulping the night air,
> sobbing it out again, running lopsidedly like Jim, pushing now
> with this leg, now with the other, flailing with his head for
> extra speed. He had no thought for where he was heading.
> All his awareness was behind him; fixed on the black revolver
> and the bands of chamois leather; on the pen tops that
> turned to bullets as Jim threaded them methodically into the
> chamber. (221)

Even though his knowledge causes a rush of adrenaline, Roach cannot run away fast enough. He fears that knowing about Jim's gun jeopardizes his life. Yet fear, instead of accelerating him across the landscape, makes him live as if in a dream where everything happens in slow motion. In all of these instances of chases, the potential for capture is genuine or felt to be genuine at a psychological level. Beyond capture, the chase implies other outcomes: disappearance, entrapment, torture, conversion, defection. Chases have two fundamentally opposed positions: one either chases or is chased. Certain espionage narratives assume only one of these perspectives; others switch from one to another. These positions are simultaneously psychological, physiological, and political.

The narrative that focuses on the pursued man invokes discourses of conspiracy and paranoia. In *The Thirty-Nine Steps*, Richard Hannay is relentlessly chased. "I reckoned that two sets of people would be looking for me—Scudder's enemies to put me out of existence, and the police," says Hannay. "It was going to be a giddy hunt, and it was queer how the prospect comforted me" (20). Hannay wants to be the object of attention. The more enemies who treat him as quarry, the better. As a South African adrift in London, he has no social standing. A giddy hunt, in which both German spies and British police pursue him, affords Hannay the luxury of being visible, of having a recognizable identity. The chase brings him into being as a subject, albeit one bred of conflicting forces. Hannay has a psychological predisposition towards loneliness (or lonerness) that prohibits him from confiding to the police as soon as he is implicated in Scudder's death. In flight from his enemies, Hannay runs and pedals through the Scottish highlands. Only when no other human being is in sight, no one at all to chase him, does Hannay finally feel terrified: "oddly enough, for the first time I felt the terror of the hunted on me. It was not the police that I thought of, but the other folk, who knew that I knew Scudder's secret and dared not let me live. I was certain that they would pursue me with a keenness and vigilance unknown to the British law" (30). He offers the opinion that if, when pursued, "you are hemmed in on all sides in a patch of land there is only one chance of escape. You must stay in the patch" (49). He never shakes the idea that his flight, which he calls a "crazy game of hide-and-seek" (57), transcends make-believe or play. He constantly imagines his quandary in terms of games or theater, as if he cannot take it seriously, or as if the repertory of images for describing interpellation derives from infantile and representational sources. Disbelieved by policemen in London, he hightails it through dense traffic, "put[ting] on a spurt" (87) from time to time.

To occupy the position of the pursued is to exist within a circuit of paranoia and vulnerability. At some layer of ideological subjectivity, the pursued person understands himself to be guilty beyond redemption.

Guilt so profoundly defines Hannay's sense of self that he imagines an end to fear in the act of being discovered, caught, accused, and hanged. He is, in effect, too solitary. Hannay has "no real pal to go about with" (7) in London, and consequently he feels disappointed and dislocated in the city. The chase reveals ulterior motives intended to remedy Hannay's sense of dislocation. *The Thirty-Nine Steps* uses chase scenes to establish desirability and undesirability among immigrants. The South African has to prove his loyalty through an adventure that saves Britain from German invasion. South Africans are worthy immigrants because they are wily and willing to go outside the law; Germans, the villains of the piece, are unworthy immigrants because they are wily and willing to go too far outside the law and establish their own laws. When Alfred Hitchcock made Buchan's novel into a film in 1935, he concentrated on chase sequences: Hannay loping across moors, sometimes in cinematic fast motion; Hannay leaping out of windows and dodging through the streets. Hitchcock exploits the narrative of the chase to show the vulnerability of the human body pitted against the law. Whereas Hannay is South African in Buchan's novel, he is Canadian in Hitchcock's film. What Hitchcock retains from the novel is a sense of the expendability of colonial subjects and the implied need to prove their worth through loyalty to Britain, which is tested again and again.

The narrative of pursuit that focuses on the pursuer implies positions of authority and menace. The pursuer sees more, at any given time, than the pursued. The pursuer, therefore, possesses more control over the circumstances of the chase. Chases often enact a contest between rationality and irrationality, though the rational force need not hold the position of authority, nor the irrational force the position of vulnerability. In *The Riddle of the Sands*, the position of power occupied by Carruthers and Davies is mitigated by the fact that they do not know what they are doing. The plot of this spy novel is, ostensibly, driven by treasure. But sunken treasure is a lure, a bit of misinformation intended to mislead the British amateur investigators. The plot of *The Riddle of the Sands* really hinges on geopolitical contests: Germany is amassing *matériel* to invade England. Carruthers and Davies inadvertently learn that the discredited navy captain named Dollmann masterminds the invasion plan. Although he acquires mythic stature from his resemblance to Wagner's Flying Dutchman, Dollmann is more duplicitous than heroic. He nearly kills Davies by leading him onto a sandbar during a storm. He surreptitiously searches the ship for clues to hold against Carruthers and Davies. Nevertheless, the two English duffers, because they possess partial knowledge of the German captain, and because they suspect more than they can prove against him, follow him. "For me," claims Carruthers as the narrator, "[Dollmann] was the central figure; if I had attention to spare it was on him that I bestowed it; groping disgustfully after his hidden springs of action, noting the evidences of great gifts squandered and prostituted; questioning where he was most vulnerable; whom he feared most, us or his colleagues; whether he was open to remorse or shame; or whether he meditated further crime" (Childers 218). Carruthers, employed in the Foreign Office in London, extends his duties as an administrator into the domains of psychology and justice. He reads Dollmann's character as a political entity, not just as a personality. By applying reason to the mystery of Dollmann, Carruthers assumes a strategic position of power. Heady with this thrilling ability to solve mysteries, Carruthers subsequently follows other members of Dollmann's entourage. Knowledge permits a narrative of pursuit. There is almost no moment of rest in the entire narrative. At times Carruthers navigates while Davies rows through treacherous waters; at times Davies marches off into fog alone in pursuit of information about Dollmann. Engrossed in the chase, the Englishmen expose themselves to danger, confusion, and hardship. Carruthers knows when to relent and when to lose "sight of [his] quarry" (Childers 239). As in *The Thirty-Nine Steps, The Riddle of the Sands* presents political enigmas as the engine of plot. The political allegory is again one of planned German invasion and the defeat of that plan by amateurs. Duty to the state begins with the individual; cleverness cannot be too valuable when it keeps enemies at bay. In both novels, the trope of pursuit implies a fable of the proper latitude for action. The private individual may exceed the limits of lawfulness, may pursue supposed enemies, in the service of nation. The plot hurries forward by virtue of the positioning of characters as quarry or assailant, with the ulterior assumption that the individual has a civic responsibility to enact justice by arrogating the authority of the state.

In contradiction of the Althusserian analysis of political subjectivity, the hunter-and-hunted scenarios of espionage fiction permit two opposing relations to power. Subjectivity emerges from passivity and fugitive understanding of the law; subjectivity emerges from taking the law into one's own hands and stirring fear in others. Espionage narratives excite thrills in readers and spectators as so-called entertainment value. In his preface to *The Third Man,* Graham Greene confides that he and Carol Reed, director of the film version, "had no desire to move people's political emotions; we wanted to entertain them, to frighten them a little, to make them laugh" (11). The crucial insight here is not that *The Third Man* is an entertaining narrative. Rather, Greene identifies in passing that "political emotions" exist and can be manipulated. Laughter and fright go hand-in-hand in the realm of representation. Fear makes an audience giddy, especially when an audience can distance itself from the action being represented and feel secure.

The chase sequence in spy narratives has value in that it promotes thrill in excess of the representation, that it can effect a moment of conversion or compliance in an audience. Greene is a master of such effects. The dominant trope of Greene's novels is the chase. In *A Gun for Sale,* Raven runs from the police, cowers in darkness in a train car, hides in a warehouse, gets killed. In *Brighton Rock,* a gang of boys hunt down Hale and are hunted in turn by an amateur do-gooder named Ida Arnold. The protagonist of *The Confidential Agent,* designated only as "D," alternately thinks he will never "feel anything again except fear" (18) and suffers from the returning "fear of other people's pain" (140) as he flees from several enemies. In *The Ministry of Fear,* pursuit has less athletic qualities. Rowe, having purchased a cake containing microfilm at a village fund-raising carnival during World War II, is shadowed by a group of spiritualists, Austrians, tailors, and collaborators. Confined to an asylum after he loses his memory, Rowe lives in darkness. He haunts dark apartments, dark trains, rooms darkened for séances, London darkened against Nazi bombers—places that can be understood as the emblem of his not knowing. He has no understanding of why intriguers chase him. All of these chase narratives foment fear as a political emotion.

The purgation of pity and fear, Aristotle claims, happens after an audience identifies with a character. In espionage narratives, catharsis is also an ideological intervention in the audience. Catharsis effects closure by asserting a restrictive and unopposable position: there is no room for dissent or doubleness. Spies are unmasked and right prevails. According to the Aristotelian conception of purgation, the audience, having expelled pity and fear, emerges from the experience as exemplary, "purified" citizens.

They will not enact dangerous emotions in civil discourse and governance. This licenses theorists to treat aesthetic forms as essentially liberal forms in which narrative permits a play of ideas, a margin for action, and a tolerance for eccentricity in character. This interpretation of catharsis places reasonableness after emotion. In the Aristotelian formulation, drama permits an interplay of ideas from which the audience may or may not learn. As Andrew Ford says in an explication of this view, "the *katharsis* of pity and fear is a complex but finally irrational pleasure of the quintessentially democratic art form" (124). Bertolt Brecht, however, objects to the emotionalism of catharsis-oriented drama because irrational pleasures distract from the intellectual work of drama. Emotion is counterproductive to clear thinking. And this is the key to a reinterpretation of catharsis as a bodily effect that transforms thought: "catharsis marks and remarks a sentient convergence of body and meaning, when the material body, in all its otherness, makes itself felt to consciousness even as it enters discursive categories that make it mean" (Diamond 154).

If pity and fear get incited then eliminated in symbolic fashion within art forms, if, as we sit in the theater with our knuckles white and our eyes glued to the screen watching a feat of derring-do, of some impossible heroics, as when Arnold Schwarzenegger single-handedly combats snowmobiles, skiers, guard dogs, and various other assailants in the opening chase sequence of the movie *True Lies,* we have conformed to the intentional structure of the narrative to behave as docile subjects of authority and not to become terrorists or secret agents. As readers or viewers of espionage narratives, we experience catharsis as confirmation of ideological authority, since the murderous, foreign agents lose in this power struggle. Catharsis results from the expulsion of otherness, not its integration into a political process. The moment of suspense—when our sensibilities get caught in the tempo of watching—differs from tragic drama of the Aristotelian kind, insofar as espionage thrillers calculate their effects to make the audience, in a state of fright, accept the logic of justice without question.

"Without all doubt," writes Edmund Burke, "the torments which we may be made to suffer, are much greater in their effect on the body and mind, than any pleasures which the most learned voluptuary could suggest, or than the liveliest imagination, and the most sound and exquisitely sensible body could enjoy" (305). The suffering body learns more, registers more, than the voluptuary's body, according to this formulation. Burke's emphasis on suffering provides a crucial insight into the mass-market appeal of espionage narratives: addressing the body, thrillers move by pain, not by pleasure. Suspense—a bodily effect—urges conformity in a flash of brainwashing. In *Aesthetic Theory*, Theodor Adorno comments that emotion and reason, or "feeling and knowing" (454), cannot be disentangled and that "aesthetic behaviour might be defined as the ability to be horrified, and goose-pimples as a primordial aesthetic image" (455). "Shudder is a kind of premonition of subjectivity," Adorno continues, "a sense of being touched by the other" (*Aesthetic Theory* 455). In the moment of suspense, we are forbidden to think for ourselves. We abide by emotional response. We react according to the reality or the threat of pain. Pain instructs, as Burke makes clear: "When danger or pain press too nearly, they are incapable of giving any delight, and are simply terrible; but at certain distances and with certain modifications, they may be, and they are delightful, as we every day experience" (305–6). After terror subsides, we extract the lesson that conformity is expected. This conformity and this recognition of conformity have been achieved through threat to the body.

At the moment when the reader is most thrilled, he is interpellated. He becomes the subject of ideology, even a convert to the predominantly restrictive and conservative ideology of espionage narratives. Thrilled, the reader abandons his body. He grips the arm of his chair. He clenches his fingers into balls. He hides his eyes. He recoils. Thrilled, the reader or filmgoer forgets that he witnesses a representation instead of an event. He identifies with the pursued outcast more than he identifies with the pursuer, for the thrill depends for its effect on psychological patterns of submission, humiliation, defeat, and, thereupon, conversion. Thrilled, the reader or spectator anticipates accidents, destruction, or death—not his own, but death as a specter all the same. His hair raised, his breath held, he loses track of time and causal sequence. Only when the last moments of rapture pass off and a certain calm is restored can he evaluate the meaning of the thrill. Only then can he reinhabit his body.

Such is the logic of spy fiction.

You fear me; therefore you run.

I chase you; therefore you are doomed.

You want to be chased.

You fear that you will not be caught.

You will die alone in a sewer or a warehouse. You flee not because you are afraid, but because you need to be pursued, because you want to be caught. Pursuit gives point to existence; it sharpens the senses. If you were never caught, you would never know that you had lived. And for this reason, following the rationale of predation, you become a spy.

You may not be able to live a useful life without losing your way, without mismanaging your ethics from time to time or without feeling vulnerable, without cloaking your fear and seeing it surge up in a novel or a film.

The thrill you feel is the shock of what must be assimilated (the knowledge of death, the knowledge of vulnerability) or the shock of what will never be assimilated and will never be known: your place within a political order.

CHAPTER THREE

Codes

SELF-EVIDENT MEANING IN NARRATIVES OF INTRIGUE

Language, in a manner of speaking, is a type of algebra consisting solely of complex terms.

Ferdinand de Saussure, *Course in General Linguistics* (122)

WORDS[2]

Like the Enigma machine used by Nazis for encoding messages during World War II—a gizmo with rotors, scramblers, and plugboards permitting approximately 10 trillion key settings to encrypt messages (Singh 136) —the spy novel demands deciphering because it always means something other than itself. In *Enigma* (1995), Robert Harris's best-selling novel about events at Bletchley Park in England, where cryptanalysts broke the Enigma code during the War, the all-knowing historical narrator points out that the Enigma machine "had only one tiny—but, as it turned out, crucial—flaw. It could never encipher a letter as itself: an *A* would never emerge from it as an *A,* or a *B* as a *B,* or a *C* as a *C.* . . . *Nothing is ever itself*" (Harris 65). Characters, actions, numbers, and words in spy narratives have to be translated into other representational systems and contexts before they yield meaning. The clever interpreter—whether an agent within the text or a reader outside the text—moves adeptly among metaphorical, literal, and numerical systems to read aright. An interpreter of the signs around him, Richard Hannay, as the hero of four thrillers by John Buchan, travels through the world solving puzzles. In *Greenmantle,* Hannay deciphers three hastily scribbled words to know who his chief enemy is and what sort of conspiracy he faces. From the slenderest evidence, he extrapolates theories and meanings. "My mind had nothing to work on but three words of gibberish on a sheet of paper" (18), Hannay despairs. Poverty of evidence does not inhibit him from solving the mysteries before him. In the codes of espionage literature, words point to other referents, sometimes in other languages. A word is never a word, just as a number is never a number plain and simple. Nothing is ever itself. Breaking a code ushers a reader or a spy over a threshold of ignorance and into the domain of knowledge. In spy novels, codes mystify political realities. In *Greenmantle,* a Muslim jihad in Turkey threatens the balance of power during World War I. Hannay's cracking the three-word code preserves political and social order. Similarly, in John le Carré's novels, communist aggression during the Cold War is aggrandized through codes. Protected information, tautologically, is more valuable because it is protected. Spy novels promote themselves as codebooks, or at least coded books, offering political possibilities based loosely on political probabilities. These possibilities are disguised as mathematical problems, wordplay, or logical puzzles. Whereas solutions to mathematical equations or brainteasers promise knowledge, cracking such codes often leads to the death of the agent. In short, according to the sinister logic of espionage fiction, every code must be cracked, even if knowledge endangers the interpreter.

Codes have several attributes. They are symbolic representational systems. They encrypt secrets. They presume shared knowledge, as in social codes, by which *those in the know* abide. Codes therefore exclude. They imply internal coherence of structure; meaning compacts around a set of numbers, a shibboleth, a specific memory, an alphabet, a logo, a sign, a PIN, or an acronym. To have access to codes means to have access to some form of power. Characters are sometimes encoded as a function within a structure. In *Enigma,* a chief, called simply "C," organizes cryptanalysts at Bletchley Park. In John le Carré's *Tinker Tailor Soldier Spy,* the former head of the Intelligence Office is known only as "Control" (26). During World War II, the head of MI6, General Sir Stewart Menzies, was "always referred to only as 'C'" (Cline 23). In James Bond narratives, "Q," "M," and "007" assume existence as linguistic or numeric ciphers. As isolated figures in sequences, they promise progression. "R" could replace "Q" and "008" or even "1025" could replace "007." Such codes defy attempts to nail down either a spy's or a spymaster's identity. Numbers stretch to infinity; letters, too, can be recycled ad infinitum like so many settings on the Enigma machine. Similarly, personnel may change but their function in a system remains the same. Various people could execute the authority of Q, M, or C, since they serve as nearly algebraic symbols signifying bureaucratic roles. Joseph Conrad spoofs the tendency to mystify identity with mathematics when he calls Verloc in *The Secret Agent* "the famous and trusty secret agent, so secret that he was never designated otherwise but by the symbol Δ" (63). Such codes lock up personal identity or convert personal identity into an icon that assumes its place within a larger system of meaning. Such codes of identity, regulated by the Pentagon or MI6 or CSIS, require conformity. They limit identities to specific profiles. They also require knowledge of systemic functioning: what is the relative power of Q to M, if any? Are these identities, like figures in an algebraic equation, subject to speculative solutions? Solve for M. Solve for Δ.

Richard Hannay, who narrates *The Thirty-Nine Steps,* likes "chess and puzzles" and reckons himself "pretty good at finding out cyphers" (25). He puts his puzzle-solving abilities to use when he acquires a top-secret codebook written in cipher, "the numerical kind where sets of figures correspond to the letters of the alphabet" (25). Through skillful reasoning, he deduces the keyword that will unlock the code: "A was J, the tenth letter of the alphabet, and so represented by X in the cypher. E was U = XXI, and so on" (34). But he finds other enigmas embedded within the unscrambled code. The whole story, he concludes, occurs "in the notes—with gaps, you understand, which [Scudder, the spy who wrote the code] would have filled up from his memory" (37). The central mystery of the novel, the one heralded by the title, does not readily yield to interpretation: "'(Thirty-nine steps, I counted them—high tide 10:17 p.m.).' I could make nothing of that" (38). Hannay's exercise in reading moves him from numbers to words and back into numbers. One representational system merely displaces another, as if the solution to one puzzle is another puzzle. In this novella, Hannay's act of interpretation is an allegory of hermeneusis. What logical leaps does a reader make in order to synthesize information into meaning? If no text, whether written as figures or numbers, represents itself, if it cannot be taken at face value, what knowledge must be brought to bear to interpret it correctly? Hannay has to solve the puzzle of 39 at 10:17. To succeed at this task, Hannay has to read precisely and figuratively. The penalty for failing to do so is death: "from the scribble of a dead man I was trying to drag a secret which meant life or death for us" (96). The voice of the dead, possessing an authority that the living do not have, needs to be unscrambled before it can be put into effect. The dead speak in secret codes. *Caveat lector:* the secret of 39 at 10:17 might harm those who carry it or figure it out. The code might doom the reader just as it doomed Scudder. Although solving the puzzle is vital to national security, the answer may produce further casualties, including Hannay and his cohort.

In *The Thirty-Nine Steps,* as well as its sequels—*Greenmantle, Mr. Standfast,* and *The Three Hostages*—Hannay ventures outside the law in order to affirm the legitimacy of empire and its power structures. A contra-distinction with the detective novel needs to be drawn here. As Franco Moretti points out, the dominant opposition in detective narratives is between "the individual (in the guise of the criminal) and the social organism (in the guise of the detective)" (134). In espionage fiction, the individual repairs the social organism by taking the law into his own hands. Whereas crime fiction emphasizes domestic malfeasance, spy fiction emphasizes problems of racial integration, threats from other nations, and armament. Murders occur, but not, as in crime fiction, because of implacable hostilities between husband and wife; rather, homicide is cast as political necessity. Homicide "purifies" society of contrarian elements. In this fashion, spy fiction enacts a conservative political fantasy of wholeness and like-mindedness within nations. For this reason, militant nationalism and anti-Semitism underlie the genre. Hannay worries about "Jew-Anarchists" and "the killing of a Dago" (*Thirty-Nine Steps* 37). Fiedler in *The Spy Who Came in From the Cold* is a "Jew of course," with a tendency to be "remorseless in the destruction of others" (107). Deeply distrusted because of his undeclared allegiances, Fiedler, a German communist Jew, exponentially compounds the duplicity manifest in all agents. Religion, whether Jewish or Muslim or Hindu, is a label for doubleness within narratives of intrigue. Civil society has less homogeneity than supposed. As in *The Secret Agent,* London swarms with displaced Eastern European anarchists, nihilists, and revolutionaries of all stripes. In Doris Lessing's *The Good Terrorist,* a hodgepodge cell of activists and politicos holds, in London, "the first National Congress of the Communist Centre Union" to formulate revolutionary principles on the model of "the Russian Revolution, the Chinese Revolution, and, if necessary, the French Revolution, for it was not too much to say that the lessons of the French Revolution had by no means been exhausted" (221). Revolutions abroad animate the London Congress, which is a way of claiming that radical social change has to be coded as foreign for it to undermine domestic security. Spy and terrorist narratives exaggerate revolutionary zeal within society in order to justify its extirpation. The spy, as an encrypted and allegorical figure, embodies latent contradictions in British or American or Russian society. To dispatch a spy is to dispel contradiction, especially the contradiction of multiple allegiances or multiple nationalisms.

Or the spy must labor tirelessly to prove his nationalistic mettle. Although a South African, Richard Hannay is a zealous patriot. Perhaps *because* he is South African, Hannay is a zealous patriot—for Britain. His differences of outlook and accent prompt him to go to great lengths to integrate. (Arnold Schwarzenegger's many roles as the overbuilt, Austrian-inflected Über-American provide a cinematic equivalent to Hannay's complex nationalist position.) Patriotism does not prevent Hannay from slipping into and out of numerous disguises. Indeed, his background facilitates his theatrical talents. His identity—rooted in his narrating voice and the personal pronoun "I"—remains essential, a constative as opposed to a performative self, or so he wishes readers to believe. His ability to enact various roles and to maneuver through conflicting systems of representation allows him to crack codes, presumably because he can occupy numerous subject positions. He imagines himself in different disguises, in different countries, in different languages. He reacts speedily to dangerous circumstances because he can think outside of his own worldview. In *Greenmantle,* Hannay is handed a piece of paper with these words written on it: "'*Kasredin*,' '*cancer*,' and '*v.I*'" (15). Possible solutions for "Kasredin" and "cancer" are immediately offered. The third cipher evokes no specific meaning. It could be the "number of a motor-car" (25). It could equally be, in its combination of letter and Roman numeral—or is it a capital I? —shorthand for something more recondite. "Kasredin" means "house of faith" in Arabic; or it may be a misheard rendering of the name Nasr-ed-din (24–25). It touches pointedly on the mystery of "Greenmantle," a coming prophet (147–48). "Cancer" refers to disease or a sign of the zodiac. Hannay, during a bout of illness, realizes that "v.I" is a shorthand for "von Einem" (98), a formidable woman who rallies support for the jihad among Germans and Turks alike. Solving such language puzzles requires building theories from "the slenderest evidence" (117).

Often about codes, secret languages, and encrypted meanings, narratives of intrigue require reading beyond the surface. Spy novels mislead readers by planting false clues or clues not fully understood. In John Barth's *Sabbatical*, footnotes ostensibly substantiate the narrative with background information, character dossiers, and news-blotter facts, yet the reader has no assurance that this information has validity unless he or she undertakes research to prove or disprove it. *Sabbatical* presents odds for strange coincidences, couched in mathematical terms. In a Washington department store, two friends, Fenn and Dugald, run into each other by pure chance, even though they are scheduled to have lunch together at the opposite end of town later the same day: "According to the 1980 census, the Washington D.C. metropolitan area is home to more than two million people; it is visited by more than fifty thousand tourists on an average day. There are two other customers at Woodward and Lothrop's beret counter: one, a lady, leaves just as Fenn arrives; the other, a gentleman, arrives just as Fenn is leaving. No mathematician, Fenn will nonetheless calculate, once he finds an almanac, that gender aside, the odds against one of those two's being Dugald Taylor are at least 1,025,000 to 1. Yet the gentleman-arriver-as-Fenn-is-leaving is his old friend and mentor [Dugald]" (139). Rendered as statistical probability, the encounter acquires cachet. Barth parodies the tendency to read meaning into encounters that are novelistic contrivances; he equally parodies the tendency of spy novels to confer probability on themselves by resorting to complex numerical calculations, in which mathematics looks like technical exposition. Other information, regarding government expenditures and aliases and undercover intrigues, spills from *Sabbatical* as a jumble of probability and impossibility, odds and ratios. Statistics disguise truth as much as they tell truths. Numerical bafflegab authenticates the narrative for certain readers, or at least gives a whiff of credibility to this story of unlikely occurrences. Every event inexorably leads to another event the way that numbers succeed each other in sequence. Every incident functions like an indispensable piece of a carefully worked-out plot. The plot appears rational because measured and divided into incidents.[1]

As coded books, spy thrillers suggest that true interpretation is a deviation from standard or word-for-word interpretive practices. Hannay's companion-in-intrigue in *Greenmantle*, Peter Pienaar, undertakes a mission to deliver an important map showing enemy positions across a battlefield. As he crosses enemy territory, he acquires information in code. Lying in the absolute blackness of the night, Peter hears someone tapping out Morse signals: "The sound was regular and concerted—dot-dash, dot-dash, dot, dot. . . . This was where Peter's intelligence work in the Boer War helped him. He knew the Morse, he could read it, but he could make nothing of the signalling. It was either in some special code or in a strange language" (238). Just as Hannay has to fall ill in order to discover the meaning of "v.I," Peter has to lie still in a place of death in order to understand what the code may be. Throughout all four Hannay thrillers, the protagonist and his allies brush against death to find the solution to codes that will alter the course of international politics. Messages of life and death are so dire that they cannot be fully absorbed by the living. Although Hannay frequently ventures out on his own recognizance, he does so, allegorically speaking, to suggest that the limits of interpretation must be pushed further, that the reader of codes cannot comfortably abide by what he or she already knows.

Codes need keys or keywords that permit decipherment, like a Rosetta stone that makes translation possible or an agreed-upon clue that unlocks an entire message. Codes communicate, yet, self-evidently, they are intended to prevent information from being intercepted. In this sense, codes are secrets that float through public space. The logical problem with most codes is that both the sender and receiver must possess the key that unlocks the encrypted message. There has to be reciprocal knowledge. Technically speaking, a cipher is letter-by-letter substitution, whereas a code substitutes words for other words or symbols. A codebook could be elaborated in which all words would appear as something not themselves: General = ∞ and Agent = μ and so forth. Elaborate systems could spring up around such substitutions. One language replaces another entirely. All nouns, for instance, could be mathematical icons; all verbs could be numbers; all adverbs could be Japanese characters. 12 ∞ ⼑ might mean "Kill General immediately." Such encoding has the downside of being laborious to concoct and torturous to read. The agent either has an infallible photographic memory or carries about a cumbersome codebook delineating the meaning of individual icons. Once an enemy intercepts these codes and codebooks, they have to be abandoned. Letter-by-letter encipherment, as opposed to symbol-for-word encoding, is therefore often more handy for military and other purposes (Singh 30).

Computer technology has altered the symmetrical arrangement of encryption. It is now possible to have asymmetrical encryption: "asymmetric cryptography can be thought of in the following way. Anybody can close a padlock simply by clicking it shut, but only the person who has the key can open it" (Singh 270). The sender encrypts a message using a public encryption key; the recipient opens the message using a private decryption key. Spy narratives, being ultimately modernist in their conception of rational worlds, have not caught up with such encipherment techniques. The implications of asymmetrical encryption for reading are limited: no novelist writes a book for only one reader. Nonetheless, one reader at a time unlocks the enigma of the thriller narrative. Traditional one-time keypads and sourcebooks are still stock-in-trade for fiction writers. In Graham Greene's *The Human Factor,* the mole named Castle encrypts messages using *Clarissa* or *War and Peace* as the source for coding (29). The mole Pym in John le Carré's *A Perfect Spy* uses a copy of Grimmelshausen's *Simplicissimus,* an eighteenth-century volume of verse written by a man obsessed with "false names" (340). Such encoding depends on symmetrical arrangements. The cryptographer invents a code, knows how to encipher and decipher, and distributes the key for the code to all those who need to open it. Linguistic and numeric competence are equally apportioned between sender and receiver.

The fluidity of movement from language to code to language points out that all languages are codes, not just in the degree to which signs arbitrarily designate meaning, but also in the degree to which languages get personalized by users. Like the "little language" that Jonathan Swift creates in *The Journal to Stella,* a weird hybrid of anagrams and baby talk and *l*'s substituting for *r*'s, personalized language looks forbidding: "Must loo mimitate pdfr, pay? Iss, and so la shall. And so leles fol ee rettle. Dood mollow" (210). Loosely translated from pidgin into grown-up English, this means, "Must you imitate Presto [Italian for Swift], pray? Yes, and so you shall. And so there's for your letter. Good morrow." James Joyce, influenced by Swift, makes this point forcefully in *Finnegans Wake* (Bishop 453–54), and especially in the lisping sections concerning Issy: "Has you pusy a pessname? Yes, indeed, you will hear it passim in all the noveletta" (561). Few people read *Finnegans Wake* without several guidebooks in hand to elucidate its obscurities. Modernist literary language is often the little language of the self—the odd locutions that individuals use, the personalized vocabulary and invented words that express identity. Joyce intimates as much in *Ulysses*, filled as it is with puns and pettish prattle: "I called you a naughty boy because I do not like that other world," declares Leopold Bloom's coy mistress Martha (63). As in Swift's little language, a hint of perversity clings to private exchanges. Swift and Joyce elaborate codes for naughtiness in which the sender and the receiver of the code share the key to meaning.

Little languages require translation into linguae francae. As both Swift and Joyce recognize, there is something inherently regressive and infantile about such languages. They repeat sound patterns rhythmically and, once decoded, yield little sense: *coochy-coochy-coo, ga-ga-goo-goo, higgledy-piggledy-pop*. Made-up languages are fundamental to identity, especially to erotic life, where little languages flourish as nicknames, pet phrases, and gibberish. Such languages, between lovers or within families, assert tribal belonging. They create intimacy and regulate it. Coded messages within novels likewise assert affiliations, with the corollary that secret agents learn to speak several languages or get by heart many codes in order to expose doubleness in others. Based on the same principles of substitution and condensation that little languages possess, codes in spy narratives present themselves as vital to national security. Spy novels advertise their codes in titles. John le Carré's *Tinker Tailor Soldier Spy* and Len Deighton's *Twinkle, Twinkle, Little Spy* play on nursery rhymes and songs, suggesting that the most commonplace phrases are replete with secret meaning. Numeric titles such as *The Third Man, The Tenth Man*, or *The Thirty-Nine Steps* activate the suspicion that numbers, like words, open up mysteries or, put otherwise, that numbers are as arbitrary as words.

Because spy narratives advance the proposition that meaning is detectable within codes, the most successful spy-catchers are drawn from the ranks of Oxford and Cambridge dons. These academics are useful not just for their ability to teach, but for their ability to deduce information from encoded, sometimes foreign, languages. Versed in arcana, linguists, medievalists, and epigraphists are accustomed to solving puzzles that seem to have no solutions. They infer information from the smallest scraps of evidence. George Smiley, who figures in all of John le Carré's early novels and assumes spymaster preeminence in the "Karla" trilogy comprised of *Tinker Tailor Soldier Spy, The Honourable Schoolboy*, and *Smiley's People*, is a linguist by training. Even minor characters in this series have a smell of the library about them: Roy Bland, in *Tinker Tailor Soldier Spy*, spends years "plodding the academic circuit in Eastern Europe" and thinks a fun evening is spent "talking Wittgenstein" (92). The cryptanalysts in Robert Harris's *Enigma* are drawn from the ranks of mathematicians and linguists at Cambridge, supplemented with deft crossword-puzzle solvers who responded to a newspaper contest during the early days of World War II and found themselves recruited willy-nilly to work at Bletchley Park. In a variation on this motif, Richard Hannay is a geological engineer by training, an applied rather than a liberal arts education. Like the best of the academics, Hannay is a dab hand at deduction. He also admits to speaking "pretty fair" German and fluent Dutch (*Greenmantle* 30–31). Sometimes he affects a broad Scots brogue and a Yankee drawl as required by the touchy circumstances in which he finds himself.

Spymasters, such as Smiley or Somerset Maugham's Ashenden, typically conserve a donnish inquisitiveness—softness of voice and suaveness of manner—that teases out a confession or a vital statistic from double agents. The bumblingness and ordinariness of the scholar-spies grant them perfect cover. Often they need no disguise because they in no way call attention to themselves in dress or voice. More important, the recondite knowledge they have at their fingertips allows them to make leaps of deduction that appear intuitive but are the result of logic. The spy-catcher does his homework. Smiley, for instance, sits up until the wee hours in search of specific information (*Tinker Tailor* 261–66). He tracks, then backtracks, through dossiers until he finds "the corroboration of a theory" (*Tinker Tailor* 217) that previously had no footing in fact. With their linguistic competence always at hand, even agents taken out of the field can count on day-school placement teaching French or German: Jim Prideaux in *Tinker Tailor Soldier Spy* teaches French and marks student papers through the night "because correcting kept his mind in the right places" (270). Magnus Pym in *A Perfect Spy* excels at German and loves Oxford so much that he vows, "I shall become a don and be a hero to my pupils" (340). Careful spies and their operators burn the midnight oil. All of them are blessed with fine-tuned analytical skills. All of them think before they act. Hermeneutically inclined, all of them read the signs of the world— whether in clothes, or letters, or books, or gestures—as a set of codes.

Narratives establish the parameters within which spies and readers interpret codes. In *Tinker Tailor Soldier Spy,* the arrival at a boys' school of a new master with an odd name elicits comments on the open secrets of language: "'A linguist,' Thursgood told the common room, 'a temporary measure,' and brushed away his forelock in self-defence. 'Priddo.' He gave the spelling 'P-R-I-D'—French was not Thursgood's subject so he consulted the slip of paper—'E-A-U-X, first name James.' . . . The staff had no difficulty in reading the signals" (9). The staff reads this name as suspiciously foreign. Not sharing the biases of the teachers, the reader of the novel may not interpret the signals the same way. Jim Prideaux's presence at the school is enigmatic, as is his past. The novel elaborates numerous codes, including a system of leaving milk bottles on a stoop "to signify, in the eclectic language of [housekeeper] Millie McCraig, that you may come in and all's well" (336). Smiley blinks a flashlight into the garden to send messages to his back-up assistant. Clothes too are a code: "'If I wore my collar open she knew I'd had a look around and I reckoned the coast was clear. If I wore it closed, scrub the meeting till the fallback'" (68). Identities and passports and bodies are rife with meaning in this narrative. A plethora of details challenges the reader to sort meaningful signs from meaningless ones. Readerly aptitude is at stake. Moreover, this degree of encryption promotes a conception of character as enigma. At the microlevel of words and at the macrolevel of narrative, character is the sum of complex codes of clothing (open collar or closed?), gesture (was that a flashlight beam I saw in the garden?), and language (P-R-I-D-E-A-U-X?). "The more identities a man has," we learn later, "the more they express the person they conceal. The fifty-year-old who knocks five years off his age. The married man who calls himself a bachelor; the fatherless man who gives himself two children. . . . Few men can resist expressing their appetites when they are making a fantasy about themselves" (209). The observation, homespun though it is, indicates that the codes of character interpolated within espionage narrative may ultimately be about surfaces, not secrets. The more encoded an identity, the more it approaches authenticity. The greater the number of identities, the more closely they express one single identity.

Aficionados of spy literature keep reading novels not for the sameness of the stories but for variations on recognizable motifs. We understand codes because the structural limits of the genre dictate that some threat to national security will be uncovered; an agent will be dispatched to confound that threat; an agent will succeed or not; another agent will be a mole; calm will prevail in the end. Roland Barthes, writing generally about the activity of interpretation, claims that codes "are themselves, always, ventures out of the text, the mark, the sign of a virtual digression toward the remainder of a catalogue . . . ; they are so many fragments of something that has always been *already* read, seen, done, experienced; the code is the wake of that *already*" (*S/Z* 20). Barthes is speaking here of the ways that a narrative can summon meaning in a reader's mind by virtue of resemblance and difference. The reader recognizes actions, character, and meaning because other narratives manipulate similar material. One cinematic code for bad guy is dark glasses (such as the computer-programmed agents wear in the film *The Matrix*), though this code has acquired nuance and, indeed, flipped into positive encoding (Arnold Schwarzenegger, a good guy, wears sunglasses in *The Terminator*). One televisual and cinematic code for connectivity is the phone booth (characters in *The Matrix* regain their mother ship by being sucked as strings of code through phone lines, just as Maxwell Smart in the 1960s television show *Get Smart* accessed his underground headquarters through a phone booth).

A panoply of codes interweaves to produce variants of "formulaic" spy fiction. Espionage codes include disguise, abduction, chases, gadgetry, ghosts, disappearances, foreign accents, maps, ennui, homosexuality, and so on (Cawelti and Rosenberg 219–20). Because these codes are so recognizable, they can be mixed in various ways, as in most James Bond films, without much attention to narrative continuity. The plots are episodic, we might say, or they are held together through the interweaving of codes already familiar. As Barthes claims, the code is "already" common property. The keys for unlocking meaning are in public hands, which implies that all decoding is merely a discovery of the self-evident. In some ways, codes, because they mean something more than themselves, can be solved. Only one solution fits all the conditions that create the code. One true answer emerges from a host of possibilities. In this regard, spy fiction defies the notion of hermeneusis as the generation of endless chains of meaning. Correct meaning does exist "outside of its realization in the mind of a reader" (Tompkins ix). Unlike deconstructionist musings that emphasize reading as a re-encoding of meaning—Paul DeMan claims that "interpretation of the sign . . . is a reading, not a decodage, and this reading has, in its turn, to be interpreted into another sign, and so on *ad infinitum*" (9) —formulae in spy novels admit one correct, ultimate interpretation. Having said that, I will add that decoding puzzles in spy narratives generates multiple alternatives. The reader searches among possible answers to find probable solutions. Moreover, the reiteration of codes in spy fiction draws attention to what is not already known. If readers and spies automatically deciphered all codes, there would be no point in undertaking the dangerous mission of reading. The capacity to live in a state of not knowing animates both readers and intelligence-gatherers.

Codes require accurate reading, as do clues, though codes and clues are not the same thing. A code is immaterial; a clue is material. A code refers to something not itself, whereas a clue, like a hair left at a crime scene, synecdochically relates to the crime. Codes are, in C. S. Pierce's terms, "symbols," that is, signs that neither resemble the thing they represent (an icon), nor have a causal or existential relation to the thing they represent (an index), but exist as a system of arbitrary designations (Mitchell 56). By the same classification, a clue usually is indexical, insofar as the object has a causal or existential relation to an event or character. Blood stands for crime. Hair stands for murderer. Hammer stands for weapon. Nonetheless, clues, like codes, require sequencing and interpretation. In *A Perfect Spy*, for example, word codes trigger readerly interpolations. Magnus Pym, also known as Mr. Canterbury, mentions two posters affixed to a notice board, "both to the passer-by as dreary as cups of cold tea. Yet to those who know the code they transmit an electrifying signal" (39). In and of themselves, the posters signify nothing, unless the reader can convert their meaning into an electrifying signal. These particular posters elicit personal memories for Pym, not secrets pertinent to espionage. The billboard codes pertain to psychology rather than political machinations. The reader of the novel, who has to organize Pym's feverish jottings into a personality that makes sense, only later learns that these are not prearranged signals—such as the tinny tappings on a telephone receiver that Pym listens to and comprehends. In a narrative that makes much of acts of reading, of calling the reader's attention to details, no degree of vigilance suffices. By the end of the novel, when a small light switches "on and off" (602), the vigilant reader understands this as an interpretable sign: Pym has been surrounded in his lodging house and defeated in his scheme to flee from his life as a double agent. From the single flicker of light, the reader extrapolates an intelligible system, a world dazzling with meanings so plentiful that it is impossible to know what degree of interpretation will prove adequate to organize those meanings.

In *A Perfect Spy*, le Carré toys with the possibility that all words, including names and advertisements, function as codes to be read correctly, with neither too little nor too much emphasis placed on facts in themselves. Actions encode meaning about character that the spy does not regulate consciously: "Sometimes our actions are questions, not answers," Magnus Pym writes (39). Behavior, then, cannot be used as a reliable guide to character. As a mole spying for the Czech government against his British employers, Pym acts according to the context in which he finds himself. He performs. Even the passion he feels for Mary his wife—however authentic it may be at the beginning of their marriage—dissipates. In his final minutes of life, he addresses Mary in his head: "'Sorry I married you for cover. Glad I managed a bit of love along the way. Hazards of the trade, m'dear. You're a spy too, remember?'" (605). Having "managed" his love, Pym has not been entirely truthful about the degree of passion he felt for Mary; she loves him wholeheartedly and goes to great lengths to protect him. Some actions, including, apparently, acts of love, may be performative, a trying on of potentialities within personality, an actor's reflex based on instinct or unspecified need. Pym claims that he has "never taken a conscious decision" in his life (35). Codes of character lie at the heart of espionage narratives. The genre makes a virtue of rationality: puzzles yield to reason. At the same time, the genre promotes the indecipherability of character: character is a puzzle that is nigh on impossible to crack. Although we, as readers, discern through Pym's narrative that he places his oldest friend, Axel, in an unimpeachable position, and that his belief in one true friendship causes Pym to doublecross his British handlers, this psychological explanation is baffled by the realization that Axel, understanding Pym's need for one true friend, toys with his friend's tenderheartedness. Pym does not have full appreciation of his own character. He is, to himself, a cipher.

QUADRATIC EQUATIONS

Because spy narratives revel in the complexities of algebraic substitutions, let us express this character problem mathematically: $x \neq x$. A character is not what he seems. Pym serves as a double agent, a false husband, a con man, a lonely schemer without fixed political convictions. Nonidentity extends to all facets of the novel. A radio broadcast is not just a broadcast, as when Pym tunes into a Czechoslovakian station to hear publicly announced private messages: "Sound of page turning, signal for get ready" (171). In all such instances, $x = y$, something not itself. A page turning means take up your pencil. Or perhaps $x = x^n$, in which x raised to the power of n stands for the potential surplus of meaning that x yields when placed within different contexts. A page turning means nothing at all to those who don't know the code, but it means any number of things to the agent who has his shortwave dial tuned to Brno. Magnus Pym decrypts messages using a keybook: "Opening his Grimmelshausen at page fifty-five he found five lines down without even counting and on a fresh sheet of paper wrote out the first ten letters of that line, then converted them to numerals according to their position in the alphabet. Subtract without carrying. Don't reason, do it. He was adding again, still not carrying" (171). Don't reason, argues Pym's inner voice of betrayal. The message has nothing to do with thinking. It has only to do with action.

Spy narratives dictate that character cannot move too far outside a set of established options. Spy fiction relies on rationality, logic, linguistics, and precision to consolidate its status as "real" within the possibilities of representation. Mathematics within such narratives enhances effects of certainty and precision. Like words, numbers are signs that form systems. They are symbolic structures (Ifrah 23–24).[2] Numbers represent reality; they account for objects and events in the world without causing them to materialize, just as words do. To put it curtly, numbers are not real, but representational. They are an elaborate code useful for defining problems in reality. Numbers mean nothing to those who don't count. What is the meaning of "one" or "2,397"? What or how does "zero" signify except as an abstract concept of a void? Zero, in other words, is an emblem for the idea of nothing. Typically, spy narratives play numbers off against words. When words can no longer be trusted, narrators resort to numbers. "Thirty-nine steps" is a measurement, but of what? The "third man" is a missing person, but who? The numbers seem to offer stability insofar as they point to something that must exist. The third man, having been seen, is assumed to occupy a place in the world but has, in his disappearance, left a hole in reality where number 3 should be. As codes, the numbers require interpretation.

John le Carré's novel about a mole who has infiltrated the British Intelligence Office, *Tinker Tailor Soldier Spy,* quantifies character and action, time and terror, probability and potentiality. Interrogating a former member of staff, George Smiley discounts certain extravagances in her narrative: "to Smiley's tidy mind her speculations, in terms of the acceptable arithmetic of intelligence, seemed even wilder than before" (109). Smiley discredits those details that have been added for the sake of the story. Stories begin in facts and work outwards through deduction. "Learn the facts," one intelligence officer proposes, "then try on the stories like clothes" (302). He implies that if the clothes don't fit, go back to the facts. Narrative concatenates facts logically. Facts and intelligence have more inherent value, according to this model of storytelling, than elaboration and point of view. This adherence to rational fact tyrannizes characters. Le Carré treats numbers and their functions as metaphors throughout *Tinker Tailor Soldier Spy*. For instance, Bill Haydon surpasses George Smiley at the intelligence game, at least temporarily, because he is "better at the arithmetic" (149), which means he connives and plays favorites. Deceit coded as *calculation* (in both senses of the term) is not restricted to Haydon. One "mathematical-looking boy" (328) in Paris seems capable, despite his eggheadedness, of capturing a wily agent. Another character, Peter Guillam, snoops through files in the Intelligence Office archives, worrying all the while about the passage of time, which is a different form of numerical tyranny. "Don't look at your watch," he counsels himself, "look at the clock and do the arithmetic, you idiot. Eight minutes. . . . Still eight minutes" (174). Time measures and quantifies duration in an apparently rational manner. Guillam works against the clock, which is to say that he works against the constraints of numbers. Rebellion against the regime of numbers is possible. In *Tinker Tailor Soldier Spy*, gamblers "play" numbers. A casino manager claims about his establishment, "'We get all the help we need from the arithmetic'" (228). He is lying, of course, merely to prove that his establishment is aboveboard. Human intervention contradicts the strict objectivity of number-based chance. The human element alone confounds arithmetical rationality.

Tinker Tailor Soldier Spy poses the problem of defining character within the rational limits of logic and numbers. Time in Guillam's mind seems elastic—too fast, yet static. Smiley discredits stories that deviate from logic, which may, in truth, limit his ability to discover the traitor within the intelligence hierarchy who understands how to abide by logic and yet must, because he is two-faced, prove self-contradictory in some way. Smiley examines reports for logical inconsistencies, rejecting those that have been filed in the archives purposefully to deceive sleuths such as himself: "Having listed the topical reports, he set down their dates in a single column and threw out the rest. At this point, his mood could best be compared with that of a scientist who senses by instinct that he is on the brink of a discovery and is awaiting any minute the logical connection" (217). While adhering to such rational standards, Smiley can also open his mind "to every inference, every oblique connection" (148), since what he needs to find is an inconsistency, a telltale pattern, a fake, a code, anything that will unlock the mystery of the mole in the Intelligence Office. Looking over a technical report, Smiley appreciates the "higher mathematics of the balance of terror" (139). Such mathematics involve the statistical capabilities of missiles balanced against the terror inspired by nuclear war. The mathematical metaphors of *Tinker Tailor Soldier Spy* heighten the "logical" aspect of narrative yet are contradicted by the improbabilities of behavior derived from terror or subterfuge.

The mathematics of personality are more complex still.[3] Certain agents never exist except on paper, as contrivances to foil counterespionage incursions or to throw internal sleuths off the trail of moles. In *A Perfect Spy*, unreal agents are invented as covers, the way a hypothesis is advanced to prove or disprove a point. In this case, where an agent is no one, $1 = 0$. Sometimes, as in *Tinker Tailor Soldier Spy*, one person has two categorically distinct personalities. In this "devious arithmetic" (94) of doubleness, $1 = 2$. After examining classified documents, Smiley discovers corroboration for a theory that two seemingly different people are actually the same person: "between the mole Gerald and the Source Merlin there was an interplay that could no longer be denied; that Merlin's proverbial versatility allowed him to function as Karla's instrument as well as Alleline's" (217–18). Since Smiley's thinking is relatively obscure as a deduction, let me express this deduction as an equation. A mole infiltrates a British secret service organization headed by Alleline. The mole occludes his secret identity with the code name Gerald. At the same time, a leak, code-named Merlin, sells information to Karla. Gerald is a variable as is Merlin. If x, in algebraic fashion, signifies mixed motives, Gerald $= x$. By contrast, Merlin, a British member in good standing at the Intelligence Office— let us designate him as y for the time being—proves to be a Czech or Russian infiltrator. Smiley, in a flash of insight, proves that $x = y$. Gerald is Merlin. Bill Haydon is Gerald is Merlin. If $x = y$, can the mole sustain both identities indefinitely? Does x sometimes take precedence over y in the eagerness with which he avows allegiance, in which $x = y^{-1}$? The factors may multiply, not equal, each other: Bill = xy. Or Bill = (Merlin × Gerald). Gerald's credibility increases in proportion to the value of x and y working in tandem. The more esteem attached to him by the British, the more prized will be the information he can trade to the Russians. A narrative that presumes $x + y$ = Bill is less skill-testing all around. If both variables have an ideological cast to them, x = imperialist, Western, democratic, militaristic values and y = Marx-inspired, utopianist, soviet, authoritarian, militaristic values, then xy multiplied produces, as the numbers rise, greater ideological frottage, or hysteria, or importance. Lacon tells Smiley that 600 agents are operating in the field at present—the novel is set in the early 1970s—and 120 agents are behind the Iron Curtain: "With numbers, with facts of all sorts, Lacon never faltered. They were the gold he worked with, wrested from the grey bureaucratic earth" (78). Once the variables of character have been conned, intelligence officers deal with nuggets of verifiable fact. At the same time, the novel undermines the certainty of all numbers. Abiding by the possibility that $2 = 1$ in an erotic sense, two men, like the yolk and white of an egg, can potentially combine into one perfect being. Bisexual Bill Haydon extols the virtues of Jim Prideaux: "'He's my other half, between us, we'd make one marvellous man'" (263). Bill is possibly Jim's lover (343). Jim, we learn, also loves Bill (360). Thus the blending of two personalities yields a single "marvellous man": $2 = 1$ in the Platonic sense that halved souls seek their lost partners. Character that seems single and unitary is, in truth, fractionalized and fragmentary.

Although a mathematization of narrative seems fanciful, an algebraic hypothesis that accounts for encoded material might help us see why espionage is called a "formulaic" genre (Sauerberg 78–81). To arrive at a formula for the character of a spy, elements such as education, xenophobia, gender, fluency in foreign languages, voyeuristic tendencies, nationality, sportsmanship, capacity for consuming alcohol, and sexual expertise have to supplement the basic silhouette of personality. The exact measure of those qualities cannot be taken, not even by the spy himself. Psychology is an imprecise science. Bill Haydon, for instance, ranks highly in United Kingdom intelligence gathering, yet he has other qualities that contribute to the complexity of his character. He paints extremely well at an amateur level. He is "blueblooded" (90). He has a "queer colour" in his cheeks that makes him look slightly like "Dorian Gray" (92). He sleeps with a "snotty little sailor boy" (356) as well as a "flat-faced girl" (355). He also seduces Smiley's flibbertigibbet wife. These attributes of eros, class, secrecy, and artistic inclination cohere in a psychological profile. Character, however, has to move through actions in order to acquire meaning. To create an equation that allows for character and action both, we will have to consider experience in the field, coincidence of events, theft, doublecrossing, chases, false accusations, inauspicious encounters with wanted agents, recruitment, illness, and disguises. Character reveals itself through choices and actions.

In *Poetics,* Aristotle observes that a good plot depends on "the law of probability or necessity" (54). He elaborates by saying that "within the action there must be nothing irrational" (58). Because all imitation duplicates reality, actions must show "consistency" (58), by which Aristotle means appropriate language, gesture, and motive. If something unlikely gets represented, it has to be challenged as artistically incorrect: "With respect to the requirements of art, a probable impossibility is to be preferred to a thing improbable and yet possible" (65). Aristotle seems to swerve here from his insistence on probability over possibility by introducing the feasibility of impossibility under probable circumstances. Probability depends on the parameters established by action and character up to that point. In Alfred Hitchcock's *North by Northwest,* Cary Grant, playing an ad executive named Roger Thornhill, abducted under a weird pretext of being a military intelligence officer named George Kaplan, ends up running across an Indiana cornfield and sliding down Mount Rushmore with Eva Marie Saint. Given the hinging together of events (abduction, mistaken identity, pursuit), scrabbling over the stony visage of George Washington begins to look probable, even if physically impossible. Eva Marie Saint nearly falls to her death, in part because she has on the wrong shoes. Another twist further complicates probability. George Kaplan does not exist; the FBI fabricated him to catch a criminal. Roger Thornhill is George Kaplan who is a dummy: $1 + 1 = 0$. The requirements of art determine the suitability and plausibility of the action.

Somerset Maugham, in his introduction to *Ashenden, or the British Agent,* comments that: "The work of an agent in the Intelligence Department is on the whole extremely monotonous. A lot of it is uncommonly useless. The material it offers for stories is scrappy and pointless; the author has himself to make it coherent, dramatic and probable" (ix). In his

suite of spy stories, Maugham casts Ashenden as a playwright who works
as an agent during World War I. Ashenden constantly resorts to his writerly
knowledge to fend off the more dangerous aspects of his undercover work:
"Ashenden reflected that had he known anything of the technique of the
theatre Bernard would have been aware that it was useless to make a gesture that had no ulterior meaning" (16). The theater teaches useful lessons
in character reading, bluffing, and restraint. The probability that Maugham
endorses in his introduction is, then, the a priori probability of the theatrical world. Maugham's intention, clearly, is to uphold an Aristotelian conception of the logical linkage of events. He supplements the "law of necessity" with the law of representation. Genre establishes its own rules and
those rules assert probability. Such predetermined probabilities serve as
codes. The ingenious and athletic spy will escape his pursuers. The bisexual
is a traitor. The woman is a dupe. Such are the characterological paradigms
of the genre, with a few variations.

"Probability" and "possibility" coincide in literary representation and
resemble abstract calculations. Readers weigh likelihood against far-fetched
premises. Constant adjustment of expectations during the act of interpretation constitutes hermeneusis. The reader decides whether adventures
as improbable as Richard Hannay's reveal an allegory of politics that an
imitation of "real life" would not fulfill. Hannay improbably eludes his
captors, whether Scotland Yard or German agents, with uncanny ingenuity.
George Smiley, going over reports stolen from the Intelligence archives,
establishes the probability of finding an inconsistency—methodical research pays off—whereas the discovery of inconsistency without methodical research or patience or due suspicion would be absurd. Le Carré always
prefers necessity over accident, pattern over chance, ordinariness over
heroism. Just as chase scenes in thrillers cause readers and viewers to
regress, through fear, to vulnerability, codes in espionage narratives intimate that readers lack information. They inexpertly decipher codes. The
reader, susceptible to being duped in any event, condones improbability
for the sake of arriving at a better understanding of political allegiances.
Thus the genre resorts to mathematics to make improbability seem coherent. Odds are that a narrative of intrigue delimits improbability through
a numbers game.

Robert Harris, in *Enigma*, raises the possibility of a mathematical code
for narrative:

"The cipher machine converts the input (plain language, P) into cipher (Z) by means of a function f. Thus $Z = f(P,K)$ where K denotes the key. . . ."

He sharpened his pencil, blew away the shavings and bent over the sheets.

"Suppose K has N possible values. For each of the N assumptions we must see if f^{-1} is the deciphering function which produces P if K is correct . . ." (15)

Plain language emerges as cipher through the intervention of a machine. The machine regulates ciphered language, and therefore it regulates narrative itself to some degree. The idea of the story-generating machine is a deeply held modernist fantasy. V. I. Lenin promulgated literature-as-machine in *Party Organization and Party Literature:* "Literature must become *part* of the common cause of the proletariat, 'cog and wheel' of a single, great Social-Democratic mechanism brought into motion by the entire politically-conscious vanguard of the entire working class" (qtd. in Zwerdling 6). By extension, writers serve as machine operators, as assembly-line propagandists who keep the cogs and wheels of the Social-Democratic state oiled. In Lenin's view, literature needs to be partisan, to adhere to an aesthetic of social realism and an advocacy of the working-class movement. Lenin, however, does not reject the cultural products of the past. In fact, he does not think a proletarian culture can be decreed into existence, but builds instead on previous culture. Lenin's view of literature differs from nineteenth-century practice, especially in its representation of labor. In Dickens's *Hard Times,* machines destroy the will of the workers and the best that characters in that novel can hope for is to run away with the circus or to repudiate toil in factories. By sharp contrast, Lenin sees literature as an apparatus, a cog and wheel in the mechanism of the state. The novel-writing machines in George Orwell's *Nineteen Eighty-Four* bring this vision of propaganda to fulfillment. Julia, in Orwell's novel, runs a "powerful but tricky electric motor" in the Fiction Department of the propaganda bureau, and she "could describe the whole process of composing a novel, from the general directive issued by the Planning Committee down to the final touching-up by the Rewrite Squad" (108). The collective fantasies of Orwell, Lenin, and Harris suggest that novels have formulae. They conform to mathematical laws.

So, too, in *Enigma,* the encoding machine and the decoding *bombes* clatter along, irrespective of human feeling, creating lines of text that defy instantaneous understanding: "BSTUXNTXEYLKPEAZZNSKUF" (66). Numbers abound in this novel: "five hundred pieces of information every week, 25,000 in a year" (301); "20:46: ten" (306); "he twirled III and set it at the letter G, V at A and IV at H" (324). Every object, every clue, gets reckoned as a statistic by cryptanalysts and readers. Like a reader, a cryptanalyst looks for patterns of repetition and probability within strings of letters. All aspects of the world, including sounds and military maneuvers, have a numerical structure subtending them. To amuse himself as a child, Jericho factors hymn numbers in church: "number 392 in *Ancient and Modern* came out very prettily, he remembered, as $2 \times 7 \times 2 \times 7 \times 2$" (165). Hermeneusis, like decoding, begins at nodes of repetition. The Enigma code breaks under close scrutiny not because the machine repeats itself, but because the keys for scrambling and decoding messages, distributed to weather station managers and U-boat commanders, among others, require that a four-letter call be repeated at the beginning of each transmitted message—to prevent human error in reception and interpretation of the message. The machine itself remains a masterpiece of mathematical ingenuity. Human foible alone, specifically the need to forestall error in the act of interpretation, deprives the code of its invincibility.

In the Enigma machine itself, "there were five different rotors to choose from (two were kept spare) which meant they could be arranged in any one of sixty possible orders. Each rotor was slotted on to a spindle and had twenty-six possible starting positions. Twenty-six to the power three was 17,576. Multiply that by the sixty potential rotor-orders and you got 1,054,560. Multiply *that* by the possible number of plugboard connections—about 150 million million—and you were looking at a machine that had around 150 million million *million* different starting positions" (Harris 65). The "sublime" (Harris 64) element of numbers translates into a surplus of technical exposition. Such exposition aims at maximum precision through mathematical reference: "Convoy HX-229A. Left New York Tuesday. Twenty-seven ships. Similar cargoes to the others. Fuel oil, aviation spirit, timber, steel, naval diesel, meat, sugar, wheat, explosives. Three convoys. A total of one hundred and seventeen merchant ships, with a gross registered tonnage of just under one million tons, plus cargo of another million" (Harris 82). This passage suggests that the spy plot depends on synchronicity and calculability. Food and *matériel* have no expressiveness beyond tonnage, although quantity registered in numbers has a certain sublimity. To extend this enthusiasm for numbers to the patterns of narrative itself in spy fiction would, theoretically, generate a set of strict algorithms that the novelist could adhere to.

A workable formula for spy fiction would, in the first instance, allow variables of action and character. Hence, an equation, for which one could solve for "character" and "action," should express potential, probability, and event through algebraic and logarithmic means. In the following formula, x and y stand for antagonistic components. These antagonisms may be within the character's own personality (Pym is the product of a con man father and a merciless, Protestant, preaching grandfather) or may be between characters (*Spy vs. Spy*, as *Mad* magazine characterizes it). In the equation that follows, "Eros" signifies erotic attractions, which have been defined by infantile development and exacerbated by subsequent experience. Eros plays a part in political antagonisms, insofar as it muddies friendships and disrupts bureaucratic efficiency. (Bill Haydon sleeps with George Smiley's wife.) Eros, ever and always a cipher, should take into account homosexual and heterosexual experience, number of lovers, libidinal drive, and capacity for distraction. (James Bond sleeps around, yet his libido scarcely interferes with his duty.)

Furthermore, the number of languages spoken fluently by the spy will arithmetically, as opposed to exponentially, enhance opportunities for espionage, since speaking one language does not grant any particular advantages in speaking other languages, although the size of linguistic groups (Norwegian versus English, for example) will affect opportunities for interaction. Language complicates recruitment procedures and encoding of messages. You might intercept a German code, but if you don't speak German, deciphering the code will not be useful. Let l therefore signify languages. "'Amazing what people will tell you if it gives them a chance of showing off their languages,'" says a character in *Tinker Tailor Soldier Spy* (255). Arnold Schwarzenegger in *True Lies* slides through English, French, Arabic, and German with equal facility. His linguistic capacities confer authority on him in sticky situations. The more languages the spy speaks, the more power he has to negotiate the complexities of global politics. Foreign languages liberate unactualized parts of the self. What can never be expressed in one's mother tongue finds release in French, or Persian, or Sanskrit. Pym, in *A Perfect Spy*, "needed to be able to close the door on his Englishness, love it as he might, and carve a new name somewhere fresh. He even went so far on occasion as to affect a light German accent" (187).

To converse brilliantly in a foreign language but to say nothing of consequence is far worse than to converse adequately in a foreign language about matters of moment. Therefore, education (technical, philosophical, general) enhances linguistic authority, whether education pertains to a stock of general knowledge (Grimmelshausen was an eighteenth-century mercenary, poet, and falsifier) or to more specific information (the range, in kilometers, of an ICBM). Years of higher education can polish general and specific knowledge, though the number of years spent pursuing a degree has no necessary correlation with competence under pressure. Let e stand for education, with the proviso that e can include elements of class (did the spy go to Eton, Oxford, a red-brick university, an Ivy League institution?) as well as street smarts (did the spy acquire his savvy on the job? in the military? elsewhere?). At this point, we should concede, language and innate intelligence merge with action.

Pym performs his Germanness just as Schwarzenegger performs his Americanness and Richard Hannay performs his many identities. Character, we remember from Aristotle, manifests itself through action. Action takes precedence over traits of personality and modifies traits of character. For this reason, an "adventure" or "action" coefficient always qualifies personality, either by compromising or amplifying it. Such a coefficient will not be constant, since happenstance and periods of reflection interrupt the forward thrust of the thriller plot. Hannay falls ill, as do Leamas in *The Spy Who Came in From the Cold* and Pym in *A Perfect Spy*. Productive as these periods of flu or fever prove to be, they alter the rhythm of the narrative from headlong to sedate. Bearing in mind the alterations in narrative pacing, let the coefficient for adventure indicate hazard. The frequency and intensity of adventures will be proportional also to global conflict. The perception of communist threat in 1963 will heighten the urgency with which spy missions are undertaken, as opposed to the perception of communist threat in 1989. Traits of character will emerge during a secret operation conducted during wartime that might not have emerged under any other circumstances. The logarithm denotes external conditions that accelerate or decelerate the rate of adventure. Taking all these elements into account, I offer the following equation for character:

$$\text{Character} = \frac{[(xy) + (l^n \times e)]^\circ}{\text{Eros}}$$

With factoring, we might solve for Eros or l as well. Similarly, action might generate a formula in which "character" has its place. Action unfolds over time and modifies character as it does so. Therefore we can solve for "character" and introduce that solution into the equation for action.

$$\text{Action} = \frac{[(\text{character}) \times (\text{coincidence})]^{time} + \text{gadgets}}{\text{Duty}}$$

Both of these formulae have, of course, no validity. They merely take to an extreme the latent wish of all spy novels: to be as logical and precise as an equation. The inner logic of the machine of narrative resembles the inner logic of language. Both aim at controlling variables and making all details cohere into a whole. Yet in language and narrative, a wide margin of possibility remains.

Codes generated by machines break down because of human intervention or human error (Seife 1–3). Characters buck the system, hack into a network, defy the numbers and the machines that encrypt privacy. Behind such actions lies the human need to respond disruptively to systemic control. Conflicts between programmed machines and human beings register another conflict within spy narratives, namely, the one between perfect, machine-written plots, in which every detail falls into place and every event synchronizes faultlessly with all elements of the plot, and resurgent human passions, such as love, betrayal, and loyalty, that the perfect plot has forbidden. In *Enigma,* Jericho, a cryptanalyst, falls in love with Claire, who has been assigned the task of routing traitors from the cryptanalysts' ranks by seducing them and monitoring their behavior. Jericho unwisely thinks Claire loves him for himself, when she loves him because she has to do her job. Quite suddenly, she disappears from Bletchley Park (169). Because she disappears, she's presumed to be "a spy" (227). The "hunt" (273) for Claire yields no physical trace of her beyond a pile of clothes at the side of a lake. Jericho and Hester discover that she is not who she pretends to be. *Nothing is ever itself* in code. This maxim translates into the affective life of Jericho, Hester, and Claire as well. Claire impersonates a girl who died in infancy; Claire takes over her name and upper-class identity as credentials for her espionage work. Claire ≠ Claire. Even her name, with its implications of lucidity and transparency, misleads. Jericho sentimentally believes that Claire authentically loved him: "'He never suspected she was betraying *him* all the time'" (383). He fails to translate the first rule of codes into his emotional life where he would have been able to discern the difference between love and love as a pretext for duty during wartime. A romantic trapped in a spy plot, Jericho cannot operate both code systems simultaneously. He dreams of machines fitted with "pentode valves and GT1C-thyatrons to create computers, machines that might one day mimic the actions of the human brain and unlock the secrets of the soul" (165). Vain as this wish may be, it registers his discomfiting fantasy of being relieved of emotion. To rid himself of the ghost of Claire, he imagines himself a machine. Computers would drain character from its human container. Formulae covering probabilities and possibilities could predict actions. Meanwhile, characters vanish without a trace. No equation covers such eventualities or recuperates the human body. No formula forecasts the treasons and disillusionments that comprise erotic life.

DEATH

Jericho solves the mystery of Claire's disappearance without solving the mystery of her character. He knows she is not the person she claimed to be. He knows she was planted among the cryptanalysts to unmask traitors. He knows that she coaxed him into an erotic liaison not because she loved him but because she had to perform her job as a spy-hunter. Knowing all this does not prevent Jericho from being haunted by Claire. To figure out that she behaved doubly, Jericho courts death; he recognizes that his erotic passion for Claire, having ebbed away, leaves only melancholy stasis. As one character tells Jericho apropos of secrets, "'it's possible to know too much'" (365). Knowledge does not soothe Jericho's longing for Claire. It merely brings him closer to the knowledge that he cannot possess her. Decipherment leads him to despair. Solving puzzles (like doing a crossword or factoring a number) produces no reward. If anything, demystification produces baleful sadness. Indeed, code-cracking resembles grave-robbing. To understand a code is to encounter death, as in *Treasure Island* when Captain Bill is tipped a sheet of paper called a "black dot," a "summons" (Stevenson 15) that means either he gives up his treasure or he dies. The black dot, inked completely on one side, warns the captain that he has to surrender his booty by a certain time. The captain understands the code of the black dot. Taken by apoplexy, he dies instantly, before delivering the treasure. Similarly, in *Enigma,* Jericho and a colleague joke about the etymological proximity of decryption to crypts:

> "The Latin *crypta,* from the Greek root κρύπτη meaning
> 'hidden, concealed.' Hence *crypt,* burial place of the dead,
> and *crypto,* secret. Crypto-communist, crypto-fascist. . . .
> By the way, you're not either, are you?"
>   "I'm not a burial place of the dead, no." (13)

Jericho lies. He becomes a burial place of the dead in that Claire continues to haunt him. He hears messages about her "from the edge of the grave" (383). Jericho hopes that she still lives; he presumes that she has resumed her own name and identity in London: "'to say that she's still alive is not an act of faith, but merely logical. She *is* alive, isn't she?'" (383). The language of logic, Jericho should have learned, has no relevance to character. Claire disappears but Claire is not dead. She is two people; she is one; she is none. Although as good as dead, she does not remove the problematic erotic melancholia that Jericho suffers when she disappears. If anything, his sense of frustration compounds when she leaves because he will never be able to get her to love him again. He holds out the vague hope that she may return because he wants to revive his passion for her, even if it is a passion based on illusion.

The trope of disappearance raises the problem of bodily representation in spy fiction. In thrillers, as in other narrative genres, the body gives off meaning. To cause a body to disappear is to erase it as a signifying entity, to deny that the body functions both as a physical fact and as a code constituted of words, disguise, or gesture. The missing body generates a different kind of meaning. Rather than gestural evidence, the missing body becomes the ultimate cipher, a figure of deathliness. What makes someone want to disappear? In *The Secret Agent,* Winnie Verloc leaps from a ferry while crossing the English Channel. Because Winnie leaves behind her wedding ring and no statement of why she drowned herself, the tabloids call her death *"an impenetrable mystery"* (Conrad, *Secret Agent* 266). In *The Riddle of the Sands,* Dollmann leaps from a cruising ship into the North Sea and his body is not found: "'He must have slipped over quietly. . . . He had an ulster and big boots on'" (Childers 259). Missing bodies typically return in narratives of intrigue. While absent, they are, for all intents and purposes, dead bodies. Having disappeared from representation, bodies may transform or evanesce (Christ in Joseph of Arimathea's tomb; the Duke in *Measure for Measure* who abdicates then comes back in disguise). Thus disappearance encodes a hidden story of resurrection, of fleshly decay overcome. In spy novels, the body that disappears comes back as a warning that death cannot be outrun. The "peculiar power" (Goodwin and Bronfen 9) of a corpse augments when the corpse, mysteriously hidden, rematerializes. In spy narratives, the corpse is both clue and code. Like the skeleton of a man carefully laid on the ground in *Treasure Island* to indicate the location of buried loot, the corpse speaks, albeit mutely and in code. Rather than transforming into something else while missing, the spy's cadaver signifies that all bodies are dispensable, especially in the realm of political games and brinkmanship.

At first glance, disappearing bodies seem to deny the rational structures of spy fiction. It is not impossible that a body go missing and not be found, though it is, by the logic of global intelligence and intensive surveillance, improbable. Manhunts retrieve bodies, dead or alive. If the body is dead, dental records and DNA tests will ascertain identity. Anterior to such a presumption of rational structure and the place of bodies within espionage narratives lies the problem of the body as itself a code. In *Greenmantle*, Hannay, escorted by a kindly German, reads gestures as a language: "he ... wanted to tell me that he was my friend, and he had no other language than a pat on the back" (68). The body produces a language of gesture that exceeds words. In this instance, Hannay, pretending to be an Anglophobic Dutchman who speaks no German, finds comfort in physical touch. Where words fail, touch confers meaning. Beyond gestural languages, the body signifies pain, death, and history. Richard, a veteran of trench warfare, has a shrapnel wound at the back of his neck that "hurt[s] like hell" (81) when Stumm cruelly prods it. These wounds tell a story of suffering that Richard himself does not narrate in words. The ultimate code of spy fiction may therefore be the body itself: indecipherable, multiply storied, costumed, scarred, agonized, kinetic. The body, as a container of personality, allows emotion to register on its surface. Stumm reads a look of dismay on Hannay's face as "fear" (80). Because it signifies so powerfully, no one imagines a body can disappear without leaving a trace. Rare indeed is the spy narrative that allows a body not to be recovered. Exceptions to the rule include *Enigma* and *Sabbatical*. More usually, the bodies of missing people have to be found and acknowledged as dead in order for them to cease to have agency. Survivors have to bear witness to the truth of death in order to persevere.

Disappearance sometimes prefigures the death of the body. In the vanishing world of *A Perfect Spy*, everyone and everything disappear. Magnus Pym, on the pretext of burying his father, slips away from all surveillance systems to a boarding house on the English coast. He vanishes from view. Neither his wife Mary nor his English boss Jack knows where he has gone. Prone to disappear "for two days" (153) and return with a lie on his lips, Pym follows a pattern of evanescence established by other characters: "Everybody vanished, everybody out of touch. . . . Conger's daughter is not reported present, is not reported sicklisted. Vanished" (402). Disappearance runs in Pym's family. His mother "sort of vanished" (192). The floozies who hang around his con-man father "were fickle and liable to sudden disappearances" (133). When Pym, as a young spy, reports that his friend Axel has gone "missing" (459), that he has "vanished" (466) definitively, the police do not respond. Axel's disappearance remains an unexplained mystery. The pattern of having family members and friends who disappear underlies Pym's own decision to absent himself from his wife, his son, and his various chiefs. The narrative advances towards Pym's capture—he is a double agent—and simultaneously moves backwards to disclose why he betrayed his country. The "ghost of Axel" (352), which is really the ghost of a friendship with Axel, causes Pym to commit acts of betrayal.

Pym also suffers from an acute sense that personality seeks its complement in another person: "Axel was his keeper and his virtue, he was the altar on which Pym had laid his secrets and his life. He had become the part of Pym that was not owned by anybody else" (583). Within this novel, le Carré represents psychology as complementarity. Pym imitates the mannerisms and speech of Axel. He patches together a public persona out of other people's behaviors. " 'Magnus is a great imitator,' " says Axel, " 'Really I sometimes think he is entirely put together from bits of other people' " (501). A composite personality, Pym has no authentic self. He is merely a set of interlocking gestures, speech patterns, and civilities acquired from others. Mary notices that Axel's gesture of looking over the brim of his glass during a toast has insinuated itself into Pym's habits: "That's what Magnus does, she thought. And it's you he learned it from" (496). Mary consequently realizes that she has lived with a husband who has borrowed "style" (497) from Axel. Pym has never been himself with her, merely a conduit of personalities. The formula for character in this case could be expressed as Pym $= a + b + c$, and so on to infinity. With the exception of his attachment to Axel, Pym has no discernible individuality. Together they establish their "own country with a population of two!" (478). His personality interlocks with Axel's so thoroughly that, by implication, Pym cannot disappear without Axel and the ghosts of all the other personalities that make up his own. Having disappeared, Pym must be hunted down because he has deceived so many of their private selves. His betrayal of England seems less crucial than his exposure of the fundamental inauthenticity of personality.

Moreover, the narrative technique of A Perfect Spy reverses the role of person and phantom. In his coastal boardinghouse, Pym writes the story of his life to various interlocutors. They appear in turn—father, son, wife, friend, chief—conjured from Pym's memory. They exist as ghosts. Occasionally, while "writing his meticulous reports on tomorrow's revolutionists, the ghost of Axel materialised before him and Axel's cry of 'Pym you bastard where are you' whispered in his ear" (352). He sees the "ghost" of his father "in every shop window and autumn doorway" (169). Sections of third-person narrative detailing the manhunt for Pym—Pym as quarry —intercut the first-person segments narrated by Pym. In alternation, Pym's interlocutors, then Pym himself, act as ghosts. A perfect spy dematerializes. He is everywhere and nowhere, someone and nobody. While Pym reaches into the past to justify his actions, the manhunt aimed at finding him moves relentlessly forward through a series of interrogations and meetings. Where past and present converge, the body of Pym materializes—dressed in pajamas, swaddled in towels, ready to commit suicide. Once the spy disappears, he cannot reappear as he was. Once the narrative presents a plausible account of Pym's character, once the code of espionage has been broken, Pym dies. Propelled by the desire to decrypt information, which is akin to a desire to enter a crypt, interpreters encounter dead bodies. Although the mathematical impulses of espionage fiction propose that everything can be accounted for, equations do not account for disappearance and death. While upholding rationality as a desirable motivation for action, spy narratives such as Greenmantle, Enigma, and A Perfect Spy permit irrationality to enter representation in the form of ghosts.

PART TWO FRONTS

CHAPTER FOUR

Ghosts

ILLEGITIMACY AND COMMITMENT IN
UNDER WESTERN EYES

UNCANNY POLITICS

Ghosts are relics of desire. They incarnate covert erotic or political wishes that have gone unrealized and that come back to haunt the divided subject. They are also, sometimes, estranged elements of subjectivity projected as alien shapes. Ghostliness characterizes partisan roles or acted-out identities that have been violently repudiated, or just as violently endorsed, that is, a suite of identities adopted to suit changing circumstances. Ghosts stand for those aspects of character most fully realized during moments of terror: who are we when we are frightened out of our wits? For the bereft, ghosts stand as figures of obstructed mourning. More specifically, in espionage fiction, specters express the uncanny return to consciousness of false commitments, betrayals, or collaborations tainted by error. Ghosts flit about scenes of crime, including assassinations and terrorist attacks. Such phantoms recall incidents of trauma, in the sense that Freud uses the term in the *Introductory Lectures on Psychoanalysis* to define an excess stimulation that the mind cannot shed: "an experience which within a short period of time presents the mind with an increase in stimulus too powerful to be dealt with or worked off in a normal way" (275). But the ghostly, and sometimes ghastly, representations of trauma in the novels of Joseph Conrad, especially *Under Western Eyes,* a seminal novel in the literature of double agency, yoke personal psychology with political affiliation.

A ghost recalls not just a personal act of betrayal, of the student Razumov turning Haldin over to the police, but also a forcible integration into a conspiracy, of Razumov being recruited as a police spy in exchange for what he imagines will be a secure bureaucratic position. In a manner entirely new in the repertory of the thriller, Conrad demonstrates that modern subjectivity is predicated upon a split between being and doing—of character and action, or plan and praxis—that allows the spy to believe in meritocracy and to agitate for revolution at the same time.

Modernism is crowded with the ghosts of repudiated affiliations and renounced friendships. Not all these ghosts represent false political commitments. Many of them reflect hysterical disruption or inexplicability. A roll call of modernist fictional specters would necessarily enlist Oscar Wilde's "The Canterville Ghost," Henry James's *The Turn of the Screw,* Edith Wharton's *Tales of Men and Ghosts,* the wet apparition of Michael Furey in James Joyce's *The Dead,* Stephen Dedalus's theory of authorship as ghostly infiltration of character elaborated in *Ulysses,* M. R. James's tale of moonlit abduction in "The Mezzotint," Yeats's yarns about wailing banshees and Irish supernaturalism, the wan ghost of Mrs. Moore in E. M. Forster's *A Passage to India,* and Freud's interpretation of trauma in "Mourning and Melancholia." Some of these ghosts serve aesthetic purposes. Some answer psychological needs for remembrance and justice; they bedevil authority or confound the senses. Some acknowledge murder or strange disappearance. Some stand for the terrifying aspects of the unknown. More often than not, they recall mortality. The Canterville ghost appears just "before the death of any member of the [Canterville] family" (Wilde 193). Ghosts figure modern facelessness and anonymity. "So many, / I had not thought death had undone so many," sighs the speaker in "The Burial of the Dead," the first section of *The Waste Land,* as he surveys urbanites drifting across London Bridge (Eliot 62).

A distinction needs to be drawn, however, between phantoms of the living and phantoms of the dead. Some of the most importunate ghosts of the twentieth century include the troops killed in the trenches during World War I. These ghosts force a confrontation with death as a reality beyond comprehension. "We are the Dead," writes John McCrae in the sonnet, "In Flanders Field," the most widely read poem of World War I. The speaker in this poem beckons his audience from beyond the grave: "To you from failing hands we throw / The torch; be yours to hold it high. /

If ye break faith with us who die / We shall not sleep" (qtd. in Fussell 249). The dead pass the torch of leadership in battle to those who still live, but those same dead troops also transmit a threat that they will stalk the living for breaking faith with the past. The soldier-speaker seeks justice for untimely death. The stratagem of hailing "you" demands readers to see the dead, to acknowledge their sacrifice, and to honor them ceremonially. The tradition of conversing with ghosts has precedents in Homer's *The Odyssey* and Dante's *Inferno,* though typically the living call up the dead. In McCrae's poem, the ghosts of recently dead soldiers hail living soldiers to preserve faith with and do justice to their common cause.

Communication with soldiers killed in action during the Great War— seemingly an entire generation—involves insurmountable grief, grief on a scale that exceeds the capacity of one person to define. Yeats confronts this problem in "All Soul's Night," a poem written in Oxford in 1920, a town populated by the ghosts of men who lost their lives during the war and who ought, had history been fair, to have formed the undergraduate body by 1920. "A ghost may come; / For it is a ghost's right," writes Yeats in a spiritualist mode (256). Unable to think of so many ghosts in the abstract, he then summons up his many dead friends by name. "But names are nothing. What matter who it be," he concludes, for the hosts of the dead so outnumber the living, and because death undid an entire generation of young men (259). Yeats's point, like Conrad's a decade earlier in *Under Western Eyes,* bears on the nature of public experience and mourning. Conrad shares with other modernists, especially Yeats, the sense that ghosts represent the incomprehensibility of political actions. Only the dead can answer for their actions. Motives and meaning slip into obscurity when not narrated either by sufferers or by witnesses. In *Under Western Eyes,* Razumov observes that "'a soul when it is seen is just that. A vain thing. There are phantoms of the living as well as of the dead'" (224). Authority resides with those who can *see* such emanations. One must be predisposed to witness and talk with the dead in order to hear their belated messages of caution and commitment.

Especially in spy narratives, repression of political alternatives induces haunting. In John le Carré's *Tinker Tailor Soldier Spy,* an informer declares that a double agent, supposedly dead, turns up haphazardly at an airport lounge: "Not a ghost. Flesh" (26). The informer implies that the materiality of the agent's body is always doubtful. The spy does not differ physically from other travelers. Blending in, he is just not recognized as a spy. Anthony Hyde's *The Red Fox,* a thriller about a missing person, opens in a cemetery because, as the narrator states, "I was to learn that all the real secrets are buried and that only ghosts speak the truth" (3). Spies' bodies are typically apparitional. Spies inhabit louche spaces: sewers, alleys, basements, bunkers, tunnels. They understand hidden, connecting passageways and move from place to place freely, heedless of walls. Haunters of shadows, spies depend on insubstantiality as a cover for information gathering. Moreover, the ghostly spy strikes a pose of indifference towards foes in political conflicts. Equivocal, the spy could belong to any party. In political terms, we think that we understand our convictions perfectly, but situations of danger force unexpected actions that contradict our beliefs.

As a recurrent trope in spy narratives, ghosts signify ethical dilemmas that have no resolution. Furthermore, spy fiction strains realist credibility by admitting phantoms that disturb the illusions of closure that realism promotes. Relying on realist techniques of psychological complexity and moral assurance, spy narratives allow readers to indulge in fantasies about the tidiness of history, that villains die and that countries possessing the most up-to-date weapons win disputes and wars. The reader participates in a complex thrill brought about by "the hero's triumph over history . . . and the resolution of complexities of the external world" (Wark, *Spy Fiction* 7). If this is so, the ghosts in spy fiction reintroduce unresolvable complexities. They represent nodes of unassimilable traumatic matter. They need to be read allegorically rather than literally.

Despite its many phantoms, *Under Western Eyes* is a realist novel riven with contradictions about revolution and conservatism. Both the revolutionaries in "La Petite Russie" (4) in Geneva and the police in Russia misunderstand Razumov's politics. The "puppet of his past" (362), Razumov feels "he no longer belong[s] to himself" (301). He betrays the revolutionaries by filing a spy report. He betrays autocratic rule by confessing that he spies on the revolutionaries. Critics construe his self-division as duplicity because he initially fools both sides. He scarcely knows what he believes because he has never been tested in his commitments. Whereas readers of *Under Western Eyes* beg for a definition of political engagement that caters to such contradictions, Conrad offers only irony. Avrom Fleishman claims that Conrad never stopped hoping for "human community" (242) in his political representation of autocracy and Rousseau-inspired freedom.

Such a formulation makes Conrad a social liberal, but it does not quite describe his expansive political vision. The freedom from politics that Razumov seeks ushers in tragedy. Human community remains an illusion. Razumov integrates into society by returning to Russia at the end of the novel as a deaf, crippled, forgotten, former spy. From the opening pages of the novel, his actions pose an ethical dilemma. Abstractly stated, the dilemma concerns "'complicity'" (301), a word that irritates Razumov like a splinter under his skin. Should Razumov turn the assassin, Haldin, over to the police or should he aid him in escaping the law? Should he abide by the law even if he distrusts the law? Should he betray his country or his friend? What agency does he have to act or not to act?

The agent enacts the dilemmas of political engagement where character merges with praxis. Action in spy fiction, however, always occurs in support of an ideology. Because ideology supersedes individual initiative or revolt, the thriller plot curbs the freedoms of the individual. As such, thrillers are typically conservative. They eliminate, as far as possible, reason, doubleness, duplicity, and liberality from the representation of character. Even physical uniqueness is undesirable because telling details (color of hair, DNA, blood type, fingerprints, eye color, distinguishing scars) betray the agent. In the good guys versus bad guys dialectic of the spy narrative, characters tend not to change over time or with experience. Once a Brit, always a Brit; once a fighter, always a fighter. They may pass over to the enemy side as a matter of going bad or going out in the cold. The spy embodies dangerous doubleness, the possibility of opting for an alternative that upsets stability, or the possibility of behaving independently that the spy holds in reserve. Although characters may not evolve through a spy novel, spy fiction represents the contradictions of the free-thinking, rational, democratically able individual recruited into ideology. The paradox of abiding by principles and translating them into human action obsessed Conrad. In *Nostromo*, the narrator states: "A man haunted by a fixed idea is insane. He is dangerous even if that idea is an idea of justice" (322). Ideals should not be pitched above human difficulties, for ideals brook no deviation. The spy tolerates, even welcomes, paradox as a form of conviction.

In *Heart of Darkness* (1899), *Nostromo* (1904), *The Secret Agent* (1907), and *Under Western Eyes* (1911), Joseph Conrad represents political agency through ambiguous male doubles. The double projects sexual energies and uncertainty. As Freud writes in "The Uncanny," the double emblematizes "possible futures" (358) projected as otherness. The double telepathically shares thoughts, feelings, experience, and knowledge with his *semblable,* to the point where "the subject identifies himself with someone else, so that he is in doubt as to which his self is, or substitutes the extraneous self for his own" (Freud, "The Uncanny" 356). The double haunts the subject who regrets actions not performed. Leggatt, the criminal pulled from the sea by a novice ship captain in "The Secret Sharer," which Conrad wrote in November 1909 while struggling with *Under Western Eyes,* casts missed opportunities as homoerotic longing (Najder 353). The Captain stashes Leggatt behind the bathroom door and feeds him tinned delicacies from a private larder. The two men whisper sotto voce in the dark to avoid detection. Leggatt stows himself in the Captain's bed, in a manner reminiscent of Haldin's throwing himself onto Razumov's cot. Yet Leggatt may not exist at all. The Captain may hallucinate him to compensate for his lack of authority; an inexperienced commander, he barely controls his crew. Always appearing in the dark, always weary with fatigue, always whispering, Leggatt, whose name hints at legalities and legs to stand on, consolidates the authority of the Captain by demonstrating that uprisings can be quelled through proper management. As the head of a mutinous crew, the Captain needs authority, even if he obtains it by consorting with an accused murderer who, on the run, boards the Captain's ship in dark of night. The phantom double therefore incarnates the doubts held by the Captain about his own ability to govern. As the story ends, Leggatt disappears into the sea, effacing in a gesture the problematic phantom. Not an espionage story, "The Secret Sharer" nevertheless registers homoeros as a subtext extinguished by the assertion of authority. Although the Captain gives his pajamas and his hat to Leggatt, he keeps his head. Expelling the phantasmatic, murderous stowaway from the ship underscores the homosocial or homicidal bond between Leggatt and the Captain. The ghost of mutiny vanishes.

Whereas the doubles in "The Secret Sharer" express ambiguity of sexuality and authority, Razumov and Haldin, the doubles in *Under Western Eyes,* express the traumatic consequences of political commitment. The conservative protagonist Razumov repeatedly sees the silent phantom of revolutionary Haldin lying in the snow or living anew in the form of his sister Natalia Victorovna. After brutally assassinating Mr. de P—, the head of the Repression Commission in czarist Russia, Haldin enters Razumov's room unbidden under the mistaken apprehension that Razumov is a noble-minded liberal. More strangely still, he lies uninvited in Razumov's bed, where, hands over his eyes, he discourses on the nature of revolution and eternity. Without having sanctioned Haldin's action, or without having welcomed the revolutionary into his rooms, Razumov is implicated in a plot that he finds repugnant. Outraged at being dragged into a situation beyond his control, he turns Haldin over to the police. Haldin is tortured and summarily hanged. Even before Haldin is executed, Razumov has a "morbidly vivid vision" (32) of him as a martyr to political freedom. In the snowy streets of St. Petersburg, Razumov envisions the spectral body of Haldin "stretched on his back . . . solid, distinct, real, with his inverted hands over his eyes" (36–37). Irate, Razumov walks across the "phenomenon calmly" (37). He commits an act of violence against the specter that he hopes will counteract Haldin's bomb blast and aggressive misinterpretation of Razumov's character. Violence begets violence. At the moment that he realizes his future has been compromised and that conspiracy has rendered him passive, Razumov conjures this phantom of the not-quite-dead but soon-to-be-executed Haldin. The ghost returns ceaselessly throughout the novel. Razumov fears that "the corpse hanging around his neck would be nearly as fatal as the living man" (32). Even the ticking of the clock reminds the student of "'the time when I returned and found him standing against the stove'" (300). Denying the ghost substance and interpreting the ghost as a sign, Razumov thinks, "It was what the miserable phantom stood for which had to be got out of the way" (302).

The problem of the return of the repressed is not solved so easily. Haunting is a narrative and structural issue in *Under Western Eyes*. Chronological fracturing—time stops and starts throughout the novel—enacts traumatic return. Part 4 resumes where part 1 leaves off. Instants of betrayal and recruitment play over and over in Razumov's mind. Only violence can quell this haunting, he concludes. He tells Mikulin that the whole affair is "'a comedy of errors, phantoms, and suspicions'" (99). When Mikulin asks about the phantoms, Razumov replies, "'I could walk over dozens of them'" (99). Conrad attaches to the ghost narrative a startling innovation: the ghost represents futurity—possibilities unrealized in the realm of action—rather than history. The moment of recruitment, when Haldin confides in Razumov, betrays future happiness for both of them. The ghost represents not a single person, but the haze of politics

—ties, complicities, treacheries—that envelops all those who interact socially.

Although several critics have observed the motif of the phantom in *Under Western Eyes,* few have connected this motif to the problems of political commitment and agency in the novel. Frank Kermode links phantoms to secrets that will come out in the course of the narrative (96–99). Pointing out that the double narrative of the novel, by Razumov and the Professor of Languages, enacts a way out of the bind of complicity, Penn Szittya concludes that this narrative doubling gives "internal conflict form by projecting it into an embodied dramatic conflict which may appear in dreams or in hallucinations, or psychoses" (835). Criticism of Conrad's fiction dwells on his complex psychological portraits as contradictions of his sardonic political views. Daniel Schwarz astutely argues that Conrad "realized that political activity fails because most men are selfish; those who are not selfish are victims of their own obsession, and thus are incapable of sustained activity on behalf of the community" (105–6). Tracing Dostoevsky's impact on Conrad and the thrilling suspense of the novel, Aaron Fogel concludes that the novel sets up "a grammar of political language" in which no "community" is achieved (188). While it is true that Razumov suffers from internal conflicts that cause hallucinations, those conflicts occur when plot exceeds personal agency. Every character shares some measure of guilt, which, as Althusser acknowledges in his exemplum of the policeman hailing a citizen, is the inevitable work of ideology. Guilt is one aspect of citizenship, even if that guilt derives from being a good citizen.

The logic of commitment determines that no individual can claim innocence as a viable position. Within a plot that governs all individuals, no individual stands beyond the law. Mikulin, the head of the repressive czarist police, ensnares Razumov because of his passivity. He forces the young student to act as a spy in Geneva. Razumov's only alternative is to explain why he consorts with revolutionaries like Haldin: "Everybody Haldin had ever known would be in the greatest danger. Unguarded expressions, little facts in themselves innocent would be counted for crimes" (20). Razumov has no choice, as he sees it, but to betray Haldin and cut a deal with Mikulin. Innocence as a character trait is invalidated by necessity as a narrative device. Not knowing about a law, like not knowing about a conspiracy, does not nullify the law or the conspiracy. Ignorance is no excuse against ideology. As a young man, Conrad worried about the "notion of life as an enterprise that could be mismanaged" (*Personal Record* 127). His fiction proves, at least in *Under Western Eyes,* that no degree of management, no exertion of will, can necessarily prevail against the forces of conspiracy. The novel demonstrates political inevitability as the imposition of plot over character. Yet Razumov remains a wild card. He acts of his own volition. When he denounces himself to the revolutionaries, he foils the plot of intrigue hatched by Mikulin in Russia. Although Razumov's anger and treachery would never have sprung forth if circumstances did not permit, when the circumstances do arise in Geneva, his personality gets the better of him. In general, certain predispositions or traits of personality (willfulness, submissiveness, obstinacy) force a character to fulfill certain actions. Certain situations demand the manifestation of traits (cowardice, heroism, ingenuity) that would remain hidden in less exigent circumstances. The plot must exist for a character to act. These problems abide at the center of espionage narratives as problems of instrumentality and agency.

Bureaucracies thematize agency and power in Conrad's narratives. Verloc in *The Secret Agent* toils for a foreign, presumably Russian, embassy in London, and also sells his services to the London police. Lazy by nature, Verloc disguises his double identity by keeping a stationery and pornography shop. Both the foreign ambassador and the British police bully Verloc. The agent merely executes the will of bureaucracies that purchase his squibs of information. The whole plot of *The Secret Agent* hinges on the foreign ambassador's caprice of seeing some mischief raised in England that will provoke a clampdown by the police. Conrad habitually designates characters by function to emphasize their social utility: Lawyer, Accountant, and Director in *Heart of Darkness;* Assistant Commissioner, Chief Inspector, Privy Councillor, Comrade in *The Secret Agent;* Prince, General, and Professor of Languages in *Under Western Eyes.* Each character exists as an instrument within governmental or corporate organizations. Professions, Conrad implies, deform character. Instrumentality overwhelms individuality to the point that character cannot be distinguished from job. This instrumentality, exemplified in the tendency to assign characters titles, appears throughout twentieth-century spy narratives and, as such, owes a debt to Conrad's political fiction. Instrumentality allows the bureaucratic handler to force an agent into circumstances that require athletic prowess or intellectual ingenuity. In part a master-servant convention, the handler-agent dynamic implies degrees of sadistic trickery and masochistic passivity. As Umberto Eco points out about the M-Bond relationship, "M represents to Bond the one who has a global view of the events, hence his superiority over the 'hero' who depends upon him and who sets out on his various missions in conditions of inferiority to the omniscient chief" (147). Omniscience, in this case, requires street smarts. The division of knowledge and action, or information and agency, exaggerates the secret agent's submissiveness. Never able to comprehend the entire plot that determines his or her actions, the agent acts as a conduit for and defender of ideology. Ideologies haunt the agent even when the agent cannot articulate their value. The agent defies, through the emptying out of individuality, the notion of character as destiny or character as psychological complexity.

Spy plots more or less disable initiative and agency. To act as a double agent is to enter into a situation of bad faith, to perform according to ideological necessity rather than personal ethics and choice. Espionage narratives qualify the capacity to act as an inalienable character trait. Spies routinely find themselves bound, gagged, lassoed, or otherwise immobilized. They cannot always specify what mechanism causes them to act in the first place within the machinelike universe of the thriller. If spies serve ideological functions only, and do not heed their own desires, they act as instruments. Even the Professor of Languages realizes this when he calls himself a "dumb helpless ghost" that "could only hover about without the power to protect or guide by as much as a whisper" (126). Translating Razumov's notes, the Professor views himself as only the transmitter of narrative, or as the spectator at a drama, but never as an agent who can assist the protagonist.

Plot encompasses and generates characters. Webs of intrigue prohibit individuals from making a difference (because they feel impotent before the vastness and invisibility of ideological might). They lapse into indifference (because no course of action exists that has not already been mapped out in advance according to the scripts of covert operations). For this reason, espionage is often figured as game-playing, as in *The Secret Agent*, where both policemen and agents provocateurs abide by the "rules of the game" (69). In *The Political Unconscious*, Fredric Jameson, thinking of Conrad's characters within capitalist modes of production and class, hypothesizes that a character system presupposes another hypothesis, namely, that a "subject, in the immediacy of his or her consciousness, has no meaning, but that when a given subject is endowed with meaning . . . , then that particular meaning can be traced back to the system that generates it" (243). Meaning derives from the systemic production of characters. Characters do not fabricate meaning within the narrative framework. When the combinations of actions made possible by the system alter, characterological types that "embody and manifest such contradictions" emerge (Jameson, *Political* 254). In the case of *Under Western Eyes,* Conrad invents a character who embodies qualities of romance, adventure, conservatism, commitment, and illegitimacy in response to a political system that allows contradictions to coexist.

The political critique offered by Conrad in *Under Western Eyes* takes this insight into plot as overriding structure further. Whereas liberty allows individuals to act from conviction, Conrad advances the observation that action proceeds from inertia, laziness, dread, or entrapment. Razumov wants only to live a sedate, unremarkable life. He does not want his motives questioned. When all avenues of rescue have closed on Razumov, when Haldin recruits him to the revolutionary cause, he commits acts of violence, such as tramping across Haldin's phantom body or beating the sleigh driver Ziemianitch nearly to death with a pitchfork (30). His acts of self-assertion revert to barbarous physical abuse. When Razumov later reflects that "all revolt is the expression of strong individualism" (264), he accepts a doctrine of engagement that begins with the individual yet has punitive consequences for the individual, including himself. Even though standoffish Razumov despises revolution, he comes around to seeing himself as a potential revolutionary: a conservative and rebel uncomfortably housed within one body. He never entirely accepts his instrumentality within an espionage plot. In this sense, the ghosts of two political philosophies at loggerheads with each other struggle to take over and haunt Razumov. As if inhabited by unavowed political beliefs, Razumov experiences repressed political action as uncanny repetition that he can eliminate only through confession. As the embodiment of ambiguous allegiances, the spy, to conform to the overweening demands of ideology and plot, ultimately commits himself or dies. Spy stories end with the confirmation of ideological rightness, not with the enlightenment of the protagonist.

GESTURES

As psychoanalyst Nicolas Abraham says in "Notes on the Phantom," "what haunts are not the dead, but the gaps left within us by the secrets of others" (75). Abraham supplements Freud's notion of the ghost as traumatic return of the repressed. We live out the secrets of others, even if those secrets remain unarticulated. What we do not know can, nonetheless, affect our behavior. Secrets devolve from generation to generation. They become ghosts that have no name but possess a vital presence. Unspoken and unacknowledged, ghosts remain gestural. Their language is untranslatable into the language of the living. The ghost stands as a cipher for what we do not recognize in ourselves, whether those ciphers signify covert desires, unintentional crimes, or political doubts.

Razumov, seconded by the Professor, observes that "the dead can only live with the exact intensity and quality of life imparted to them by the living" (304). The dead vampirically suck strength from the living. Mortals imperfectly understand ghosts' motives. The lines of communication between the kingdoms of life and death are never static-free. Talking with the phantom world has other liabilities. It is never clear what language ghosts speak. They channel their voices through mediums at séances, as in Graham Greene's thriller *The Ministry of Fear.* They rap on tables. They speak subvocally. More often than not, they communicate through gestures. Gesture suggests performance in the sense that gesture demonstrates the vulnerabilities of character on stage. *Under Western Eyes* constantly tropes on the theatricality of all action, not least in its title and in the Professor's tendency to think conspiracies "theatrical" (110) and to believe that "it was only on the stage that the unusual was outwardly acknowledged" (54). As a form of theatricality, gestures translate psychology into bodily display. In *Nostromo,* the heroic, athletic, suggestible protagonist, Nostromo, reflects on the death of Daniel Decoud by occupying exactly the same physical space and exactly the same posture as Decoud assumes just prior to his suicide. Both sit in the prow of a cargo boat in the calm waters of the Golfo Placido. Nostromo assumes this position to investigate Decoud's mysterious death—to reenact what Decoud might have thought or felt. The specter of Decoud troubles Nostromo so much that he subsequently compromises his heroic virtue by hiding stolen silver and abandoning the cause of revolution. Decoud does not return as a ghost per se, but his physical presence is replicated by Nostromo in shadow gestures.

Gestures obsessed Conrad. The short story "The Informer," included in the volume *A Set of Six,* was initially called "Gestures" because of the artificiality and pretension that society women show in their political affiliations; they merely toy with anarchist politics as a "pose and gesture" (*Set of Six* 78). Gestures for Conrad are apparitional, as they were for Shakespeare: the ghost in *Hamlet* beckons his son to parlay with a wave of the hand. In *Under Western Eyes,* Haldin's mother sits in tragic immobility, as if watching "a beloved head lying in her lap," which the Professor of Languages calls a "gesture [that] had unequalled force of expression" (355). Razumov grabs Natalia's hand fervently, as if about to kiss it, then shakes it "by the finger-tips in his great paw" (130). Razumov clasps the Professor's arm at the elbow. He crosses his arms in defiance. He purses his lips in an effort to contain the violence of his emotions. The narrative relies on shrugs, salutes, waves, crouches, finger-pointing, and other physical postures to convey meaning. Gesture may even permit communication with the dead. Although Razumov claims he "'can't speak for the dead'" (261), he acts sometimes on behalf of, and sometimes in avoidance of, the dead. Razumov cannot sleep in his own bed once he sees the dent in the pillow left by Haldin's head. He cannot fill the body of Haldin or duplicate his gestures, at least not initially. Haldin permanently contaminates Razumov's sense of unapproachable isolation. "It was what that miserable phantom stood for which had to be got out of the way" (302), Razumov thinks. Still, he catches himself lying in the same position as Haldin (70). He even narrates details of Haldin's light-footed departure from his room from an ambiguous point of view, neither his own nor Haldin's: "There is a staircase in [the story], and even phantoms, but that does not matter if a man always serves something greater than himself—the idea" (353). This curt speech recalls Haldin's commitment to an ideal of revolution. Haunted by Haldin, Razumov lives over and over the traumatic repercussions of the evening in his rooms when his life becomes public property, when he is interpellated into conflicting political positions. As Freud would have it, the emotional stimulus provoked by Haldin's appearance cannot be worked off by Razumov in the normal way. Even when leaving the Château Borel in Geneva, Razumov suddenly pauses on the staircase and remembers Haldin's nocturnal escape; the staircase intimidates him with its "great power of resonance" that echoes with "footfalls and voices" (226). In his mind, he revisits the moment of betrayal again, the trauma that has been reduced to the gestural disappearance of Haldin sneaking down the darkened staircase. The only exorcism available to Razumov is a physical replication of the traumatic moment. So, "at the very stroke of midnight," the hour when Haldin fled his rooms in St. Petersburg, Razumov, in Geneva months later, "jumped up and ran swiftly downstairs" (362). Like an understudy who steps into a role after much rehearsal, Razumov performs Haldin's disappearance. More than theatrical, this replication compounds trauma. Repetition of gesture brings no relief from haunting, but instead, only the "suspense of plotting, by which each betrayal solicits a false reading" of bodily clues (GoGwilt 168).[1]

In a novel that broadcasts distrust of words as the "foes of reality" (3), gestures assume prominence as clues. But clues are not always seen as clues. They may be lost amidst the redundant heaping up of other clues, or they may bear more significance than words can convey, or they may be grossly misinterpreted. Gestures originate in and act out the body. They require an acute consciousness of the performative potential of the body, the potential to substitute one body for another, just as Razumov inserts himself into the bodily place of Haldin. Since *Under Western Eyes* is, like many spy narratives, about a missing body, gesture supplies a clue about where that body has gone. It has, in this case, been absorbed into the gestural repertory of the living. As a clue, Razumov's body is misread. In an act of self-betrayal, he points an accusatory finger at his own chest: "He pressed a denunciatory finger to his breast with force, and became perfectly still" (354). Yet neither Natalia nor the Professor of Languages knows exactly what this gesture means. The physicality of Razumov's torment, of his haunting by Haldin, cannot be put into words. Gesticulation communicates far more to Razumov than it does to those who witness the gesture.

Touch speaks. Gesture warns. Just as the deceased child communicates with his sleeping father by touching his arm in Freud's telling of the "dream of the burning child," a dream reinterpreted by Lacan as a case of avoidance of the Real in the essay "Tuché and Automaton," the gestures of covering one's eyes or of sitting in the same position as a dead man at the instant he meditates upon suicide, which occur in *Under Western Eyes* and *Nostromo*, respectively, suggest that living out the secrets of others happens at a physical level, through imitation. Lacan maintains that "trauma reappears, in effect, frequently unveiled" (*Four Fundamental* 55). Traumatic return, in fact, may occur in gestures. Gestures unveil disorder or irregularity. Gestures bring about discovery, as in the "dream of the burning child," when the child touches the arm of the sleeping father to awaken him. "The real may be represented by the accident, the noise, the small element of reality," writes Lacan, "which is evidence that we are not dreaming" (*Four Fundamental* 60). Spies observe a strict regimentation of the body, down to tics, gestures, accents, and gait, in order not to betray covert allegiances. In spy narratives, the "small element of reality" has a political valence and points to larger conspiracies at work in the world. Conspiracy theorists and paranoiacs read clues as overdetermined intrusions of the Real. Interpreted neutrally, spy fiction promotes scrupulous reading of the body as a site where ideology declares itself. In Buchan's *The Thirty-Nine Steps,* Richard Hannay unravels a German conspiracy to invade Britain when he observes a tiny, nearly unnoticeable gesture executed by a spy posing as an old man. The tapping of fingers against the impostor's knee—the moment when the Real, as political plot, reveals itself despite disguises and carefully modulated accents—tells Hannay what he otherwise had prohibited himself from knowing. Seeing the man's "fingers tapping on his knees" grants Hannay an "absolute recognition" (109) of the plot and its dangers. Gesture betrays conspiracy: "A little thing, lasting only a second, and the odds were a thousand to one that I might have had my eyes on my cards at the time and missed it" (109). Gesture declares what otherwise cannot be spoken, namely, enmity within. Spy fiction requires a meticulous reading of bodies to discern foreignness.

Heart of Darkness offers a more familiar example of the spectral as gestural. When Marlow returns to the sepulchral city after his journey to the Congo, he approaches the house of Kurtz's Intended (90) with trepidation. On the threshold, he suffers a bad case of the heebie-jeebies brought about by a hallucination of the ivory agent Kurtz: "before the high and ponderous door, between the tall houses of a street as still and decorous as a well-kept alley in a cemetery, I had a vision of him on the stretcher, opening his mouth voraciously, as if to devour all the earth with all its mankind. He lived then before me; he lived as much as he had ever lived —a shadow insatiable of splendid appearances, of frightful realities" (90). Reputed for his oratory, Kurtz does not speak when he comes back from the dead. He lives as mouth, as the more-than-real ghost of colonial rapacity and personal ambition, the death drive made into a presence.

Kurtz's return is more complicated still. While in the jungle, Marlow refuses to witness the ivory trader's death. Everyone else runs off to see dead Mister Kurtz while Marlow sedately finishes eating his meal. Marlow subsequently displaces eating into the dread of being swallowed alive. The next day, seeing Kurtz's cadaver tossed into a muddy hole, Marlow comments that he too is very nearly buried by the grave-diggers. "'I did not go to join Kurtz there and then,'" observes Marlow. But that has not prevented him from worrying over the significance of death: "'I have wrestled with death. It is the most unexciting contest you can imagine'" (87). This casual dismissal of death belies Marlow's terror of being haunted by Kurtz. In his later hallucination on the stoop of the Intended's house, he transposes fear of death into the ghastly return of devouring Kurtz. Mister Kurtz never dies, certainly not in Marlow's traumatized consciousness. Failing to exorcise the ghost of Kurtz, Marlow hopes to make the Intended the legatee of Kurtz's memory. He wants to appoint her the inheritor of death in order to swerve from that role himself. The Intended loves and misunderstands Kurtz. Because she misunderstands him, because she does not glimpse the extent of his criminal rapacity in the Congo, she can devote herself to preserving his memory. By contrast, Marlow has glimpsed the forces of annihilation manifest in Kurtz's character and career. Both Kurtz and Marlow confront the horror of death. Unable to fathom the political implications of Kurtz's commodity trading and ignominious demise, Marlow casts the dead man as a ravenous ghoul come back to consume all the living. This spectralization of Kurtz alleviates Marlow's guilt over his own complicity in the ivory trade in the Congo and his own repressed recognition of omnivorous death. In short, Kurtz's phantom stands for the gap in Marlow's self-understanding. His voice replaces Kurtz's in the narrative as the voice of authority. Marlow shadows Kurtz, who lives on in the legend obsessively recited by Marlow.

The apparitional implies violent denial in *Under Western Eyes*. Summoned by General T— to a meeting, Razumov suddenly sees his enemy loom before him:

> the familiar phantom, Haldin stood suddenly before him in the
> room with the extraordinary completeness of detail. Though
> the short winter day had passed already into the sinister twi-
> light of a land buried in snow, Razumov saw plainly the narrow
> leather strap round the Tcherkess coat. The illusion of that

hateful presence was so perfect that he half expected it to ask, 'Is the outer door closed?' He looked at it with hatred and contempt. Souls do not take a shape of clothing. Moreover, Haldin could not be dead yet. Razumov stepped forward menacingly; the vision vanished—and turning short on his heel he walked out of his room with infinite disdain. (84–85)

Having learned how to repudiate this ghost by menacing it, Razumov feints. Unlike Marlow who cowers before the reverberant apparition of Kurtz, Razumov behaves with disdain and contempt. The phantom embodies Razumov's hatred. The traitor's body may vanish, but the body never goes away because it is the projection of hatred. At stake in *Under Western Eyes* is the recoverability of the lost body, of the body resurrected out of the grave. Gestures dissolve almost as soon as they are performed. But, as ways in which the body establishes itself in space, these gestures conjure up vanished bodies. The pattern of ghostly return in *Under Western Eyes* speaks to this problem of eliminating the body of the spy or the revolutionary once and for all. " 'People do disappear. Yes, they do disappear' " (109), says Natalia, but they invariably return as the incarnation of repressed death drives, or visceral emotions. Like the dead child who rouses the sleeping father in the "dream of the burning child," ghosts deliver messages of silent agony.

THE TRAUMA OF ILLEGITIMACY

The question of haunting in *Under Western Eyes* centers not on the repressed knowledge of death and commodities as in *Heart of Darkness*. Haunting expresses instead the uncanny effects of illegitimacy and political obligation. Razumov cannot fathom Haldin's familial security and his willingness to sacrifice that security for the political goal of liberty. Haldin embodies Razumov's unacknowledged desire for liberty and family connection. Freud's definition of the "uncanny" as the unfamiliar lodged within the familiar—or, in Schelling's definition quoted by Freud, " '*Unheimlich is the name for everything that ought to have remained . . . secret and hidden but has come to light*' " ("The Uncanny" 224; Freud's ellipsis)—is usually applied to traumatic experiences that the mind cannot assimilate. The uncanny breeds fear and hair-raising horror. Unaccustomed to uncanny events himself, Freud confides that he "must start by *translating* himself" (220;

emphasis added) into a state of mind receptive to horror. Fear, especially in spy narratives, testifies to the presence of the unnameable that characters translate into intelligible terms. After Razumov betrays himself to the revolutionaries at the end of *Under Western Eyes*, his story passes into the hands of the Professor of Languages who narrates the novel, based on personal observation and involvement, supplemented by written notes and confessions left by Razumov. Razumov's uncanny commitment occurs through translation from Russian to English, as well as from Razumov to the Professor, a translation that mitigates the representation of political actions.

Conrad's treatment of the public sphere, emphasizing ambiguity, demonstrates that all actions become interpretations of actions. In other words, we live out a relation to our fantasies about the Real rather than living the Real itself. Cathy Caruth argues in *Unclaimed Experience* that "inherent forgetting" (16) or the will not to know characterizes trauma: "history [may] arise where immediate understanding may not" (11). The trauma in *Under Western Eyes* redounds to the survivor, the Professor, who inherits the story and has to make sense of it, not Razumov, who sheds the story through confession. Yet confession cannot alleviate trauma: "the witness-appointee cannot relieve himself by any delegation, substitution or representation" (Felman and Laub 3). Trauma remains outside narrative or other representation. Indeed, the person who suffers trauma may delegate a witness who does not understand the resonance of the tale of violence, destruction, or catastrophe precisely because traumatic occurrence needs to be *translated* into words or images to avoid duplicating the initial calamity. Although he narrates the tale, the Professor also wishes to avoid knowing too much about commitment and duplicity, which, the reader suspects, deform the Professor's character as much as they alter Razumov's. The Professor of Languages confesses that he speaks English as a first language and never quite understands the peculiarities of Russians. He disclaims possession "of those high gifts of imagination and expression" (3). Yet he makes a priori judgments about Razumov because he is Russian. Narrated by the Professor, the traumatic story does not go away. It ripples in widening circles of misunderstanding as it passes from Razumov to the Professor to the reader. Never domesticated or brought home, the uncanny merely disperses, as Conrad represents it, into misapprehension.

Unassimilable and untranslatable, ghosts require exorcism. Razumov violently attacks the unfamiliar even when it serves his own interests. What Razumov most wants is the thing he vehemently denounces. Believing in meritocracy, he nevertheless champions autocracy, a political regime that denies his merit. Yet when confronted with authority, Razumov rebels. His resentment expresses itself in enraged, jerky gestures. Interviewed by General T—, Razumov instantly loathes him. Razumov speaks to him "angrily" (45), "with suppressed irritation" (46), "violently" (47), "with malicious pleasure" (50). Later, Razumov scrawls five conservative slogans on a paper and stabs the paper to the wall with a knife tip. When he hallucinates the phantom of Haldin lying in the snow and tramples it, he relieves his pent-up rage through fantasized aggression. Furthermore, the Professor of Languages shows animosity towards his subject and competes with him erotically for the attention of Natalia Victorovna. The logic of violence in *Under Western Eyes* dictates that aggression return to its perpetrator. After Razumov confesses his duplicity, another spy, Necator, bursts his eardrums with two stunning blows to the head. Deafened, Razumov falls beneath a tram and is nearly killed. Later, Necator, a double agent, dies for his duplicities (381). In short, Haldin's phantom instigates violence instead of curing the original act of violence—the bomb blast and assassination of the President of the Repression Commission—with which political representation begins. The bombs that explode in both *The Secret Agent* and *Under Western Eyes* tear apart social fabrics and ruin lives. Terrorism requires a narrative structure that can accommodate the unspeakable or bridge the gap in consciousness opened up by physical threat and fear: "The violent event enacts a temporal rupture within mimetic representation itself, a split between a 'before' (unviolated) state and an 'after' (violated) state" (Mageean 236). Espionage fiction often shows violence diffused through uncanny structures of authority, agency, and conspiracy. Although the secret agent kills, he does so, putatively, in the interests of the greater good. Yet *Under Western Eyes* treats the greater good ironically, as the attempted elevation of personal conviction into doctrine. Brutality and political commitment cause estrangement of individuals from communities and from themselves. Politics, in Conrad's fiction, emerges as uncanny, a phenomenon capable of inspiring terror and endless repetition.

Uncanniness especially crisscrosses gender relations in *Under Western Eyes*. When Razumov meets Natalia Victorovna, Haldin's sister, in Geneva, he brusquely confesses to her with "visible repugnance" (346) in a "convulsive, uncontrolled tone" (349). In her resemblance to her brother, Natalia reminds Razumov of his own treachery. As the ghost of her brother, Natalia attracts and repels Razumov. When he lays eyes on Natalia, Razumov remembers "the very sound of his [Haldin's] voice" (358). Sibling doubles trace an eerie subtext in the novel. Natalia's presence goads Razumov. She substitutes as ghost, always herself and always in part her brother, in Razumov's fantasies: "while shunning the sight of you, I could never succeed in driving away your image. I would say, addressing that dead man, 'Is this the way you are going to haunt me?'" (358). She brings to light every violent, erotic, and bipartisan sentiment that he wishes to keep hidden. She also points towards one of the enduring roles for women within the espionage genre: the ingénue whose worth lies in her tangible reminiscence of enmity and compromise. Loved as woman but hated as ideological foe, the merit of Natalia, in the codes of the novel, is her ability to translate Razumov's own conflicted allegiances into physical form. She jolts him into recognition of his betrayed life. She locks him in a past that he can never leave.

Jacques Derrida argues in *Specters of Marx* that the specter desynchronizes and recalls anomalies in systems of governance and justice (50). *Hamlet* illustrates this anomaly: not only has Claudius usurped Hamlet as king, the kingdom of Denmark has an ongoing territorial dispute with Poland that resolves only when Fortinbras smashes his way into the Danish state in the last scene of Shakespeare's play. The ghost of Hamlet's father, the anomaly of time and mortality, disappears when conflicts about governance get arbitrated through force. In one sense, Derrida's formulation of the *revenant* as an atemporal phenomenon does not move us much beyond Freud's estimation of the ghostly as traumatic revisiting of the unassimilated past. Derrida means that the ghost speaks of the future as much as it speaks of history and that its emblematic authority, like the authority of the taciturn ghost of Hamlet the father in Shakespeare's tragedy, has a jurisdiction wider than the individual. Derrida implies that the *revenant* expresses a disequilibrium in justice, in honor, and in legitimacy, through asynchrony (22).

Ghosts figure national quandaries. The greatest ghost story of the nineteenth century, perhaps, is *The Communist Manifesto*. "There is a specter haunting Europe, the specter of Communism [*das Gespenst des Kommunismus*]," chant Marx and Engels (33). In *The Eighteenth Brumaire of Louis-Napoleon,* Marx resorts to a similar image cast as a bad dream: "The tradition of all the dead generations weighs like a nightmare on the brain of the living" (15). The image of history as a phantom entrances Marx. He resorts tirelessly to images of corpses and phantoms as political tropes: the "ghost of the old revolution" stirs national consciousness; revolution is "the awakening of the dead" (*Eighteenth Brumaire* 17). History cannot be suppressed forever. Similarly, throughout his essays, Conrad compares nations to phantoms. In part, Conrad may have acquired this metaphor from the play, *Forefather's Eve Part III,* by Polish nationalist Adam Mickiewicz. The ghosts of the past rise up in *Forefather's Eve* and inspire the protagonist, Konrad, to sing "Vengeance, vengeance on the foe" (Mickiewicz 98).[2] As Conrad points out in "The Crime of Partition," Poland, divided between Germany and Russia, had the status of a spectral country in the nineteenth century. In "Autocracy and War" (1905), Conrad spits out his contempt for Russia in images of weird apparitions. Russia perches like a ghoul on the grave of Russians. Russia exists as "a fantasy of a madman's brain . . . seated upon a monument of fear and oppression" (*Notes on Life and Letters* 91). Siding with the Japanese in the Russo-Japanese War of 1905, Conrad likens Russian autocrats to life-sucking demons. He hopes the Japanese destroy the "oppressive ghost" (*Notes* 111) of Russian autocracy. His vituperation reaches such a fevered pitch that his syntax spins out of control:

> It may be said the twentieth [century] begins with a war which is like the explosive ferment of a moral grave, whence may yet emerge a new political organism to take the place of a gigantic and dreaded phantom. For a hundred years the ghost of Russian might, overshadowing with its fantastic bulk the councils of Central and Western Europe, sat upon the gravestone of autocracy, cutting off from air, from light, from all knowledge of themselves and of the world, the buried millions of Russian people. . . . We have seen their blood freezing crimson upon the snow of the squares and streets of St. Petersburg; since their generations born in the grave are yet alive enough to fill the ditches and cover the fields of Manchuria with their torn limbs; to send up from the frozen battlefields a chorus of groans calling for vengeance from Heaven; to kill and retreat,

> or kill and advance, without intermission or rest for twenty
> hours, for fifty hours, for whole weeks of fatigue, hunger,
> cold, and murder—till their ghastly labour, worthy of a
> place amongst the punishments of Dante's Inferno, passing
> through the stages of courage, of fury, of hopelessness,
> sinks into the night of crazy despair. (*Notes* 86–87)

The ghoul that demands blood sacrifice from Russians does not result in their release from the underworld. On the contrary, the murderous imperative of Russian politics sinks them deeper into a Dantean inferno. So entranced is Conrad by this metaphor of Russian politics as vampire that he conjures it up as the best expression of his undying resentment. In *Notes on Life and Letters,* Russia figures as a "ravenous ghoul" (89), a "monster" (94), and a "phantom" (113).

In *Under Western Eyes,* familial belonging, or not belonging, compounds the specter of patriotic allegiances. Conrad implies that political engagement arises from psychological needs. Razumov has no family: "Others had fathers, mothers, brothers, relations, connexions, to move heaven and earth on their behalf—he had no one" (21). This periphrasis avoids saying outright that Razumov is illegitimate, a bastard not acknowledged by his biological father. Yet Conrad draws attention to Razumov's illegitimacy in the preface to the novel: "He has an average conscience. If he is slightly abnormal it is only in his sensitiveness to his position. Being nobody's child he feels rather more keenly than another would that he is a Russian—or he is nothing. He is perfectly right in looking on all Russia as his heritage" (xxxi). Razumov's alleged father, Prince K—, will not openly claim him. Illegitimate Razumov goes out of his way not to irritate his father Prince K— at the same time as he inserts himself into his father's regard. By contrast, Haldin has a family—a mother and sister—but no father to speak of. Haldin characterizes his father, with no particular acrimony, as "a Government official in the provinces" with "the soul of obedience" (23). Haldin does not identify with his conformist father. Rather, he stakes his personal and political identity on the character of an uncle, an army officer, shot by czarist executioners in 1828 for an unspecified crime (23). The uncle replaces the obedient civil servant as the symbolic father who imbues Haldin with revolutionary zeal, regardless of the crime committed by that surrogate father. Haldin's father has a negligible place in his identity, but his transferred allegiance to the politically disturbing uncle leads the reader to conclude that Haldin's revolutionary behavior stems from a desire to rectify old family wrongs. To do so, he must perpetuate civil disobedience.

The only family connection Razumov can genuinely claim is the "parentage" of Russia (11). A small-time lawyer pays the hard-up student a quarterly stipend from an unknown benefactor. Because of Russian patronymics, however, Razumov's illegitimacy appears in his very name. Lacking a father, he acquires his full name, Kirylo Sidorovitch, from two Russian saints, "Cyril son of Isidor" (3), rather than from a biological father. The assertion of this orphan's religious patronymic in the first paragraph of the novel disguises illegitimacy.[3] Razumov is, indeed, the son of the state and the church. By chance Razumov meets Prince K— one day at his lawyer's offices. The aristocratic and gouty Prince squeezes Razumov's hand with "a light pressure like a secret sign" (12), which causes the parentless student to designate the Prince as his father. The transmission of paternity—a squeeze of the hand as interpreted by the son—occurs as a gesture that transpires outside language. In this case, physical touch, not language, confers identity. The bastard son picks his father as an alignment with the "aristocratic and proud" (12) class that Prince K— represents. The parentless child opts for a parent who fulfills psychic needs for order, aristocracy, bloodlines, continuity, security. In this sense, Razumov and Haldin complement each other. Haldin rejects one father and chooses another more suitable to his ambitions. Razumov, prone to hero-worship, extends his fantasy of aristocratic legitimacy to a compensatory conviction about imperial fathers and public position. He accepts the inevitability of a Nietzschean *Übermensch,* an autocrat, who will rule Russia: "But absolute power should be preserved—the tool ready for the man—for the great autocrat of the future" (35). Guided by a bold conviction in his intelligence, which he mentions to everyone, Razumov wants only to rise to eminence as a "celebrated old professor, decorated, possibly a Privy Councillor" (13). The legitimate child, Haldin, orphans himself, whereas the illegitimate child labors to make up for, and make up to, the absent father. Haldin neglects his "obedient" father; Razumov squirms to attract notice from Prince K—. Curiously, no one's father is directly represented in *Under Western Eyes,* except Prince K—, who denies paternity. Fathers exist outside representation, yet they govern the behavior of sons by symbolic law.

On the day of the assassination, Razumov visits Prince K— to seek advice and to betray Haldin. This visit may seem like a solution to Razumov's dilemma about how to exonerate himself from the unwanted complicity Haldin has foisted on him. The visit may also be self-serving insofar as Razumov can elevate himself in Prince K—'s esteem. Prince K—'s acceptance of a son manqué expresses itself in a second gesture that bonds father and son. Razumov feels "unexpectedly in the dark a momentary pressure on his arm" as he and Prince K— ride in a carriage to General T—'s house (42). This second, identity-bestowing touch confirms, in Razumov's mind at least, that Prince K— is his father. Only much later does the reader, but not Razumov, learn that the eager-to-please student is truly "the son of Prince K—" (306), as Mikulin and General T— surmise.

The knowledge of paternity comes too late. In treating filial fantasies ironically, the novel exposes paternity as fraudulent. It exists in the mind of the son as a phantom. A compound, familiar ghost, the father assumes powers beyond the mere capacity to create sons. Fathers become also the object of derision, resentment, and secret longings for authentic existence. In the most stark counterexample to Razumov's illegitimacy, the father of Kostia, a student at the university, supports the madcap antics of his champagne-drinking, hedonistic child. The father, "a very wealthy and illiterate Government contractor" (78), pays off Kostia's gambling debts and bar bills with only the mildest rebukes. Ever the bounteous father, Kostia's dad can be robbed and shown no respect, yet he never loses patience. As Kostia says, " 'I have my rich dad behind me. There's positively no getting to the bottom of his pocket' " (80). When Kostia steals money from his father to pay Razumov's way out of Russia, the action inspires nothing but contempt in Razumov. He throws the packet of stolen money out a train window. " 'For the people' " (315), Razumov mutters, as he tosses away the money. Throwing away stolen loot means that Razumov does not abet a second crime by virtue of his contact with it. The repudiation of Kostia and his crime against his deep-pocketed father expresses the degree of contempt that Razumov has for the ideal, benevolent paterfamilias. He requires an immediate, physical parent and resents abstract, generous paternity. The father must be tangible. The father, to exert authority, ought to remain a ghost.

This absent parent combines Razumov's need for authority and his need to refute authority. Throwing away "dad's" money expresses resentment of the regime that coerces Razumov into acting as a double agent. Having been forced to abandon his hopes to be a privy councillor, Razumov gestures at being individualistic, which is what he has sometimes been but pretends not to be. By betraying Haldin, Razumov sacrifices all pretenses of intellectual "liberty" (90) that might threaten Russian autocracy. Instead of liberty, he faces a politically lawless world. His true life, we learn, is located "in the determined future—in the future menaced by the lawlessness of autocracy—for autocracy knows no law—and the lawlessness of revolution" (77). Since neither autocracy nor revolution abides by laws, Razumov finds himself confronted by an insecure political future that requires him to improvise roles: spy, student, revolutionary, anarchist, lover, confessor. His tragedy hinges on his inability to make these roles authentic or practicable. Since none of them is legitimate, each of them disintegrates.

IMPROPER COMMITMENTS

Often called a conservative novel that aims at nullifying all political positions, *Under Western Eyes* more subtly qualifies political engagement by exposing the self-interest that underlies commitment. Eloise Knapp Hay claims that the novel expresses a conversion experience from an "ideology of political liberty and personal freedom" to "the organic bonds that tie [Razumov] to others" in an autocratic state (226). This formulation needs modification. Razumov is never liberal by conviction. Although he does turn to the state, he does so only when trapped by suave, sadistic Mikulin. The dynamic tension of Razumov's character centers on his reluctant double agency. Understanding Razumov's "unsettled mind and shaken conscience" (307), Mikulin makes the floundering student feel that "he had committed himself" (308). This recruitment plays off Razumov's desire to belong to some community, some organization that provides a sense of security and place and that will prove he had nothing to do with the assassination of Mr. de P—. The autocratic Russian regime offers the security that a missing father cannot.

In an insight that cuts to the heart of modernism, Conrad sees ambivalence and changing alliances as the fate of political subjectivity. Conflict resides within the individual. Now liberal, now autocratic, now illegitimate, now legitimate, the political subject best expresses himself as a double agent internally riven. The pattern manifests itself most strongly in a spy who cannot bear his divided allegiances. Razumov stands as a prototype for espionage fiction in that his double agency signifies indecision, potential betrayal, shifting allegiances. Jon Elster has argued that improvised political identities are characteristic of postmodernity. Individuals, Elster claims, make rational choices based on personal needs and common interests: "agents face *choices under constraints*. . . . If the agents are rational, they will choose the element in the feasible set that best satisfies their desire" (*Political Psychology* 163). By "agents," Elster simply means political subjects who act. Desire to conform modifies self-serving choices. Speaking of the chances to maximize personal gain versus enhancing collective strength, Elster comments that "each agent prefers to cooperate if the others can be expected to do likewise, but if he suspects they will not, he won't either" (*Making Sense of Marx* 362). Political identity is always in transition because it is based on personal interest set over and against public virtue. We sometimes act for the public good if we think others expect us to do so. In such quandaries of whether to magnify self-interest or appeal to civic ideals, every individual, or agent, weighs the gratifications that each move in the game of political choice brings. Hence political subjectivity is extemporized, much as an actor, or a spy, extemporizes a role. One could call this enlightened self-interest or opportunism. Either label impugns the sincerity of commitment.

Conrad anticipates the notion of improvised subjectivity based on rational choice by making Razumov's psychological need for recognition underlie his desire for political authority. Razumov believes in autocracy, yet he acts as a revolutionary. He pretends to be sympathetic to the expatriate Russians in Geneva yet spies on them for Mikulin and for Russia. He refuses to commit himself absolutely to either side. Political indeterminacy undoes him. Where can Razumov possibly go? When he says he wishes to retire from this unspeakable quandary of complicity and treachery, Mikulin asks him, "Where to?" (99) The question returns, like the repressed obstacle to happiness, late in the narrative (293). As Mikulin knows, and as Razumov slowly understands, the uncommitted student can go nowhere. Conrad begs the question of what fate the double agent has in spy fiction. Is it possible to be a conservative who performs as a genuine revolutionary? Is there truly a connection between intention and action in politics? Barely in touch with Mikulin, Razumov operates according to an ideological mandate without interference from bureaucratic authorities. This freedom contains the tragic possibility that the agent, once freed from the burden of serving the state, may never be readmitted to his homeland where, at least, he recognizes the workings of ideology.

If *Under Western Eyes* is one of the "powerful counter-revolutionary" novels of modernity, as Fredric Jameson claims (*Political Unconscious* 268), it nevertheless gets built around a curious refraction of *ressentiment*. Jameson declares that the novel emits messages of *ressentiment* "obsessively" (268). Resentment as political expression stems from the Nietzschean conception that those underclasses who wish to rise up in rebellion find they cannot and thus express vengeance in imaginative forms. Novels unleash and manage resentment. In *Under Western Eyes*, Razumov unquestionably resents Haldin and government functionaries such as General T—. Razumov's resentment of privilege stems from the repressed fact of his illegitimacy. His illegitimacy confounds his membership in either elite or unprivileged classes and makes his particular brand of *ressentiment* a hybrid of dislocation, merit, outrage, and conservatism. He dreams of winning a silver medal at university in order to elevate his status until it reaches the place that he believes he deserves in society. His resentment of Haldin springs from the compromise that the revolutionary inflicts on his plans for security and success in the public world. Adapting conventions of sensation, romance, and adventure narratives in *Under Western Eyes*, Conrad makes political representation both urgent and complex. Jameson writes in *The Political Unconscious* that "the modernist project" intends to "'manage' historical and social, deeply political impulses, that is to say, to defuse them to prepare substitute gratifications for them" (266). On the contrary, there is a crucial continuity between those historical impulses and the representational modes of modernism. The "gratifications" proposed by Jameson are not substitutions but cultural articulations of disturbing impulses. Conrad's fiction attempts to imagine the political not as a surrogate for action, nor as the manifestation of resentment, but as an effort to work out the contradictions of psychological motives latent within action.

Modernists themselves worried endlessly about the relation of politics to intention and intention to representation. This dilemma sometimes gets cast as a question of loyalty. "If I had to choose between betraying my country and betraying my friend," E. M. Forster postulates in 1939, "I hope I should have the guts to betray my country" (78). The choice pits one-to-one valor against abstract national loyalties. Betrayal of a country has far more onerous penalties than betrayal of a friend. Conrad, in a letter written to his agent R. B. Cunninghame Graham in February 1899, states the question of allegiance abstractly: "Si l'idée nationale ap[p]orte la souffrance et son service donne la mort ça vaut mieux que de servir les ombres d'une éloquence qui est morte, justement par ce qu'elle n'a pas de corps" [If nationalism brings suffering and serving a national ideal brings death, that is better than serving the shadows of an eloquence already dead, that is merely a phantom] (*Letters* 117; my translation). The sentiment might be paraphrased thus: *if I must choose one or the other, give me patriotic politics that cause actions rather than empty rhetoric.* But for Conrad, all commitment bears illusion. Belief brings death or a batch of dead words. In the same letter, he calls democracy a beautiful phantom: "l'idée democratique est un très beau phantôme" (*Letters* 116). This figuration of democracy suggests the flimsiness of belief, of pursuing something that can be neither captured nor proven.

The question of commitment anguished many twentieth-century writers according to the degree to which they felt complicitous in regimes of political authority. Jean-Paul Sartre delineates the necessity of engagement for writers and intellectuals, especially in such essays as "Why Write?" and "What Is a Collaborator?" written shortly after World War II. A writer is free to choose and promote political convictions but may in fact promote convictions that inhibit the freedom of others. By advocating a political position, the writer risks being collaborationist, as was the author Drieu la Rochelle, who published Nazi propaganda during the war and who is decried by Sartre in "Why Write?" for having done so. Speaking of those who supported the fascists, Sartre admits that ambition and self-interest motivate collaborators. Collaborators hold something in reserve, act from personal motives irrespective of ideology, just as Razumov acts in part out of necessity, not conviction. Sartre claims in "What Is a Collaborator?" that the collaborator becomes a conduit of ideology: "quelle étrange ambition: si, vraiment, cette passion est, en son fond, la recherche d'un pouvoir absolu sur les hommes, il y avait une contradiction manifeste dans l'ambition du collaborateur qui, l'eût-on mis à la tête du pseudo-gouvernement français, ne pouvait être qu'un agent de transmission" [what a strange ambition: if this passion is, at bottom, a search for absolute power over mankind, there was a manifest contradiction in the ambition of the collaborator who, had he been placed at the head of the French pseudo-government, would have been only an agent of transmission] (*Situations* 3 50; my translation). The ambition to hold absolute power is flawed because another country confers and reinforces that power. The collaborator in the political sphere can never fully possess himself or his power if he merely belongs to a "pseudo-government." The same applies to writers who cater to political regimes and satisfy their desire for power by doing so. Therefore, Sartre distinguishes between those committed writers who transmit ideology without necessarily believing it *(un collaborateur)* and those who exercise freedom by writing *(un écrivain engagé)*. Some forms of commitment, according to Sartre, are improper because they compromise freedom. Answering Sartre's call for commitment in artists and art, Theodor Adorno claims that "commitment in itself remains politically polyvalent so long as it is not reduced to propaganda, whose pliancy mocks any commitments by the subject" ("Commitment" 302). In effect, Adorno switches the point of discussion from the engagé writer to representations of politics. Whereas Sartre refers to politics as praxis, Adorno refers to politics as resource for art. The question of politics as gestural, as transmissible, as collaborationist, or as representational underlies the narrative of *Under Western Eyes*. Does Razumov believe in what he does or does self-interest motivate him? How does one interpret Razumov's convictions, and, by extension, how does one interpret Conrad's political position? To put the matter briefly, how do we read ghost stories?

Ghosts insist on remembrance as a threshold to understanding. They flaunt opportunities for apprehending the full reach of political plots, then snatch them away. In Conrad's fiction, ghosts stand for concussive history, for traumatic occurrences and their repetition. Abject and silent, ghosts point to what has been repressed and forgotten. Razumov in *Under Western Eyes* neither speaks fully for the dead nor speaks competently to the dead. In his novels, Conrad wrestles with the political ambiguities of agency, similar to the way that Sartre calls collaborators possible transmitters of ideology who reserve shades of individuality within the constraints of a committed position. What remains beyond expression for Conrad, and for Conrad's readers, is the political itself, the great haunted house of modernism where importunate ghosts continue to rattle their chains and gesture dumbly to those who might remember them and put them, at last, to rest.

CHAPTER FIVE

Sewers

FANTASIES OF DEATH AND DISGUST IN
THE THIRD MAN

A CORPSE

Whereas ghosts will not leave Razumov alone in *Under Western Eyes,* corpses will not stay in the ground in *The Third Man.* Harry Lime dies twice and is twice buried in Graham Greene's novella. On the lam for selling impure penicillin on the black market in post–World War II Vienna, Lime moves through the sewers of the city to escape detection. In many ways, the sewer is "a place of definition for Harry" (Evans 39). Calloway, the police inspector who narrates Lime's case, draws a connection between street-level and subterranean realms: "the gravediggers had been forced to use electric drills to open the frozen ground in Vienna's Central Cemetery. It was as if nature were doing its best to reject Lime, but we got him in at last and laid the earth back on him like bricks. He was vaulted in" (13). Rejected by nature, Lime reappears in the streets of Vienna after his obsequies. If, according to Calloway's description, nature lies below ground, above ground stands for culture, denatured space, or unnatural behavior. As Greene notes in his preface, Rollo Martins's sighting of Lime's ghost provided the point of genesis for the story (9). In the finished novel, Martins does not see Lime in the flesh until three-quarters of the tale has passed, then discounts this sighting as "an illusion caused by a shadow" (88). Nevertheless, the shock of seeing a man who is supposedly dead induces a sense of eeriness in Martins. His quest to solve the identity of the third man, who turns out to be Lime himself, issues from foreboding. Inconsistencies accumulate around his death. Were two men present or three? Did Harry die instantly or afterwards? Uncanniness propels the narrative towards the killing of Lime as a rectification of the disturbance in nature that he causes. Living, he inspires dread. Dead, he allays Martins's need to make his image of Lime correspond with reality. Martins also kills Lime to negate his own death drive. Rather unconvincingly, Martins, who cannot stop mourning Lime, thinks, "'The dead are made to be forgotten'" (62). But the novella emphasizes remembrance and an outburst of repressed feeling rather than forgetting. Although *The Third Man* falls between adventure, western, detective, and espionage genres—its classification is made more complex by virtue of its having been written as a template for Carol Reed's film version in 1949 before being published as a novella in 1950—the narrative figures fear and disgust as aspects of political representation, embodied in a plot of hunter-and-hunted. The obsession with underground spaces in this narrative raises auxiliary problems of masculinity, political representation, capitalism, spirituality, and urban intrigue. Sewers in *The Third Man,* with their swirl of dreck and garbage, analogize the unconscious of modernism as that which cannot be known about political allegiance, or as the necessary obfuscation of commitment within the genre of the thriller.

The Third Man is far from being Greene's most overtly political novel. *Stamboul Train,* with its diagnosis of 1930s anti-Semitism and xenophobia, addresses the jitteriness of prewar Europeans. *The Confidential Agent,* though it never names the continental country from which its protagonist hails, conjures up the Spanish Civil War and the urgency injected into that conflict by the Munich Agreement of 1938, as Greene makes clear in *Ways of Escape* (69). *The Comedians* takes the violent regime of Papa Doc Duvalier in Haiti as its backdrop. *The Quiet American* anticipates American involvement in Vietnam. *The Human Factor,* modeled after various Cambridge spies such as Kim Philby, Guy Burgess, and Donald Maclean, recounts the subterfuges of a mole in the British intelligence service who, when nearly caught, defects to Russia. If not as preoccupied with Cold War intrigue as *The Human Factor* is, *The Third Man* nevertheless demonstrates Greene's understanding of Cold War policies of containment at the moment of their inception in the late 1940s. While cognizant of its shortcomings as a spy novel (it has policemen and army officers but no spies per se), I view *The Third Man* as a quintessential narrative of intrigue in its preoccupation with death, political inscrutability, and containment.

Containment, in practical terms, demands comprehensive surveillance: wiretaps, infiltrations, spy-versus-spy maneuvers, defections, dossier keeping. Yet containment is also a narrative problem against Lime. In *The Third Man*, Calloway contains the tale by scrupulous documentation of the case. A Scotland Yard inspector seconded to an army detective unit, Calloway obsesses about the tidiness of his files and the finer points of "police procedure" (93) as a way of distinguishing between good guys and bad guys. He has Martins followed through Vienna and keeps "a very careful record of his movements" (76). Nevertheless, he does not record that Martins fires the close-range shot that kills Lime (98). The city, divided according to international zones, teeters on the brink of Cold War catastrophe, with Americans battling Russians for the lives of Austrians and foreign nationals. "Senseless kidnappings" (14) go nearly unremarked though they violate international boundaries. Calloway, as narrator, emphasizes the single criminal rather than national crimes. Although Graham Greene had published nearly twenty books before *The Third Man*, this novella features his first extended use, not counting short stories, of first-person narration (Hoskins 140). Told retrospectively, the narrative implies an ethics of responsibility in a political crisis.[1] The first-person witnesses who recount Lime's racketeering, rebirth, and second death are, inevitably, those who survive and who feel compelled to draw lessons from their experience. As readers, we assume that the survivors' worldview—Calloway's, Martins's—prevails, yet fear and mixed motives crisscross that worldview. Fear, as an element of political motivation and response, rattles Martins. If fear motivates an action, is that action rendered null by virtue of its irrationality? Does fear invalidate ethical engagement? Is fear ever completely contained in political discourse or fictional narration?

In general, Greene's thrillers represent the dilemmas of commitment in the face of danger. Influenced by Conrad, Buchan, Maugham, and Le Queux, Greene thoroughly transmutes the thriller genre into a mode of unabashed political speculation. Quoting Browning's "Bishop Bloughram's Apology" in his autobiography *A Sort of Life*, Greene locates his novels in a zone of danger: "Our interest's on the dangerous edge of things" (117). Coming from a family of spies (Shelden 292–309), Greene undertook a prewar espionage mission to Germany. Between 1941 and 1944, he worked directly under the supervision of Kim Philby. Michael Korda claims that Greene "maintained his shadowy connections with the British Secret Intelligence Service until near the end of his life" (50). Korda, who first met Greene in the 1950s, states that "it was always difficult to tell where the spy novelist left off and the spy manqué began" (50). Norman Sherry hypothesizes that Greene's espionage activities permitted him "knowledge of the lives of others so necessary to a novelist and especially this novelist born into the irksome restrictions of his class" (133). Writing overlaps with spying. In his dream archive, *A World of My Own,* Greene links acts of espionage with papers: "passports" (24), "a compromising letter" (39), or "top secret information" left open "for anyone to read" (19). Spying generates paper, just as novel writing does. Confusion about the relation of spying to writing also emerges because Greene offers conflicting reports about the goals of intelligence gathering. In *A Sort of Life,* Greene distinguishes between spying in order to obtain information and "spying for spying's sake" (104). Placing espionage in a category of pure disinterest where spies spy irrespective of what they learn, Greene seems unconcerned about declared allegiances. Having joined the Communist Party briefly in 1925, having been a self-professed liberal during his adult life, and having numbered several dictators among his acquaintances, Greene understood divided commitments. The spy-novelist's interest in spying has no single etiology. Spying eases boredom; spying reenacts the primal scene; spying fetches an income; spying aids national security; spying, like chess, involves games of cunning that prove intellectual superiority. "Espionage today is really a branch of psychological warfare," Greene writes in a 1968 review of Philby's memoir *My Silent War (Collected Essays* 414). As Greene makes clear in this review, the spy, regardless of his biases, has many facets to his personality and these should be judged objectively, without reference to local treacheries. He admires Philby, somewhat perversely, for his unflappable management of counter-Russian espionage teams. A good spy lives by a set of standards not applicable to average citizens or to national interests. A good spy demonstrates the gaps and inconsistencies within ideology, as a novelist might.

Understanding Greene as a novelist-cum-spy who feels scopophilic pleasure in his intelligence gathering leads us away from the more crucial question of how Greene makes thrillers into political allegories. Although Roger Sharrock claims that "Greene's great technical achievement has been the elevation of the form of the thriller into a medium for serious fiction" (12), he does not specify how that elevation comes about. Greene himself argued that he did not write for political reasons (Allain 78). The comment is disingenuous insofar as he writes about contemporary trouble in far-flung locations. He acknowledges in an interview that his fixations include "the melodramatic, the contemporary and later the Catholic novel" (Hynes, *Graham Greene* 160). Melodramatic thrillers on contemporary themes have the advantage of conveying specific political ideas "to readers who would otherwise not be reached by more conventional political discourse" (Diemert 13). Aimed at exciting the reader, the thriller promotes action rather than character development. Protagonists chase or run away, as if fear and aggression cap all human instincts. Characters win or lose, escape or die. The thriller, with its limited roster of outcomes, reveals the fundamental grimness of life and the irrationality of choice made during moments of panic. By utilizing thrillers as a genre, Greene critiques the rationality that is alleged to underlie political decisions. In his autobiography *Journey Without Maps,* he implicitly connects "brutality" with gangsters in novels "who have so agreeably simplified their emotions that they have begun living again at a level below the cerebral" (21). Readers follow suit. Arousing emotions rather than intellectual engagement, the thriller dramatizes the narrow self-interest that underlies choices made by characters and readers. It needs also be said that nearly all of Greene's protagonists are men who prove their masculinity through chases and combats. Most of them die in the end (D in *The Confidential Agent,* Castle in *The Human Factor,* and Martins in *The Third Man* prove exceptions to the rule). Although thrillers represent the fierce attempts by characters to subdue panic and survive, this rarely comes to pass. Allegorically, Greene's thrillers imply that fear must be reckoned as integral to, but does not override, political representation. Working out a paradigm of political thrills requires a constant shifting among considerations of contemporaneity, psychology, nonconformism, masculinity, and self-interest.

Hate, in particular, animates characters in Greene's thrillers. Hate, even if personal, can have public consequences; national hatreds, too, boil down to personal vendettas. Cates Baldridge suggests that Greene's mature political thought cross-fertilizes Christianity, liberalism, and Marxism, yet Baldridge qualifies these public allegiances by observing that "there are for Greene *only* private motivations for political engagement" (169, 179).

The Third Man bears out this conclusion. Hatred spurs actions. Rollo Martins initially trusts Harry Lime, whom he hero-worshipped when they were schoolboys together. When Calloway shows Martins the files amassed on Lime's penicillin racketeering, Martins's boyhood love turns to hate. The ghastliness of Lime's actions supersedes intense personal admiration, converting, at the same time, Martins into an information-gatherer working on behalf of the police. Yet Martins's profile suggests that self-interest forces him into that position. Accused of killing Herr Koch by a mouthy child named Hansel, Martins lurks in the half-light of suspicion. Indirectly responsible for Koch's death because of an indiscreet interrogation, Martins has no alternative but to "'turn policeman'" (107), as Lime conjectures he might do. Recruited by his need for exculpation, Martins exterminates Lime. If we read *The Third Man* as a parable of behavior, Lime represents repressed fantasy elements in the imaginative life of Martins: originality, superiority, authenticity. Martins thinks Lime "'a wonderful planner'" who "'knew the ropes'" (24). He even believes that Lime writes a corny melody that, in fact, he has plagiarized. Riding the Prater Ferris wheel, Martins realizes for the first time "without admiration" that Lime had "never grown up" (104). The past shifts for Martins. He renounces his allegiances—to Lime, to authenticity, to cleverness. Subsequently, the western-style shoot-out in the sewers seems to vindicate Martins's alignment with the police. At this point, the political allegory of the novel, theoretically expunged with Harry's death, really begins, in that hatred spills over into murder. Only by a perverse psychological torque can the death of Martins's illusions justify the death of Harry Lime.

Because of its postwar setting in "smashed, dreary" (13) Vienna, *The Third Man* allegorizes the afterlife of commitments: "Vienna is a microcosm of international politics; and the character relationships become symbolic of national political relationships" (Carpenter 58). Conflicted characters replicate the territorial zones of the occupied city. Political and psychological divisions overlap and reinforce each other. The segregated city represents divergent aspects of identity (communist, opportunistic, democratic, ex-Nazi). Russian, British, American, and French forces battle for civilians' allegiances. In particular, Anna Schmidt, the actress for whom Harry fixes false documents and then betrays to the Russians, suffers because of her hazy background: "'She was Hungarian and her father had been a Nazi, so they said. She was scared the Russians would pick her up'" (58). Indeed, "dumb with fear" (94), Anna, pretending to be Austrian, gets driven by two Russians towards the Russian sector, until Calloway stops the car at a roadblock and demands Anna's release. Anna, as a pawn in a territorial battle, signifies political contamination: she associates with Harry Lime; she has a tainted Nazi past; she carries false papers. Split in her loyalties, she responds with fear.

In Greene's representation, fear is a threshold for action, and that action may have enlightened self-interest or dumb panic at its core. Fear, however, cannot efface former allegiances. An action, once committed, cannot be retracted. It permanently defines character. Paradoxically, actions agglomerate into character, yet after death, lessons about character take precedence over actions. Calloway tenders the opinion that "One's file, you know, is never quite complete; a case is never really closed, even after a century, when all the participants are dead" (22). The statement means several things. Crime has an afterlife. Characters alter history by their actions. A traumatic event necessarily produces ghosts that cannot be assimilated into patterns of rationality. Notwithstanding the capacity of the dead to live in ghostly fashion, *The Third Man* requires that a missing body be produced in order officially to close the dossier on Harry Lime. Although he's dead, his crimes add another horrifying chapter to the history of evil that the police dossier does not regulate. Martins pointedly says he will never forget what has happened (118). As he rises from and disappears back into the sewers, Lime embodies Martins's dread of what will never go away. As the objectification of Martins's horrified incapacity to grasp circumstances, Lime can never be completely contained. He exceeds storytelling. Amoral, freewheeling, ruthless, he stands as a cipher for fear.

Whereas Lime exists as an externalization of Martins's fear, and the Russians embody Anna's fears, *The Third Man* also represents identity as internally divided, as fearful in itself. Such characters as Anna fear that their internal division will attract attention; the subject who lacks unity of personality worries that incoherent political affiliations will arouse the suspicions of governmental powers. Martins intuits this and therefore aligns himself with the police as a means of diverting attention away from his own incoherent identity. Spreading his internal uncertainties onto others, Martins ascribes a second identity to Calloway by calling him Callaghan (27). Likewise, he misnames Dr. Winkler as Dr. Winkle (102). Anna multiplies her identity through passports and cheesy theatrical roles. Martins, similarly, atomizes into several identities. He publishes under the nom de plume Buck Dexter. In the comic subplot of the novel, he is confused with a Jamesian literary author named Benjamin Dexter. Division extends to his sexual identity. A sentimentalist, swaggerer, drinker, and puritan, Martins seduces women indefatigably yet refers to them as "incidents" (16), as if they had no connection to him. Calloway observes that "There was always a conflict in Rollo Martins—between the absurd Christian name and the sturdy Dutch (four generations back) surname. Rollo looked at every woman that passed, and Martins renounced them forever" (18). In my interpretation of Martins's case, internal divisions take on a hysterical cast in which he makes women culpable for his lack of self-knowledge. Seducing women in Dublin, Amsterdam, and elsewhere, he offloads his hysteria onto women. Calloway calculates that Martins has at least six ex-girlfriends ready to assail him at unguarded moments (16). Martins's troubled devotion to Harry translates into a troubled seduction of Anna. Instead of stemming from or manifesting itself in womanizing, Martins's hysteria may be causally connected to grief, in the sense that symbolic codes of friendship disintegrate when a death occurs (Bronfen 16). The death of Harry causes Martins to confront his guilt for trusting and defending a false friend. At the same time, Harry's death brings Martins into a triangulation of desire, implicit in dating Anna as a means of coping with and overcoming his guilt. He loves Anna because he does not know how to deal with his conflicted feelings for Harry.

Once loved, Harry never really dies. After converting boyish love to adult hate, Martins projects his vestigial love for Harry into a love for Harry's girlfriend. Initially, Martins conceives of Harry as the "'best friend [he] ever had'" (23). In a dream, Martins wonders why "only the two people [Anna and Rollo] who loved him seemed to have been missing" from Lime's funeral (42). Yet their friendship relied on Martins's taking the blame for Lime's pranks at school. "'I was always the one who got caught,'" Martins says (24). The conclusion of the novel reverses this pattern: Martins catches Lime. The dead friendship becomes a dead friend, according to the intrinsic narrative logic of The Third Man. The sense of inferiority that Martins displays vis-à-vis Lime in the past culminates with his vanquishing of Lime. Allegiances have to be renounced in order to assert independence from the specter of the past. By contrast, Anna continues to love Harry as "'the man we knew'" (86) despite her limited knowledge of his evil deeds. She wishes "'to be dead too'" (42) in order to reunite with him. Anna sees death as an orphic potential for rescue: she adheres to her old convictions and sentiments because she distinguishes Lime the man from Lime the racketeer. For both Anna and Martins, Harry exists as a figment of ideals. Moreover, Anna loves Martins in reminiscence of Harry; Martins loves Anna in compensation for the loss of Harry. Seducing Anna, Martins resurrects the ghost of his love for Lime. Through her, he can rid himself of Harry and hold on to him too. Because he cannot square death with his idea of the past, Martins conjectures that killing his old friend will resolve incongruity: "'Maybe I'd kill him myself under these circumstances'" (87). He wants Harry alive. He wants Harry dead. He doesn't know what he wants. His fear compels him to investigate. Greene, in *A Sort of Life,* distinguishes between terror and fear in ways applicable to the conflicts inherent in Martins's identity: "From terror one escapes screaming, but fear has an odd seduction. Fear and the sense of sex are linked in secret conspiracy, but terror is a sickness like hate" (31). Fear of Harry, linked to covert attraction for Harry, delivers Martins over to wide-eyed, nervous curiosity about his friend.

An agon between men, *The Third Man* mystifies masculinity in the portrayal of bodies. Harry is a corpse, a ghost, a living person. The interplay between bodies and their apparitions produces two representational strategies for corporeality: first, bodies are immobile, unreal, frozen, statuesque; second, bodies are fragmented, spectral, anonymous, incomplete. The emblem of immobile bodies, "statuary" lines the Innere Stadt (14). The Russians erect "statues of armed men" in their part of the cemetery (20). In central Vienna, statues of Titans balance "great globes of snow above their heads" (68). These memorialized bodies make the past seem heroic, partly buried beneath snow and unchanging. Male bodies are also incomplete or fake. A "toupée of snow" (20) that slides over an angel's stone face anticipates the "flat and yellow" ill-fitting toupée worn by Kurtz (35). The wig disguises malevolent Kurtz, who looks made up "to express charm, whimsicality" (35). The wig eerily detaches from his body. Martins spots Kurtz's toupée "hanging sedately on a peg" (101). Like the saints' relics available in Dr. Winkler's shop, including "little bits of bone marked with saints' names" and a chunk of "Saint Susanna's knuckle" (45), bodies survive in bits. Synecdoches for whole but missing bodies, these relics and hairpieces morselize and spectralize bodies.[2] The body fragments under the pressure of multiple identities. The cinematic cropping characteristic of Greene's narrative exposition accentuates the tendency to see the body in parts. Looking down on the so-called accident that kills Harry, Herr Koch sees only the tops of heads, especially the man in the toupée. They have, from Koch's perspective, "foreshortened" bodies (51). Anna, first glimpsed by Martins as a "face" (40), seems cut off from her body. She has "a face for wear" (62), yet Martins and Calloway resist talking about her as an integral human form beyond her free-floating face. Similarly, Martins gazes out at "the earnest and cheery faces of constant readers," including "a woman's face shiny with exertion" and "two young men with the happy intelligent faces of sixth-formers" (68). The audience shrinks to rows of faces. The faces, hypothetically, belong to bodies. Nevertheless, those hidden bodies exist phantasmatically, as entities that have dwindled into spectral anonymity. So, too, characters disappear then come back into focus. Martins vanishes from Calloway's purview for stretches of time, just as Lime disappears and returns.

In an extension of the principle of bodily disintegration, everyone is always already a corpse. Characters shed body parts in preparation for death. Nor should we forget that Harry Lime trained as a doctor, without practicing, and that the adulterated penicillin he sells causes death and madness for some victims and requires the amputation of infected limbs for others (80–81). Lime deals death. Whether death arrives at the hands of others or not, the body carries within it the seeds of its own decay and demise. Quite apart from the ethical imperatives that cause Martins to hunt down Lime, Martins kills his old friend to externalize and rid himself of his own sense of mortality. In this sense, then, the body of the agent in a narrative of intrigue incarnates the death drive—the radical diversions and displacements of the agent's knowledge of mortality get foisted onto his quarry—just as the hunted criminal also incarnates the death drive that must be confronted and defeated. The body, as vessel of death, flickers in and out of view in morselized pieces or appears in memorial statuary in *The Third Man*: slightly unreal, slightly spectral.

Greene often concludes his narratives with death. His novels return obsessively to funerals, suicides, murders, shoot-outs, accidents, morgues, hostages, cadavers. Pinkie leaps off a cliff to his death in *Brighton Rock*, which might provide unusual satisfaction to Ida, who "liked a funeral—but it was with horror—as other people like a ghost story. Death shocked her" (35–36). An atmosphere of corruption hangs over *The Power and the Glory,* culminating in the execution of the whisky priest; "I might just as well have never lived," the priest thinks with existential gloom (210). Scobie kills himself in *The Heart of the Matter.* Anna-Luise dies in a ski accident and her father Doctor Fischer lies like "a dead dog" (138) on the ground after he shoots himself in *Doctor Fischer of Geneva or the Bomb Party.* Dr. Czinner in *Stamboul Train* reasons that "'Life has not been so good as that. I think I shall be of more use dead'" (166), as if death had utility for those who continue to live. To enumerate corpses prompts a secondary question about the manner in which characters die: solitarily; violently; suicidally; homicidally; publicly; deliberately; reluctantly; happily; emptily; agedly; youthfully; comically; impiously; contritely. No death resembles any other. Furthermore, death and corpses signify according to the narrative context in which they are located (Stewart 6). In *The Third Man,* Lime's alleged corpse is a body double. Harbin, who snitches on Lime to the police, is killed and buried in Lime's coffin. Lime has two bodies. He dies; he rises again; he is killed; he lives in memory.[3] Death is not restricted to the body. Whereas the ghost of Haldin in *Under Western Eyes* reminds Razumov of his betrayal and lack of engagement, the ghost of Lime reminds Martins of the irreducibility of the body. Harry engineers the ruse of substituting another body for his own in the coffin, yet Harry is only ever himself. One body cannot replace another.

In *The Third Man,* the living mingle with the dead. Knowledge of death, however, gets pushed underground, where Lime and Martins confront each other one last time.

SEWERS

Other narratives by Greene began as books before becoming film scenarios, but *The Third Man,* from its inception, was written "only to be seen" (9). Image precedes text. The film offers "the finished state of the story" (10). Instead of considering the novella as an artifact independent of the film, we can interpret them as supplements to each other. Both serve as cultural documents in the midcentury evolution of narratives of intrigue. *The Third Man,* as film, takes place mostly in darkness. The first glimpse that film-watchers have of Harry Lime reveals his face caught in a sudden sweep of car headlights. His body, swaddled in a black greatcoat, remains obscure. Paradoxically, the long chase sequence through the sewers of Vienna that ends with Rollo shooting Harry depends on not being able to see. Although meant "to be seen," *The Third Man* withholds visual information. Drawing on film noir conventions of down-and-dirty gutter life, of hardened criminals, of nighttime obscurity, the sewer scenes in both novella and film address a cultural preoccupation with the underground world. This preoccupation has antecedents in Odysseus's speaking to the souls of the dead in Homer's *The Odyssey* or Dante's guided tour through the circles of Hell in *Inferno*. Via associations with Dostoevsky's *Notes From Underground*, underground has connotations of countercultural alienation. Dostoevsky's underground man is an anonymous, despicable antihero. And the fascination with troglodytes and underground adventures in Jules Verne's *A Journey to the Center of the Earth*, Kenneth Grahame's *The Wind in the Willows*, or J. R. R. Tolkien's *The Hobbit* speak to an abiding concern with netherworlds in literature. *The Third Man*, film and text, alludes to a network of literary underworlds while preserving the cultural specificity of the subterranean fantasies active in post–World War II Europe.

Greene likes dark places. Dark places are not necessarily subterranean, yet they can approximate the coffinlike blackness of underground spaces. Greene's protagonists frequently enter closets, railroad cars, sheds, outhouses. In *Stamboul Train*, Josef Grünlich slips through shadows; indeed, most of the characters in the novel, compartmentalized in train cabins, loiter in darkness, where "betrayal" occurs (12). Certain rooms seem more oppressive or treacherous in the dark, whereas outdoor spaces at night provide opportunities for escape. "Misery is worse in the darkness" (57), thinks Scobie in *The Heart of the Matter* about indoor confinement; this misery yields to precarious happiness as he sets "out in the darkness, in the rain, alone" on his nightly patrol (140). Criminals seek haven in darkened rooms. Fugitive Raven hides in the "close cold darkness" of a shed in *A Gun for Sale* (117). Raven struggles to see Anne's face through the gloom. As such, darkness covers erotic intentions while prohibiting men and women from really knowing each other. In the dark, they communicate through language and touch, not image and gesture. Greene's male-female couples often talk in darkness with a candor not possible in lit rooms. As Freud says about infant anxiety, people "are afraid in the dark because in the dark they cannot see the person they love" (*Three Essays on the Theory of Sexuality* 224). Darkroom conversations do not always promote intimacy. Rowe and treacherous Miss Hilfe speak nervously through a bombardment in *The Ministry of Fear* in a "darkening" room (102). Blackout darkness inspires dread. In *The End of the Affair,* darkness during the Blitz becomes the emblem of mortal terror. Bendrix, "puzzled by the darkness" (71) that follows a direct bomb hit, lies under debris scattered by the blast. Moments in darkness, whether implicated in scenes of intimacy or terror, signify in Greene's oeuvre a recollection of death or near-death experience. Subterranean worlds trigger phobias about live burial. For D in *The Confidential Agent,* hiding in darkness reminds him of "the air raid of December 23 when he was buried for fifty-six hours in a cellar" (13). He cannot tolerate the idea of "going underground" (80) and thinks about his countrymen who "would die in company in underground shelters" (106). In *The Third Man,* Martins dashes into a dark room. Hearing a parrot scratching on its post, he realizes that "he was far less afraid of the police than he was of the darkness" (74). The darkness cloaks these characters with existential panic, a panic exacerbated by the retreat into subterranean spaces, such as the sewers of Vienna.

At the end of *The Third Man,* policemen, like watchmen of the unconscious, guard all entries and exits to the sewers. They are ready to ambush Harry Lime when he pushes his way into the aboveground city. Orson Welles, in the film version, extends a trembling, whiter-than-white hand upwards through a manhole cover in a bid for freedom. As he does so, Joseph Cotten as Holly, aka Rollo Martins, shoots him. Lime sinks back into his sewery milieu. If the ideal of contemporary urbanism is *"un espace propre"* [a clean space], in which rational organization represses "all the physical, mental and political pollutions that would compromise it" (De Certeau 94), then a movement below ground preserves the potential for irrationality within the city. The sewer system maintains "a dangerous but fascinating network of often subterranean relationships in need of decipherment" within the city (Donald 79), even if the darkness of subterranean worlds thwarts complete decipherment. The underworld eclipses reason and ideology. Although mapped (111), subterranean realms in *The Third Man* have the allure of freedom from law and postwar politics. Because of fiercely partisan commitments above ground, politics moves into murk. Underground, one dodges the barbed wire fences that divide zones. Above ground, territorial sectors perpetuate political squabbles. In the 1950 docu-feature *The Big Lift* (shot on location in the rubble of Berlin), American, British, Russian, and French forces divide the city into bezirks that may not be crossed. In a graphic example of ideology in action, peace-keeping militia pull a woman back and forth between sectors, just as, in *The Third Man,* Anna fears that Russians will drag her into their zone. Dissociated from battle lines in the city, the sewers of Vienna become a zone where nonaligned, antiheroic Harry Lime can skirt political skirmishes with his capitalistic sell-to-the-highest-bidder ethos. The sewers form an unconscious to the city. In that unconscious, capitalism reinvents itself as an apolitical force.[4]

Sewers defy simple cultural categorization. They metaphorize filth and pollution as well as crime, as Calloway makes clear when he says that burglars and deserters hide in them (98). Sewers evoke hidden, labyrinthine structures, even though sewers were uncovered runnels trickling through streets until the mid-nineteenth century. Murky and smelly, they also inspire rhapsodies. "What a strange world unknown to most of us lies under our feet," Calloway muses; "we live above a cavernous land of waterfalls and rushing rivers, where tides ebb and flow as in the world above" (113). The "obscurity of the sewers" (112) induces perverse sublimity from Calloway: "The main sewer, half as wide as the Thames, rushes by under a huge arch, fed by tributary streams: these streams have fallen in waterfalls from higher levels and have been purified in their fall, so that only in these side channels is the air foul. The main stream smells sweet and fresh" (113). Sublime because inaccessible and cascading, the sewers intimate that nature lies beneath the cobbles of the old Hapsburg capital. Although Greene usually specializes in locales degraded by "the weary feeling of waste and human failure" (R. Stevenson 94), in *The Third Man,* where waste is the object of exposition, the rhetoric effusively reverses expectations about foulness and sweetness in order to suggest that the urban unconscious can renew political thought. Renewal might come from disintegration. Sweetness and freshness notwithstanding, sewers excite fears of breakdown and contamination. Elsewhere in his fiction, Greene demonstrates scatological keenness that can be metonymically connected to the semiotics of sewage. In the short story "The Destructors," an elderly gentleman gets locked in his outhouse while a gang of boys saws his house apart (*Collected Short Stories* 19–21). D slips into "an outside lavatory" while being chased in *The Confidential Agent* (172). And Martins pretends to need the men's room to escape the police (73). Rowe confronts Hilfe in a men's room in *The Ministry of Fear* (214–20). The most resplendent of Greene's miscreants all carry within them "'the secrets of the sewer,'" as one character in *Brighton Rock* calls villainous knowledge (211).

Sewers recall Greene's fascination with the incomprehensibility of death. The human body finds a provisional grave in the sewer. Like the dark railway cars and abandoned factories that provide cover for Raven in *A Gun for Sale,* the sewers in *The Third Man* signify conditions of unknowing, whether about death or about the body. Calloway tells Martins that "for some reason" (97) the Russians object to the sewer entrances being locked. Colonel Calloway lacks historical perspective: "in the days of the workers' uprising in Vienna before the war, when Philby had helped communists to flee, the sewers had been their escape route" (W. J. West 128). Sewers provide asylum because authorities hardly think to search them. Already foul by nature, Lime amid slime disappears through self-abasement. His name alludes to "lime," or calcium oxide, the chemical used to treat sewage and to neutralize gases released during the decomposition of bodies. In a misguided analysis, Martins conjectures that Lime tries to crawl up to a manhole before he dies: "[a man] wants to die at home, and the darkness is never home to *us*" (117). Martins falsifies Lime's personality. In fact, Lime prefers darkness. He thrives in it. In the final chase scene, a constable flashes a searchlight into the dark as Lime "took a flying jump into the deep central rushing stream" (116). Apart from this fugitive glimpse, the gurgling, seeping sewers admit no observation, but they do carry sound, as does, earlier in the novel, the darkened closet where Martins hears the rustling parrot. Martins identifies Lime in the dark by his customary trite whistle, but at the moment of death, Lime mumbles something that Martins doesn't understand. Lime's passage into death, in the final analysis, remains mysterious, a knowledge that Martins cannot translate into intelligibility. In both *The Third Man* and *The Heart of the Matter,* underground rivers recall Stygian passages into oblivion. In the latter novel, when Scobie dreams about a boat adrift on an underground river, he smells decay and realizes "that it was not the dead body that smelt but his own living one" (222). As the figuration of the body itself—its organs, its demands, its diseases— the sewer system permits speculation about bodily corruption and demise. In the sewer, Martins and Scobie encounter deathly versions of themselves. The sewer provides a trial run for death. Although the sewers lead to "disintegration of the self" for Martins (Thomas 11), his descent into darkness also marks a point of disillusionment. The sewer clarifies his fears.

To speak of dank, dark sewers is to elevate to consciousness the democracy of bodily functions: foul excretion, unspeakable waste, toxins on the loose. All segments of society get equalized by the secret conduits and dark tentacles of plumbing that link a city. The sewer opens into private water closets and public toilets. The sewer unites urban-dwellers in unmentionable ways. We disavow our sewage as soon as it leaves our premises. Roaming through the sewers, Harry slops through unhygienic international detritus. A particle of urban effluvium, he brushes against "a scum of orange peel, old cigarette cartons, and the like" (114). The sewer refers metaphorically to ways in which cities manage criminals, public works, and poverty. The trope of the city as a complex sewer system can be traced to Eugène Sue's *Les Mystères de Paris* and Victor Hugo's *Les Misérables*. In both those Parisian novels, the underworld seeps and trickles. The denouement of Charles Dickens's *Oliver Twist* occurs among the "dirt-besmeared walls and decaying foundations" of Folly Ditch, where "every loathsome indication of filth, rot, and garbage" befouls its inhabitants (404). Many nineteenth-century narratives of cesspools and sewers are implicated in class biases, such as Dickens's *Our Mutual Friend,* where impoverished corpse-hunters fish a cadaver from the "slime and ooze" of the Thames (43). Marx, who felt no charity for the *Lumpenproletariat,* catalogues this class of homo sapiens in *The Eighteenth Brumaire of Louis Bonaparte* as "scum": "Alongside decayed *roués* with dubious means of subsistence and of dubious origins, alongside ruined and adventurous offshoots of the bourgeoisie, were vagabonds, discharged soldiers, discharged jailbirds, escaped galley slaves, swindlers, mountebanks, *lazzaroni,* pickpockets, tricksters, gamblers, *maquereaus,* brothel-keepers, porters, *literati,* organ-grinders, ragpickers, knife-grinders, tinkers, beggars—in short, the whole indefinite, disintegrated mass, thrown hither and thither, which the French call *la bohème*" (75). Peter Stallybrass and Allon White point out that Marx's fascination with this "disintegrated mass" conceals "links between slum and suburb, sewage and 'civilization'" (130). The more perfectly sewers function, the more the bourgeois citizen can conceive of his purity and his hygiene as separate from slums. This class distinction was less easy to make before the mid-nineteenth century. Until Haussmann's reorganization of water supplies and construction of sewers in Paris after 1852, Parisians dumped ordure into the Seine, then pumped drinking water from the same place (Des Cars and Pinon 154–55; Reid 9–15). In

Paris, London, Vienna, or anywhere else, filth diminishes social distinctions. Although no one likes to acknowledge it, everyone is a bit soiled. Social niceties merely repress personal filthiness. The good bourgeois covers his mouth when he sneezes, does not fart in public, does not allude to his bowel movements. The body sloughs its skin, pus, nails, snot, sweat, earwax, feces, blood, and urine into sewers and immediately abjures them as products of the body. In this sense, the grubbiness of the body defies ethnic distinctions; everyone's body, regardless of ethnicity, requires upkeep. Marx's vocabulary intimates that filth knows no ethnicity. He resorts to an international lexicon to describe the *Lumpenproletariat*. French and Italian border-crossing terms converge with other European words in the excremental mass of Marx's catalogue of fringe capitalists and the down-and-out. As Victor Hugo writes in *Les Misérables,* in the sewer "all things converge and clash. There is darkness here, but no secrets. . . . Every foulness of civilization, fallen into disuse, sinks into the ditch of truth wherein ends the huge social down-slide, to be swallowed, but to spread" (qtd. in Stallybrass and White 141). "Spread" activates Hugo's fear of sewage as fear of mixing nationalities and ideas. This idea of international contamination endures until the post–World War II period. In an autobiography about growing up in Florida, Clark Blaise remembers digging in the sludge of a ditch where he finds a cable: "So there I sat, trowel in hand, arms brown to the elbow in scummy groundwater, blushing over having uncovered secret equipment: German, Japanese, ours, or Russian" (44). A cable in a ditch must, de facto, be foreign. In the Cold War, the sewer breeds the danger of internationalism. Americans in the 1950s even feared that bathroom bacteria might breed bolshevism (Ross, *No Respect* 45–47). Politics spreads through sewers.

Sewers and subterranean recesses—where Mutant Ninja Turtles, the Phantom of the Opera, legendary alligators, swarms of rats, and freed piranhas congregate—typically provoke disgust and fear. The heroin-addicted protagonist in the film version of Irvine Welsh's *Trainspotting* dives headfirst into the fetor of a backed-up toilet in a disgusting, but not frightening, encounter with filth. What disgusts us does not necessarily frighten us, or vice versa. William Ian Miller in *The Anatomy of Disgust* suggests that fear causes flight; disgust, less kinetic, causes aversion without movement. "It has been proposed," writes Miller, "that the difference [between fear and disgust] is that fear is a response to harms threatening the body, disgust to harms threatening the soul. That contrast strikes me as implausible. Many of our fears are not about our bodies" (25–26). A grimace of disgust registers alarm about contamination of soul by body; bruising of one leads to bruising of the other in Miller's estimation. Like the chamber pot filled with shit and piss under the breakfast table that forces George Orwell to vacate a boarding house in *The Road to Wigan Pier* (14), disgust arises when boundaries between in-place and out-of-place filth collapse. Orwell sees class lines quiver and nearly shatter. Fear of the working classes edges his disgust, which he transfers to full chamber pots. Disgust, when allied with class, functions as a "powerful anti-democratic force, subverting the minimal demands of tolerance" (Miller 206). Disgust may be permanent, low-grade fear. Disgust erupts where unlikely categories, whether of nation, class, or bodily excrescences, commingle. In *The Third Man*, the desperate chase through the sewers—idiosyncratic in its uniting of filth with flight —is an escape *into* fear where the disintegrated mass of postwar Vienna burbles. Harry Lime lives in the milieu of contamination by choice. In other words, the postwar sewer has a different metaphorical valence than the festering sewers of nineteenth-century Europe.

The divided city, subject to occupation by foreign forces and to restructuring, develops downwards in sewers, subways, torture chambers, and fallout shelters. In a reversal of most other portrayals of underground space (as hell, as crypt, as trolls' warren), the postwar netherworld offers refuge from devastation, as with the building of bunkers. Underground is a dream space.[5] Subterranean zones offer sanctuary: Londoners descended into tube stations during the Blitz because below ground was safer than above ground. "O dark dark dark. They all go into the dark," writes T. S. Eliot in "East Coker," a meditation on precautionary wartime blackouts and imminent death (Eliot 180). The sewer sometimes substitutes for political situations, as when in the opening scene of Virginia Woolf's *Between the Acts*, conversation turns on the subject of "the cesspool" (3). German refusal to think about sewage, except derogatorily, allowed Jews incarcerated in the Warsaw ghetto to flee underground and to retaliate from within the sewer system. In Leon Uris's *Mila 18*, Nazis drop barbed wire into the sewers when they discover that incarcerated Jews traverse the ghetto underground, but "Sewer Rats" quickly learn "to duck beneath the running sewage and cut barbed wire in the main sewers" to restore passageways (Uris 383). The way down is the way out of politically desperate situations, or at least the way down establishes a redoubt from which to make incursions against oppressors. The nineteenth-century sewer represses; the sewer during World War II camouflages.

For two decades after the end of the War, the trope of underground in literature and film evoked a blend of abnegation, shelter, disappearance, disaster. No longer a place of camouflage, subterranean space became a place of conflict. The constricted, hellish rooms of Sartre's *Huis Clos*, a play that opened in Paris in May 1944 while Nazis still occupied the city, recalls underground chambers of interrogation and torture. In the play, Garcin, executed for some political crime, anticipates "les pals, les grils, les entonnoirs de cuir" (stakes, pyres, leather torture devices shaped like funnels) (15) behind the bolted door of his room in hell. The chamber in *Huis Clos* prefigures the bunker, the fallout shelter, the subterranean war room, where space is measured out and divvied up, where every survivor or occupant has to get along with everyone else despite inbred antagonism. Such underground rooms, pressed in on all sides by earth, are spaces of horror, like the underground torture chamber in *Nineteen Eighty-Four*. Below-ground spaces recall live burial. They recall catastrophe and apocalypse, usually of the nuclear sort. Traces of underground dystopia are present in Samuel Beckett's *Endgame* (1957). Hamm, in a reflective mood, asks Clov, "Did you ever think of one thing?" "Never," replies Clov. "That here we're down in a hole. *(Pause.)* But beyond the hills? Eh? Perhaps it's still green. Eh?" (Beckett 39). Nature flourishes in an unreachable place beyond the hills, not underground. Among the resonances of this passage, one hears the possibilities of a lost paradise, of the landscape before it was devastated by nuclear bombs. The bunker is, in the last analysis, no haven. Death crosses its threshold. The constricted room of *Endgame* "stinks of corpses" according to Hamm (46). Underground remains a place of burial, but the grave may provide the only refuge from apocalypse. Holing up in places of death may be the way to face further calamity.

Subterranean spaces therefore register the fear that no place, anywhere, is safe, either above or below ground. Postwar writers and architects invent alternative, underground spaces that embody fantasies of survival against all odds. Subterranean spaces, however, in the postwar period are bolted shut and watched over. These places seem suspended in time. For instance, Chris Marker's 1963 short film *La Jetée* takes place in a bunker after World War III: "The survivors settled beneath Chaillot in an underground network of galleries. Above ground, Paris, as most of the world, was uninhabitable, riddled with radioactivity. The victors stood guard over an empire of rats" (Marker n.p.). Torturers reminiscent of Nazis in *La Jetée* live among giant ventilation pipes and conduct time-travel experiments by injecting men's veins with memory-enhancing, mind-altering drugs. Underground space becomes nightmarish: after global annihilation, bunkers provide no respite from crypto-Nazi torturers. Underground spaces in the postwar period express fear of technology. Missiles rise out of underground silos. Control rooms are subterranean. One retreats to a bunker with tinned vegetables and condensed milk, enough for a few months or until ground-level radiation recedes somewhat.

By the mid-1960s, the sense of underground changes again, towards comedy. In, for example, the quirky television comedy series about international POWs incarcerated in a German camp, *Hogan's Heroes* (1965–71), the prisoners dig their way past the perimeter of the camp, spoonful of dirt by spoonful of dirt. Colonel Klinck and Nazi guards patrol the camp. They do not, however, govern the dirt under their feet. The underground passage allows comic stealthy diversions. Stanley Kubrick's political satire *Dr. Strangelove*, released in 1964, stages confrontations between a Russian spy, a war-mongering American general, and a nervous president in a vast underground "war-room." When a fight breaks out, the president innocently announces, "there'll be no fighting in the war-room." The underground headquarters enters the image repertory as a joke in *Dr. Strangelove* and becomes a commonplace in 1960s Cold War television programs. Emma Peel and John Steed cruise down a ramp to their underground headquarters in *The Avengers* (1961–69) or descend by standing in a particular phone booth that is a secret entry to HQ. In the American parody of this sequence, Maxwell Smart gets into a phone booth in front of a federal building that magically drops him into a maze of corridors in the credit sequence of *Get Smart* (1965–70). These trapdoors to the underground all recall the entry to sewers in *The Third Man*, through a secret door in a kiosk in the middle of a cobbled plaza. In general, intelligence—whether shrewdness or espionage control—goes into bunkers. Batman and Robin leave their bat cave through a movable lawn in *Batman and Robin* (1966–68). Thought-control centers are protected from encroachment or bomb blast by virtue of their subterranean locations. Strength in postwar culture is chthonic: it derives from contact with the earth or from being in the earth.[6]

Underground is a place of intelligence. Pertinent to *The Third Man,* Vienna immediately after the war was the site of "Operation Silver," an American and British scheme to tunnel under the Russian sector and tap phone lines for intelligence purposes. In 1954, Allen Dulles, director of the CIA, authorized "Operation Gold," a tunnel in Berlin masterminded by British Secret Intelligence Service (MI6) but paid for and built by the American CIA. After attending meetings about the tunnel, an MI6 officer named George Blake, who was also a spy for the KGB, reported to his Russian operators that the tunnel was being constructed. The tunnel went ahead. The KGB disseminated disinformation to the German and American agents listening to Soviet conversations. As a propaganda coup and media sensation, Soviet and East German soldiers broke into the tunnel on April 21, 1956. The listening post was declared a breach of international law and an act of gangsterism (Polmar and Allen 61–62). In Ian McEwan's *The Innocent,* set in Berlin in 1955 in and around the tunnel, the English agent responsible for electronic surveillance smells "earth, and a lurid dampness, and shit not quite neutralized by chemicals" (21) as he stands at the lip of the hole leading underground.

The Third Man participates in polyvalent meanings of underground: sewer, shelter, control center, escape route, dream space, threshold, passageway. In their depiction of death and subterranean spaces, the novella and film sketch a relatively apparent division of conscious and unconscious behaviors. Compromised, inquiring Martins circulates in the streets of Vienna while murderous, fugitive Lime roams through the city sewers. For Greene, the spatial design of *The Third Man* enables an understanding of emergent Cold War breakdown of cooperation and anarchic self-interest. After the Soviets admitted in 1946 that they had spied in Canada during World War II, and after Churchill's "iron curtain" speech in March of the same year, the Cold War unofficially began as low-intensity combat among nations who had previously been allies against Nazi Germany. Instead of out-and-out warfare, espionage contained animosity to specific incidents. The formation of the CIA in the United States in 1947 out of the existing Central Intelligence Group, coupled with the formation of the KGB (Committee for State Security) in Russia in March 1954, institutionalized espionage as an inevitable state activity. Yet spying was, of course, already widespread during World War II. The defection of Igor Gouzenko in Ottawa in September 1945 with documents that proved Russian espionage activity in Canada during the war triggered an international outcry. The Gouzenko incident established a conception of Cold War enemies *within* host nations. Rooting out those enemies was hampered by the fact that the Cold War was ostensibly waged in peacetime. Local fracases signify larger ideological differences. *The Third Man* depicts international tension within and across the bezirks of Vienna. The Russians will not cooperate with the British or Americans. Literary councils wage wars of words about artistic merit. Personal desires override public good. The Cold War disputes about who will strike first, who speaks for whom, on whose side justice falls, all appear in *The Third Man*.

Even the narrative form of first-person dossier betrays Calloway's uncertainty about the meaning of Lime's criminality. He recounts the tale as an undecidable case that requires readerly arbitration, as a case not fully closed. Calloway, acting in the name of law, nevertheless allows vigilante justice to take precedence over justice when he conveniently omits from his official report that Martins shoots Lime. Consequently, guilt shades his character, as it does Martins's. Greene brings to the representation of this political melee an acute awareness of the failure of systems of justice: Anna's deliverance into the hands of the Russians serves the interests of Lime and Calloway, just as Calloway's rescue of Anna does not occur because he feels any sympathy for her or sense of duty towards her. She is helpful in the Lime case. Hence, fear and self-interest underlie ethical choices. Martins, in part, shoots Lime because of a conflict over the affections of Anna and over a sense of having lost his illusions about Harry's schoolboy know-how. He does not necessarily shoot Lime because of the violent deaths that Lime's contaminated penicillin have brought about. This urgent sense of irrationality in action, of character not functioning according to standards of law but according to impulse and psychological involvement in a criminal case, inflects the representation of underground, where lawlessness holds sway and where anarchic impulses produce action.

The underworld disintegrates official procedures that obtain in the occupied city, but this disintegration potentially leads to a reinvention of citizenship and justice. Unlike the representation of Razumov in *Under Western Eyes*, whose status as recruited and reluctant spy vexes him while he infiltrates a spy cell in Geneva, the representation of Lime and Martins amounts to two halves of the spy's personality, working within and outside structures of justice simultaneously. The division of character into villain and police stooge allows insight into the psychology of commitment. Nothing compels Martins to pursue Lime except his entanglement in and obligation towards the past. By contrast, Lime speaks for an ethos of selfish amorality that has to do with the future, not the past: "'In these days, old man, nobody thinks in terms of human beings. Governments don't, so why should we? They talk of the people and the proletariat, and I talk of the mugs. It's the same thing. They have their five-year plans and so have I'" (106). If, as I have maintained, *The Third Man* provides an allegory of political behavior, Martins, turned towards the past and the "memories" (102) that flood him when he sees Lime, betrays his old commitments in order to satisfy a personal sense of justice, whereas Lime, turned falsely towards a totalitarian future of five-year plans, obliterates the past and plans his own survival. In this cagey representation, Martins's and Lime's motives can be neither fully justified nor fully condemned. Greene intimates that the hidden self-interest of political behavior, the underground motives that harm others, have to be brought into a discussion of Cold War commitments. In a peculiar way, acknowledgment of unconscious motives could potentially refresh political discourse. To breach the threshold between street and sewer is potentially to introduce the disintegrated international mass of unthinkable matter—rivalry, hate, border crossing—into the factionalism of aboveground discourse instead of pretending it doesn't exist. To go underground is, therefore, not necessarily a subterfuge, but an avowal of the psychology of death that political discourse typically forbids: *you hate me, therefore I fear you; I fear you, therefore you'll chase me and I'll run away. This game can only lead to our demise.* Given Greene's fascination with pursuits and darkness, we can conclude that fantasies of dread and death are invariably about the desire to make fear a component in political discussion.

*

You are caught not just because you are an object of the law who has been interpellated. You are caught, rather, because you've grown weary of trying to flee from your own fears and the tithe you owe to death. So you descend to the sewers, site of disgust and obscurity, where you find your past incarnated as treachery: buried but not dead, not yet. In the sewers, you touch the very object of your disgust—the waste products of the body, the parts of yourself you've rejected—and you grasp the need to acknowledge that you embody laws and convictions. You are not just the interpellated victim of justice. You pull the trigger. Doing so, you have not really stilled the profound disquiet of your past commitments, which have turned out to be treacherous. Flush them away as you might, they just won't disappear. You remember the war and its upheaval, its collaborations and its blackouts.

CHAPTER SIX

Collaborations

LOVE AND WAR IN *THE HEAT OF THE DAY*

DOUBTFUL COMPLICITIES

The Heat of the Day, a literary espionage novel published in 1949, directs attention towards treacheries within love as a consequence of treacheries within public service. In this narrative of traumatic discovery, emphasis falls not on the spy's duplicities, but on the ethical dilemmas that love affairs create for women during wartime. Falling in love is, in this case, a subset of political collaboration. Set principally in London between 1940 and 1942, *The Heat of the Day* traces a love affair between Stella Rodney, a translator in the Ministry of Information, and Robert Kelway, who, after being wounded at Dunkirk, works in the War Office and passes information to the Nazis. All evidence points to his being a "leak" (35). Kelway withholds his treasonous activities from Stella. Harrison, a counterspy, informs her of Robert's treachery yet offers to remain silent if Stella will sleep with him. Harrison puts Stella in the morally ambiguous position of betraying the duplicitous man she loves in order to rectify her ignorance. In a novel, as in a war, Bowen claims, we are "deeply implicated in what we do not yet even know that there is to know" (*Afterthought* 157). Not knowing conditions behavior and determines action. The novel thus poses a series of dilemmas about action, character, commitment, disloyalty, and espionage. If you love a spy, are you a traitor by association or is your lack of knowledge an airtight alibi? Can you love someone for his character irrespective of his political allegiances and actions? Is action separable from character? To love someone on false premises does not necessarily nullify your sentiments for that person. You may not have loved the whole person, but to love only a part does not negate the intensity of passion. In *The Heat of the Day*, both men and women are guilty of illusions in love. Stella conceals the fact that her husband Victor left her. Robert conceals the extent of his "disaffectedness" (271) while pretending that, all along, Stella knows about his secret dealings. The moral complexity of *The Heat of the Day* hinges on Bowen's astute handling of the late 1940s renouncement of history and allegiance as a personal renunciation: to give up a loved one is to cast off contaminating affiliations with fascism. But this concern implies that survivors bear the burden of grief that accompanies abandoned commitments. And in *The Heat of the Day*, those survivors are principally women.

Often considered the best novel about World War II, *The Heat of the Day* represents the relation of women to war. By shifting emphasis away from political abstractions to a love affair, Bowen accounts for "the complex and ambiguous conditions of middle-class privilege, the blitzing of middle-class private life," and the unease of public events determining private lives (Lassner, *British Women* 11). The novel also contains, according to Bowen, touches of "melodrama" (Glendinning 188). Stella herself has "melodramatic fears" (30) about her relationship to Robert. She eschews farfetched theories until she sees proof of Robert's betrayals. For a moment, when Harrison confronts her with information about Robert's espionage activity, Stella thinks the whole plot "unreal": " 'it's immaterial, crazy, brain-spun, out of a thriller. Am I passing stuff across? No, of course not: how could I be, why should I, what do you take me for?' " (190). Stella answers questions even as she asks them. The syntax sputters. Roundabout utterance in the novel—the transposition of clauses, the reluctant use of commas for clarification, and the curious accenting of words that do not appear to bear meaning—registers discomfort about the place of individual actors in the drama of war. The greatest contortions of language occur at moments of historical grandiosity, moments irrevocable in their significance (Di-Battista). Stella may well be passing stuff across without knowing it. Her plea, " 'what do you take me for,' " does not exonerate her. She cannot be taken for anything at all: everyone in the novel misinterprets her, especially her ex-husband's relatives who believe her to have been a *"femme fatale"* (83) with a lover. In truth, her husband abandoned her for the woman who nursed him through injuries sustained in World War I. For years, Stella pretends to be something she is not: an adulterous woman. She performs roles that disguise her affective life. Her hair—a streak of gray sweeps up from her forehead—looks "artificial" (25) but is perfectly natural. She appears false but is genuine. This confusion between real and seeming, reinforced throughout the novel by a motif of lipstick and other cosmetics, touches on the larger problem of discerning Stella's allegiances. Loving Robert inculpates her. She collaborates by being in love. Her character profile exaggerates the split between her emotional and intellectual selves: "by temperament she was communicative and fluctuating. Generous and spirited to a fault, not unfeeling, she was not wholly admirable; but who is?" (26). Rather than relying on the skillful handling of guns in chase scenes, thrill in this novel of intrigue depends on the skillful handling of moral quandaries.

Bowen's knowledge of thrillers is circumstantial, conditioned by the cultural currency of espionage plots in the 1930s and 1940s. Notwithstanding her literary propensities, Bowen took thrillers seriously. She knew John and Alice Buchan well; she often wrote at their house in Oxford and completed the story "Reduced" in John Buchan's library (Glendinning 57). As a moviegoer, she no doubt saw cinematic thrillers by Alfred Hitchcock and Alexander Korda. In fact, John and Alice Buchan's son Billy lived with Bowen and her husband, Alan Cameron, in the late 1930s, on Clarence Terrace, the outer ring of Regent's Park in London. At the time, Billy Buchan was employed by Hitchcock "learning to make films," as Bowen wrote to her friend Virginia Woolf on July 31, 1935 (*Mulberry Tree* 211). Hitchcock, incidentally, released his cinematic version of John Buchan's *The Thirty-Nine Steps* in 1935 and his version of Joseph Conrad's *The Secret Agent*, renamed *Sabotage*, in 1936. Hitchcock's *The Lady Vanishes* followed in 1938. Aside from Hitchcock's films, intrigue—spies, fog, shadows—was the order of the day in movie theaters and bookstalls in the late 1930s. In Stevie Smith's 1936 spy tale, *Novel on Yellow Paper*, the narrator issues caveats to the reader—"You all now have been warned" (40)—within a labyrinthine set of stories that require decoding. In a 1956 broadcast about "Truth and Fiction" on BBC radio, Bowen cites Graham Greene's thriller *Brighton Rock*, about a man convinced he will be murdered, as the epitome of "the novel of action," which features "tautness, quickness, and what Sartre has called 'the extreme situation'" (*Afterthought* 118). Distinguishing the novel of action from character novels and social novels, she praises "the under-tow of suspense and fear" in *Brighton Rock* (*Afterthought* 118), trademarks of Greene's style. Bowen knew Greene personally. She wrote theater reviews for his short-lived weekly magazine *Night and Day* in 1937–38. On a lecture tour after World War II, Bowen dined with Greene in Vienna, where he was collecting atmosphere for *The Third Man*. Using connections, Greene staged a raid at a seedy nightclub with a British sergeant who "demanded to see Elizabeth's passport" (*Ways of Escape* 107), a stunt that impressed her even though it was contrived.

Spy narratives in the late 1930s captured the perils of commitment at a time when no one knew what the consequence of any particular allegiance might be. Passage to the 1940s meant the jettisoning of previous political commitments by a generation of writers—Auden, Spender, Greene, Pym—who found wartime inhospitable to vacillation. In *The Heat of the Day*, characters carefully parse the meaning of betrayal while living with the intensities of warfare. W. H. Auden, sitting in a dive on 52nd Street in New York on September 1, 1939, the day German forces invaded Poland, cannot harmonize the "strength of Collective Man" with the individual "faces along the bar" clinging "to their average day" (Auden 87). Auden asserts the averageness of these American faces while reflecting on the mixed motives of 1930s politics. Meanness and betrayal come down to in-dividuals' actions. Public causes do not square with personal biases after all. The average man may be much more sinister and far less heroic than socialist sympathizers in the 1930s imagined. With the advent of war, per-sonal actions had, potentially, international repercussions. Anyone might be a turncoat. This movement from national or partisan politics to inter-national and personally felt commitments appears in Graham Greene's fiction as well. His 1930s novels largely document domestic betrayals and crimes committed by gangs: Myatt's betrayal of Coral Musker in *Stamboul Train*, the flight of hare-lipped Raven in *A Gun for Sale*, the death of Hale at the hands of small-time thugs in *Brighton Rock*. But during and after the war, Greene's attention to the problem of betrayal turns international: a German spy ring operating in wartime London in *The Ministry of Fear*, the murky world of policing Sierra Leone in *The Heart of the Matter*, the terrors of postwar Vienna in *The Third Man*. Bowen reassesses the problem of betrayal in light of combat. In *The Heat of the Day*, disloyalty may mean adherence to outmoded commitments.

From a midwar perspective, Bowen acutely felt that prewar literary ambitions had been exhausted: "And to what did our fine feelings, our regard for the arts, our intimacies, our inspiring conversations, our wish to be clear of the bonds of sex and class and nationality, our wish to try to be fair to everyone bring us? To 1939" (*Bowen's Court* 92). After 1939, all changed insofar as the past had to be forgotten or reorganized along principles of loyalty and patriotism. Civilized, Bloomsburyish conversations of the prewar period were only so much fine feeling that disregarded brutal, intolerant agendas elsewhere. A coterie's desire to be fair is not necessarily answered by others' desire to be fair. Bowen, however, is making a conservative point about the relation of culture to politics. Pursuit of feeling, art, and conversation for the sake of freedom in culture disguises the possibility that such freedom resembles the fascistic rhetoric of "freedom" (268) that Robert tosses about. For Robert, freedom stops when one authoritarian will establishes a law that cannot be broken, and for him, fascism embodies that absolute law. One reason to make Robert a Nazi spy, a choice that gave pause to many of Bowen's early readers (Watson 88), is to critique political allegiance as pure, unambiguous freedom. By contrast, Bowen implies that all political positions involve degrees of collaboration. As Alan Sinfield puts it, "the precise project of [*The Heat of the Day*] is to entertain the thought that vulgarity dwells with the democratic victors of 1945, and civilization with fascism" (17). Robert's discourse derives from prewar rhetoric of civilization. In the postwar period, the desire to assert civilization became a conservative impetus. E. M. Forster in his 1940 "Three Anti-Nazi Broadcasts" argues that "creation lies at the heart of civilisation," but that artists have to submit to censorship in time of war for reasons of security (*Two Cheers* 43). To make politics "aesthetic" (Benjamin, *Illuminations* 242), as German fascism did, blunts the sharp edge of discriminatory, racist, nationalist policies that animate fascism. A fascist spy makes sense in *The Heat of the Day* insofar as such an allegiance raises alarms about the highbrow commitment to culture and edifying conversation as fine things in themselves, irrespective of content. Thriller plots of the 1930s emphasizing *individual* quandaries, plots rendered obsolete by global carnage, get reinvented in *The Heat of the Day* in order to come to terms with new relations of culture to politics. In particular, Bowen indicts the British middle class, embodied by Robert, for shifting positions and displaying shallow attachments. She represents the magnitude of horror in relation to five principal characters who are, following the example of Stella, not wholly admirable.

As Bowen thinks back through models of literary espionage, summed up by Conrad, Buchan, and Greene, she alters the genre to include considerations of gender within political representation. Women accumulate, sift, purvey, interpret information, especially Stella, whose work requires knowledge of several European languages (25–26). Men defer to her interpretation of events. Roderick asks her to decipher the meaning of his cousin Francis's will (87–88). Robert, because of his elusiveness, obliges her to interpret his motives. Men place the onus of understanding on Stella. To deal with their demands, she more or less has to bury the secrets of her emotional life and develop a "habit of guardedness" (26). Most spy plots treat love as a pesky distraction that befalls male spies. By contrast, in *The Heat of the Day*, Bowen places love at the core of narrative. Whereas emotions of hate drive many spy thrillers, love is the animating force in *The Heat of the Day*. Women, in classic espionage paradigms, are to blame for erotic entanglements with the wrong men. Instead of choosing whether women will be love objects (duplicitous Vesper, who betrays James Bond in *Casino Royale*), traitors (calculating Madam von Einem in *Greenmantle*), or moles (pliable Charlie in *The Little Drummer Girl*), Bowen demonstrates that equivalent roles are not only irrelevant for Stella, but limit the subtleties of her political position. Love is a political effect, in that war breeds love and kills it. Robert's duplicity destroys Stella's love for him. He puts her in an ethically untenable situation. Although their final night together proves the impossibility of her continuing to love Robert, Stella does not renounce her feelings for him in explicit terms. She despises his actions, without decrying his character. In the *Casablanca*-like contradiction of love in a time of war, *The Heat of the Day* suggests that giving up a lover does not mean that you love him less, just that you have to cede your personal interests to the greater good.

Bowen's reconfiguration of espionage conventions in *The Heat of the Day* poses a challenge to critical interpretation. Hermione Lee acknowledges that the novel "looks like a peculiarly unconvincing or sketchy 'spy story,' if set against the work of Conrad or Kipling, Buchan or Greene, Fleming or le Carré" (168). More accurately called a novelist of contemporary mores, Bowen is concerned in her novels and stories of the 1920s and 1930s with betrayal inside families. In *The Death of the Heart*, for example, Anna snoops through Portia's diary, and Eddie and Daphne betray Portia when, at the cinema, they hold hands "with emphasis" (195). *The Heat of the Day* ups the ante by making betrayal an international concern. Adam Piette aptly claims that "Bowen translates Proustian jealousy into fifth-column paranoia and spy-fiction suspicion to show that history can equally shed and create false identities and life-stories" (166). Phyllis Lassner argues that every meeting between Harrison and Stella, or Stella and Robert, "diffuses the meaning of personal and political loyalties, indeed, explodes the representation and definition of spying itself" (*Elizabeth Bowen* 126). The novel questions conventional definitions of loyalty and guilt "by situating a female character at the centre of a spy story, reversing our expectations of a conventional genre which usually places female characters on the periphery" (Lassner, *Elizabeth Bowen* 129). Harriet Chessman interprets Stella's dilemma in terms of silence that women deploy to avoid becoming "objects of narration" (70). To my mind, the problem of *The Heat of the Day* centers on complicity by association, the co-opting of Stella into a spy plot by virtue of her affections and the stresses of living through the Blitz. The novel treats love as a secret. Or, more accurately, Stella loves the secret that Robert represents, just as he loves her secrets. At their first meeting, they see in each other "a background of mystery" (95) that attracts them. They love in each other what they cannot grasp: the secrets that define their identities and that remain unarticulated. The novel raises the possibility that all love is a form of secrecy with potentially harmful effects.

Although it concerns wartime London, *The Heat of the Day* requires reading against intellectual and cultural contexts after the war. In 1949, the aftermath of collaboration was being thrashed out in legal tribunals, films, and philosophy. In his essay on collaboration first published in 1945, Jean-Paul Sartre claims that people do not recognize their own collaborative dispositions, whether because of their biases of class or because of their psychological tendencies to yield to the forces of history as a means to protect personal interests. Sartre mockingly concludes that "*la collaboration est une vocation*" (collaboration is a vocation) (*Situations 3* 45). Anthony Eden, foreign secretary to Winston Churchill from 1940 to 1945 and prime minister of Britain from 1955 to 1957, says in *The Sorrow and the Pity*, Marcel Ophuls's 1971 documentary about collaborators in Vichy, "it's one thing if France cannot fight; it's another thing if she collaborates with the enemy." In short, not raising arms could be construed as a form of collaboration, of yielding to the force majeure of the occupying power. By the same token, resistance in France, or elsewhere, could be understood as a mental act rather than the more narrow definition of acts such as harboring persecuted people, raising arms against the Nazis, or fighting for freedom. Such degrees of cogitated (as against enacted) resistance and collaboration, get worked out in the representation of Stella's and Robert's respective positions in *The Heat of the Day*. Robert betrays his country, not in the passive, Vichy manner of accommodating himself to an authoritarian regime, but in the active, Quisling manner of selling secrets. Collaboration by spying is not the same as collaboration by erotic involvement. Stella suspects she may be guilty of complicity because she loves Robert. In the 1940s, representation of collaboration is affected by predisposition of character, recruitment to a committed position, and the participation of women in the war.

Collaboration, as many argued after the war, may contain degrees of resistance. In the postwar years, France addressed the problem of collaboration with greater urgency than England for the obvious reason that France had negotiated a treaty with the Nazis and had established Maréchal Pétain at the head of the Vichy government. Other European countries, including Norway, Belgium, and Holland, set up governments-in-exile, mostly in London, in resistance to Nazism. Naming Dutchmen, Norwegians, Belgians, Frenchmen, and Poles, George Orwell confidently broadcast propaganda on May 9, 1942, to the effect that "the people of the occupied countries have refused to collaborate with the enemy" (*War Commentaries* 91). On October 17, 1942, Orwell claimed that "nearly all classes of Frenchmen" held the Vichy regime in "loathing and contempt" (*War Commentaries* 167). *Nearly all classes:* not all Frenchmen showed animosity towards the Nazis. The collective will to exorcise the ghost of collaboration resulted in an *épuration* or "purification" of real and suspected French collaborators in 1945. Proving their patriotism, Frenchmen hastened to round up collaborators, often killing them without legal proceedings of any kind (Beevor and Cooper 84–92). Women who had had German lovers were publicly humiliated by having their heads shaved. The legendary French film actress Arletty, who had taken no pains to disguise her affair with a German Luftwaffe officer and lived luxuriously at the Ritz during the Occupation, was imprisoned and shorn (Lord 47). The stigma of her *"collaboration horizontale"* clung to her for the rest of her life (Beevor and Cooper 141).

Although the issue of collaboration meant far less in England, the role of women as accomplices in espionage, whether horizontal or vertical, had a considerable cinematic presence.

As Bowen worked out the significance of collaboration in the making of character in *The Heat of the Day*, she was responding to a culture that took the problem seriously. Three films, *Casablanca, Notorious,* and *Hiroshima Mon Amour,* released during and after the war, address the cultural complexity of collaboration. Sentimentally understood as a tough-love film featuring the owner of a nightclub in Morocco, *Casablanca* indicts American noninvolvement in World War II. Rick Blaine feigns political neutrality. Dapper French Captain Louis Renault epitomizes vacillation. "I have no conviction," Renault tells Nazi Major Heinrich Strasser. Rick asks Renault, "Are you pro-Vichy or Free French?" Renault gives the impression of bending to prevailing attitudes: rounding up suspects to assist the Nazis; siding with Rick and the Americans when he realizes they have more going for them. The collaborator, as opportunistic as a spy, is the victim of ideology rather than its agent. The best lack all conviction. Everyone performs a doublecross in *Casablanca.* Renault arrests Laszlo, which foils Ilsa and Laszlo's plans. Rick doublecrosses Renault, which foils Renault's aspirations for promotion. Renault calls Major Strasser on the phone, which nearly capsizes the escape plot. Ilsa doublecrosses Rick at the train station at the planned moment of their departure from Paris. On the horns of a dilemma, Ilsa wavers between the ignoble, self-serving love affair she has with Rick and the noble, freedom-serving marriage she has with Laszlo. Although Rick has run guns to Ethiopia and fought fascists in Spain, he practices, as he leads everyone to believe, a hands-off, nonpartisan capitalism in Casablanca. Yet he shoots Major Strasser at the end of the film in an unequivocal declaration of commitment.

Casablanca perpetrates the notion that war creates variants of love and allegiance that do not apply in peacetime. Love is aggrandized by unbearable distance. Ilsa is romantically alluring; Rick loved her in Paris and he needs to go as far as Casablanca to forget her. Love arises in the uncertainty that one's lover—or husband—will return; he may die under torture or in battle so why not love someone else in the meantime? Ilsa hedges her bets against a solitary future by having an affair with Rick. Love, an act of desperation, flourishes amid uncertainty. Ilsa's attraction to Rick's nonaligned position, simply because of its nonalignment, is romantic love, as opposed to committed marriage; Ilsa loves Rick because he is not Laszlo. Rick represents freedom. Laszlo represents having freely chosen. The film promotes the surprising conclusion that one can pretend not to be in love in order to administer justice. Rick denies that he and Ilsa love each other so that Laszlo and Ilsa can leave and continue their freedom-fighting mission. A moral lie safeguards the truth. Present necessity overrides sentimental allegiance to a past liaison: "we'll always have Paris," now let's move on to more pressing matters. Although Renault calls Rick a "sentimentalist," the categories of "sentimentalist" and "collaborator" remain vague in *Casablanca*. Rick's initial noninvolvement in political turbulence suggests a degree of laissez-faire compliance with the occupying Nazi regime. Although a mercenary in Ethiopia and Spain, he ends up committing a politically astute maneuver that serves the Allies' ends. By contrast, vacillating Renault claims that he "will take what comes." Renault collaborates with Strasser, then sidles up to a less administratively rigid regime, embodied by Rick, who is willing to cut deals and abet Renault's on-the-side amours. Renault's attachment to Rick in the fog on the tarmac at the end of *Casablanca*, far from being value neutral, is a parasitical cozying up to the most cunning person left standing. Even though Renault tosses away his Vichy water, his obedience to those with authority could be taken as pure Vichy collaboration—moral pliancy in the face of adversity. Unsurprisingly, given the allegory of French dependence on American heroics, the film was used propagandistically to encourage Americans to enter the war (Caruth, *Unclaimed Experience* 126). Notwithstanding the companionship of Renault and Rick, the film is really about the difficult position of Ilsa, who tries to see romance as a form of ignorance: "We knew very little about each other when we were in love in Paris. If we leave it that way maybe we'll remember those days, not Casablanca." Romance grows from mutual illusions: Ilsa's failure to disclose her marriage; Rick's failure to disclose his past activities. The remarkable conclusion of *Casablanca*, however, is that present danger negates a sentimental, illusion-filled past. Romance does not win out. When Rick lies, Ilsa does not contradict his lie. Renault rounds up suspects who could have nothing to do with the shooting of Strasser. The war continues. Collaboration is a story jointly fabricated and brought to life. Collaboration is an ensemble of treacheries mutually sustained.

In Alfred Hitchcock's 1946 thriller *Notorious*, the cast of *Casablanca* returns, with the roles of villain and collaborator transformed. In *Notorious*, Claude Rains (erstwhile Captain Renault) plays suave Alex Sebastian, part of a recidivist Nazi-capitalist consortium in Rio de Janeiro trying to reanimate Third Reich plans for world domination. Uranium provides the key to their ambitions. Rains's vacillations in *Casablanca* are replaced in *Notorious* by firm fascistic convictions. Ingrid Bergman comes back in *Notorious* as Alicia Huberman, daughter of a Florida-based, Nazi-sympathizing, German father. Alicia, an American patriot (her house was bugged and her pro-American declarations were recorded), is pressed into service as a Mata Hari-style seductress who marries Sebastian in order to infiltrate his cadre of friends and ruin his plot of world domination. Cary Grant, as American agent T. R. Devlin, assumes the role of hard-edged intelligence man and slick manipulator of Alicia's sentiments. Alicia falls for Devlin romantically. He resists open declarations of affection in return—until he rescues poisoned Alicia from the evil Nazis and admits, finally, "it tore me up not having you." Devlin forces Alicia to collaborate with American intelligence because the taint of fascism might be genetically present in her, subtly transmitted from father to daughter. In Rio, Alicia tells Alex, "I'm allergic to American intelligence agents. Their fine points don't particularly appeal to me." She lies and she tells the truth. She's angry at Devlin for placing his intelligence duties ahead of their romance, but she's also acting her part as infiltrator of a spy ring and as a collaborator. With her mildly foreign accent, Alicia is either a patriotic traitor or a treacherous patriot. Because she can never rise above suspicion, the Americans manipulate her ruthlessly. Relying on paradigms of treachery instead of paradigms of authentic love, Devlin accuses Alicia Huberman of sluttishness even though the American intelligence crew force her to marry Sebastian on the grounds that "it's a perfect marriage for us." Alicia's alleged sluttishness is a metonym for guilt: her father's treason may suddenly break out in Alicia as Teutonic sympathies. Never able fully to clear herself of such suspicions, she has to collaborate with both Sebastian and Devlin, whatever her romantic inclinations might be. Her alleged sluttishness arises out of exigencies that she cannot control. As a Frenchwoman who had slept with Germans during the Occupation shouted at her persecutors in 1945, "'My ass is international, but my heart is French'" (Beevor and Cooper 80). Alicia's heart may belong to an American, but the American treats her badly and jeopardizes her safety for the sake of antifascism.

The Truman Doctrine of intervention in far-flung locations to secure democracy legitimates itself in the American undercover operation in Rio. The operation is coded as an intervention by off-shore parties. Alicia's foreignness is an expedient for American intelligence operatives, and they nearly abandon her when she accomplishes her mission. As a political allegory, *Notorious* impugns cavalier, ad hoc American alliances. The Americans arrive and leave according to a timetable of shady self-interest. Without rationale, they lend aid, then withdraw it. In this allegory, foreign Alicia stands for reformed, abject democracy who loves America with zeal but who is not loved back with unconditional acceptance. She can be loved only to the extent that she has utility. The movie raises the simplistic question of whether women, led astray by romance, can make independent political choices. As Harrison flippantly says in *The Heat of the Day,* "a woman's always a woman, and so on" (41). Or as Alicia Huberman puts it in *Notorious,* "Once a crook, always a crook. Once a tramp, always a tramp." She mocks the stereotypes of women agents: "Mata Hari. She makes love for the papers." Unlike male plots that emphasize the intrinsic value or political sensitivity of information, *The Heat of the Day* and *Notorious* demonstrate the risks of information gathering for women. In both instances, collaboration is a by-product of romance. Although Stella *fears* that she puts information across to the enemy through Robert, Alicia knows that her usefulness *depends* on putting vital information across to the Americans. In both narratives, collaboration presumes compliance on the part of women.

Collaboration as a deeply embarrassing historical event that cannot be banished from French culture surfaces in *Hiroshima Mon Amour,* the 1959 film by Alain Resnais with a screenplay by Marguerite Duras. In the film, a French actress in Hiroshima has a transient sexual encounter with a Japanese architect. For the first time, she tells the story of the German soldier who was her lover in the town of Nevers during the Occupation. Flashback montages reveal their giddy love-making near riverbanks, in potting sheds, among ruins, in fields, haphazardly. In these montages, reminiscent of the happy-go-lucky montage of Rick and Ilsa in Paris in *Casablanca,* the German soldier never speaks. Zippy soundtrack music escorts the Frenchwoman and the German to their trysting places. They are never shown in dialogue. He is her first love. Because they do not share a language, their love seems to exist outside language. The German, shot on the day that the couple planned to run away together, which happens to be the day Nevers is liberated, lives within the actress's mind as an unacknowledged, secret, protected love. Reviled by the townspeople of Nevers, locked in the basement by her parents, her hair shorn for her horizontal collaboration with the enemy, the young woman cannot talk about her erotic entanglement because no discourse allows such memories to circulate openly. The past distresses her. Distress defines her. About *Hiroshima Mon Amour,* Cathy Caruth comments that "the possibility of knowing history, in this film, is thus also raised as a deeply ethical dilemma: the unremitting problem of *how not to betray the past*" (*Unclaimed* 27). Indeed, the narrator of *Hiroshima Mon Amour* asks, "Why deny the obvious need for memory?" The question answers itself within the context of the film: because memory for the thirty-four-year-old French actress is intimately connected to wartime collaboration. Consequently, the problem of the past is not about its betrayal but about acknowledgment of its shamefulness. The past is already dishonorable, already deceptive. Thus to narrate the tormenting love affair does not betray the past, but therapeutizes humiliation. Narrative releases the collaborator from the torments caused by harboring a secret. As in *Casablanca* and *Notorious,* the woman in *Hiroshima Mon Amour* finds that love positions her politically in ways that can be controlled only through other kinds of emotional engagement.

As in these three films about collaboration during World War II, love is a traumatic event in *The Heat of the Day.* The novel suggests that love during the war had a specific resonance not possible at any other time in history. Love arises at the conjunction of darkness, timelessness, terror, combat. Stella and Robert fall in love in a moment of desperation. They cannot recall their first words, spoken during a bomb attack in September 1940. A glissade of bombs drops through darkness. Stella and Robert exchange a glance in a bar or a club, "afterwards they could never remember which" (95). They are about to speak when a bomb whistles down "a shaft of anticipating silence. . . . With the shock of detonation, still to be heard, four walls of in here yawped in then bellied out; bottles danced on glass; a distortion ran through the view. The detonation dulled off into the cataracting roar of a split building: direct hit, somewhere else" (96). Relief arrives only in the final two words of this sentence, but those words contain the recognition that "somewhere else" has suffered damage and someone else may have become a casualty. Love is premised on a stranger's death.

Interior space almost blows to smithereens. Roar deafens human speech. The attack induces amnesia. Trauma, we might say, is the suspension of consciousness in the face of terror. The couple cannot remember what they intended to say. They cannot remember if they were in a bar or a club. They hardly remember meeting. They remember only that Stella had raised her hand to wave goodbye to an acquaintance.

The gesture of waving goodbye is telling insofar as almost every meeting in *The Heat of the Day* moves towards a wrenching farewell, whether the "amputation of [Stella and Robert's] 'good night' as lovers" (126) or the "disheartening farewell" (144) that Harrison makes to Louie in Regent's Park. Robert's niece tells him, "'You're always going . . . , always going away'" (266). He constantly takes his leave, as if he cannot be held in any one place. The last encounter between Stella and Robert, ending with an ambiguous "'good night'" (289) rather than a definite goodbye, is implicit in their very first meeting, coded in the goodbye wave: "That gesture of good-bye, so perfunctory, was a finalness not to appear till later" (95). Justifying his escape into darkness, Robert tells Stella, "'Better to say good-bye at the beginning of the hour we never have had, then it will have no end'" (288). He forestalls the heartbreak implicit in farewells by emphasizing intensity—of saying goodbye before the affair loses its fire. In any case, his affair with Stella always grouped itself around the gesture of farewell, encoded in their first nearly forgotten meeting. The terror of the bomb raid, synchronous with their encounter, "was the demolition of an entire moment" (96). Their encounter occurs as a hole in reality. Trauma is about *not knowing* the extent of horror that one faces, as Cathy Caruth argues in *Unclaimed Experience* (37–38, 40). The lovers prefer to know less not more about each other. Nor do they ever learn much about one another; "life-stories were shed as so much superfluous weight" (95). Love incarnates, from the beginning, not knowing, which leads to catastrophe.

Trauma cannot be measured with the mind. "There is no language of destruction for / The use of the chaotic," wrote Philip Larkin in 1940 (249). The war generally was perceived as an event beyond description, "an ungrasped, ungraspable mystery" (Piette 111). "'But then there's a deal in life you don't understand at the time,'" someone tells the memory-afflicted veteran in Henry Green's war novel *Back* (16). Overwhelmed by the accumulation of "dead matter" during the Blitz, a character in Bowen's story "Summer Night" tries to sum up the inexpressible horror of the war: "'There's been a stop in our senses and in our faculties that's made everything round us so much dead matter—and dead matter we couldn't even displace. We can no longer express ourselves: what we say doesn't even approximate to reality; it only approximates to what's been said'" (*Collected Stories* 590). Reality chokes expression. Confronted by monumental destruction, Stella and Robert lose language and memory. Their joint past cannot be betrayed because it scarcely exists. They do not speak as if dead but as survivors who need each other to validate that they have endured against all odds. Possible annihilation binds them together. Their sensation of timelessness, a symptom of trauma brought on by bombardment and accentuated by pervasive darkness, is a symptom of being scared to death.

From the start of their affair, time sits "in the third place at their table. They were the creatures of history whose coming together was of a nature possible in no other day" (194–95). Their love is predicated on the specificity of disaster brought about by war. The war in *The Heat of the Day* induces a perpetual present. A secure "place in time had been lost" (176). Characters forget time while remaining acutely aware of it. Working in an underground air-raid warden's office, Connie loses track of time: "'it might be any time of year or of day or night neither'" (154). Wristwatches "belie" time (97). Alarm clocks don't work (242). Time clogs the ticking of a grandfather clock (108). Even when time and date are precise, places seem to have "no given hour of time" (21). Time plies back, or in, on itself. Even the chronology of the novel is out of joint. The narrative begins in September 1942, moves backwards to a funeral in May 1942, then further backwards to the meeting of Stella Rodney and Robert Kelway in September 1940, then ahead to autumn 1942, before concluding with a chapter set between 1942 and 1944. In its asynchrony, the novel meditates on time and memory. Flashbacks supply information about death and love as well as repeating events that have not fully been integrated into consciousness by the characters. In retrospect, Stella begins to understand the implications of Cousin Francis's death. Atemporal organization suggests that Stella and Robert love each other because of their terrified survival. Like all Londoners, they experience time as a vacant immediacy. During the Blitz, "everybody in London was in love" (95), presumably because they needed to anchor themselves in an emotion of being remembered when they might be killed imminently. They are suspended in the present: "The extraordinary battle in the sky transfixed them; they might have stayed for ever on the eve of being in love" (96–97). Although the title of the novel flashes forth intimations of brightness at high noon, it more accurately describes the problem of intensity in love and war. The heat of the day may occur in the middle of the night. Given the pervading darkness of *The Heat of the Day,* the title implies that love that arises at times of crisis may not outlive crisis; therefore, it is better to abandon love at the moment of intensity, just as Stella and Robert say goodbye in darkness at the height of their affair, than to let that passion peter out into sentimentality or nostalgia. If Stella continues to love Robert, his nefarious politics will contaminate her further. If she does not continue loving him, she will forego the intensity of the situation. She will live through bombardments alone, on the verge of extinction and being forgotten. She has, as she acknowledges, no one left in London to love.

Love seems like a cure for the traumatic afflictions of war—homes in rubble, families dead in explosions, accumulated memories disintegrated in a single blast. Yet love perpetuates the conditions of trauma: not seeing, not knowing, not feeling. When Stella discovers a mislaid letter in the pocket of Robert's dressing gown, she tears it up after scanning it briefly, because learning some incriminating bit of information might compromise her love for Robert. She prefers to believe in his integrity. This definition of love in chaos, of shared intensity and unquestioning trust, infuses other war narratives. Indeed, one definition of communal trauma involves experiences that "work their way so thoroughly into the grain of the affected community that they come to supply its prevailing mood and temper, dominate its imagery and its sense of self, govern the way its members relate to each other" (Erikson 190). War binds people afflicted by the same external occurrence into a community, of sorts. Intensified emotion leaves little room for reflection. In October 1940, André Gide lamented in his journal, "doubtless the greatest harm this war is doing to culture is to create a profusion of extreme passions, which by a sort of inflation, brings about a devaluation of all moderate sentiments" (51). War exacerbates reactions into feelings much larger than peace permits. This includes hyperextended states of mind, such as camaraderie in duress or sympathy with criminality. "Wasn't it better to take part even in the crimes of people you loved, if it was necessary hate as they did, and if that were the end of everything suffer damnation with them, rather than be saved alone?" speculates

Digby in Graham Greene's *The Ministry of Fear* (132), a novel that treats love as a contingency of memory, and loss of memory as a contingency of war. In "London in War," a notebook she kept in 1940, Virginia Woolf writes, "The sensation of fear very soon evaporates. Everybody is feeling the same thing: therefore no one is feeling anything in particular" (n.p.). Bowen expresses much the same sentiment in a postscript to her collection of stories *The Demon Lover*: "In war this feeling of slight differentiation was suspended: I felt one with, and just like, everybody else. Sometimes I hardly knew where I stopped and somebody else began" (*Mulberry Tree* 95). George Orwell's *Nineteen Eighty-Four*, inspired by the war and set against a state perpetually at war, treats the affair between Julia and Winston as, initially, sympathy between the like-minded, though the narrative hinges on Julia's coerced collaboration with Big Brother and his agents.

In each of these cases, a third element, unnamed, often secret, intervenes in the love affair: war, hate for Big Brother, fear, crime. As such, feelings of affinity or belonging have about them an aura of unreality or ghostliness. Between Stella and Robert, secrets, even when not specified, color their relationship. Having met in extreme circumstances, they pretend that they exist outside time, amid the ruins of the city. As in *Casablanca* and *Notorious*, characters lie about love in *The Heat of the Day*, not by denying feeling, but by denying other conditions that establish or breach trust. Robert likes to believe that his sense of hollowness in the political sphere, his sense of belonging to no particular race or country, his sense of being "born wounded" (272), can be remedied through erotic commitment. Similarly, Stella's repudiation of what really happened between her and her husband Victor, a traumatic knowledge that she doesn't discuss, allows her to love Robert without questioning him. Love thrives in vacuo. When Harrison volunteers to tell her about Robert, he plays on Stella's implicit adherence to the ideology of love as trust. But love might be based on secrets, not trust. Despite Robert's refutation of seeing love in the same light as dangerous espionage work (279), Stella and Robert are drawn to each other because they both have secrets—a third, unspecified term— that they do not divulge. Indeed, Harrison is for her a third term in their relationship, as Stella concedes after the fact (320). By not telling Robert that she knows about his spying, Stella takes on his secret. Love predicated on mysteries rankles. Stella doubts that " 'there's any such thing as an innocent secret' " (228). Digging up another person's secret is " 'malignancy,'" whereas exposing one's own secrets would be "'madness'" (229). Secrets, however, generate characters and narrative (Rashkin 44–45). Stella recognizes that Roderick loves a particular version of her that he has assiduously assembled over years, an idea of motherhood that excludes secrecy (229). Having sacrificed knowledge about Robert's past to the intensity of need that war demands, Stella must decide whether character precedes action as a determinant of political accountability, whether the illusion of love is more important than the fact of betrayal.

Stella meditates on her own relation to secrets while visiting Mount Morris on behalf of Roderick, who has inherited the property. She hasn't been in the house since her honeymoon. Consequently, she's living partly in the past, partly in the present, partly nowhere. Her oil-lamp reflects in various mirrors in the dark drawing-room. Holding up her lamp, she sees her reflection "against the drapery of darkness. She wore the look of everything she had lost the secret of being" (174). She often looks into mirrors. When Harrison visits her in London, she momentarily plans to watch him in a mirror as he enters her flat (24). At Mount Morris, she turns away from her reflection. Her face sports an ambiguous look in the mirror, yet what look is it? "She wore the look of everything she had lost the secret of being." If she no longer possesses that way of looking, how can she suddenly have it flicker back into her face? The syntax, lacking commas, hides meaning. She looks as if she has lost everything, including the secret of *being*, as if this were an existential crisis. She looks as if she has lost everything, including the secret of *her* being. She has lost everything and that is the *secret* of her being. Back in Ireland, she regains the *look*, which reveals the secret of her being, despite everything she has lost. She was not aware that this is the way she once appeared; her image has been, to herself, a secret that she didn't know she possessed. Inspecting her image as if it were an ancestral portrait hung on the wall, she moves into history by a theatrical gesture of holding a lamp up to the mirror and staring at her face. She wears an inquiring look not exclusively her own, but a look that queries those who come after, and that artifice, that consciousness of history, especially in the turbulence of World War II, is the key to being. By assuming her place within a family lineage at Mount Morris, as the mother of the man who inherits the house, she recognizes that she doesn't fully belong to the place. History, furthermore, gets falsified in mirror images, or by too much concentration on the faces that one loves. The whole story of a character is never told in a face. Most probably then, the ambiguous sentence, correct without commas, means that Stella catches this unawares glimpse of herself as if she were a portrait; the reflection shows her as she thought of herself before Harrison strips her of romantic illusions. She wears the look of what she once was. Emphasis falls on the direct object in the sentence: "She wore the look of *everything*-she-had-lost-the-secret-of-being." What disappeared has come back for a second. This identity, not just an image, was, however, a secret, even to her. Before knowing about the dangers of love and war, Stella's relative naïveté showed in her face. Time had, in this younger version of her being, not caused her to behave as she has had to do during the war. Emphasis may fall on the secret: comportment with regard to the world of betrayal that lay coiled within her until necessity caused her to act. She is thinking about her complicity, about "her espionage" (172). She thinks that Robert, a spy for the Nazis and a traitor to his country, may well have pretended to love her: "*If* actor, to her and for her so very good an actor, then why not actor also of love? Incalculably calculating, secretly adverse, knowing, withheld had Robert been, all this time, from the start?" (173). She thinks that she has never read his face aright. Moreover, she never entered his consciousness as the iconic face of love: "'from the very beginning I've had no face'" (228). The secret of her being, resting on slender principles, yields to the information that love, like political behavior, is a sham: "Bowen's novel suggests that love is fundamentally *affected* by the impossibility of knowing how far one's own behaviour—and the behaviour of one's lover—is 'merely' acting, merely 'the appearance of love,' and the impossibility of extricating the recognition of such an impossibility from a sense of spying and fiction, a logic of fictional espionage" (Bennett and Royle 88–89). Bowen couples the espionage commonplace of gathering politically sensitive information with the novelistic motif of gathering information about the person one loves. From this one can deduce that all love affairs require some degree of performance. Scripts determine how one will act during a romance. No love affair is authentic, nor should be, since one never knows if the loved one is acting in turn.

Something may always remain hidden in a loved one.

Someone will always be left to betray.

INTENSITY AND CHARACTER

During the war, Bowen volunteered her services as an intelligence-gatherer for the British Ministry of Information. A property owner in County Cork, she traveled to Eire and filed reports about the possibility of establishing British naval bases in neutral Ireland (Fisk 352–67). She talked unofficially to acquaintances in Dublin who didn't know that she was writing up their conversations and filing them to London. Owing to this casual espionage, Bowen developed a fairly acute sense of "the distinction between being a traitor and a spy" (Jordan 156). Bowen's experience of traveling to Ireland partly informs Stella's trip to Mount Morris in *The Heat of the Day*. Relatively "impervious" (Halperin 109) to Irish nationalism and suspicious of fascist sentiment in Ireland (Fisk 356), she found the substrates of Irish politics "a craggy dangerous miniature world" (*Mulberry Tree* 218). In her disapproval of Irish small-mindedness and British insensitivity to Irish positions, Bowen raises the question of which loyalty ought to take precedence in times of duress: loyalty to writing, loyalty to Ireland, loyalty to England, loyalty to democracy, loyalty to self, loyalty to a lover. In an essay titled "Disloyalties," she posits that the writer who remains too faithful to one idea, too loyal to particular social values, misses intricacies in character, "the doublings and twistings of mankind under the grip of circumstance and the pressure of life" (*Afterthought* 195). Bowen hypothesizes loyalty and disloyalty as a false opposition, certainly when it comes to writing, though the leveling of that opposition may well apply to the moral dilemma of Stella as she wonders whether she has committed a crime. *The Heat of the Day* neutralizes antitheses, which are usually the heart's-blood of intrigue. Instead of playing "lurid oppositions" (Caserio 280) against each other, such as Nazis against Allies, villains against heroes, or nations against each other, the novel resists settled answers about who or what is right. Very little gets resolved. As a concrete example of this refusal to settle ambiguities, Robert's "fall or leap from the roof" (291) is never clarified. Distinctions between wholesale collaboration, passive complicity, and out-and-out resistance are equally blurry. Everyone is, or ought to remain, a bit suspect, since, as Bowen argues, the novelist documents the "individual as he himself is, behind the social mask" (*Afterthought* 195). The shading of disloyalty that Stella exhibits—she never tells her son Roderick about his father's real motives, she doesn't immediately notify Robert that she thinks him a spy—reinforces the grip of circumstance in *The*

Heat of the Day. Loyalty may be essential to "survival" (*Afterthought* 196) during the war, but such patriotic loyalty does not forestall everyday treacheries of the heart.

For Bowen, the grip of circumstance is indissociable from the craft of novel writing. Circumstance is the force of events in a narrative structure, not just historical reality. Seldom does Bowen write novels set in the past; *The Last September,* about a girl's maturing during the Irish Troubles in 1920, is an exception to Bowen's general practice. Concerned with perception of the present, Bowen is manifestly a writer of intense vision. How one sees and remembers events determines how the grip of circumstance will be managed. Bowen calls herself a "visual writer" (*Pictures and Conversations* 60). In *The Heat of the Day,* seeing as a form of knowing is thematically represented in the motif of eyes. Harrison has uneven eyes that seem to look people over from two angles. In his unfeelingness towards Stella, Harrison imposes "his psychic, his moral blindness" (143). Robert avoids the eyes of his father. "'Very often I did not know which way to look'" (119), he says about his childhood, and he takes up photography so that he can retreat to a darkroom. When Louie dusts her husband's photograph, she picks it up and stares at it without taking it in. "To see, however, is not to look" (159), the narrator warns. Vision requires intensity to bring it to the point of knowledge. For Bowen, this is a writer's imperative. In her preface to *A Day in the Dark* she writes, "Of vision, one asks only that it should not lose its intensity—and I would say that if vision is there at all, that wish is usually granted" (*Pictures and Conversations* xxii). Intensity of vision means the power to sustain the writing of a novel, of seeing how characters will comport themselves. Intensity of vision does not extend to heightened powers of observation in characters. Louie and Stella see the world before them without grasping what's happening. In the pervading black atmosphere of the novel, seeing anything at all presents a challenge. Nevertheless, not seeing does not mean that retrospect cannot usher in increased understanding. In the case of writing, the writer "sees what he did not intend to see; he remembers what does not seem wholly possible" (*Afterthought* 191).

Bowen makes seeing a confrontation with reality. During an evening party in 1941, at the height of the Blitz, she commanded her guests, among whom was Stephen Spender, to step outside and watch bombs fall on the city. She "assembled her guests on the balcony overlooking Regent's Park, kept them there drinking coffee, without comment, throughout an air raid, and only remarked, as they went indoors, that she felt she ought to apologize for the noise" (Craig 110). Spender calls London in the Blitz, with its eerie conjunction of civilized supper parties and ear-splitting bombardment, "a little island of civilization surrounded by burning churches" (Spender 91). The episode on Bowen's balcony reveals her ironic discomfort with war. A charismatic hostess, she cannot keep the noise of war out of the drawing room. She forbids her guests, however, to forget about bombs shattering the city. She drinks coffee yet remains aware of the need to cling to rituals, mementos, friendships. She comments that "The violent destruction of solid things, the explosion of the illusion that prestige, power and permanence attach to bulk and weight, left all of us, equally, heady and disembodied. Walls went down; and we felt, if not knew, each other" (*Mulberry Tree* 95). The intensity of the war meant intensity, first and foremost, of feeling. Sympathy displaced knowing. That feeling radiates to other people and other classes. Bowen and her guests look across Regent's Park in the direction of St. Pancras and Euston stations and, farther still, to the working-class neighborhoods of the East End, which suffered heavy casualties during bombing. The scene on the balcony that made Spender so conscious of civility and its fragility touches upon acts of witnessing and the necessity of taking responsibility for catastrophe by writing. When a writer looks, what does she see? When a writer feels, what does she remember?

In all of Bowen's fiction, including *The Heat of the Day*, the motif of ghosts and haunting suggests heightened seeing or clairvoyance of perception. Those who see ghosts have more power of insight. Ghosts point to the inadequate absorption of visual material into consciousness. Things incompletely seen come back to haunt the seer. Ghosts figure gaps in reality or gaps in vision. In this regard, Bowen's ghosts are unlike Conrad's ghosts: Conrad politicizes apparitions; Bowen historicizes them. Twentieth-century ghosts, Bowen claims, haunt "for the sake of haunting" (*Afterthought* 102) and bespeak the enormity of violence that characterizes the times. The violent past asserts itself through ghosts who beg to be remembered. Bowen's characters often re-enact past events. "Life works to dispossess the dead," claims the narrator in *A World of Love* (44), a novel about the recovery of forgotten love letters; in this novel the dead cannot be appeased. In *To the North*, a novel about boredom and departures, lovers look for "a ghost of that first charming strangeness" (232) that brought them together and fail to find it because strangeness gets bred away by familiarity. The protagonist in *Eva Trout* keeps returning to scenes of her troubled youth as if "time demolished itself" (240). As in *The Heat of the Day*, where the membrane between "the this and the that" thins (195) and "the wall between the living and the dead" crumbles (92), in *Eva Trout* the wall "'between dead and living'" is tenuous (173). And in *The Little Girls*, Dinah has a flash of memory that makes her, with Proustian intensity, live fully in the past: "'I've been having the most extraordinary sensation! Yes, and I still am, it's still going on! Because, to remember something, all in a flash, so completely that it's not 'then' but 'now,' surely *is* a sensation, isn't it?'" (20). In all of these instances, history encroaches on conscious-ness. The past punctures the present moment, allowing the dead to consort with the living. These moments are violent in their repercussions. *The Last September* in particular resembles *The Heat of the Day* in its background of cataclysmic upheaval. In a central episode in *The Last September,* an Irish guerilla shoots Marda's hand but neither she nor Lois speaks afterward of the wound (132). Violence remains unspeakable. Gerald's death in the novel, predicted in his early appearance to Lois "as though he were dead, as though she had lost him" (52), ultimately does not receive direct represen-tation because violence is too bewildering to fathom, for Lois and for the entire Anglo-Irish class.

Ghosts stand for disturbed memory or the desire to live beyond current anguish. The ghosts in *The Heat of the Day* wander disconsolately about London. The trope of ghosts to describe those dispossessed by warfare is legitimated in other war narratives, such as Rose Macaulay's short story "Miss Anstruther's Letters."[1] A "ghost" whose flat has been bombed and whose personal letters have been obliterated, Miss Anstruther never re-assembles her life; she becomes a "drifting ghost" because of the war (S. Jameson 299, 308). Macaulay lost her house on May 10, 1941, in a raid that damaged the British Museum, the House of Commons, and West-minster Hall. Her library was incinerated. She recalls in a 1949 BBC broad-cast called "Losing One's Books" that losing culture means losing every-thing: "haunted and troubled by ghosts . . . I can still smell those acrid drifts of smouldering ash that once were live books" (qtd. in Piette 48). War divides characters from their former identities. Either ghosts or memo-ries hold together prewar and postwar selves. Memory is a problematic pillar of identity: uncertain, fragile, suspended during bombardment. Stella, her past feelings having "miscarried" (133), resists remembering or talking about her husband and marriage. Her former husband accuses her of not understanding love at all. Never actualized in love, she represses her past. Her "helpless progress towards disaster" (134) coincides with her entry into history defined as disaster. The ghosts that flock around her include her brothers who died in the Great War. Indeed, the dead "from all the wars" (177) enter her consciousness as the figures of what has been abandoned in history. Just as marriage to Victor did not complete her, her love affair with Robert becomes the relic of what can never be fulfilled because of his treachery.[2] When she meets him at Euston Station after being in Ireland, she thinks they have taken their place among the "shades in Hades, the new dead scanned dubiously by the older" (181). Less fortunate still, Nettie, married to Cousin Francis, declines into imbecility after meeting her "own ghost" at Mount Morris (217). Locked in a nursing home for the feebleminded, Nettie turns ghostly to avoid the torments of daily existence. Other ghosts are less personal. In London, the "unknown dead reproach the living" (92) just because they survive. For Stella, after she learns of Robert's treachery, love is a matter of time-limited opportunity. Love becomes something like touching with her fingers "some unknown dead face in the dark" (192). The idea of loss haunts Stella's intimate life, for she loses her husband and then Robert. Loss permeates *The Heat of the Day* in the survivor's sense that one is glad to be alive, but uncertain how survival came to pass and whether it is deserved. Stella thinks of herself as partly dead, as being able to communicate with the missing as if they were, in some degree, already dead. "'The more wars there are,'" she says ironically, "'the more we shall learn how to be survivors'" (317). Ghosts in the novel address decisions made by characters under duress and alternative decisions never pursued. The ghosts represent not just the potential for anyone in London to have died suddenly during the Blitz, but the potential for any character to absorb the lessons of the past into a program of conduct for the future.

The Heat of the Day offers an unusual sense of survival in that character is the remnant of actions that have been lived through but renounced. If character is not the consequence of actions, is it the statement of beliefs, loves, hates, politics, attitudes that one affirms or denies willy-nilly? Connie and Louie speculate loudly on the topic of character: "'You saw,'" Connie queries Louie about the newspapers, "'where it says how war in some ways makes our characters better?'" (153). "'Character's getting us there'" (155), says Connie apropos of success in Stalingrad. Character, she supposes, precedes action and predicts success. Through perseverance, the Allies will win. Character prompts action. Whereas the spy novel typically defines character strictly through action, *The Heat of the Day* conceives character as an entity detachable from action. Even if she starts to feel compelled to play "*her* part" as a listener and watcher (127), Stella initially chooses to overlook evidence of Robert's espionage for the Nazis because she loves him for himself, not because of what he does.

As we have already seen, Aristotle proposes a similar definition about character and action in *Poetics:* "tragedy is an imitation, not of men, but of an action and of life, and life consists in action, and its end is a mode of action, not a quality. Now character determines men's qualities, but it is by their actions that they are happy or the reverse. Dramatic action, therefore, is not with a view to the representation of character; character comes in as subsidiary to the actions. . . . Again, without action there cannot be a tragedy; there may be without character" (53). Actions reinforce character, just as character traits manifest themselves in actions. The man who claims to be the soul of generosity and who refuses to give money to a beggar refutes his claims by his actions. Action qualifies character. Concomitantly, aspects of character that may have been latent arise from certain actions. Valor or cowardice exhibited during war might never have mattered in peacetime. In the post–World War II milieu, deliberations about character centered on the existential, anti-Aristotelian conjecture that character remains independent of action. Can a good citizen be a collaborator? Is a collaborator simply facing facts? Is accountability in one aspect of character transferable to another? Many Europeans rationalized and thereby dismissed their activities as peculiar to times of fear and domination. Janet Flanner, attending the postwar trial of Maréchal Pétain, records this ironic bon mot of Admiral Leahy, the former American ambassador to Vichy: "'ambassadors are polite enough to forget the truth. *C'est la courte mémoire qui fait la courtoisie diplomatique*'" (A short memory makes for diplomatic courtesy) (37). Diplomacy entails overlooking unsound past actions.

A short memory, however, may lead to another version of collaboration, namely, collaboration by consensual forgetting. Rebecca West probes the conflict between the origins of character and the nature of sedition in her

1947 trial analysis, *The Meaning of Treason,* about the prosecution of traitors John Amery and William Joyce. Joyce, better known as the propagandist Lord Haw-Haw, loved "an obsolete England" out of sync with contemporary England; in West's opinion, this discrepancy between ideal and reality "made him a Fascist" (17, 18). Injury to Joyce's ideals compels him to act. Like Robert Kelway, Lord Haw-Haw was a middle-class, educated man with a powerful sense of displacement in British society. His fascistic leanings were not idiosyncratic. In June 1935, Chips Channon confided to his journal gossip about "the Prince of Wales' alleged Nazi leanings" (35). Oswald Mosley's British Union of Fascists had visible presence in England until after the outbreak of World War II. Mosley's vilification of Jews continued unabated until his internment in 1940. British misunderstanding of Nazism sometimes bordered on flippancy, as in *Pigeon Pie,* Nancy Mitford's 1940 spoof about propaganda broadcasting during the phony war. One might also consider the jaunty representation of British officers stationed in Naples in Barbara Pym's novel *A Glass of Blessings* and contrast it with Pym's prewar liaison with an SS officer named Friedbert Glück (Holt 68–72). While living in Germany in the late 1930s, Pym made a scarlet box with a swastika on it, bought a swastika pin, and never bothered to investigate Nazi principles. In 1941, "she expressed some regret for past excesses, but her self-condemnation never sounded entirely convincing" (Wyatt-Brown 33). In all of these instances—with the exception of Mosley who returned after the war with heinous, racist ideas such as forbidding all nonwhite immigration to England—allegiances in the past had to be dealt with as shameful legacies.[3] The dilemma is ontological. When it comes to wrongheaded commitments, character *(I am a good citizen)* shaves off from action *(whose acts I disinherit because they were necessitated by the times).*

Bowen vehemently opposes the idea of action without characters, of the kind that Aristotle hints at when he claims that tragedy may happen without character but can never happen without action: "One cannot 'make' characters, only marionettes. . . . Characterless action is not action at all, in the plot sense. It is the indivisibility of the act from the actor, and the inevitability of *that* act on the part of *that* actor, that gives action verisimilitude" (*Mulberry Tree* 37). One actor cannot substitute for another. Stella loves Robert not someone else, definitely not Harrison who manipulates her into an untenable position. The problem dilates to greater proportions when memory is added to the paradigm of action and character. Is it possible to have character if one has no memory? In *The Heat of the Day*, Bowen draws attention to forgotten time, dimly remembered alliances and entanglements—Stella's failed marriage and Robert's involvement in trench warfare. His sense of having served his country already in a futile cause makes Robert work for the Nazis. His character manifests causal continuity. Nevertheless, he isolates love from patriotism: "What country have you and I outside this room?" Robert asks Stella (276). As an assessment of commitment to country and to lovers, *The Heat of the Day* raises the possibility that all love affairs are incomplete and needfully so. We love only those aspects of another person that we recognize, and even then we don't love them on their own terms but as we see them. In that case, the political allegiances of a beloved person are irrelevant. Stella could go on loving Robert as a person instead of loving him as a spy. She could love him for his character, not his actions.

The crisis of character as brought into being by the war gets elaborated by Sartre in works published in the 1940s, such as *Being and Nothingness* and *Anti-Semite and Jew*. Sartre, in a reversal of literary and philosophical conventions such as Aristotle's, magnifies the distance between character and action. This philosophical division of being from doing addresses, in part, the legacy of collaboration in France, in that collaborators denied their pasts or declared they were the victims of circumstance. Sartre wants to hold collaborators accountable at the same time as he wants to preserve the freedom of choosing. Sartre mounts an inquest into human agency that empties itself of responsibility after the fact. He deplores self-defined character based on contingencies rather than principles. He argues that political suppleness need not be the only means to realize a goal—even if that goal is laudable, such as the defeat of the Nazis through resistance. Sartre makes a parallel case about the character of the anti-Semite who controls others through fear. The anti-Semite therefore is "nothing save the fear he inspires in others" and this prevents him from looking for his personality within himself (*Anti-Semite and Jew* 21). He confounds facts with prejudices. In both cases, character splits between constatation and action. Self-identification (the anti-Semite claims to be a good person) has nothing to do with agency (the anti-Semite reviles Jews). Similarly, collaborators distinguish between personality and action. The collaborator transmits authority while refusing to commit himself absolutely to any position.

Or the collaborator claims to act expediently and provisionally at the same time as he or she claims not fundamentally to be altered by such self-interested behavior.

Bowen answers the Sartrean position about character and action in a different way.[4] As we have seen in *The Heat of the Day*, character is a symptom of ideology. Character is a symptom of trauma. Character emerges at nodes of impossible-to-master circumstance. Love, for example, arises as an urge to cling to life. The idea of character, whether essential, performative, or self-defined, troubles Bowen not only because she spied during the war, but also because she represents Robert as a collaborator and Stella as a secret sharer. Ethics, too, determine character and action in *The Heat of the Day*. Action does not happen in any novel as the expression of unique character, as Bowen points out in "Notes on Writing a Novel"; instead, "characters are there to provide the action. Each character is created, and must only be so created, as to give his or her action (or, rather, contributory part in the novel's action) verisimilitude" (*Pictures and Conversations* 170). In accordance with Aristotle's observation that action determines character, Bowen sees characters as "expending potentiality" in the course of a novel (*Pictures and Conversations* 188). A completed action is marked by the exhaustion of character. A contradistinction can be drawn from Sartre's *Being and Nothingness*. Sartre claims that "to act is to modify the *shape* of the world" and that an act, which decides its own ends and motives, "is the expression of freedom" (559, 565). Motive is defined by the act itself. The person who acts does not necessarily control the intention of the act committed. Action expresses freedom according to Sartre the philosopher; according to Bowen the novelist, action expresses overweening situation, place, inevitability. Novelistic "characters are called into existence by the demands of the plot" (*Afterthought* 124). They have inevitability according to the design of the action that envelops them.

One could claim, *pace* Aristotle and Bowen, that character exists independent of action in two ways. First, to say one is a spy without ever committing an act of espionage is to make an unfulfilled action a determinant of character. Let me give another example. *I am a writer, but I have never written a word.* This may simply be bad faith: the ruse of claiming to be something that one manifestly is not can be used as a marker of potential rather than accomplishment. The verdict can hang for a long time. Should a writer publish, late in life, after long tribulations and infinite revisions, one piece of writing, his constatation becomes truth. The action retrospectively justifies the claim. But the principle is less clear-cut when the action has moral heft to it. *I am a murderer, but I have never killed anyone.* It would be silly to prosecute everyone who ever uttered such self-remonstrations, though doubt always shadows such constative statements. In this sense, both Aristotle and Bowen are right in asserting that action precedes, defines, and modifies character.

Whereas the case of self-identification and its fulfillment has relatively obvious ramifications, character and action might intertwine in a negative dialectic. A spy may commit an action of espionage but claim not to be a spy. This may be the essence of espionage: to act (inadvertently, unintentionally), then claim that the action never happened. Again, degrees of ethical responsibility affect such a statement. In a neutral case, one might say *I have published a great deal of material, but I am not a writer.* One could attribute this claim to false modesty. More seriously, the constatation nullifies the performance of the action, or would seem to. Despite performing regular actions that amount to the fabrication of character, the character refuses to be defined by those actions. Character exists elsewhere, an ontology apart from actions. In the political sphere, such a statement becomes hazardous: although one might have collaborated, the act of collaboration did not leave permanent traces on one's character. Past and present are not continuous. Action does not define identity. *All evidence of my espionage to the contrary, I am not a spy.* Although one commits a treacherous action, it does not fundamentally change character. Put otherwise, you can love a spy, but his political duplicity does not change his ability to love you back. You love him for what he is, not what he does.

THE FACE OF THE BELOVED IS THE FACE OF HISTORY

In *The Heat of the Day,* characters concentrate identity in their faces, whether masks of terror or masks of duplicity. Louie herself claims never to forget a face (13) and later attributes the remark to Harrison (238). Harrison recognizes Louie when she turns up at a bar and interrupts him, to his immense irritation. Faces, as "the place where the coherent mind becomes an image" (Elkins 200), herald identity, but that doesn't mean that every meaning written into a face is controlled by the possessor of that face or that faces are ever wholly known. As when Stella looks at herself in the mirror at Mount Morris, a face retains secrets. Faces register contradictions of feeling and memory. Although Bowen manifests interest in people's physiognomy in all of her fiction, face reading assumes exaggerated importance in *The Heat of the Day*. Everyone enters the narrative through an exposition of facial features. Stella has "one of those charming faces" that "look either melancholy or impertinent," and she wears a "pale, fine, soft bloom of make-up" (24–25). Harrison has out-of-true eyes and "a face with a gate behind it" (12). Louie has a "sun-coarsened face" (11). Connie "has bags under her eyes under the powder, a bull fringe, and a brick-red postbox mouth" (147). Blue-eyed Robert evades Stella's glance (98). Laughter makes his "face a mask of shut eyes and twisting lips" (285). These thumbnail descriptions do not provide authentic portraits. Faces lie. Cosmetics in the novel should not be construed as a falsification of the face, but as an application of lipstick and powder to faces that are already misunderstood by people who look at them. The human face in *The Heat of the Day* cannot express all the motives of behavior: Robert's espionage, Connie's bossiness, Louie's desperate leading of servicemen back to her apartment. Faces are more remembered than actual. Stella, fearing that her lover has died, sees "Robert's face with hallucinatory clearness" (93). "Loving no particular person now left in London" (93), Stella despairs of feeling love anymore at all. She sees Robert's face when love deserts her. The most clear image of a face occurs not in the presence of the loved one, but in the moment when the loved one seems lost irrevocably. His is a recalled face, an object onto which Stella cathects despair. She views his face according to desire mixed with memory, not according to fulfillment achieved through his presence. On the last evening that Stella and Robert spend together, she connects betrayal with the memory of his face—"that crystal ruined London morning when she had woken to his face" (274).

The pervasive darkness of atmosphere in *The Heat of the Day* hides faces. During a confrontation with Robert, Stella closes blackout curtains. Behind her Robert's voice blends in the unlit room: "In something more powerful than the darkness of the room the speaker had become blotted out: there occurred in the listener one of those arrestations of memory which made it impossible to conceive not only what the look on the face might now be but what the face had been, *as* a face, ever" (269). As if expunged completely from time and history, no detail of the face can be summoned up. Darkness obliterates the face from the present (whatever look it might be wearing) and from the past (whatever grimaces and gestures it habitually wore). Far worse, darkness obliterates the *loved* face, the face that the woman wants to remember before any other face and yet cannot because of this syncope in memory brought about by the traumatic discovery that the beloved face belongs to a spy. She has endowed this face with a surplus of meaning: "To have turned away from everything to one face is to find oneself face to face with everything" (195). To have relied on this one face as the repository of certainty during war is to expose the flimsy ideology of love: no face, just because it is loved, is authentic. The loved face, in any event, is never just itself. A repository of secrets, the face condenses history, destiny, treason, desperation, complacency, misunderstanding, happiness.

The "genius of the beloved face" (Barthes, *Camera Lucida* 66) exists in certain physical features, not all of them. Love affairs leave behind only images of faces—and only for those who survive. Stella is left with Robert's photograph, the memory of his face. Something once magical (a jawline, an ear, a habit of frowning, a smile) becomes puzzling in its banality. *How could I ever have loved such a face?* Writing about the genesis of her short stories, Bowen states that "history suddenly appeared to me in some tiny act or a face had begun to haunt me before I glanced at it" (*Afterthought* 78). Stories emerge from an act (gesture, movement, change) or character (face, body, silhouette, appearance). Action and character "haunt" her. They epitomize "history." Although Bowen distinguishes here between short stories and novels, she implies that history incarnates itself in individuals. The principle applies to *The Heat of the Day* as well. Stella and Robert call themselves "creatures of history" (194) whose love affair begins because of the war. Time runs in their veins. Bowen divides the elements of fiction into "story," "people," and "time" in "Truth and Fiction." Time has overwhelming presence. "Time acts on people; they react to it," she claims (*Afterthought* 135). The relation of time as historical imperative is thematized at various levels in *The Heat of the Day*. Ernestine denies responsibility for her opinions on the grounds that an idea "is *plus fort que nous*, it was in the air" (186). Robert argues that he spies because of necessity that he cannot control: "'I didn't choose them: they marked me down. They are not mine, anyhow; I am theirs'" (272). Robert's self-defense sounds dubious because he posits an absolute limit to his personal freedom. He could not but choose to spy because freedom was, in his estimation, always a sham: "'Do you suppose there's a single man of mind who doesn't realize *he* only begins where his freedom stops?'" (268). Individuals absorb historical currents and express them. The face abbreviates these historical exigencies into an image. Every face is historical.

The Heat of the Day is structured around face-to-face conversations, each of which contributes to the making of history. Characters square off in twosomes for confidential chats. If a third party breaks in, general discomfort follows, as when Ernestine accompanies Robert and Stella in a car ride through London, or when Louie gauchely joins Stella and Harrison in a bar. Some tête-à-tête conversations occur in darkness that cloaks both speakers and listeners. Connie and Louie, sharing a bed, talk in the dark (243–50), as do Robert and Stella (267–76). Darkness erases other methods of communication, such as gesture and glance. Even remembered faces lose definition in the dark. Louie feels "a fog of abhorrences" settle over Harrison's features (244); she hopes never to see him again. And Stella, on her final night with Robert, turns his photograph to the wall (277) so that she needn't be confronted by even so much as his image when she knows he is about to disappear for good. As in the portrait of Tom that Louie keeps on her mantle, the photographed face does not conquer absence, nor does it compensate for an imminent goodbye. Tom's portrait, taken as one of his "farewell acts," records "the face of a man already gone" (159). Photographs recall that all loved faces are essentially phantoms.

Stella expresses no regret or loss after Robert dies, which is not to say that she feels neither, just that she doesn't express any feeling one way or another.

What does any love affair mean?

"Every love brings to light only what is to it relevant" (99).

Roderick, alone, lies in bed at Mount Morris and wonders if he should "aspire to be the final man" (312), the one who embodies and makes sense of history. For the first time, he feels afraid.

Harrison returns after time abroad. It is 1944. Bombs fall on London.

Stella, in a rented flat, listens for the All Clear.

On a crystal ruined morning in London, I awoke thinking with hallucinatory clearness about the face of the person I love.

No face, because loved, is true. Some faces, like Harrison's, never have been loved.

"'Perfect love'" cannot cast out fear (200).

Someone will always be left to betray.

CHAPTER SEVEN

Walls

IDEOLOGY IS A GAP

John le Carré's *The Spy Who Came in From the Cold* allegorizes the genre of spy fiction. More specifically, allegory expands the range of political meanings in this novel that represents conflict between East Germany and Britain at the height of the Cold War. In allegories, signs and characters possess meanings in excess of themselves, meanings that play across historical, political, and semiotic registers. In allegory, nothing is self-identical. "Cold" in *The Spy Who Came in From the Cold* initially means snow and freezing temperatures, then enlarges in scope to include emotional frigidity, intellectual *froideur,* political chilliness, and wintry death. Not just a signifier of weather, coldness invokes all these meanings at the same time and requires readerly agility to see correspondences among competing alternatives. Meanings falsify or contradict each other. The title, for instance, betrays expectations. At the end of the novel, Alec Leamas does not come in from the cold—that zone on the other side of the Berlin Wall where, left to his own resources and ingenuity, he has no contact with his operators. He fights Mundt without knowing that he is, as a double agent, *more or less* on the same ideological side. "Cold" is a no-man's-land of choice. Although Alec comes in from the cold of East Germany before the novel begins, he never manages to come in from the cold of disillusionment. He cannot cross that wall. As an allegory of reading, *The Spy Who*

Came in From the Cold invites an ironic interpretation of events that transpire in the gaps between promises and eventualities. Far from being a realist novel about the Cold War, *The Spy Who Came in From the Cold* represents anti-Semitism, thrills, codes, violence, hatred, waiting, walls, and silence as aspects of complex political engagement.[1]

To read Leamas's career allegorically—his going on the dole, his decline into seediness and alcoholism, his tardy understanding of being set up—invites the question of what Leamas's decline allegorizes. In one interpretation, his trajectory of doom speaks to the conflicting demands of capitalism: he has no money at all (26); he seeks credit at the grocery store (41–42); his pension has a lien on it (25); he wonders who will buy drinks (58); George Smiley pays his bills (186). A fringe capitalist, the spy manifests virulent "hatred for the boss-class" (98). In another and not mutually exclusive interpretation, Leamas's decline addresses the soul-crushing littleness of bureaucracies. In other novels, le Carré criticizes English institutions and types, such as élite public schools *(A Murder of Quality)*, diplomatic pettiness *(A Small Town in Germany)*, World War II nostalgia *(The Looking Glass War)*, capitalist burnout *(The Naive and Sentimental Lover)*,[2] Kim Philbyish traitors *(Tinker Tailor Soldier Spy)*, religion *(A Perfect Spy)*, Cold War policies *(The Secret Pilgrim)*, and corporate corruption *(Single & Single)*. Most of these narratives concern espionage. Le Carré's spies, as character types, figure differences within bureaucracies. Connected to but not wholly endorsed by official institutions—embassies, corporations, intelligence agencies, public schools—the spy is a vehicle for social critique because he preserves individual agency. Never just acting on his own behalf, never speaking in propria persona, the spy switches between public and private selves without warning. These shifts are necessary to discern treachery in others, such as Control's false promise that after one last mission Leamas can retire with a pension. Both the perpetrator of corruption and the victim of corruption, the spy emblematically unites paradoxes of civic duty and free will.

Le Carré's obsessive representation of spies, whether as moles, defectors, double agents, sentimentalists, men, women, veterans, or neophytes, suggests that spies stand for the "various paradoxes in which we live," as le Carré told a BBC interviewer in 1965 (qtd. in Monaghan 571). From his student days until his Foreign Office posting to the British Embassy in Bonn that ended in 1964, le Carré acted as a spy, "in one way or another, for sixteen formative years, between the ages of seventeen and thirty-two" (Ash 41). He describes himself as an "espiocrat" ("Spying . . . the Passion of My Time" 270). Spying provides metaphors and material for fiction in that espionage is always about make-believe. All of life, le Carré says, either is made up or is "material . . . for fabulations" (Ross, "Master" n.p.), in which disappointments get exaggerated and unhappiness gets rewritten. Beyond le Carré's personal involvement in the realm of intrigue, the spy embodies the coalition of conflicting interests that comprise twentieth-century political affiliation. The spy, like Leamas in *The Spy Who Came in From the Cold*, lives out the dangers of insufficient knowledge. Or like impetuous Leiser in *The Looking Glass War*, the spy suffers for his rash actions; Leiser kills a border guard for no discernible reason and sleeps with a German woman against the dictates of good judgment. Adhering to technique and tradecraft rather than intelligence and spontaneity, the spy "sacrifices any claims to maturity and at worst becomes totally dehumanized" (Monaghan 570). The spy justifies means by results, which causes him to perform actions as if he were another person. Never just himself, the spy challenges ways that character is represented and whether character can be represented at all.

In analyzing le Carré's thrillers, critics usually opt for one of three approaches: exegetical; generic; historical. Either they disentangle the complex doublecrosses that constitute plot (who betrays whom), or they discern a commingling of realism and thriller conventions (how does le Carré resemble John Buchan, Ian Fleming, Len Deighton), or they interpret le Carré's narratives as historical documents about Cold War Realpolitik (how closely does fiction approximate reality). All of these are valid approaches, yet they rarely let le Carré off the leash of mass culture to consort with writers from nonspy traditions.[3] Without doubt, *The Spy Who Came in From the Cold* adapts thriller conventions to Cold War predicaments. Peter Lewis usefully summarizes events contemporaneous with the writing and publication of the novel, such as the shooting down of a U-2 plane over the Soviet Union in May 1962 and the Cuban missile crisis in October 1962 (61–63). Other critics isolate the gritty realism of the narrative—the narrator's manifest fondness for smells, stains, decrepitude, and decay (Beene 52). John Cobbs, detecting this preoccupation with grime, links the novel to naturalism (57). David Monaghan reveals "realistic and mythopoeic elements" in the narrative (115). Other critics view the narrative as a study in human failure. According to Cawelti and Rosenberg, le

Carré changes the spy genre "from a story of heroic, or at least, accidental triumph into a much more complex and ambiguous narrative of ironic failure in which the protagonists succeed only at the cost of becoming as dehumanized, as distorted in their conception of ends and means as their adversaries" (179). In such analyses, the novel focuses on character, with special attention paid to Leamas's romance with Liz Gold and his bid to rescue her as they scale the Berlin Wall. Leamas blinds himself to "ethical inconsistencies" (Beene 52) in Control's plan because of his rugged he-man devotion to action. Notwithstanding his efforts, upside-down morals in the novel make Leamas a "victim" (Wolfe 114). He safeguards the "moronic mass" (210) of people, as he contemptuously describes Western democracies. Leamas learns that his putative freedom is "illusory" (Barley 34), because his actions compromise his own safety and produce no change. Likewise, Liz Gold "is the paradigmatic naïve victim" (Aronoff 117). Worse, she suffers from "stupidity" (Beene 56). The parables drawn from these analyses conspire to suggest that, in the Cold War, ethical action and justice cannot be disengaged from shoddiness and illegality.

Political representation in *The Spy Who Came in From the Cold* does more than demonstrate victimization and shoddiness. If, as we have seen already in *Under Western Eyes, The Third Man,* and *The Heat of the Day,* spies suffer from an excess of memory arising out of conflicts about commitment, the willful eradication of memory in *The Spy Who Came in From the Cold* produces characters who function like chess pieces rather than rational, sentient creatures. Without memory, a character behaves as if all situations were unprecedented. Without memory, character may not exist. Alec Leamas, who runs agents in East Germany for ten years, sheds his memory in order to defect. Only rarely, at night, alone, in bed, does Leamas "allow himself the dangerous luxury of admitting the great lie he lived" (127). He particularly applies forgetfulness to his relationship with Liz Gold. He tells Control that he wants Liz "'forgotten'" (52). Memory erasure does not happen. Liz returns as a catalyst of catastrophe. She exposes Leamas's ruse and causes his death.

Obtuse though Liz might be, she is not solely to blame for these failures. Leamas, too, shares responsibility, because he unsuccessfully tries to negate his romantic inclinations. On the night that Liz and Leamas first sleep together, Leamas leaves "ashamed" (36) at five in the morning. An unnamed man observes this departure. This hasty retreat is an effort to suppress romance, just as later Leamas refuses to tell Liz that he loves her on the grounds that he doesn't "believe in fairy tales" (41). In prison, Leamas thinks about Liz perfunctorily, then puts her "from his memory. Leamas was not a man accustomed to living on dreams" (43). Leamas represses romance as the entanglement that jeopardizes his operation. Leamas does not master romantic impulses. Memories of Liz surge up at inopportune times. Just because Leamas wants Liz forgotten does not mean that others, such as the anonymous watcher, will forget her.

Leamas wants to eradicate intimacy in order to work efficiently, without encumbrances. Hence he restricts his contact with Liz to a sexual minimum. Almost all of Liz and Alec's encounters occur in intimate spaces. He sleeps in her bed (35). She creeps up to his sickbed (40). He speaks to her intimately for a long time at his bare apartment, presumably in a disclosure of his secret life (41). In his prison cell, he remembers the touch of her body (43). He thinks about her while he lies in his bunk. She signifies masturbatory pleasure, a private indulgence of memory and fantasy that Leamas consciously forbids himself. Intimacy, however, provokes hostility in Leamas. Encounters with Liz or recollections of her conclude chapters (35, 82, 95). Chapters snap closed as willful attempts to delete her from memory. The narrative, imitating Leamas's repressive tactics, stops short of admitting that Leamas loves Liz. So fierce is his repression that he associates Liz with dead Elvira (82). He remembers Liz *as if* she were no longer alive. Perversely, because Leamas loves Liz, he wants her dead. This repressed desire to see her dead in memory yields to the double death at the end of the novel.

Having unsuccessfully mastered his romantic feelings, having unsuccessfully become a purely functional character who serves his political masters first and foremost, Leamas nevertheless turns back at the Berlin Wall to face a hail of bullets. His death repeats a familiar pattern. The betrayal of Leamas by Liz duplicates the betrayal of Riemeck by Elvira: "'Just as Karl Riemeck did. He's made the same mistake'" (189). *Cherchez la femme:* although one could fault Elvira and Liz for treachery, the repetition of the "mistake" of love demonstrates that sentiment and memory are never adequately brought under control by agents. Leamas's commitment to duty never completely dehumanizes him. However much he quells his feelings for Liz and unconsciously projects her death, she connects Leamas to life. Although Leamas snorts with suspicion and fury about Riemeck's relation to Elvira (10), his own love affair blinds him. He does not learn from others' mistakes and tells Liz about his secret life, "things she only dimly understood" (41). Although codes of Cold War masculinity determine that men should not leak information during pillow talk, the leaking of information is also inherent in the representation of macho Cold Warriors. Eventually, they all seem to tell more than they should, and this leakage, paradoxically, becomes the proof of their masculinity. Pressured into keeping silent, male spies reveal their sentimentality to short-term girlfriends and mistresses. A victim of a romantic ideology that equates love with trust, Leamas fails to see that love affords betrayal either innocently or deliberately. In short, his need to repress is contradicted by his need to feel and to remember. Although he says he doesn't believe in fairy tales, he behaves as if he lived within one.

As much as he strives to forget, Leamas counts on his perfect memory to fulfill his mission. As part of operation Rolling Stone, he pretends to be down-and-out, sullen, unemployed, violent, abandoned by his operators in London, in order to create a cover for himself in East Germany, where he ferrets out the anti-Semitic ex-Nazi Mundt. Leamas does not know that Mundt has been previously recruited by the Circus. Not possessing all the facts, Leamas operates under false assumptions in order to reinforce security—if not his own, then at least the security of British intelligence. While ostensibly exposing Mundt, Leamas preserves Mundt's cover. Ideology asserts itself as false consciousness, figured as double-agency. Although Leamas has to forget allegiances, he also has to remember quantities of information about his prior operations in East Germany to create an alibi: "His memory was . . . remarkably precise considering the amount he drank. He could give dates and names, he could remember the reaction from London, the nature of corroboration where it existed" (80). His consistency as a storyteller determines his authenticity as a defector. The various demands to repress and to recollect point to a split in Leamas's consciousness. He struggles with his own sentimentality and ruthlessness. Although he neglects to mention his ex-wife and two children (100), he cracks up over the image of a carful of children who nearly get crushed on the Autobahn (102), which provides the treacly final image of the novel (219). Leamas cannot expunge family commitments or fellow feelings from his affective life. Gaps open between his functionality as an agent and his sentimentality as a man.

Ideology manifests itself in the gaps between remembering and forgetting, pretense and action. The novel plays on various gaps—in space, in remembrance, in narrative, in knowledge—that cannot be breached. The opening of the novel presupposes gaps in time and space. Several guards survey the strip between East and West Berlin at Checkpoint Charlie, where Riemeck is scheduled to cross. Not just a frontier, the no-man's-land is a physical gap between here and there, us and them. This spatial anomaly is also a warp in time. Nine hours delayed in his designated arrival, Riemeck calls attention to the gap between expectation and fulfillment. This gap in time ought to permit reflection for Leamas, but instead it creates nervous agitation. The temporal gap, filled with cups of coffee and tense chitchat, inhibits Leamas's ability to see how Mundt has duped him. Leamas, having failed to keep his network of spies alive in East Germany, keenly feels "the gap between then and now" (13), which could be otherwise characterized as Leamas's misunderstanding of the operation. In the gap between past and present, no one has bothered to keep Leamas up-to-date. In the stories fed to him, as well as the stories that he tells himself, gaps occlude truth. The fabrication of cover stories requires patching over gaps. For instance, Leamas toys with his interrogator, allows him "to fill in the gaps" (86) in his alibi. Control advises Leamas to make the East Germans *"deduce"* (103) details. False inferences permit interpreters to assert their own beliefs. Because the East Germans want to believe that Leamas defects, they make deductions based on their convictions. Hence disinformation leaks out in the gaps between what is left unspoken and what is surmised. Ideology seeps through such fissures. Far from being neutral, silences manifest duplicity.

Silences in *The Spy Who Came in From the Cold* are places of wounds, accusations, betrayals, rumors, disinformation. Speculation about links and causes occurs when information is withheld. The tactic of remaining silent—sometimes construed as tactfulness—encourages false surmises in one's interlocutors. Leamas's characteristic retort to difficult situations is silence. He stares at Elvira in silence that indicates his suspicion (7). Some of his silences repress truth. When Control asks him about Liz, Leamas responds with "a very long silence," followed by "another silence" (51). By not talking about his love affair, Leamas presumes that everyone will forget it. Leamas tacitly names Liz his next of kin, a legal maneuver that Liz does not discover until after the fact (100). The narrator delivers this information tactfully, though such delays also demonstrate that Liz, like the reader, is not fully informed. Abiding by Leamas's silences, the narrative does not disclose the full extent of Leamas's romantic commitment to Liz. When Liz asks Leamas a few direct questions about his mission, he says "nothing" (206). The silence makes Liz deduce what is going on. The victim of silences, Liz has diminished chances of survival because she does not know how to evaluate her role in the game. The silences inflicted on Leamas by Control and Mundt are repeated in the silences that Leamas inflicts on Liz. Doublecrosses happen at moments of silence, when motives are left unexplained and wishes are not articulated.

Silence justly inspires terror in Liz when Fiedler tosses her into a prison cell (203). Structurally, her imprisonment duplicates Leamas's earlier imprisonment. She is put in a cell as part of a ruse. Silences—like the ominous pauses in Beckett's or Pinter's plays—inspire fear and consternation because one knows that certain information is withheld. Without knowing the content of repressed information, one is powerless to act. Furthermore, communication continues in silences, but information transacted in silence is often misinformation. When rumors circulate about his having embezzled money, Leamas says nothing to contradict them (25). Thus silences and omissions cut both ways for Leamas. He uses silence to further his ends, yet he is also the prey of others' omissions. Le Carré asserts in his introduction to *Philby: The Spy Who Betrayed a Generation* that "we should never forget the gaps" (10) in any spy's career. Strange things transpire during silences. Allegiances change. Secrets are exchanged. Soviet recruiters, whose "influence" and "shadow" (le Carré, "Introduction" 10) are recognizable but whose faces and names remain unknown, lurk in the gaps of a spy's life story. Recruitment and treason occur in the blank between what is known and what is not known.

Gaps also prefigure death. Silent, imprisoned, amnesiac, the spy slips into a half-world of forgetting and invisibility. Typically le Carré views spies as ghosts. In "To Russia, with Greetings," he calls Cold Warriors "tragic ghosts, the unfallen dead of the last war" (6). As we have already seen in *Under Western Eyes,* ghosts recall asynchronic jolts brought about by trauma. In a speech to the Boston Bar Association in 1993, le Carré claimed that "the law was the ghost at every clandestine feast" when he entered the secret world ("Tinpots, Saviors, Lawyers, Spies" 25). Like ghosts, spies vanish. Numerous characters disappear in le Carré's narratives: Leo Harting vanishes with secret files in *A Small Town in Germany,* leaving "an empty chair" (33) and one of those "'gaps'" (68) in space that unremarkable office drudges create with their passing; spies suddenly disappear "'off the face of the earth'" in *Tinker Tailor Soldier Spy* (107); George Smiley's wife Anne goes AWOL early in their marriage and pops up now and again when it pleases her; Magnus Pym slides from official purview and becomes the subject of a massive MI5 dragnet operation in *A Perfect Spy.* Le Carré conceives of character as not altogether present, as neither completely alive nor completely dead. In *The Spy Who Came in From the Cold,* Leamas disappears from Liz's life, just as he disappears, with official sanction, from his job. He is as good as dead. Liz, busting into his apartment when he is ill, initially thinks "'he's dead'" (38). He smells like decayed fish oil and the fetid "smell of death" lingers about his clothes and hair (27). Leamas links himself with Riemeck: "'He was dead—what else was there to say?'" (83). In effect, he posits death as an absolute limit. Yet this refusal to elaborate on Riemeck's death, like Leamas's other baffling silences, does not mean that death has no meaning. On the contrary, death has too many meanings for Leamas, none of which he can articulate. He lacks an understanding of his own hauntedness.

Like the Stygian sewers in *The Third Man,* the environment and characterization of *The Spy Who Came in From the Cold* generate metaphors of death and corpses. Disburdened of material possessions, stripped of dignity and attachment, the spy recalls the anonymity and death that lurk at the heart of modernity. The spy incarnates the death drive insofar as he seeks quiescence or stasis that he can bring about only through his own demise. Leamas's death at the Berlin Wall fulfills that death drive. The wall stands as the absolute barrier between life and death, the partition between conscious and unconscious that ineffectively seals off knowledge of death.

THE WALL IS A BARRIER OF REPRESSION

In one last defining gesture, Alec Leamas turns back to help Liz Gold scale the wall that separates them from the West. He executes his gesture of salvation out of romantic reflex—he hopes to save his girlfriend—or out of foolhardiness—he plays the hero in order to escort Liz back to the land of doublecrosses and treacheries. An ubiquitous presence, the wall dominates *The Spy Who Came in From the Cold* as an impediment to understanding.

Approaching the wall, Liz and Leamas look for "'a small gap'" (215) cut in the barbed wire. Allegorically, the slit in the wire at the top of the wall figures not just the narrowness of the passage between East and West, but also the narrowness between the subject positions of sentimental communist Liz and toughened sentimentalist Leamas. The attempt to escape fails. Gap or no gap, the wall asserts itself as an absolute threshold that cannot be crossed. Narrow though the chances of escape may be—they have about ninety seconds to scale the wall (212)—the wall represents a point of obdurate unchangingness. A "dirty, ugly thing of breeze blocks and strands of barbed wire, lit with cheap yellow light, like the backdrop for a concentration camp" (9), the wall epitomizes the point where allegory fails, in that Leamas manifests romantic tendencies in his rescue attempt of Liz: he deliberately turns back to save her and causes both of them to die. He cannot live in Germany without compromise and he cannot live in the West without Liz. Whereas Leamas imagines he lives in truth, he lives in illusion. He thinks of himself as antiromantic, but he is really amorously afflicted. The wall thus stands for the illusory boundaries around genres—romance and realism, thrillers and literary fiction—that artificially divide literature.

Twentieth-century literature features a maze of walls, including walls of execution, wailing walls, hollow walls, fourth walls, and walls reduced to rubble. Walls in World War II fell: houses blown to bits, public buildings blasted to rubble. Very quickly after the Blitzkrieg started in 1940, the landscape of London transformed into a city without walls. Mounds of bricks, craters, and partly destroyed buildings dominated the cityscape for years after the war. Anthony Powell's novel *Casanova's Chinese Restaurant* begins with a postwar perspective on the grim, not-yet-rebuilt architecture of London:

> Crossing the road by the bombed-out public house on the corner and pondering the mystery which dominates vistas framed by a ruined door, I felt for some reason glad the place had not yet been rebuilt. A direct hit had excised even the ground floor, so that the basement was revealed with a sunken garden or site of archæological excavation long abandoned, where great sprays of willow herb and ragwort flowered through cracked paving stones; only a few broken milk bottles and a laceless boot recalling contemporary life. In the midst of this sombre

grotto five or six fractured steps had withstood the explosion
and formed a projecting island of masonry on the summit
of which rose the door. Walls on both sides were shrunk away,
but along its lintel, in niggling copybook handwriting, could
still be distinguished the word *Ladies*. Beyond, on the far side
of the twin pillars and crossbar, nothing whatever remained
of that promised retreat, the threshold falling steeply to an
abyss of rubble; a triumphal arch erected laboriously by dwarfs,
or the gateway to some unknown, forbidden domain, the lair
of sorcerers. (7)

The pub has sentimental significance for Nick Jenkins, narrator of Powell's
twelve-volume *Dance to the Music of Time*. The ruin, as in the beguiling
romantic ruins that gothic writers in the eighteenth century and landscape
designers in the nineteenth century contemplated, is the shape of memory.
The blasted past can never be put back together again as it was. Violence
in the material world is the ground zero of identity, the point at which
identity becomes uncertain of itself: *Did I once live here? Did I once inhabit
such a space?* Graham Greene makes the bombed landscape the place
where gratuitous gangland cruelty takes root in his 1954 story, "The Destructors." Gang members meet near a leaning house that "had suffered
from the blast of the [last bomb of the first blitz] and the side walls were
supported on wooden struts. A smaller bomb and incendiaries had fallen
beyond, so that the house stuck up like a jagged tooth and carried on the
further wall relics of its neighbour, a dado, the remains of a fireplace"
(*Collected Stories* 9). The man who lives in this house cannot give it up
and will not fix it up. The boys saw away its joists and pull out its mortar
until the house collapses with the slightest nudge. The near-ruin becomes
a complete ruin. Not a wall is left standing.

In a 1940 poem entitled "Ultimatum," Philip Larkin writes, "But we
must build our walls, for what we are / Necessitates it" (Larkin 243). The
poem does not spell out "what we are," though the British wartime reader
might infer that "we are" a nation under attack. The wall, whether of
bunker or seawall, provides shelter from enemy forces. In this poem, the
consolation of boys' adventure stories and the peaceful days of commerce
have given over to walls of defense. The poem ends with a dire choice and
a shift in pronoun away from "we" to "you," as if some act of exculpation

has occurred: "You must escape, or perish saying no" (Larkin 243). "You" cannot live in perpetual denial behind your walls. Undefended walls become prison walls. The poem, though arguing for some putative spiritual freedom through metaphors of ships, is a subtle bit of versified propaganda about the necessity of fighting for freedom since "escape" means one thing and one thing only in 1940: battle.

At almost the same time as Larkin wrote this poem, Virginia Woolf noted in her diary for July 24, 1940, "All the walls, the protecting & reflecting walls, wear so terribly thin in this war" (304). The walls of an audience who could reflect back some of Woolf's opinions, the walls of a shelter that keep out the noise of bombs, disintegrate. Adam Piette suggests that "History [manifest in World War II bombing raids], with its empty, booming sounds, was making too much noise, threatening to break down the walls to the private rooms of the writer and her circle"; this breakdown undoes middle-class securities in Bloomsbury as well as the "substance, standards and identity" of the writing self, threatened with death "behind invisible walls" (Piette 178). By October 1940, the walls had crumbled. Woolf went to look at her bombed house in Russell Square: "I cd just see a piece of my studio wall standing: otherwise rubble where I wrote so many books. Open air where we sat so many nights, gave so many parties" (*Diary* 331).

Walls destroyed in World War II became, in European culture during the 1950s and 1960s, political walls: the Iron Curtain, the Berlin Wall. While *The Spy Who Came in From the Cold* evokes the tensions in Berlin in 1961 when the wall was first constructed, it also alludes to novelistic and theatrical walls. Pyramus and Thisbe whisper through a chink in a wall in Shakespeare's *Midsummer Night's Dream*. In Diderot's *The Nun* and Abbé Prévost's *Manon Lescaut,* women are immured in convents. In Honoré de Balzac's *L'histoire des treize* and Henry James's *The American,* walls divide heroes from the heroines they hope to save. As such, walls segregate genders. The legacy of such walls returns in Albert Camus's *The Plague:* in the quarantined Algerian city of Oran, the journalist Rambert searches for "a rift in the walls" (130) that cut him off from his absent beloved in Paris, whereas Dr. Rieux sends his ailing wife to a quarantine hospital for a cure. These walls hold some people in and keep others out. As in André Brinks's *The Wall of the Plague,* the wall defends and sequesters, provides imaginary security and reinforces apartheid. Fictional walls preserve distinctions between inside and outside, knowledge and its inaccessibility. Applicable to the allegorical sense of a wall in *The Spy Who Came in From the Cold* as the boundary between life and death, Jean-Paul Sartre's short story "Le Mur [The Wall]" contrasts prison walls with a wall of execution: "On allait coller un homme contre un mur et lui tirer dessus jusqu'à ce qu'il en crève; que ce fût moi ou Gris ou un autre c'était pareil" (They were going to stick a man against a wall and shoot at him until he died; whether that man was me or Gris or another didn't make any difference) (36; my translation). The story reverses expectations about a wall of execution. Sartre's protagonist, expecting death, is set free. The wall of death becomes the wall of ambiguous freedom, in which the inevitability of death conditions all subsequent actions.

Walls are barricades against the decipherment of meaning. In *Smiley's People*, a novel that also ends at the Berlin Wall, "the wall between safety and extreme hazard [for a secret agent] is almost nothing, a membrane that can be burst in a second" (331). The wall in *The Spy Who Came in From the Cold* sustains Leamas in his illusions about efficacy and agency. According to le Carré, the Berlin Wall serves as a "perfect theatre as well as a perfect symbol of the monstrosity of ideology gone mad" (qtd. in Cobbs 62). The wall as a "theatre," in which and on which Liz and Leamas enact their last hurrah, is "an empty stage" (217). The attempt to cross the wall occurs as part of the performance of ideology. No one else appears on the stage, but Liz and Leamas are more vulnerable for that emptiness. In any event, the escape has been scripted by Mundt and Control. Though the guards "hesitate" (219) momentarily before killing Leamas, his death is foretold. Hesitation, that little gap in time that opens a vista upon freedom, merely accentuates the dramatic inevitability of the moment. That drama occurs within the shadow of a wall already overdetermined with meaning.

Dying at the gap in the Berlin Wall, Leamas hardly qualifies as a tragic figure. He arrives at understanding belatedly. He admits no overt allegiances, except to his agents and to his job. Ambiguity defines his role vis-à-vis Control and Fiedler. He does not know what he is doing. In his representation of Leamas, le Carré does not valorize Western politics. In fact, le Carré rebuked a Soviet critic in 1966 who accused him of fueling mistrust between East and West. Speaking of *The Spy Who Came in From the Cold*, le Carré argues that "in espionage as I have depicted it Western man sacrifices the individual to defend the individual's right against the collective. That is Western hypocrisy, and I condemned it because I felt it took us too far into the Communist camp" ("To Russia, with Greetings" 5). Twenty years later, le Carré resumes this theme. He asks if anyone has the right "to suspend his individual conscience in the interest of some mistily perceived collective" ("Le Carré: The Dishonourable Schoolboy" 18). For le Carré, political engagement entails thoughtfulness and responsiveness, not naive adherence to party programs. He ridicules those who read spy novels to uphold a putative notion of superiority against Russians or other designated enemies. With pre-*glasnost* irony, he claims in 1984 that "spy books should celebrate our incompatibility, specialness, insularity, superiority" ("Why I Came in From the Cold" 35). Le Carré implies that, while reading, devotees of spy novels entertain contradictions and form alliances with inimical forces. Reading provides an occasion for wide-wheeling thought and radical inconsistency.

THE READER IS A DOUBLE AGENT

The Spy Who Came in From the Cold allegorizes acts of reading as acts of death and violence. In *The Origin of German Tragic Drama,* Walter Benjamin aphoristically asserts that allegory "declares itself to be beyond beauty. Allegories are, in the realm of thoughts, what ruins are in the realm of things" (177–78).[4] Allegory points to what is missing, not what is present, of the spirit that has vacated objects, not the aura of beauty that enlivens objects. In J. Hillis Miller's gloss of this Benjaminian principle, allegory entails "the giving of a human mask and a voice to what is dead or inanimate. The essence of allegory is the way in which this process exposes itself as an unsuccessful projection" (365). The dead remain dead. Verbal signs—narrative, dialogue, exposition—lack materiality. Narrative is always ghostly insofar as it conjures up characters and places that do not exist. Allegory hypothesizes similitude between unlike categories, but in the end the gap between categories draws attention to dissimilarities among analogous categories. A spy is not a ghost. A reader is not really a double agent. Similitude facilitates understanding but should not be confused with things that are identical.

In this regard, we can speak of *The Spy Who Came in From the Cold* as an *allegory* of death, not just death as the undiscovered kingdom from which Leamas cannot return, but also as the impossibility of reproducing the nihilistic impulses that underlie Cold War representation. The experience of death cannot be translated into language. An allegorical mask or voice merely ventriloquizes death. By indirection, allegory addresses the apocalyptic threats and retaliations that constitute arms buildup and superpower standoffs. In effect, violence and death enter representation obliquely as phenomena that undo the principles of mimesis. Because death signifies negation, nonbeing, the not-known, it disrupts representation. Violence undermines the control of narrative by forbidding coherence. A narrative that incorporates a violent act—the assassination of a Russian minister, an air raid that destroys central London, a shoot-out in a sewer in Vienna—has to find the means to avoid incoherence. For this reason, the representation of death and violence has to be allegorical. Whereas the spy tradition returns again and again to violence as a viable, necessary precondition for change, le Carré indicates in *The Spy Who Came in From the Cold* that acts of violence merely sustain the status quo. Cold War brinkmanship means possessing weapons that hold enemies in abeyance. Stockpiling of missiles and the invention of fail-safe systems preclude randomness: "in terms of actual strategy and in the basic understandings of everyday life, chance or contingency became compelling in a powerful and historically distinctive way, became an element of the conscious and unconscious atmosphere of that period we call the Cold War" (Jackson, "Postmodernism" 332). Within a structure of uneasy neck-to-neck competition, violence occurs as a prelude to apocalypse or as a reminder that violence can be kept under control. The carefully planned assassination or bombing thus has a ritualistic quality. Every so often, an agent dies or a car blows up to reiterate the point that other, larger-scale kinds of violence—thermonuclear war or military invasion—do not occur.

Violence is therefore staged as violence in Cold War representation. The death drive that Leamas embodies creates an atmosphere of death around him. Vopos shoot Riemeck as he peddles towards the West Berlin border. A gunman slays Elvira (81). Leamas kills an East German with a blow to the throat (145). Fiedler dies for knowing too much (206). Leamas's death recapitulates Riemeck's as a fatality without importance. Although Leamas understands that Control has duped him and that Mundt, as a double agent, has killed every man in Leamas's DDR network, this knowledge cannot be transported back into the West. In the allegory of the novel, the Berlin Wall contains information that the West cannot assimilate, namely, that within an ethos of individualism, such as the West adheres to, individuals are dispensable. Not all aggression leads to death in this narrative. Sometimes violence causes grave bodily injury. Alec Leamas punches a grocer in the face twice, fracturing his cheekbone and dislocating his jaw (42). In prison, Leamas jabs a hoe into another prisoner's stomach (44). On his mission in East Germany, a guard bashes Leamas in the head (146). Barely conscious, Leamas rams his head into a guard's stomach (148). As a figure who inflicts and sustains injury, Leamas expresses himself through, and takes punishment on, his body. Violent behavior is justified in pursuit of an abstract ideological goal and has no meaning in itself. Leamas does not hold personal grudges against the guard and the grocer. Already scripted in the spy's program of action, violence causes no real change. Leamas abides by a plan in which he pretends to be a disaffected former agent to let communist agents recruit him. His acts of violence follow this script. Violent reactions, like the tears of an actor, spring from cues, not passion.

In this regard, le Carré brings the conventions of realism to an impasse. Passion is put on. Character is motivated by ideology, not a quest for authenticity. Raymond Williams, defining nineteenth-century realism, observes that "Society from being a framework could be seen now as an agency, even an actor, a character. It could be seen and valued in and through persons: not as a framework in which they were defined; not as an aggregate of known relationships; but as an apparently independent organism, a character and an action like others. Society, now, was not just a code to measure, an institution to control, a standard to define or to change. It was a process that entered lives, to shape or to deform; a process personally known but then again suddenly distant, complex, incomprehensible, overwhelming" (13). In realist literature, society masters and deforms the individual. The individual in turn puzzles out his relationship to amorphous society. If society is "a character and action like others," if it has an "agency" of its own, the individual, as agent, responds to and rebels against social intrusions. Realist characters such as Dorothea Brooke or Lucien de Rubempré negotiate their wants over and against the exigencies of making a good marriage, thriving in a career, doing charitable deeds, upholding morality. Passions, already cast as antithetical to social norms, become the stuff of realist narrative—as nodes of unresolvable conflict or thwarted ambition or unfulfilled desire. To apply Williams's formulation, therefore, we view realist characters as having or not having credibility by virtue of their dissent from social norms. By contrast, le Carré represents characters as torn between functionality and authenticity. Leamas, having grown too old to work as an agent in the field, accepts his position as a doer in the intelligence hierarchy. His acts of violence conform to the plot of disaffection. Even though he cannot define Western ideology—"'we're not Marxists, we're nothing. Just people'" (120)—he obeys his controllers to the letter. The expectations of his job as a spy create his personality. He plays along and pretends that ideologies of various types do not merit discussion.

By the same token, Leamas preserves romantic resistance and romantic ideals that suggest that he has not entirely fallen into lockstep with the scripts supplied to him. He dissents from popular standards through negation. Anger defines him. He tells a CIA agent to "'Shut up'" (6). He snaps at a West German guard (8). He speaks "fiercely" and persists "ruthlessly" (60). "'Who the hell are you?'" (47), he asks Ashe, when Ashe tries to recruit him. He answers Ashe "savagely" (54). He raises ire in those around him. The people in his neighborhood dislike him (27). Working at a library, Leamas cultivates hatred in his boss: "He had become an enemy of Miss Crail, and enemies were what Miss Crail liked" (33). Kiever, accompanying Leamas to Berlin, grows irate over dirty dishes (66). Kiever speaks "shortly" and "savagely" (63). Anger is a threshold of action for these characters. They thrive on adversity. Hostility motivates other spy narratives. In *Democracy*, Jack Lovett blows up at Harry Victor for not knowing about anything that has not appeared in American newspapers. In *The Third Man*, Rollo Martins tries to punch Calloway for insinuating that Harry Lime is a criminal. In *Under Western Eyes*, rage governs Razumov's behavior. Anger releases these characters from frustration or inanity. *When I get mad, I get things done.* Violent actions or verbal abuse vent hatred. Liz Gold diagnoses a "core of hate" (35) in Leamas's personality. He lists his manifold dislikes: Americans, public schools, military parades, people who play soldiers, and people who tell him what to think (35). He hates being touched (134). Hatred exhilarates him. Like many Angry Young Men of the 1950s and 1960s, he exists because he abhors. Or, like Miss Crail who needs to be hated, Leamas exists because others abhor him.

Being hated is a twentieth-century prerogative. In Albert Camus's *The Plague,* Tarrou tries hard "not to be the mortal enemy of anyone" (206). Tarrou does not claim to be successful, just that he tries. He means that someone somewhere, not anyone in particular, hates him. To be human is to be someone's enemy. *I exist because others hate me and that hatred defines my identity, if inimically. I know they hate me and therefore I hate them in turn.* This logic pertains to *The Spy Who Came in From the Cold*. Consequently, hatred triumphs over romance. Instead of viewing love as the expression of character and desire, we could interpret love as merely functional, a motive for doing something, just as hatred instigates action. Liz wonders if governmental agencies manipulate love affairs for their own ends (208). Love facilitates blackmail and other kinds of social governance. Love, like any other emotion, rather than existing for its own sake, has utility within the regimentation of the state. Love limits characters rather than frees them. Fiercely riven by his repressed love and his virulent hates, Leamas cannot see that he is a realist character living inside a functional plot. Whereas Leamas ought to fulfill his duty and act according to the mission that Control has enlisted him for, which would require that Leamas function irrespective of his feelings, he adheres to sentimental notions of family and love, as when he tries to protect Liz at the communist tribunal or remembers the children watching him from their car window on the Autobahn. In a functional narrative of intrigue, action conducted in the service of ideology supersedes personal sentiment. Therefore, le Carré represents an allegory of realist and functional modes of narration in *The Spy Who Came in From the Cold*. Leamas's defeat at the Berlin Wall implies that neither realist nor thriller conventions strictly control his actions.

Leamas's ignorance and hostile negation establish the rudiments for an allegory of reading in the novel. Stripped to a "barebones" (Wolfe 112) austerity of style, as if an assiduous editor had removed all superfluous words from the narrative to make the prose as "sinewy" (Lewis 68) as possible, *The Spy Who Came in From the Cold* represses significant information. Assiduous readers *deduce* the identity of George Smiley, who may or may not appear beside park railings (36), at London flats (98), near kiosks (105). He is not always introduced by name. The reader, like Leamas, fills in the gaps of exposition. Characteristic of allegory, whether by Edmund Spenser or John Bunyan, "there are disjunctions in [the] surface, or illogical juxtapositions of sequence, which tempt translation as a means of bridging the gaps" (Quilligan 235). Like Leamas, the reader knows only as much about the Rolling Stone operation as the narrator divulges. As a substitute for the reader, Leamas suggests that some interpretations, furiously enforced, violate facts. When interpretation fails, a rousing punch-up alleviates frustration. Anger, too, is instrumental in interpretation. Breakage inflicts meaning in hermeneutical exercises, just as hitting the grocer and head-butting the guard bring them into the plot of Leamas's irate miscomprehension. In less roistering moods, the reader has to interpret allegorically in order to arbitrate conflicts of ideology. The reader, like Leamas, resembles a double agent, practicing shiftiness and duplicity, deducing meaning from ambiguities. The reader is doomed to inadequate knowledge of the pressures that direct his or her reading of the novel. As a cryptic double agent, the reader evaluates his or her interpellation into ideology by scrupulously examining Leamas's alternatives.

Opportunities for expressing subjectivity, narrowly restricted by Cold War demands in *The Spy Who Came in From the Cold,* make characters allegorical rather than realistic or romantic. Character does not produce ideology, but vice versa: ideology produces character. The clearest demonstration of allegorical tendencies in the novel appears in characters' names. *Mund* in German means "mouth," and it nearly approximates the name of the fast-talking double agent Mundt. "Control," the head of intelligence-gathering operations in London, assumes an allegorical function without a fallback identity anchored by a specific name. He is pure code as well as pure control. Liz Gold's surname connects her to the getting-and-spending motifs of capitalism in the narrative. As a name, "Leamas" evokes several meanings. A concoction of surplus vowels, his name presents itself as a code or anagram. In Spanish, *le amas* means "you love him." Or, changing the syllabification, *lea mas* means "read more," in an imperative form. Indeed, Leamas ought to read more into his situation. The name also resembles the Spanish noun *lemas,* which means "motto." His identity collapses into something completely indecipherable, a motto that is "motto," a character more emblematic than real, the way Nemo in Charles Dickens's *Bleak House* is a cipher for anonymity—in Latin, the pronoun *nemo* means "nobody." In French, *le amas* means "the heap" or "the pile," which Leamas becomes on his sickbed and at the Berlin Wall. As a heap, he scrambles identities. *Limace,* as a French homonym for Leamas, means "a slug" of the zoological sort. Anagrammatically, the letters in "Leamas" could be redistributed as "as male," the encryption of machismo, just as the name of the queer character "Ashe" could be construed, depending where the space key interrupts, as "a she" or "as he," a subject position neither wholly masculine nor wholly feminine. No one's name is necessarily genuine. Names are codes. People choose their identities by selecting aliases. Leamas calls himself Herr Thomas at the beginning of the novel (11). Ashe's real name seems to be Murphy (60)—though who can tell for sure in a novel where identities have so little certainty.

In addition to English, Leamas speaks French, German, and Dutch (23). He drifts among languages as an unfixed supranationalist. Ashe offers Leamas the opportunity of writing articles in German because of his fluency (55). Leamas's linguistic skill doubles for the reader's competence with language. Neither Leamas *(lea mas)* nor the reader ever reads deeply enough. Polyvalent allegorical meanings in *The Spy Who Came in From the Cold* fool the reader. The novel deliberately thwarts interpretation, in part by playing on silence and ambiguous dialogue. The narrative begins and ends in a *charabia* of languages. English and German intermingle in the first chapter. Shouts in "English, French and German" resound in the last scene (218). Like Leamas, the reader has to pick through these plural languages to know which voice ought to be heeded. Either the reader holes up behind the walls of predetermined reading conventions to shut out confusing, mixed signals, or the reader learns to crack the code of allegory. The task of deciphering allegory is daunting, since the narrative negotiates among competing modes of representation. The fallback temptation, then, is to read *The Spy Who Came in From the Cold* as a ripping good spy story. But such literal readings are preempted by the principle articulated by the novel and by the encryption techniques of intrigue literature: nothing is ever itself. Leamas is Thomas is *le amas.* Mundt is a double agent. Control lies. Treating the Berlin Wall or Leamas literally forces readers to produce a meaningful version of ideology—a quest doomed to failure. Allegory always beggars readerly competence. Ideology, dear reader, is not what you think it is. You have to interpret but you will never be right. As a double agent, pretending to know but not able to translate knowledge into practice, you are as doomed as Alec Leamas. You love him, even if he is a heap.

The death of Leamas does not so much figure the death of the reader as the triumph of violent indeterminacy. His last gesture remains impossible to interpret. Bearing traces of different kinds of literature—fable, realism, tragedy, detective fiction, antiheroism, romance, thriller, cryptohistory, doctrinal treatise—*The Spy Who Came in From the Cold* collapses all generic distinctions with Leamas's death. The novel encodes styles and motifs from a variety of genres; these circulate within le Carré's novel yet remain indecipherable. The blend of genres mystifies ideology. Gordon Teskey claims that "allegories do not just reflect ideological structures; they engage us in the practice of ritual interpretation by which those structures are reproduced in bodies and reexpressed in the voice. As a substitute for genuine political speaking, allegory elicits the ritual repetition of an ideologically significant world" (132). The only way out of such a closed circuit is through the destruction or collapse of allegory. Spy narratives, whether tragic or comic, end with "destruction" (*The Looking Glass War* 223), which may be a more salient feature of the genre than any other. Spy narratives represent violence as a means to an ideological end, not as an end to ideology.

As the main interpreter within *The Spy Who Came in From the Cold,* Leamas changes his tactic of inflicting violence on others by facing death at the Berlin Wall. There is no way of knowing what this action means. There is no way of getting over the wall built to hold in knowledge and to hold out interpretation.

CHAPTER EIGHT

Leaks

FIGHTING THE QUEER COLD WAR IN
THE UNTOUCHABLE

Prophecy: In a 1924 letter to André Gide congratulating him on his novel *Corydon,* Edmund Gosse conjectures that homosexuality will one day be commonplace: "No doubt, in fifty years, this particular subject will cease to surprise anyone, and how many people in the past might wish to have lived in 1974" (qtd. in Sheridan 380). Whatever fondness anyone feels for 1974—the year that Richard Nixon resigned in the wake of Watergate; the year after the American Psychiatric Association delisted homosexuality as a pathological disorder; the year streaking became a fad; the year John le Carré published *Tinker Tailor Soldier Spy* in which bisexual Bill Haydon, villain of the piece, loves a "'snotty little sailor boy'" (356)—it did not bring about the utopian queerdom that Gosse implicitly conjectures. Nevertheless, he sees Gide's novel as a harbinger of changing attitudes. Contributing to and reflecting such changes, narratives of intrigue, especially after 1945, represent gay men as protean, effeminate, deviant, enigmatic, unstable, *leaky.* The Cold War altered conceptions of queerness by aligning it with espionage, most famously in the United States because of the HUAC hearings and in Britain because of the Cambridge spies. As the Cold War progressed, all spies proved to be, in some degree, a bit queer.

*

Grim: Queer men in the Cold War expose the limits of heterosexual male-ness within plots and counterplots of espionage. Rather than being a liability, homosexuality trumps identifiers of manliness, such as Etonian suaveness, fascination with gadgetry, ordinariness, and rigidity of convictions. Invisible when not out, the queer spy takes refuge in the double closets of sexuality and political affiliation. These closets turn out to be much the same space—a magician's box with a trapdoor. In fiction, the spy's homosexuality manifests itself in character (homosexuality is innate and cannot be changed) and action (not just a character trait, homosexuality involves the performance of specific actions). The male spy who refuses to have sex with other men is not beyond reproach within Cold War standards of conduct. Pretending straightness does not shield the spy from suspicion. Proclivities alone give him away. Nevertheless, the queer spy compounds the ideological quandaries of the Cold War by his alleged susceptibility to leaking. Put otherwise, he dribbles vital information to enemies. One prototype for such leakiness is a woman, Mata Hari, wrongfully accused of spying because she slept with men of several ideological persuasions during World War I. Information also flows across and through a woman's body in "Giulia Lazzari," one of Somerset Maugham's *Ashenden* stories: under police coercion, an Italian countess lures her treacherous boyfriend from Switzerland into France, where the police catch him; Giulia Lazzari, a full-fledged romantic, is held accountable. Women's bodies symbolically substitute for points of contact. Women, uncanny in their yoking together of the strange and the familiar, terrify male spies. Rarely granted independence of thought, women in spy narratives embody the treacheries of innocence—of not caring enough about secrets. In the 1987 film *No Way Out,* a Russian spy sleeps with the mistress of the U.S. secretary of defense. By virtue of her divided sexual allegiances, the mistress is automatically assumed to be a conduit between the Pentagon and the KGB. A servile, power-mad, queer character calls her a "whore." Leaks in this instance are both seminal and informational. In any exchange of fluids, according to the dark logic of espionage, information too might be exchanged. In *No Way Out,* semen traces removed during an autopsy from the dead mistress's vagina reveal the blood type of the last man she slept with, namely, the Russian double agent.

*

Bond with Lesbians: Such women provide a lineage for leaky queer spies insofar as duplicity is thought to be grounded in sexual behavior. Whatever their other flaws, homosexual characters within an ideology of intrigue show up the grimness, cruelty even, of heterosexual masculinity. Although James Bond swigs martinis cavalierly and wears a tuxedo elegantly, his repertory of pleasure is restricted by the fact that he has no interiority, as do few men in the annals of espionage fiction. No one ever knows what Bond feels. Seldom do adjectives modify his characteristics or adverbs his actions. Fleming's sentences eschew ornament in favor of short, clipped, transitive syntax: "Bond dropped his lighted cigarette" (*You Only Live Twice* 214); "he walked purposefully" (*Casino Royale* 42); "Bond reached out and took her arm" (*The Man with the Golden Gun* 124); and so on. When qualifiers do arise, they define Bond's theatricality, killer instinct, or detachment. In *Octopussy,* he turns his "serious blue-grey eyes" on his prey (16); he leans on a doorsill "negligently" (17). In *Goldfinger,* he "smiles noncommittally" (419) and kisses Pussy Galore "ruthlessly" (639). Posturing *adverbially* affects his sexual behavior. He has sex with whichever woman throws herself in his libidinal path—*except* women who show interest in him. He goes out of his way to seduce professed lesbian Pussy Galore in *Goldfinger* because her indifference to him poses a challenge: "Bond liked the look of her. He felt the sexual challenge all beautiful Lesbians have for men" (581). After the death of lesbian Tilly Masterton in the same novel, Pussy yields to Bond, who treats her "fiercely" and sneers at her with his "cruel mouth" (638). Seducing a lesbian awakens sadism in him, a sadism excused by the notional desire that Pussy responds to *authentic* masculinity: "He said, 'They told me you only like women.' She said, 'I never met a man before'" (638).[1] Random seduction does not make Bond sexy, only opportunistic. Indeed, he treats sex mechanistically. In *On Her Majesty's Secret Service,* Bond's mind whirs "like an IBM machine" (114) while trying to remember people's names. In the same novel, after he sleeps with an emotionally fragile woman named Tracy, he switches "off his thinking about her" (36), as if shutting down a machine. He files official reports "without mention of romance" (178), in part because "he hadn't thought of [Tracy], only the job" (226). He separates sex from duty. He never falls in love with the women who admire him. He marries Tracy in *On Her Majesty's Secret Service,* though it's hard to tell what persuades him to do so: a bribe of one million pounds from her father or Tracy's declared love for him. In most of his adventures, Bond scarcely feels anything towards women. "'The bitch is dead now'" (189), he says about his erstwhile girlfriend Vesper Lynd in *Casino Royale.* Russians recruit Vesper as a professional double agent, but Bond dismisses her categorically on personal grounds, qua bitch, as if any political allegiance she might have had need not be taken seriously. He always thought her a "bitch," even before meeting her (*Casino Royale* 33, 105). "'Poor little bitch,'" he says about Tilly Masterton in *Goldfinger*, "'she didn't think much of men'" (620). The lesbian who refuses to respond to the Law of the Phallus dies. She exists only as a creation of mythic masculine authority.

*

The Trouble with Mary: Bond's adherence to phallic law and his distaste for emotional involvement preserve him from conjugal unhappiness. In *The Man with the Golden Gun,* when Mary Goodnight offers Bond a week in her Jamaican bungalow to recuperate from various wounds, he resists the "mink-lined jaws of the trap" on the grounds "that love from Mary Goodnight, or from any other woman, was not enough for him" (190–91). As her name implies, it's goodnight *to* Mary, not a good night *with* Mary, or a good night *for* Mary. Bond resists bondage by not marrying Mary. Spying trumps sensual indulgence. Moreover, Bond's achievements as a lover always get reported from the perspective of the women he seduces, for the narrator discreetly glides over the mechanics of Bond's nights of love and Bond's emotions during his manifold encounters. His legendary pleasure techniques remain obscure. Bond's pleasure is assumed, not expressed in his own words, and certainly never directly represented, as it were, in flagrant delight. The grimness of Bond's sexuality derives from the unmentionableness of pleasure. In contrast to Bond's indifference to women as political entities, the gay spy is forbidden to separate sex from politics. As we shall see, the gay spy is assumed to be *too* engrossed in sensual pleasures. Supposedly sexuality makes the gay agent vulnerable, whereas it makes James Bond invulnerable. Sexuality, whether gay or straight, does not destabilize political commitments. Sexuality merely amplifies instabilities already present within political commitments. Put otherwise, you don't have to recruit or be recruited by everyone you have sex with, as the Bond model indicates.

*

Scruffy, Dirty Things: John Banville's 1997 novel *The Untouchable* reconfigures the conception of homosexuality within the genre of espionage. The novel is based on several histories of the Cambridge spies. The chief character and narrator, Victor Maskell, is a slightly modified portrait of real-life Anthony Blunt.[2] Like Blunt, Maskell joins the Communist Party in the 1930s while at Cambridge, spies for Russia until the 1950s, and collaterally earns an international reputation as a connoisseur of Poussin's paintings. Like Blunt, Maskell goes to Germany at the end of the war to retrieve incriminating letters written by King George before the war. Like Blunt, Maskell is stripped of his knighthood by Margaret Thatcher in 1979. Like Blunt, Maskell demonstrates degrees of donnish reticence and viperish backstabbing. Like Blunt, Maskell is an inveterate cottager. He trills the glories of tearoom trade. Like Blunt, Maskell cruises the toilet near Speaker's Corner in Hyde Park in London and has a particular fondness for men in uniform and "scruffy, dirty things" (Penrose and Freeman 311). A "mixture of fear, wild hilarity and a wholly wanton exultation" overcomes him as he listens to the "dead-fish slap" of his friend Boy Bannister's stout thighs against an anonymous "red-haired young man's buttocks" in the Hyde Park lav (289). Like Blunt, Maskell poses an irreconcilable enigma about the relation of sexuality to espionage: they reinforce each other; they have nothing to do with each other.

*

Urinal: The public men's room in *The Untouchable,* even though it functions as a place for casual sex, recalls how often spies congregate around toilets. The revelation scene in *The Ministry of Fear* takes place in a train station washroom. Whenever Tom Farrell, the U.S. naval hero and Russian infiltrator played by Kevin Costner in *No Way Out,* needs to think, he heads for the toilets, though only to wash his face or scheme, never to urinate. American agents and Arab fundamentalists have a spectacular shoot-'em-up in the mall toilets in *True Lies.* Scenes in loos suggest masculine vulnerability. Calling the men's room a "theater for heterosexual anxiety," Lee Edelman concludes that public stalls lead heterosexual men, uncertain about the difference that constitutes their masculinity, towards "another 'country' whose agents are always already operating within . . . the men's room itself" (Edelman 563, 569). When zippers are down, secrets come out—or so the conventional wisdom of espionage maintains. A men's room aesthetic governs espionage narratives. Sex in the Speaker's Corner toilets in *The Untouchable* relates to, and parodies, such meanings. Flouting the fact that many men were prosecuted for homosexual acts in the 1950s, Maskell claims that those years were a very paradise for gay men: "to be queer was very bliss. The fifties was the last great age of queerdom" (321).

Sexual mores in 1979, the date that fictional Maskell tells his tale, do not allow for proper appreciation of "the aphrodisiac properties of secrecy and fear" (321) in Maskell's opinion. In contradistinction to the perceived wisdom of queer theory, that all acknowledgments of homosexuality liberate, that nineteenth- and twentieth-century discourses of psychology and sexology create the homosexual as a "species" (Foucault, *History of Sexuality* 43) and schematize his desires, Maskell suggests that fear and illegality pump up his libido and, for him, constitute pleasure. He wishes to remain a creature of secrets because they endow him with strength. By resisting the overt identification of his queerness, he doesn't shrink into the closet so much as flaunt the insight that *"identity is not serious"* (Bersani, *Homos* 18), or certainly not as serious as realist novelists and professional psychoanalysts think. After all, Maskell's desire to have sex in a public men's room is a desire to be caught, a desire to be humiliated in order to prove that humiliation factors into his character. Contrary to Edmund Gosse's wish to live in the future when homosexuality would be commonplace, Victor Maskell wishes to live in the past, when queerness was defined by subterfuge.

*

A Short, Queer Orientation:[3] Banville inverts patterns of spies' homosociality and homosexuality in *The Untouchable*. In order to locate those inversions, I am going to take a Sunday cruise through instances of queerness in history and narratives of intrigue.

*[4]

White House and Brothel: In the United States, consciousness of security risks in the Cold War coincides with an emerging consciousness of homosexuality. Gay men and women fought along with everyone else in World War II. Displacement from hometowns afforded opportunities for queerness to assert itself among aviators, sailors, soldiers (D'Emilio, "The Homosexual Menace" 233–34). "Despite the new screening and discharge policies that designated gay soldiers as unfit to fight," Allan Bérubé writes, "gay men served in combat zones during World War II as disciplined, trusted, and courageous soldiers" (175–76). Traveling servicemen encountered gay people with whom they had affinities. Gore Vidal remembers, with delight, the packed bar at the Astor Hotel in New York after the war, where Dr. Alfred Kinsey prowled in quest of interviews with demobilized soldiers. According to Vidal, "normal young men, placed outside the usual round of family and work," ran riot with each other, including "one tall golden youth, an army pilot who proved to be, on closer inspection, a much deco-rated brigadier general, in search of likeness" (102). At the same time, the war exaggerated the links between homosexuality and espionage. In Brook-lyn in 1942, a male brothel became the epicenter of a scandal that marked heightened hysteria around security and sexuality. Spies, sailors, senators, and doctors congregated at the brothel, run by a naturalized Swede. When the owner of the bawdy house was prosecuted, journalists leapt to "un-founded conclusions that homosexual men engaged in 'orgies,' could eas-ily be blackmailed, or were likely to reveal military secrets to espionage agents" (Murphy 45). In short, the war and the postwar era brought gay people increased visibility. This visibility fanned fears of homosexual influ-ence. What underlies these Cold War fears seems to be the fear that men from different classes, professions, and nationalities *get along with each other* in a bar or a bordello. They chat; they mingle. By mingling, they transgress proprieties of who belongs with whom. They cross boundaries of race, class, region, and military rank. In effect, they *leak* across borders. After the war, homosexuality, aligned with communism, was equivalent to a "national security risk" (Corber 2) that required containment. The "homo-sexual menace" (D'Emilio, *Sexual Politics* 43) led to the purging of homo-sexuals from government positions for moral turpitude. A Senate report concluded that homosexuals lacked moral fiber; indulgence in perversions made gays vulnerable to blackmail (D'Emilio, *Sexual Politics* 40–44). It hardly needs to be said that criminalizing homosexuality set the terms for blackmail in the first place.

*

On Trial: Espionage magnifies issues of trustworthiness for gay people. Indeed, homosexuality enters the American consciousness as a species of treason. As gay people were increasingly targeted during the widely broadcast House Committee on Un-American Activities hearings, "immi-gration and government employment policies based on the equation of closeted homosexuals (at risk of giving away state secrets) and hidden communists (actively betraying Americans)" sharpened (Patton 330). Part of a slightly earlier wave of Cold War suspicion, homosexual Whitaker Chambers took the stand in 1949 to testify against Alger Hiss. Chambers stoked tensions between political affiliation and homosexuality. A former communist agent himself who testified that Hiss, too, was a communist,

Chambers "lived in a time when it was easier to confess to being a spy than to confess to being a homosexual" (Blumenthal 112). Confessing to being a spy allows subsidiary disclosure of homosexuality. In an imperfect way, Chambers's renounced espionage liberated him from a narrowly defined sexuality: the good American, regardless of sexual orientation, points fingers. Identification of homosexuality, in the case of Chambers, occurs within legal structures, which is to say that to be gay is to be already an illegal subject—unless, or until, one denounces communists. The semiotic slide between communist and homosexual is endemic to the period. Perhaps motivated by semiotic confusion, but certainly motivated by the heightened consciousness of homosexuality as a phenomenon, President Eisenhower, upon taking office in 1953, ordered that homosexuals be barred from federal employment.

*

Containment: Queer citizens, analogous to communists within the United States, needed, according to the logic of containment, to be identified and prohibited from political representation, even from working in the civil service. Political containment of communism, as argued by George Kennan in his "long telegram" from Moscow and his elaboration of that doctrine in the 1947 article "The Sources of Soviet Conduct," emphasizes that political health is akin to personal health. Soviet Russia contains "the seeds of its own decay" even as it pushes communist frontiers beyond the Soviet bloc (Kennan 125). In Kennan's opinion, therefore, "the main element of any United States policy toward the Soviet Union must be that of a long-term, patient but firm and vigilant containment of Russian expansive tendencies" (119). A muted rhetoric of masculine bucking up counters Soviet aggression. Using the word "penetration" five times in the long telegram, Kennan figures "the Soviet government as a masculine rapist" and "the West as dangerously accessible" to the insistence of Russian policies (Costiglione 1309). Fearing "gender inversion" (Costiglione 1325), Kennan formulates U.S.-Russian relations as a blurring of boundaries that ought to be reinstated. The American policy of containment, by analogy, hypothesizes rampant "'leakages'" (Costiglione 1321) of the sort that characterized homosocial fraternization with Russians at the American embassy in Moscow in 1933–34 during Kennan's first posting there. Embassy official Charles Thayer feared that pervasive homosexual eroticism and the all-male get-togethers were "'almost enough to turn you pansy (there are plenty of partners in the diplomatic corps)'" (Costiglione 1323). The doctrine of containment hypothesizes, as Eisenhower's banishing of homosexuals proves, that gay men—to ascribe hydraulics to politics—leaked inordinately in comparison with straight men. The gay male body in the Cold War is invented in response to the possibility of straight diplomats turning pansy when confronted by the penetrating force of Russia.

*

A Poisoned Apple: The Cold War in Britain assumes juridical dimensions as well: "prosecutions for homosexual 'offences' rose five times over in the 15 years from 1939" (Sinfield 66). A 1957 civil service report worried about security risks posed by "suspected homosexuals about whom there is no direct evidence on which to base the charge" (Aldrich 150). Such *suspects* were routinely removed to other posts. Accelerated prosecution speaks to growing awareness that queer men exist, but increased prosecution does not necessarily speak to an increase in sexual activity among those men. Perversely, one of the victims of police vigilance was war hero Alan Turing, whose protocomputer at Bletchley Park cracked the Nazi Enigma code. Denial of security clearance to homosexuals meant that Turing could not continue working in intelligence units after the war. Filing a police report after his house was robbed, he inadvertently divulged his homosexuality and, after being charged for homosexual offences, was subjected to a cruel regime of estrogen injections designed to neutralize his libido. He committed suicide by eating a cyanide-laced apple in 1954, aged forty-two.[5] His death is explicitly recalled in *The Untouchable* when Alistair "Psyche" Sykes kills himself in the same manner (50). Legal identification of homosexuality, however, does not begin to account for the subtlety of queer politics in 1950s Britain. As Alan Sinfield argues, homosexuality in postwar Britain divides along class lines in a way that does not obtain in postwar America. Specifically, "leisure-class" gay men were reluctant to change the status quo, despite the common instance of sexual intimacy that took place across class boundaries. "Conservative and disinclined to welcome innovation" (Sinfield 78), leisure-class queers wanted a return to prewar privilege. Elite queers did not work on behalf of gay liberation that led, eventually, to the decriminalization of homosexual acts in 1967 in Britain. At the same time as persecution of gay men increased, literary representation of homosexuality made it almost banal. Aside from famous, fatalistic, drunken Sebastian in *Brideshead Revisited,* postwar British fiction also

produced (to cite just a few variants on queerness) the glittering Nova Sco-
tia-born Cedric who beds a French aristocrat and a lorry driver in Nancy
Mitford's *Love in a Cold Climate;* the middle-class couple Keith and Piers,
who shock no one except cocktail-swilling, church-going Wilmet in Barbara
Pym's *A Glass of Blessings;* and joshing Jasper in Angus Wilson's *Anglo-Saxon
Attitudes.* Paradoxically, whereas the police charged gay men with gross
indecency, novels by Mitford, Pym, and Wilson made gayness central to
the repertory of fictional characters in the 1950s.

*

Defect: The 1950s assumption that gay spies jeopardized security was con-
cretized by the defection of Guy Burgess and Donald Maclean from England
to the USSR in May 1951. (Although Blunt's involvement in the defection
is not known, Banville has Maskell drive Boy and MacLeish to Folkestone
to catch a boat for the continent [329–32].) Everyone describes Burgess
as an unkempt queer with dirty fingernails, loudmouth behavior, and a
vast appetite for sex and alcohol. Michael Straight catalogues Burgess's
slovenliness in fierce detail: "the black-rimmed fingernails, the stained fore-
finger in which he gripped his perpetual cigarette stub; the dark, uneven
teeth; the slouch; the open fly" (qtd. in Penrose and Freeman 121). Grimi-
ness advertises Burgess's status as slumming spy without explicitly naming
his peccadilloes. Filthy fingers substitute for filthy habits. No matter where
he was employed or with whom he found himself, Burgess made virtually
no effort to disguise his homosexuality. Indeed, his flagrant sexual exploits
seemed to provide cover for his espionage activities. People were so surprised
at his overt homosexuality that they neglected to be surprised by his spying. Traipsing about with his fly open, he distracted people with his virility.
As Harold Acton gossips in *More Memoirs of an Aesthete,* "Brian [Howard]
confided to me that [Burgess's] equipment was gargantuan—'What is
known as a whopper, my dear'" (Acton 87). In *The Untouchable,* Guy Burgess, rebaptized as Boy Bannister, scandalizes people because he can. Maskell sneaks a peek at Boy's "big flaccid sex lolling in its bush" (240) as he
lounges in bed. Boy pees through a window at the embassy at Rabat "into
a bed of bougainvillaea in full view of the ambassador's wife, that kind of
thing" (317). A flash of the phallus diverts attention from other activities.

*

Cambridge: Most accounts of the Cambridge spies develop some correspondence between their homosexual camaraderie and their espionage. This

correspondence has been explained by various historians and critics as a symptom of Bloomsbury snobbery, unnatural camaraderie fostered by the secret Apostles society at Cambridge, defective middle-class values, improper respect for fathers, and countless other problems (Koch 23–25; Sommer 285; Cecil 169–73; Wright 221). Andrew Boyle attributes Kim Philby's espionage to a quest for "perfect craftsmanship" rather than ideological conviction (12). These formulations obscure the fact that a spy spies not because he is homosexual but because he is a spy. No one asks, conversely, what common denominator subtends heterosexuality and espionage. Nevertheless, the Cambridge spies had a fluid sense of sexuality. Burgess and Blunt were homosexual. Donald Maclean was bisexual. Kim Philby and Guy Burgess were once caught together in bed with a bottle of champagne in Washington, although no untoward spillage, aside from some champagne perhaps, seems to have taken place (Costello 540). At issue in the Cambridge spy narratives is the representation of the queer body: how it seems to unite alterity and familiarity, how it serves as a conduit for information. During the war, Burgess presided over the meeting of a bizarre, filthy, heterogeneous salon, where he gathered "the homosexual underworld of London together with some of the most devious and despicable political operatives then at work" (Koch 41), among them a German and a Frenchman. He trespasses over class boundaries as well as boundaries of nation and heterosexuality. Honoring longstanding commitments to communism, the Cambridge spies passed information to Stalinist authorities. The porousness of the gay spy points to a postmodern conception of identity (holding conflicting opinions and values simultaneously) and away from a modernist one (rallying behind a doctrinaire cause). Despite all evidence pointing to the assorted treacheries of the Cambridge spies, no British court of law "ever pronounced them guilty of a crime"; it is particularly difficult "to pin a particular leak" on Burgess and Maclean (Sommer 288). Even Blunt, who negotiated immunity in exchange for information after Philby's defection to Russia in 1963, lost nothing more than his dignity and his knighthood in 1979. (On the other hand, Blunt's story, as told to the world at large, may be mostly "fabrication" [Steiner 191].) Queer spies in the Cold War compound illegalities: treason and homosexuality were both punishable by law. Therefore, the best spies may be the leakiest ones—those who pee through embassy windows, for example. They understand the attraction to political otherness as the expression of forbidden sexuality. They understand that sleeping around doesn't inevitably mean sleeping with an enemy. They understand that sexuality is not always a means of extorting or betraying information. By concentrating on Maskell's identity and the question of whether authenticity in identity is ever detectable, *The Untouchable* responds both to the history of the Cambridge spies and to the representation of sexuality in espionage narratives.

*

Men Only: The fictional representation of masculinity in spy novels reinforces the idea that straight men do not like sex very much. The plot of espionage novels characteristically excludes women unless needed as femmes fatales or dupes. Women "function solely as the third term in a triangle that is predicated on male rivalry and male bonding" (Silver 14). Richard Hannay works alone in *The Thirty-Nine Steps.* Women scarcely figure in his world at all, except as intruders. In *Greenmantle,* Hilda von Einem, leader of a conspiracy to rabble-rouse the Turks, appraises Richard Hannay "as a man" (171). Her gaze discomfits him. Hannay confesses that "women had never come much my way, and I knew about as much of their ways as I knew about the Chinese language. All my life I had lived with men only, and rather a rough crowd at that" (170). Hannay admires her as one admires a Wagnerian heroine: mythic, unapproachable, queenly. She has the "soul of a conqueror" (256). Hannay distrusts her, but when she threatens him with death, Hannay claims, "Never in my life had I been so pleased. I had got my revenge at last. This woman had singled me out above the others as the object of her wrath, and I almost loved her for it" (257). To be detested by a woman is, for Hannay, a mark of distinction. Hilda von Einem's death (during a shell explosion) prevents her from taking away Sandy, Hannay's brother-in-arms. Interesting as Wagnerian Hilda may be, Hannay interprets her only as a pawn of his own cunning. That she singles him out wrathfully indicates his immunity to her unconventional power. That she dies immediately thereafter justifies his repudiation of her as a woman and as an enemy. Whereas he embraces danger without being defeated, she disdains danger and succumbs. Hannay's stand against Hilda proves that masculine fitness depends on the repudiation of women and romance. "The homosociality of this world seems embodied fully in its heterosexuality," writes Eve Kosovsky Sedgwick, "and its shape is not that of brotherhood, but of extreme, compulsory, and intensely volatile mastery and subordination" (*Between Men* 66). In *Greenmantle*, such compulsory mastery entails perfect control of emotions and impulses on Hannay's part, as well as the repudiation of Hilda as the potential rouser of emotion. Hannay quells her in order to quell his own feelings, which, at a stretch, can be called merely incipient. When he chooses a woman to marry, he settles on Mary, a woman half his age who has "the free grace of an athletic boy" (*Mr. Standfast* 11). He does not marry Mary until the interim between *Mr. Standfast* and *The Three Hostages*, when the death of his buddy Peter Pienaar frees him from homosocial bonds. After marriage he all but ceases to be an agent: "the life of the secret agent is reserved essentially for single men" (Stafford, "John Buchan's Tales" 15).

*

Frippery: The independence of the men in *Greenmantle,* of Hannay from Sandy and Blenkiron and Peter, is jeopardized by the possible intrusion of a woman, certainly, but the fear of feminine softness already exists within the rough-and-tumble heart of Hannay. Hannay is a homophobe who idolizes his friend Sandy. Blue-eyed, swaggering Sandy is worshipped by his confrères as much as he is promoted as the leader of a mystical sect (Sandy is modeled on Lawrence of Arabia). Sandy's chic and intelligence elicit Hannay's homosocial admiration. While Hannay looks up to the polyglot, debonair, British Sandy, his homophobic panic erupts in the presence of a decadent, athletic, German queer. The villain Stumm, a ham-fisted, big-foreheaded brute who genuinely frightens Hannay, shows signs of *decor decadence*. He leads Hannay into a salon like "a woman's drawing room," but which is really "the room of a man who had a passion for frippery, who had a perverted taste for soft delicate things. It was the complement to his bluff brutality. I began to see the queer other side to my host, that evil side which gossip had spoken of as not unknown in the German army. The room seemed a horribly unwholesome place, and I was more than ever afraid of Stumm" (79). Hannay implies that homosexuality exists in the German army, but is—heaven forfend—unknown among British military ranks. Resembling Frederick the Great because of his military tastes or mad King Ludwig because of his arch, overdone, interior decorating, Stumm, proving his masculinity, or eager for some roughhousing, seizes Hannay by the neck. They fight on the carpet, "a wonderful old Persian thing, all faint greens and pinks" (79). His sweeping renunciation of all things feminine leads Hannay to note the beauty of the carpet before castigating it and its owner. Wholesome men eschew decor. Yet Stumm foils the codes of masculinity by being sturdy, militaristic, well built, and fond of frippery. Whereas Hannay abides by a conception of homosexuality as *that which is not heterosexual,* Stumm represents to him homosexual codes infused with heterosexual ones. The homosexual ethos of the novel, quickly raised, then just as quickly squelched, rejects the simplistic opposition of either/or. Going it alone against Stumm on the carpet in a room full of frippery (at the end of the novel he barricades himself in a *castrol* or fort with his buddies), Hannay has to rely on his savoir faire to escape. The codes of masculinity determine that two men in a room alone wrestling on a multihued carpet are enemies, but many men in a fort together withstanding shell attacks and fearing for their lives are comrades in arms. Distance from frippery, along with the manner in which the British stick up for their buddies, determines their masculinity.

*

Close Quarters: Other spies, aside from Hannay, work in pairs. Carruthers and Davies in Erskine Childers's *The Riddle of the Sands* are only fleetingly perturbed in their all-male yachting and spying expedition when Davies falls in love with a German woman, Miss Clara, daughter of the sinister Dollmann. Although this romance mitigates Davies's gruff taciturnity, it also banishes the specter of homosociality from the friendship of Davies and Carruthers, who spend a lot of time together in close quarters below decks. In similar seafaring narratives, male duos do not invariably have sex, though they might spend a lot of time loitering in pajamas and whisper-ing in "hardly audible murmurs" (93) to each other in bed, as do the Cap-tain and Leggatt in Conrad's *The Secret Sharer*. Whereas Carruthers and Davies defend Britain, even though they are amateurs with no obligation to act patriotically in situations of danger, other male agents, in tandem or singly, depart from that tradition, or work variations on the theme. For instance, Leamas in *The Spy Who Came in From the Cold* allows himself to have some feelings, however remote, for Liz: "Sometimes he thought of Liz. He would direct his mind towards her briefly like the shutter of a camera, recall for a moment the soft-hard touch of her long body, then put her from his memory. Leamas was not a man accustomed to living on dreams" (43). The passage, a forerunner of James Bond's IBM mind in *On Her Majesty's Secret Service,* makes romance an effect of gadgetry.

Leamas thinks of Liz as if his mind were "the shutter of a camera" and she the object of voyeurism. In his mind, Leamas takes her out like a picture and examines her before putting her aside. The intrusion of gadgetry into tenderness, of technology put in the service of sex, allows distance to enter between lover and loved one, a distance that might be labeled "Leamas's aloofness." Leamas consciously stages the heterosexual gaze as a performance. The passage concludes, however, with the repudiation of romance. Leamas pretends to be a criminal and is incarcerated in order to establish his bona fides as a disaffected agent who will appeal to communist operators. Leamas's cell mates "hated him because he succeeded in being what each in his heart longed to be: a mystery" (44). The core of his masculinity is his refusal to acknowledge family bonds or to give off any information whatsoever. And yet he lives with a false-true consciousness, one conditioned by its vacillation between democratic British agent and communist pretender. Insofar as an agent out in the cold can live with such dualities, he has been queered. And secretly, in his heart of hearts, he keeps thinking about the faces of some German kids looking out a car window, the picture of family-centered *Gemütlichkeit*.

*

A Little Bit of a Pansy: The ideological queering of Leamas meets with a violent repudiation of queerness in the emotional realm. Leaving prison, Leamas is tailed by a man named Ashe: "a little bit of a pansy, thought Leamas. Could be a schoolmaster, ex-LSE and runs a suburban drama club. Weak-eyed" (46). He also wears an orange tie. Those readers with ingrained 1950s fashion sense recognize orange as the color of queerness. In Robert Lowell's 1959 poem "Skunk Hour," the "fairy decorator" festoons his shop with "orange cork, / orange, his cobbler's bench and awl" (Lowell 95). In Barbara Pym's 1958 *A Glass of Blessings,* vivacious, model-handsome, chatty, tidy, queer, fabric-conscious Keith wears a "tangerine-coloured shirt" and looks "very animated" (231). Jasper in Angus Wilson's 1956 novel *Anglo-Saxon Attitudes* wears "orange suede strap shoes" (Wilson 25). Orange is late 1950s code for queer. In *The Spy Who Came in From the Cold,* Ashe of the orange neckwear ineptly shadows Leamas wearing a shabby postprison getup. When the two strike up a conversation in a bar, Leamas imagines that he and Ashe look like "a couple of cissies" (47) and Leamas later dismisses Ashe as "that cissy [who] picked me up" (61). Ashe pretends that he visits striptease clubs occasionally "to find a girl" for himself

(60). Leamas believes none of this. Nor should the reader. Donning the role of heterosexual is no more preposterous than spies' and terrorists' donning the role of homosexuals that one finds in other spy novels. Homosexual Ashe chats a bit too soothingly and sympathetically to fool anyone, except Liz, who thinks "perhaps he wasn't queer but just looked it" (141). Like James Bond who views lesbians as closeted heterosexuals, delusional Liz implies that inside every gay man is a straight one waiting to come out. Ashe tests Leamas at the strip club, a venue where Ashe himself can concentrate on the task of extorting information from Leamas, who pretends to be down-and-out. Ashe, it turns out, merely recruits Leamas for an operator higher up in the communist infrastructure. Yet the opposition of heterosexual and homosexual in the novel is not nearly so clear-cut as Leamas would like it to be. Indeed, the strip club is a theater that allows everyone to perform. Show girls dance. Ashe, playing straight, performs his role as old acquaintance from Berlin willing to help out Leamas. Leamas acts out his role as disaffected former agent with a drinking problem. Ashe's name, as we have seen, can be construed as either "a she" or "as he," among other possibilities, but in all cases he plays a part. All identities, including the role of closeted queer and feigning dissolute, are acted out in *The Spy Who Came in From the Cold.*

*

Bully: The narrator, assuming an objective knowledge of all these deficiencies of character as well as the causative continuity of plot, delivers a psychological profile of Ashe:

> Ashe was typical of that stratum of mankind which conducts
> its human relationships according to a principle of challenge
> and response. Where there was softness, he would advance;
> where he found resistance, retreat. Having himself no particu-
> lar opinions or tastes he relied upon whatever conformed with
> those of his companion. He was as ready to drink tea at Fort-
> num's as beer at the Prospect of Whitby; he would listen to
> military music in St James's Park or jazz in a Compton Street
> cellar; his voice would tremble with sympathy when he spoke
> of Sharpeville, or with indignation at the growth of Britain's
> coloured population. To Leamas this observably passive role
> was repellent; it brought out the bully in him, so that he would

lead the other gently into a position where he was committed, and then himself withdraw, so that Ashe was constantly scampering back from some cul-de-sac into which Leamas had enticed him. (48)

Softness attracts Ashe. Resistance repels him. Ashe expresses sympathy, a feeling alien to Leamas. By comparison, Leamas despises passivity; it calls out the bully in him. The characters are complementary in their relationship to power and aggression. Leamas entices Ashe into conversational cul-de-sacs, yet the metaphor of the dead-end alley hints at homosexual luring. Leamas entices. Ashe scampers. Leamas's sense of power, which he has to relinquish in order to pass for a communist in East Germany, "naturally" enforces itself through trickery and physicality. Ashe plays several roles, whereas Leamas plays only one. Leamas, more to the point, has to go further to play a role and his anger often undoes his portrayal of a down-and-out ruffian in London. Like other queer characters in spy fiction, Ashe disturbs the covert ideologies of the genre that straight guys try to keep on the Q.T.: *I like to follow other men around, I like to put on disguises, I like to watch people surreptitiously, I like transacting homosocial relations in the name of political containment.* The homosexual resolves these quandaries of masculinity through his sympathy and agreeableness. The queer spy, knowing he's queer, cannot be manipulated by the usual ploys of masculinity, such as tempting the straight spy with a female agent. Leamas ultimately succumbs to romance; Ashe dallies with picking up women at striptease clubs. He's a superior spy insofar as his sociability masks irony, whereas Leamas's irony masks romance. Ashe's narrative function, quite apart from his function as a gay character within a straight plot, has a ripple effect on the way other characters *act*. Ashe also draws attention to the body and its desires, whereas Leamas suffers for his bodily desires. Leamas contracts a dramatic fever, and his body is punished in any number of ways, such as being clubbed on the head with a revolver (146). Having made himself remote from romance, Leamas is nevertheless not immune to pain. Repudiation of feeling keeps returning as punishment of the body. The novel moves towards the disclosure that no repression of romance is ever vigilant enough. Women invariably betray men, which is how *The Spy Who Came in From the Cold* begins—an agent named Elivira, "tough as nails" (10), betrays Karl as he tries to cross into West

Berlin—and how it ends—Liz betrays Leamas by not hauling herself quickly enough over the Berlin Wall.

*

Blockage: When Leamas and Liz finally have out their respective political differences, when the jig is up for all of them, skeptical Leamas has to tell slow-on-the-uptake Liz, "What do you think spies are: priests, saints and martyrs? They're a squalid procession of vain fools, traitors too, yes; pansies, sadists and drunkards, people who play cowboys and Indians to brighten their rotten lives" (210). Although Ashe might not be the most adroit agent, he nevertheless recruits Leamas successfully, which is not hard, because Leamas wants to be recruited. But Leamas finally acknowledges what readers of spy novels have always suspected, namely, that all spies have a bit of the pansy about them. To succeed, the straight agent ought to be able to blend some homosexuality into his character profile. He ought to be able to flirt on cue with men and women. In short, the straight spy fears he will leak and tries vainly to restrain that fear. This induces a state of aggravated ambivalence in straight male spies. The gay spy knows his homosexuality will leak out; although his queerness might be used against him as, say, a ploy to lure him to an illicit tearoom tryst, he knows that duplicity is harder for him to maintain, and easier. Leamas, by contrast, rehearses his doubleness; he has to keep straight his true allegiances from his feigned allegiances, his romantic inclinations from his political fidelities. In *The Spy Who Came in From the Cold,* as in many spy thrillers, heterosexuality becomes an obstacle to double agency, not an enabler of such agency. Leamas would not die at the end of the novel were he not compelled by residual romantic feeling to help communist Liz scale the Berlin Wall.

*

Joy: In *Minima Moralia,* Theodor Adorno asserts that "Totalitarianism and homosexuality belong together" (46), not, he specifies, as synonyms, but as a dialectic of domination and dominated, a negative dialectic resembling Hegel's master-bondsman tie. Adorno continues: "In its downfall the subject negates everything which is not of its own kind. The opposites of the strong man and the compliant youth merge in an order which asserts unalloyed the male principle of domination" (46). Adorno hints that the dominator has a weakling, buried within, whom he tries to eradicate. In *The Thirty-Nine Steps,* Hannay physically hurts two people: a policeman and a fop named Marmaduke Jopley whose snobbery makes Hannay "sick"

(55). After dining with Jopley, Hannay asks a third man "why nobody kicked [Marmaduke], and was told that Englishmen reverenced the weaker sex" (55). Later Hannay punches Marmaduke because he cannot endure his "imbecile face" (87). By imbecile, he means effeminate, just as Hannay's interlocutor clearly means to call Marmaduke queer by referring to him as "the weaker sex." The joylessness of totalitarianism negates even the joy of sexuality wherever and however it expresses itself. At heart, every he-man appears a sadist (like Leamas vis-à-vis Ashe or Hannay vis-à-vis Marmaduke) but, in fact, every he-man is a masochist repressing knowledge of joy. Adorno equates the tough totalitarian tyrant with masculinity that crushes and merges with passive feminine liberals. The problematic politic of pleasure, however, escapes Adorno's leveling "negative dialectic." In mathematical parlance, masculinity does not equal passivity, and passivity does not equal totalitarianism. Pleasure reconfigures the equation. Adorno's assertion redounds worst of all to heterosexuality, which can see no other way of responding except through crushing and dominating. Beyond such grim, joyless, male totalitarianism, homosexual men appreciate pleasures of the flesh unknown to heterosexual men. In espionage fiction, the male homosexual stands for exuberant leakage, a joy that overarches the dialectic of dominator and dominated.

*

Auden: Homosexuality in espionage signifies bodily pleasure. W. H. Auden in the 1930s frequently likened the poet, as social commentator and sexual outsider, to a secret agent. Although Auden's youthful agent neglects to get "Control of the passes" for the district and does not forestall disaster in the 1928 poem "The Secret Agent," he imagines pleasures interrupted as pleasures nevertheless:

> Control of the passes was, he saw, the key
> To this new district, but who would get it?
> He, the trained spy, had walked into the trap
> For a bogus guide, seduced by the old tricks.
>
> At Greenhearth was a fine site for a dam
> And easy power, had they pushed the rail
> Some stations nearer. They ignored his wires:
> The bridges were unbuilt and trouble coming.

The street music seemed gracious now to one
For weeks up in the desert. Woken by water
Running away in the dark, he often had
Reproached the night for a companion
Dreamed of already. They would shoot, of course,
Parting easily two that were never joined.
(Qtd. in Davenport-Hines 84)

The secret agent in this sonnet imagines intimacy that never gets fulfilled just as his schemes for tapping hydroelectric supplies go unrealized. Although the poem may be about harnessing the powers of the imagination and mind, and not letting floods of emotion seep away unused (Davenport-Hines 85), it is also filled with innuendo about a homosexual encounter. "Passes" have to be controlled. The spy, "seduced by the old tricks," walks into a trap. A touch of paranoia creeps into the poem; "old tricks" entrap him, when perhaps the trained spy thought they would just go away. They menace him with blackmail. Nevertheless, he and a dreamt-of companion will just "shoot" and part. The vocabulary of this poem makes the professional spy a queer spy, one rather smitten by romantic feeling: his companion exists as a figment of a dream.

*

Alone and Bored: Auden's spy has been alone too long in the desert; too long has he been unpartnered. A certain ennui, the ennui of modernism and its manifold mind games, makes the male subject in Auden's poem seek imaginary pleasures in the dark as an escape from his solipsism. Certainly the genre of the spy thriller oscillates between tension and relaxation, between vigilance and boredom, in plot development. Even James Bond has his off hours when he's not hanging from a ledge or shooting enemies. (Bond smokes when he has nothing else to do with his hands.) Boredom, as a readerly sensation, easily translates into boredom as a symptom of character. Secret agents often succumb to boredom. Joseph Conrad in *The Secret Agent* makes Verloc a figure of ennui who craves only the continuance of physical comforts for the rest of his mortal days. Verloc, "constitutionally averse" to "superfluous exertion" and nearly incapable of winking because the "effort" strains him too much (52), lives in a state of inertia. Richard Hannay begins *The Thirty-Nine Steps* in a state of torpor; he yawns as he reads the dailies and finds "the amusements of London

. . . as flat as soda-water that has been standing in the sun" (7). Many of Hannay's associates feel the same way about the *tedium vitae* in the cosmopolis: "'She always said that you would die of boredom because nothing ever happened to you'" (107). In Auden's "The Secret Agent," pleasures remain forbidden and the prohibitions placed on the agent and his pleasures render him nerveless. He lies passively in bed listening to water running. He is alone. He conjectures that his body will never join with his dreamt-of companion. The agent's aspirations to naughty, furtive, nighttime pleasure are cut short by a gunshot. The film noir elements of the poem—running water, gunshot, reproach—mask conflicting elements of desire and violence within the poem. Pleasure, implicitly homosexual in "The Secret Agent," is nipped in the bud. In this regard, Adorno's comments on the cancellation of joy by masculine aggression can be applied to the espionage convention of *slippery* homosexual pleasure. It is not so much that homosexuals exist in novels by le Carré, Buchan, Fleming, Greene, and others; it is, rather, that homosexuals refuse to participate in the masculine orthodoxy of antipleasure that such novels perpetrate. Auden's "The Secret Agent" heralds the emergence of queer pleasure as an attribute of the spy working behind the scenes.[6]

*

Sissies Against Mass Culture: Homosexuality in spy narratives thus provokes a philosophical crisis about violence and pleasure: why does masculine orthodoxy in espionage narratives meet pleasure with violence? Joseph Litvak, in a critique of Adorno, Roland Barthes, and cultural studies generally, argues for a conception of "mass culture *as* violence, as organized, indeed industrialized, intimidation, about which it is all but impossible to write *nicely*" (118). Mass culture bullies its consumers in an ideological sense. Mass culture requires us to follow the news, the latest movies, the hippest fashions. Mass culture does not represent all sexual, ethnic, and racial minorities. Or so the Frankfurt School theory of the "culture industry" goes. To take refuge in high culture—to practice the piano or to study ballet—converts one into a sissy (Adorno, *Prisms* 131). Litvak argues that "the relations between a virile mass culture and an epicene high culture, they [Barthes and Adorno] give us to understand, obey a logic not of simple hierarchical opposition but of complicity, subterfuge, and cross-identification" (132). Litvak helpfully guides us towards a more comprehensive, less uptight idea of culture as crisscrossed with ambiguities that enable multiple allegiances. One can play the piano *and* like action films. More to the point, an understanding of mass culture as aggressive, monstrous, crushing, and virile, versus the implicit understanding of so-called high culture as passive, delicate, enlightening, and feminine, falls apart. And, consequently, the conflict between violence and pleasure can be cast in a different theoretical light. Specifically, the queer pleasure-seeking spy offers a critique of joyless heterosexuality in espionage narratives. Pleasure need not pertain only to those subway commuters who dip happily into their Ian Fleming paperbacks or Len Deighton thrillers. Pleasure, too, might extend to those James Bond characters who, weary of toughing it out with bad guys, can have a martini and snuggle between satin sheets. Homosexual characters crusade on the sly for hedonistic delight within espionage plots.

*

Terrorist: In Frederick Forsyth's 1971 terrorist thriller *The Day of the Jackal,* an urbane, blond man dons a sequence of disguises. He is a middle-aged Danish pastor. He is a muscular American student. He is a French war veteran with one leg and a sweaty, puffy face. He masquerades as a dead person by acquiring a passport for Alexander James Quentin Duggan, an infant who died, aged two, in 1931. He is a businessman. He is an arms dealer. He is a cipher called the Jackal. A group of embittered Frenchmen hire the Jackal to assassinate Charles de Gaulle in 1963. Aside from that, no verifiable information sticks to him. He lives in London, but as it turns out in the last pages of the novel, even his British nationality is doubtful. He borrows names as indiscriminately as he buys clothes. He likes to eat fine food and he spends a great deal of time shopping, mostly for disguises, forged papers, and a gun. Although the French agent who pursues him calls him "'a bit of a psychologist'" (328), the narrative style forbids any interior glimpses of the Jackal's character through indirect discourse, or even telltale verbs such as "he *envied,*" or "he *felt,*" or "he *preferred.*" Such verbs, forbidden to the Jackal, might disclose something approaching a personality. He resists interpretation. He resists realism. He has no family, no hobbies, no apparent emotion. His eyes have "no expression at all" (40). He incarnates the death drive, as do many fictional terrorists and double agents.

*

Phallus: Like most spy thrillers, *The Day of the Jackal* has a fondness for the representation of virility and violent attacks on virility. The terrorist kills a forger by crushing his testicles then breaking his neck; just before he dies, the forger thinks "his private parts had been hit by an express train" (116). A special tactics policeman suffers a "torn groin" (139) while arresting a goon named Viktor. Tortured in an underground chamber, Viktor has electrified serrated copper clamps attached to his nipples and penis (148). Even a honeydew melon, used as a surrogate head for target practice, hangs "like a weary scrotum" (128) from a shopping bag after being shot to pieces. Phallic authority is constantly mangled or disabled. Given that the Jackal lives self-sufficiently, it comes as something of a surprise that he stops long enough to seduce Madame la Baronne de la Chalonnière, a lonely country wife whose husband chases teenaged women in Paris. After a good meal at an inn, the Jackal escorts the baroness to her room. When they embrace in the doorway, the "rigid arrogance of his prick" presses against her thigh (271). And, with the mathematical precision that the narrator maintains in all matters of plot and temporality in *The Day of the Jackal,* the baroness muses that the Englishman is "hard but skilled [in sexual matters], knowing how to use fingers and tongue and prick to bring her on *five* times and himself *three*" in the course of one evening (273; italics added to demonstrate that pleasure is mathematically exact and that the Jackal places the pleasure of others above his own —he withholds pleasure from himself). The episode is a departure within the narrative: so far the Jackal has operated singly, without any hint of engaged feeling. He seems always ready to commit murder and seldom ready to have sex. Lacking interiority, his sexuality has no more meaning than a cartoon character's does. In terms of character enhancement, the night of love confirms the heterosexuality of the Jackal for whatever it's worth. This heterosexual interlude reiterates that the fruits of a well-engineered plan are passing pleasures. In such a masculinist or virilizing narrative paradigm, in which constant anxiety about castration seems paramount (crushed testicles, a weary scrotum, and so on), pleasure assumes the form of ornament or bonus, but it is not integral to the conspiratorial plan itself. By contrast, in the homosexual plot, pleasure springs from conspiracy and espionage. In Auden's poem "The Secret Agent," it may be the erotic thrill of being trapped by bogus guides and lured by old tricks that induces the trained spy to go about his business. The possibility of being found out—his paranoia—makes him think about illicit encounters. The secret agent delights in the possibilities of pleasure not as by-product to conspiracy but as the reason for conspiracy in the first instance. For this reason, homosexual men are accused, wrongly, of being security leaks, when, in truth, heterosexual men are, almost invariably, the culprits who turn over information to mistresses and traitors too readily.

*

Gadgets: Even when phallic authority in spy narratives is mutilated or disabled, gadgets replace it: guns, aerials, telephones, filing systems, cameras. Technology disperses masculine authority by extending it through space and time. In *The Day of the Jackal,* this power to manipulate or trace others through the mastery of technology disadvantages the Jackal, who fundamentally relies on his own strength, his own cunning, and his own body as a machine to get him through scrapes. The lineage of this tradition extends back to thrillers such as *The Thirty-Nine Steps,* in which Hannay has to battle airplanes and automobiles with nothing more than his ingenuity and some clever switches in disguise. In *The Day of the Jackal,* the fragility of the single outsider is set against a vast array of technological weaponry: "From the seemingly tangled web of aerials on the roof of the building the high-frequency signal beamed out across three continents, streaming high beyond the stratosphere to bounce off the ionic layer above and home back to earth thousands of miles away to another stick of aluminum jutting from a tiled rooftop" (202). If this highfalutin description of a phone call transmitted by satellite seems far-fetched, it nevertheless proves that technology works, for the investigation team traces each and every one of the Jackal's moves. Smart investigators outwit the Jackal's ingenuity. He abandons disguises before he fully exploits them because they have been found out through tracking procedures. Technology facilitates global surveillance. The isolated terrorist has no place to hide. Whereas the terrorist has complete freedom to act without interference from his employers, he has no choice but to follow through with his plot once he sets it in motion. Viktor Kowlaski, trained killer, puts it as the paradox of character and inevitability: "if his life had been different, he would have worked in an airport. But he was what he was, and there was no going back now" (135). His character has manifested itself in a set number of ways. He cannot alter character and therefore cannot alter circumstances. He is a killer; therefore he must kill. The technological apparatus that graces so many spy narratives addresses this problem of inevitability, for technology, whether a transatlantic phone call, or a card-based filing system that documents every visitor entering France, or a wiretap that catches an information leak, merely enables the capture of criminals.

*

Precision: For this reason, the simulacrum of many spy novels is a gun. It stands in for all other gadgets. (Imagine a spy thriller in which a gun does not appear. In *The Untouchable,* even thoughtful Victor owns a "six-round, .455 Webley Mark VI Service revolver, eleven and a quarter inches long, thirty-eight ounces, UK manufacture" [185], which he paws out of a drawer after long disuse in order to threaten Nick.) The gun embodies potential violence. It figures the perverse imbalance between machine and emotion since the gun, as a technology, destroys. Paradoxically, guns also express, as instruments devised to perform specific tasks, the harmfulness of precise reasoning. Descriptive details get lavished on guns: make, heft, size. In *The Day of the Jackal,* paragraphs are devoted to the "knurled end of the bolt," the "gleaming tray into which the bullet would lie" (104), the breech, the struts, the case, the scope, the weight, the material, the caliber of the assassin's gun. This precision of detail tells the reader that gun components fit together perfectly the way the elements of the plot do. Both gun and plot are created along rational principles. In *The Day of the Jackal,* precision and reasonableness get recorded in barrages of numbers, including precise records of time and date: "It was 8:17 p.m." (8); "On August 22, 1962, dusk fell at 8:10" (8); "Those twenty-five minutes were to change the history of France" (8). Numbers are meant to reassure the reader that all time has been accounted for. No moments have been lost. To indicate that time and numbers control the plot, the narrator resorts to formulaic statements of coincidence: "At the same moment" as the Jackal finishes lunch in London, "a black DS 19 sedan swung out of the gates of the Interior Ministry of France into the Place Beauvau" in Paris (159). Vice versa, "As [conspirator Marc Rodin] boarded his train [in Paris], a BOAC Comet 4B drifted down the flight path towards runway Zero-Four at London Airport" (25). An interview concludes in London as "the Jackal landed at Brussels National just after 12" (207). Everyone, everywhere belongs in a matrix of time, locomotion, date, numbers. All the world is rational and mathematically precise. The effect of crosscutting between time zones is cinematic. In a novel, crosscutting powerfully iterates the ability of the narrator to follow a grid of place and time, to move pins about on a map as it were, without losing track of any detail. Everything—weapons, characters, leaks, loose ends—must be accounted for. Otherwise, something irrational might tip the plot.

*

The Trouble with Heterosexuals: In *The Day of the Jackal,* a silly colonel allows himself to be seduced by a young woman named Jacqueline Dumas. After every security briefing, Colonel Raoul Saint-Clair de Villauban runs to his mistress and tells her everything. Initially he divulges information as Jacqueline performs fellatio on him (190). The second time, Jacqueline coaxes "a belated orgasm" (250) from the colonel almost as a reward for another tip-off. The third time, Jacqueline massages the colonel's neck while he lies facedown in bed and gives her updated news. The fourth time—not surprisingly, the security breach has come to the attention of the investigating team—Jacqueline cradles the colonel's head in her cleavage as he discloses the latest intelligence (301). The leak is finally exposed through a wiretap. The mouthy idiotic colonel resigns (324). The coincidence of sexual exchange and information exchange confirms heterosexual vulnerability, at least for the colonel. He mistakes sex for fidelity. *(Why does he insist that sex include or exact fidelity?)* He also obliges with information while engaged in four different sexual, or sexualized, maneuvers, which suggests that variety in carnal congress merits the reward of information. *(What queer character would make such a mistake?)* The colonel is almost Pavlovian in his premature disclosure of intelligence: as soon as Jacqueline touches him, he spills his guts. The colonel foolishly thinks intimacies of the boudoir are beyond politics. Such vulnerabilities expose the sentimentality of the heterosexual paradigm, specifically, that the colonel interprets women as apolitical. He mistakes sex as an expression of love—he "felt a complacent thrill of satisfaction that she was his, and so deeply in love with him" (188)—which Jacqueline takes pains to make him believe.

*

Profumo: Had the colonel paid more attention to the news (*The Day of the Jackal* is set in the summer of 1963), he would have known about the Profumo Affair in England, which broke in late 1962 and made headlines throughout the following year. British Secretary of State for War John Profumo slept with prostitute Christine Keeler, who also slept with the Soviet assistant naval attaché, Yevgeny Ivanov. (Shades of *No Way Out.*) Allegations that information was transacted across, or through, the body of the prostitute flew about the House of Parliament and eventually contributed to Prime Minister Harold Macmillan's resignation in November 1963. Such leaks of security play off fears that women may in fact be politically dangerous, no matter what profession or social position they occupy. By Cold War logic of security, therefore, the only way to prevent a leak is not to have sex at all. Or at least men should not have sex with women, if Cold War suspicions of heterosexual duplicities extend far enough. When, for example, General Jack D. Ripper hysterically worries about "precious bodily fluids" in *Dr. Strangelove,* he inadvertently parodies Cold War confusion of metaphor (information leak) with literal event (orgasm). The colonel in *The Day of the Jackal* leaks freely and without forethought. The Jackal leaks premeditatedly. In his representation of undisciplined leakage, Forsyth represents the limitations of heterosexual paradigms that were often foisted off onto homosexuals who, theoretically if not appreciably, posed security risks to espionage.

*

Les très riches heures et les sales pédés: Towards the end of *The Day of the Jackal,* the terrorist who gives his name to the novel discards his various disguises because they have been sussed out by security forces. Sitting in the Place de l'Odéon in Paris, the Jackal sees two gay men walk by. He immediately dashes off to make "a few purchases" in a women's beauty shop (328), including some lipstick, powder, and mascara. That evening he masquerades as a gay American and cruises a gay bar. He passes as gay in order to elude the police, though an observant barman has doubts about the Jackal's intentions and orientation. The question of queer identity hinges here on something beyond language and character and concentrates instead on performance and action. Since the terrorist scarcely speaks in the novel, since his real name never gets revealed (Charles Calthorp, the one name that seems to belong to him, turns out to be a red herring), since he exists as a sequence of actions rather than a sequence of conversations, he cannot be defined as an innately sexed character. His *très riches heures* with the baroness at her château allow him to hide for a few days; she is expedient, not integral, to his plan. The Jackal's willingness to pass as gay has partly to do with the 1971 publication of the novel and the cultural availability of gay liberation narratives to mainstream novelists. As a representation, passing-as-queer addresses the problem of how sexual identity may or may not be relevant to political categories. This refutes, of course, the Cold War insistence that queers automatically jeopardized security. Instead of conflating sexual identity and political identity, as Adorno and le Carré do, Forsyth presents the option that they are distinct categories. This distinction flies in the face of post-Stonewall activism that constantly politicized the sexual. Robert J. Corber argues that gay writers in the 1950s, such as Gore Vidal, Tennessee Williams, and Richard Baldwin, "helped to undermine the Cold War consensus [of making homosexuals take to the closet through persecution] by politicizing domains of experience even left-wing intellectuals tended to assume were apolitical" (192). This is true. The visibility of queers in public life—Vidal ran for Congress, lost, and thereafter declined to run for Senate on the grounds that he doesn't "like the people" (Vidal 351)—may have prepared the way for 1960s activism. But the question of queers within mass-market espionage thrillers is vexed through this period by the essential conservatism of the form: of individual men duking it out with shadowy enemies; of independent initiative being espoused in conjunction with an "ask-not-what-your-country-can-do-for-you" platform. The alternatives for representing homosexuality within espionage fiction alter between the 1950s and the 1970s towards a cautious acknowledgment of sexual otherness. Homosexuality becomes imaginable within Cold War spy plots. In *The Day of the Jackal,* the willingness of the straight man to pass as gay in order to proceed with his plot suggests that queer identities need not constellate exclusively around sexual practices. Having found an older, "artistic" man named Jules Bernard to go home with, the Jackal applies some of his newly acquired lipstick and mascara. On the way to Bernard's flat, the police pull them over but let them go. The policeman recoils "with an expression of revulsion" and mutters *"Sales pédés"* (filthy faggots) (335) through the window of Bernard's car. At another stop, the Jackal "giggle[s] seductively" (335) at a cop. Disguised as a "raving" fairy (336), the Jackal slips past the police. The Jackal refuses to have sex with Bernard and sleeps on his sofa. Although the mechanics of straight sex are set forth routinely in *The Day of the Jackal* (throbbing pricks, multiple orgasms), Forsyth draws the line at representing homosexual intercourse. The terrorist will not sleep with a man. The episode, however, opens up the possibility of representing sexuality as performative on the one hand, and largely irrelevant to political exigency on the other hand.

*

To Be, to Do, to Act: By positioning itself alongside other narratives of intrigue, *The Untouchable* invites the question of whether to read queerness
as a form of action or being. Queer spies and go-betweens pop up casually
in le Carré's, Forsyth's, and Fleming's novels. Yet not all fags in these narratives are authentic. More alarmingly, as the espionage genre evolves,
ostensibly straight characters like the Jackal behave like conspicuously
gay characters. A straight character in le Carré's *A Perfect Spy* speaks with
"faggy indignation" (29) when he needs to. Queerness for straight agents
is, apparently, an expedient, not an essential identity. Ditto, then, for gay
spies. They can perform their homosexuality every bit as well as straight
guys can. Being queer has social utility, especially in the chummy boys'-
school environment of British espionage. Although queer theory furnishes
an interpretation of homosociality constructed at the expense of homosexuality—the secret that cannot be named and which therefore yields to
muted homosocial relations rather than avowed homosexual acts—homosexuality, rather than being repressed, offers a convenient channel for
homosociality as well as the duplicities of secret agents. The queer spy
has the benefit of being always already double. He conforms and rebels;
he bears secrets and acts clean-cut; he pays his taxes and commits crimes.
Maskell connects aspects of espionage to queerness in *The Untouchable:*
"When I began to go in search of men it was all already familiar to me:
the covert, speculative glance, the underhand sign, the blank exchange of
passwords, the hurried, hot unburdening—all, all familiar. Even the territory was the same, the public lavatories, the grim, suburban pubs, the
garbage-strewn back-alleyways, and, in summer, the city's dreamy, tenderly
green, innocent parks, whose clement air I sullied with my secret whisper-
ings" (287). Maskell recognizes how to behave as a gay man because he
knows similar routines from his spy duties. He acts out his espionage activities as he acts out his queerness. Both require the performance of deeds,
since identity and action do not inevitably reinforce each other. Although
the narrative suggests that spying produces homosexuality (Victor serves
as an agent *before* he sleeps with men), the hypothesis that he is gay because he spies is not tenable. Banville's representation of Maskell deconstructs the standard representation of gay spies by suggesting that no inevitable link between spying and homosexuality exists.

*

Thriller: Although many of Banville's novels concern authenticity and enigmas, *The Untouchable* is expressly concerned with authenticity and enigmas as effects of espionage. Indeed, this is Banville's most busy novel in terms of the number of incidents. Maskell travels to France, to Ireland, to Moscow, to Bavaria, and elsewhere. Banville confesses that moving characters from place to place in *The Untouchable*—"'chaps doing things'" (Foran 21), he calls it—proved a greater challenge than did his other novels. He prefers to stay inside the heads of characters, rather than document their gadding about. Notwithstanding this expenditure of energy by Victor, *The Untouchable* suggests that thinking and feeling are modes of action as important as movement. Imagining himself in a spy adventure, Maskell explicitly recalls Henty and Buchan as prototypes (116, 286, 329). Graham Greene appears, thinly disguised, as Querell, a bulgy-eyed, buglike busybody, who writes, according to Victor, "bleak little novels" (317) and "overrated Balkan thrillers" (77). The placement of a gay spy as spokesman and narrator distinguishes *The Untouchable* from the tradition of spy novels to which it alludes. The way that Maskell thinks and feels, as queer intellectual agent, inverts expectations of action.

*

Action: Greene's, Buchan's, Henty's, and le Carré's heroes run, dodge, escape, hide, leap, flee. *The Untouchable,* in telling contrast, represents Maskell as brainy and sedentary. The closest he comes to action in the thriller mode is a slippered pursuit of Nick. Following Leninist principles, Maskell views thinking as necessary action. Intellectuals are indispensable to revolution because they articulate oppression, bring enlightenment to the masses, and limn the future. "'We must act, or perish'" (57), says Maskell, nearly quoting Auden's famous dictum from the poem "September 1, 1939": "We must love one another or die" (Auden 88). Auden and Maskell both utter stark imperatives modeled on the doctrinaire temper of the 1930s. The difference between acting and loving is instructive. Retrospectively, Maskell mocks his inflated rhetoric: "That is, I'm afraid, the way we talked" (57). Nick mocks it, too, by retaliating that words are actions for Victor. His verbal bravado hides fear. His rhetoric is part of his dramatic role. But as a role, his language establishes a base from which to act. Regardless of what motivates an action—fear, patriotism, treachery, despair—the action breeds changes and consequences. If all identity is performative, in the sense that actions modify character, then only the sum of actions counts in the making of identity. Hence, acting politically is always acting theatrically, as we have seen in the cases of both Razumov and Leamas.

*

Recruit: Victor takes the question of acting seriously. For him, slow, steady corruption works more effectively than physical heroics: "For an Englishman to rush out and get his head shot off in some arroyo in Seville or wherever seemed to me merely an extreme form of rhetoric, excessive, wasteful, futile. The man of action would despise me for such sentiments . . . but I have a different definition of what constitutes effective action" (97). His methods of recruitment, as his relation to scribal Miss Vandeleur indicates, are one-on-one. Ostensibly to write his life into history, Serena Vandeleur interviews Maskell. Like many of Banville's novels, the narrative posits a single auditor who listens and responds. Persuasion as a political effect happens at the level of the lone individual. To talk Miss Vandeleur into liking him, to find out her secret passions and to manipulate them, to wear her down with sophistries, and to convince her of his authenticity seem more important to Victor than converting large numbers of people to communism. She moves from being the interrogator in their encounters to being the subject of his questions and the object of his actions. She probably plays a role. Maskell suspects that Skryne has sent Serena Vandeleur as a surrogate. She stands in for the reader in the novel: recruited to Maskell's side, willing to listen to his story, she becomes his student (he is a pedagogue by profession) rather than his biographer. Action is negotiation of parts through talking. Action is recruitment of one person at a time. Action is acting.

*

Fear: The division between being and doing is absolute for Maskell: "We are what we are, we do what we do" (194). The twain need not meet. Despite this separation of character from action, fear (in itself not a deed but a state of being) motivates most of Maskell's actions. He fears being caught (6). He fears the telephone (7). He fears death (62). Futilely he decries fear as "banal" (73). He recognizes his brother Freddie's fear of outdoors (64–65). In Moscow, he recognizes Russians' "dull fear" (113). He sees his daughter Blanche's mouselike panic and frightened feints (229). Blanche incarnates his own unspoken fears. Fear has multiple manifestations.

Himself, he feels a "hot qualm of fear" spread up from his spine at the Kremlin (117). A "hectic, happy fear" (152) at the end of the war exhilarates him. He acknowledges the aphrodisiac qualities of fear (289, 321). Retreating from Boulogne under heavy German bombardment, he feels "the tuning fork of terror" ringing within him (199). He claims to have taken on fear, to have assumed and subdued it (200). Yet fear rattles him. Acting unafraid is a pretense. His adherence to Stoical principles causes him to stylize grief into images—facing the ocean as shells fall around him, facing his various Russian operators and pretending they are innocuous, facing the Blitz and plunging into torrid carnality with Danny Perkins as an assertion of life over fear. To act (in the sense of to do) is to act unafraid (in the sense of to pretend). Fear establishes a threshold for Victor's actions, as it does for other adventure heroes. Whereas Richard Hannay or Razumov or Leamas canalize their fear into derring-do, Victor canalizes his fear into thought. Fear however inhibits knowledge. Victor, betrayed, wonders how anyone knows anything at all. In this sense, *The Untouchable* moves towards an exposure of the factors that prevent knowledge, whereas most spy plots move towards the revelation of subterfuge or intrigue. Having aestheticized his fear into images, and having compounded his remoteness from action through language, Maskell actually exacerbates obstacles to knowledge. To act is to be. To be is to fear. To fear is to act.

*

Zither: Playing his spy role, unable to take any conviction seriously, Maskell sees his commitment to communism as a part in a play. He repeatedly refers to "music hall" theatricality (7, 190), "burlesque" (328), or "play-acting" (286) as analogies for espionage. These references all promote comic, not tragic, views of behavior. Somewhere within himself, he is never fully engaged by what he's doing, which may be a stimulus or a consequence of his intellectual pursuits. He claims to be "modesty itself" (308) and knows that he is not. His star-turn as aging memoirist has a Beckettian slapstick quality about it. (The novel is immensely funny, not least because of Maskell's plummy language.) Indeed, he thinks himself a "character in a Feydeau comedy" (193). Though Maskell has the mind of a high-toned intellectual, he has a heart of pure kitsch. He lives by conventions of cinema and farce. He lives by representations of things, not things in themselves. During a rendezvous with one of his Russian operators, Maskell suavely refers to the famous zither music in the film version of *The Third Man:* "Dear me; I could almost hear the twang of a phantom zither" (133). Graham Greene scripts his response. On other occasions, he allegorizes Russians at the Kremlin according to the way they look— as "Heidegger" and "Leathercoat" (117–19). Extending his ironic perception of identity to others, he views people as functions or costumes. He calls Miss Vandeleur "Miss Twinset" (9). He sees himself in a cowboy script as "Wild Bill Maskell" (186). For him the whole world has an animistic quality, as if he were living in a cartoon. He envisages—imagination takes precedent over reality—a German prince as a medieval warrior with "chainmail and lance and flashing tarnhelm" (301). Victor never sees anything as just itself, but as a prior representation. He is, after all, an academic. Vampire-like, allegory drains characters of life. As an expert in painting, Maskell tends to view gestures and emotions as overimbued with meaning but fundamentally static.

*

Gestures: In *Under Western Eyes*, Razumov accuses himself by wordlessly stabbing his finger in his chest. In *The Thirty-Nine Steps*, Hannay observes his disguised enemy tap his fingers on his thigh. In *The Spy Who Came in From the Cold*, Karl hunches over his bicycle handlebars, and Leamas, in a complex gesture, leans down to help Liz over the wall. In *Democracy*, Inez dances in a film loop. The gestural body in spy fiction incarnates guilt or attempts to free oneself from guilt. Inez, for instance, wishes to dance away from the red tape of Washington politics. *The Untouchable* augments the gestural repertoire of spy fiction by concentrating on one repeated gesture: a hand touching a hand or an arm. Heidegger squeezes Maskell's arm to admonish and restrain him (122). Iosif clutches Victor's arm with an "iron grip" (138). Hartmann insinuates his arm through Victor's to betoken jaunty camaraderie (145). Blanche links her arm through her father's as a gesture of daughterly love, a gesture that Victor repudiates "stiffly" (232). Danny, upon seeing Victor after a long hiatus, doesn't know whether to embrace him or shake his hand, so he settles for punching Victor on the shoulder (333). Victor fumbles with Baby's hand and longs to suck her fingernails (80). These gestures emphasize theatricality. Victor understands them as inauthentic. As a spy, "you can never stop acting, not for an instant, even when you are alone, in a locked room" (337). You develop a set of gestures and composed facial expressions that hide your real feelings. Some hand gestures in the novel are studies in leave-taking, as when Victor caresses Freddie's hand (217), or Wilson waves goodbye (220), or Boy "wistfully" waves farewell (332). No one knows how to touch Victor. He emits an aura of *noli me tangere*. He and Baby first kiss "awkwardly, like a pair of shop-window mannequins come jerkily alive" (83). And when he makes a pass at her in the taxi, he clinically dissociates her from her body parts. "I touched a breast" (84), he says, not *her* breast. When he attempts to kiss Hettie, he does so "awkwardly" again (215), and she, in consequence, turns away from him. The title of the novel concerns gesture. It ambiguously refers to Maskell's physical awkwardness and his status within the sancta of British culture and politics. Untouchable, Victor is beyond emotion (he cannot be moved), beyond displacement (he cannot be toppled from his institutional prestige and royal patronage), beyond reach (he refuses handshakes and embraces or executes them awkwardly), beyond criticism (his scholarly work is unimpeachable). The title also means, as the designation of a Hindu caste, that Victor in his downfall is unclean and defiling. He lives at both the top and the bottom of the social heap. Nevertheless, when he says, "I do not care to be touched" (354), he lies. His life is one long periplus away from and back towards the day in 1929 when Nick, at their first meeting, takes Victor by the elbow: "after half a century I can still feel that grip, light but firm, with the hint of a tremor in it" (12). Victor assumes Nick trembles with excitement. Victor ever after longs for Nick's touch. The gesture becomes the quintessence of their relationship: Nick guiding Victor lightly but firmly. As when, at the conclusion of *Paradise Lost*, Milton reverses the iconographic tradition of having Michael drive Adam and Eve from Eden (martially) and shows them, instead, hand-in-hand with the divine force that leads them (cordially) from paradise, the gesture of a hand on an elbow or a hand linked through an arm in *The Untouchable* suggests the indissolubility of bonds. As in painting, gestures in novels are an index of feeling. The first brush of Nick's hand on Victor's elbow is the grasp of the loved one whom Victor never conquers and never relinquishes. Nick, in the end, is the untouchable.

*

Sensations: The theatricality of *The Untouchable* inhibits self-knowledge. So does art. Although spy narratives concern conditions of *not knowing*—who controls whom, who outwits whom, who possesses all the material and immaterial facts of a case—*The Untouchable* raises this epistemological dilemma under the rubric of sensation. Victor relies on sensation as a guide to authenticity. He thinks bodily reactions cannot lie. When he feels strongly, his scalp prickles. His palms sweat. Ice cubes of intuitive foreboding drop to the pit of his stomach (176). He records sensations with superstitious reverence. He shivers at learning of his father's death (127), and shivers again upon returning home after the evacuation from Boulogne (202). He feels a "welter of sensations" upon Hettie's arrival at his father's bishopric (17). He has a peculiar "fluttery feeling in the region of the diaphragm and a sort of racing sensation all over" when publicly humiliated (6, 8). Sensation reminds him he's alive. When he first sees *The Death of Seneca,* he gets light-headed: "a hot something began swelling outward from a point in the centre of my breast" (40). Victor indulges sensations as if unbidden bodily reactions are different, in essence, than gestures. Yet bodily sensations are no more genuine than reason. His Poussin turns out to be, probably, a fake, no matter what light-headedness it induces in him. The painting, he conjectures, was planted at the back of Alighieri's gallery so that he might discover it. He willingly believes in the authenticity of the painting when he has forbidden himself to believe in any other kind of authenticity. The novel thus raises the aesthetic issue of whether emotion elicited by an inauthentic object is itself inauthentic. The answer is no. The emotion still occurs. Only reason shames us into thinking that emotion is value-laden.

∗

Two Muses: The novel stages a contest between rationality and sensation as two routes to knowledge. Although Victor claims that his adherence to Stoicism has caused him to sacrifice feeling (44), he has also outsmarted himself. Reason is a treacherous muse. Like Seneca, Zeno, Marcus Aurelius, and other Stoics, Victor thinks that happiness lies in freeing oneself from passions. Art therefore embodies what he does not allow himself to feel. Strangely, his irony does not extend to art, stylized, gestural, and classically composed though the Poussin paintings he specializes in may be. The sensations that art provokes in him—painting, like sex, makes him feel "tottery" (117)—exaggerate Victor's distance from himself. If he cannot be authentic, at least his Poussin can be. But the subject of the painting complicates this paradigm. The scene depicts Seneca in his death throes. Seneca's death means little in the Stoical scheme of things. Stoics believe the soul gets reintegrated into the universe but does not live on. The Stoical ideal, wrought as art in the spurious Poussin painting, has been a compromise.

In sum, Victor may be a hedonist masquerading as an Epicurean. Certainly at the end of his life as he narrates his many treasons, reliving the "peculiar thrill" of "vertiginous glee" that rushes upon him when parachuting for the first time (76), or feeling again the "secret flurry of speculative activity" prior to recruiting a candidate for espionage (102), sensation becomes a barrier between himself and death. Victor's uncertain memory complicates the probability that such emotion ever existed in the first place. Time might graft emotions onto the past. Nevertheless, to feel the thrill of recruiting someone or to feel humiliation is, at least, to remain capable of sensation. The thrill, for Victor, becomes a formal event emptied of content. He is interested in the mechanism of betrayal, its functionality. For this reason, Maskell spies for Russia, not because he believes Stalinist Russia is morally or politically superior, but because the formalities of treachery beguile him. Form matters, not content. Similarly, sensation in art is formal, encoded as gesture or stance. The Stoic, to free himself from passion, has to have some passions left, and Victor's passion is the sensation incarnated in art. In one glamorous final gesture of death, Victor imagines himself ascending in "a transport of erotic agony" headfirst into "a patch of pellucid *bleu céleste*" (6). More like Bergotte's death while staring at a patch of yellow than like Dorian Gray's fairytale death while stabbing his own image, Victor wishes to be transfigured into art, to be absorbed into the very mysteries of painting that he has parsed in his scholarly articles and monographs. He expects his death to include *son et lumière*. He expects feeling. Sensation is a treacherous muse.

*

Higher Maths: Intellectuals in Banville's novels often suffer from delusions about the relation of feeling to reason. Emblems of cogitation, mathematicians figure in Banville's scientific tetralogy: *Kepler, Doctor Copernicus, The Newton Letter,* and *Mefisto.* Mathematics affects the structure of Banville's narratives in the minute attention paid to time and sequence, as if rationality in organization keeps disorderly emotion at bay (Imhof 6). Whereas Victor in *The Untouchable* thinks in terms of images and remembers events as portraits or allegories, Banville's math-minded characters feel and remember in numbers. *"Mathematics speaks the world,"* proclaims math wizard Alistair in *The Untouchable* (190). Maskell regrets not becoming a mathematician, despite early promise in that field. The math prodigy in *Mefisto,* who learns to count before he learns to talk, "cannot see a one and a zero juxtaposed without feeling deep within me the vibration of a dark, answering note" of the mystery of entities (18). In *Kepler,* Kepler believes in "'five regular perfect solids, also called the Platonic forms'" that comprise a universal "geometry" (35). This belief regulates the five-part structure of the novel. Kepler mistakes geometry for reality. The world is not organized around five perfect shapes. Geometry—like numbers, like memory—is not true just because one believes in it. As with Victor in *The Untouchable,* many of Banville's male characters extol falsehoods and live them as truths. In *Athena,* an art heist leads a deluded art expert on an "intricate dance of desire and deceit" (219), in which everything turns out to be a lie, including the art expert's love affair, the identity of his aunt, his connoisseurship of art, and the forged paintings that he authenticates. Even in *The Book of Evidence* and its sequel *Ghosts,* where disillusionment with mathematics as a way of knowing causes a "turning to art" (Jackson, "Science" 517), specifically painting, numbers return as a modality of thought. The narrator of *Ghosts* breezily declares about physics and world formation, "it's only numbers, I know, only a cunning wheeze got up to accommodate the infinities and make the equations come out" (173). In all of these novels, feeling splits off from thinking. Numbers stand in for emotions. And, consequently, most of these narrators suffer from the ghostly return of repressed memories. Fifty-year-old Alex Cleave in *Eclipse,* playing out in his imagination the many stage roles he undertook in his acting career, feels "memories crowd in on me, irresistibly, threatening to overwhelm my thoughts entirely" (55).

*

Fakery: Cousin to these protagonists, Maskell, as narrator, is duped by his affections, scholarly aridness, and memory. *The Untouchable* is told not as a fast-paced adventure, but as a memoir. As a memoir, the narrative doubles back on chronology, blurs self-justification with treachery, withholds crucial information. Betrayed by friends and associates, Maskell has to adjust his recollections to falseness in actions and behaviors. His daughter is probably not his own progeny. Nick Brevoort, for whom Victor holds a secret lifelong passion, has strung him along for years. His accredited Poussin is probably a fake. Nothing is as it seems. Motive complicates behavior. Actions undertaken under false pretenses, which Maskell himself doesn't understand are untrue, leave him with a memory woven from lies. What he remembers is not the right version of events. For instance, he thinks he knows more than Nick about espionage, but Nick, in the end, holding the upper hand, has secretly masterminded Victor's comings and goings. The scholar who prides himself on *knowing* turns out not to know all the crucial pieces of information, even about his own activities. He has scarcely understood himself. Seen in this light, Maskell's homosexuality becomes a ruse, not in the sense that he withholds it, but in the sense that it does not explain his personality or actions. Like Anthony Blunt, fictional Maskell is a mystery to everyone else because he is a mystery to himself. Maskell's sexuality, like James Bond's or Alec Leamas's, is an improvised performance. Heterosexuality and homosexuality have more in common than one thinks. Father, husband, queer lover, art expert, royalist, spy—Maskell embodies each identity "authentically." He differs from Leamas, Hannay, Bond, and other spies in that he lives "authentically in each of his multiple lives" (174), whereas they live disingenuously in each of their roles by donning multiple disguises and names. Maskell mocks his Russian handler's attempts to foist on him the "'ridiculous code name'" John (138). He refuses to be divided into several identities. Or he allows his various selves to coexist, authentic and inauthentic jostling for place. Despite this complex commingling of selves, myriad-minded Maskell compartmentalizes activities. His British royalist beliefs do not undo his Russian communist allegiances. Maskell, like his prototype Blunt, obtains satisfaction "from escorting the president of France around the queen's pictures at Buckingham Palace, knowing that at six o'clock he had a rendezvous with his Russian controller and could then go on to a homosexual encounter with a guardsman" (Costello 28). To live a life in parts requires adroitness at seeing each part as a function within an equation. "All that I am is all of a piece: all of a piece, and yet broken up into a myriad selves," Victor says (34). He himself does not know whether his homosexuality and his espionage have anything to do with each other. Just as others have betrayed him, he may betray himself. In a principle that articulates Maskell's duplicity in all domains, a principle that recalls the fundamental tenet of spy fiction that everything, as a code, stands for something else, he says, *"everything was itself and at the same time something else"* (45). Maskell forgets this principle, even though he announces a variant of it in light of his espionage activities: "nothing, absolutely nothing, is as it seems" (131). He remembers untruths that he experienced as truths because he loses sight of the algebraic rule of substitution.

*

Panels: In any case, seventy-two-year-old Maskell lives mostly in his mind rather than in the world. In this regard, he resembles protagonists in Banville's other novels, almost all of whom are men with a scholarly bent. Scholarliness, it might be said, interferes with their appreciation of reality by making them overemphasize one theory or one way of knowing the world. As an art historian, Maskell often sees the world as static visual fields rather than dynamic interactive events. When Boy tells Victor to "'look at that,'" Victor takes in a coffee machine, the head of a girl laughing into her hand, a window framing a seascape—and misses entirely a newspaper headline announcing the Hitler-Stalin pact (150). Victor notices unimportant details or uses allusions to art to abstract himself from difficult situations. His erudition betrays him into a false connection with the world. Maskell's devotion to art is mirrored in the structure of *The Untouchable.* Like a slide show or promenade through a gallery, the novel begins with *The Betrayal in the Garden* (9) and ends with *The Agony in the Garden* (361). A triptych, the novel displays symmetry and restraint. Parts 1 and 3 each have approximately 92 pages subdivided into 4 sections; part 2, the significant central panel with double the proportions, has eight sections (4×2) totaling 184 pages (92×2). (Banville revels in this kind of mathematical planning as, apparently, does first-person narrator Maskell.) The painting *The Death of Seneca* dominates part 2. Betrayal and Agony flank Death in the triptych to create dramatic continuity that is, notwithstanding, static.

*

A Little Window: This habit of mind, of seeing everything as a static image, creeps over Victor at moments of crisis. Furthermore, he draws upon the visual convention of the window within a painting as a means of depicting his own desire to have an escape hatch from any crisis. Art is a window; and within that window, other planes open upon other zones of feeling or being. In *The Death of Seneca,* "the placid view of distant hills and forest framed in the window above the philosopher's couch" (181) opens onto stillness, the Stoical equilibrium that Victor constantly seeks. The window in the painting thus connects current agitation with promised calm. That calm, associated with the suicide of Seneca, is the factitious calm of death. That calm, associated with communist Russia, is the factitious calm of utopia. That calm, associated with Nick, first seen asleep in the garden in a hammock, is the factitious calm of affirmed homosexuality. The window is a portal of transfiguration, a threshold to another kind of existence. Patrick Quilly, Victor's "quondam catamite" (279), falls or jumps from the French window of their apartment. The windows in *The Untouchable* give upon an external world (as opposed to, say, Lily Briscoe's painting in *To The Lighthouse* of Mrs. Ramsay framed by a window). Visiting his wife at the hospital after the birth of their son, Victor walks to the window and looks "out at a blackened brick wall webbed over with a complicated geometry of drainpipes. Diagonals of sunlight and shadow on the brick bespoke the hot summer noon going on elsewhere" (163). Like people who read novels in public places in order to avoid confrontation with others around them, Victor, who could care less about his son and his wife, sees the opposite wall as a cubist painting filled with geometry and diagonals. He sees his son as "a small patch of angry pink" (163) rather than a face. With similar cubist sensibility, he pictures his stepmother Hettie "sitting squarely in an armchair by the window, like the figure of an ancient idol on display on a temple altar, with a rhomb of late sunlight smouldering redly on the carpet at her feet" (218). When Querell accosts him in a train, he gazes out the window, examines "cows, a farmer on a tractor, the sudden, sun-dazzled windows of a factory" (244). Even Querell, who, as it turns out, is Victor's wife's lover, knows more about what's going on than Victor does. Victor assumes scholarly detachment: he refuses to look at Querell and studies the scenery instead. His gaze is detached from his primary source of preoccupation. The window allows him to look askance. Similarly when Skryne interrogates him, he walks to a window and delivers a bit of exposition about a "monkey-puzzle tree, looking very black and mad in the sun, and a discouraged strip of grass with a flowerless border," as well as a fat man in the house opposite who fully fills "the window frame" (338–39). Victor walks to the window as a bit of stagecraft: he wants to avoid Skryne's questions, give himself a bit of time to think. As a painterly convention, the window within a window permits dimension and depth. For Victor, the window affords distraction, a sudden bridge to a different plane, a contemplation of death or treachery, an aestheticization of his predicaments by seeing them as painted representations. He is not who he appears to be. He is, in his mind, already a representation of himself.

*

Flow: By theatricalizing, allegorizing, and cinematizing his adventures, Victor mocks the wish to connect queerness with espionage. His personality, as he leads Miss Vandeleur to believe, has no bearing on his actions. The spy is necessary to the flow of information across borders, between nations. Queerness channels that flow but does not fundamentally change its content. The queer character graces spy narratives with ironic joy that the codes of galvanized masculinity routinely forbid to other characters. Although queer men in the 1950s and 1960s were dismissed from intelligence agencies when they were discovered, the historical construction of homosexuality as insecure needs to be investigated. Gay men are not *inherently* treacherous nor *inherently* lacking in morality. Maskell happens to be gay, happens to be Irish, happens to be Cambridge-trained, happens to be arrogant, happens to be an art historian, and happens to be a spy. Calling his life "quadruple-quintuple" (45), Victor thinks that the cheesy melodeon tune of his life could be called *"The Queer Irish Spy"* (45). Yet his queerness is not visible to others. Arthur Clegg, part of an intelligence team that unpicks mail bags on night trains during the war, calls a Portuguese diplomat in a peignoir a "friggin' ponce" (253) but does not read the semiotics of ponciness in either Maskell or his lower-class lover Danny Perkins. The *gesture* of queerness does not rise to visibility. Boy, as a model of homosexual exuberance, proves just the opposite, in that he sleeps his way through the crew of the ship *Liberation* en route to Russia (112), picks up Danny, picks up men in the public toilets, picks up a pilot who had nearly died earlier the same day while bailing out of his aircraft (287), picks up Tony the barman. Whereas Tony the barman rebuffs Victor, Boy calls him "a demon in bed" (207). Boy is Don Juan; Victor is Our Lady of Perpetual Hope. The respective queer identities of Victor and Boy are summed up in their roles at the public washrooms: Boy indulges; Victor stands guard. Boy is boyish. Victor is not victorious. Boy in his priapism prevents Victor from sexual fulfillment. When an emaciated guy walks into the washroom, he eyes Victor then leaves. After all, Victor is a character of the eye—a professional looker-on and looker-at-pictures. Whereas Boy integrates homosexuality and espionage, Victor separates them. Which leads us to the simple but un–Cold War understanding that no two spies, and no two homosexuals, are alike.

*

The Gate Is Open: Throughout *The Untouchable,* allusions to William Blake suggest revelation, an opening into other states of being. Part 2 of the novel ends yearningly before a "little window" that opens onto a dark plain

(276). Part 3 ends, likewise, openly: "Father, the gate is open" (368). The gate is open to death. The gate is open to heaven. The gate is open to new identities. The gate is open between Russia and the West. The gate is open between head and heart. The gate is open to queer identity. The gate is open. The wall is down.

PART THREE HOW BIG THE WORLD

CHAPTER NINE

Disappearances

MISSING BODIES IN *SABBATICAL*

> This, then, was the complete game—disappearance and
> return.
>
> Sigmund Freud, *Beyond the Pleasure Principle* (15)

GONE MISSING

In the foreword to *Sabbatical,* a romance-cum-spy-thriller published in
1982, John Barth acknowledges a factual inspiration for his fictional narrative: "The story was suggested by the curious death in my home waters,
Chesapeake Bay, of one Mr. John Arthur Paisley, an early-retired high-
ranking operative of the U.S. Central Intelligence Agency, who in late September 1978 disappeared from his sloop *Brillig* during an overnight solo
cruise in fair weather on this normally tranquil estuary" (3). Recovery of
Paisley's corpse a week later—decomposed, forty pounds of scuba weights
cinched to the waist—does not satisfy questions about the motive for his
death. He may have committed suicide. Alternatively, KGB or CIA agents
may have killed him for having been a double agent, or for his having uncovered a mole inside intelligence networks (98–100). Although Paisley's
body bobs out of the waters of Chesapeake Bay, Barth, working within the
romance tradition and the paranoid style of American espionage narratives, reconfigures the trope of disappearing bodies in *Sabbatical* as the
emblem of what does or does not return, of what can or cannot be proven
about conspiracies. A vanished body serves as a hieroglyph for conjecture,
crime, wish, anxiety, transcendence, conspiracy, factuality. The missing
body refuses to signify in one single way. In *Sabbatical,* missing bodies
allegorize political ambiguity.

Narratives of disappearance, whether in news or in novels, generally attribute motives to an action that is inexplicable.[1] According to contemporary folklore, people vanish because of Mafia vendettas, alien abduction, spiritual rapture, personal unhappiness, political defection, or police protection programs. Sometimes people disappear of their own volition. Sometimes they are forced to disappear in acts of retaliation, punishment, or genocide. In the absence of a body, interpretations of motive and meaning ramify. Foul play is suspected more often than not. When contrary proof cannot be produced, the missing person is coded as the agent or victim of crime. In these scenarios, bodies are implicitly understood to be the source of narratives. *If only the body were recovered, the full, true story would emerge.* Yet the law of habeas corpus pertains to such cases: there is no crime without the evidence of crime. In narrative, bodies have agency, occupy space, and express identity through a series of actions. A disappearance therefore challenges the categories of action and character as well as the categories of crime and punishment. An absent body weakens or defies opportunities for consecutive actions and undermines the tendency of realist narrative to demonstrate the effects of experience on identity. Bodies make stories cohere; when a body disappears, so do the stories that that body contains. No one can say what meaning a disappearance might have for the character who has gone missing. In consequence, whatever the motive, narratives of disappearance concern problems of knowledge. The narrative of disappearance divides the world into searchers and sought, which is to say those who do not know and the one missing person who seemingly does.

Like John Arthur Paisley's waterlogged cadaver in *Sabbatical,* the dead body itself remains an enigma, an object of curiosity and investigation, an object to be examined and autopsied until it surrenders its secrets. The knowledge sought in narratives of disappearance pertains to bodies in and of themselves. Curiosity then extends to how the body, as a gestural and kinetic entity, enacts political and narrative plots. A plot without an agent is like a task without a tool. The missing body demonstrates that actions remain subordinate to agents, which is to say, in spy thrillers there can be no thrill without ideology nor any conviction without character. The missing body or the body in hiding preserves the secret sources of action. By contrast, the body that acts openly is a body that attests to meaning—functional, partisan, ideological. A represented body remains answerable to beliefs and human business. The missing body may be either a clue or a solution, whereas a represented body must be one or the other. Not being easily categorized, the missing body marks a glitch in rationality. Especially in spy fiction, such a glitch or gap in meaning may hide a contradiction in political affiliation or a deviation from the status quo. In American espionage novels, in particular, paranoia infiltrates that gap.

As versions of paranoia, conspiracy theories join fragments of information into plausible stories. Not in possession of full evidence or missing bodies, the "we" narrators in *Sabbatical,* a married couple named Susan Seckler and Fenwick Turner who yacht around Chesapeake Bay in early June 1980, make conjectures about the interrelatedness of random events. They presume a priori that the CIA controls characters. Ideology, for them, quells individuals, although they pretend to think the opposite. With flagging skepticism, they wonder, "We don't believe that Harry Truman created the Central Intelligence Agency for the sake of this story, do we?" (352). Yes, they do. The rhetorical question belies their doubt. Truman might not have been so prophetic or so altruistic in his motives, but Fenn and Sue's story would not exist without the CIA. Espionage is a precondition for their narrative, as it is for their political consciousness. The CIA externalizes their doubts about secret convictions and complacencies that they—intelligent, bourgeois, leisured Americans—hold but cannot articulate. Fenn and Sue have a hunch that Key Island, which does not appear on any maps, is the location of a CIA safe house or compound, a surmise subsequently proven true. Paranoid Fenn suspects that he suffers a mild heart attack because an undercover agent slips poison into his bloodstream (333–34). In the course of their cruise, the Seckler-Turners frequently discuss germ warfare and CIA-developed gadgets for causing death. Sue and Fenn fret about CIA support for the shah in Iran and undercover operations in Chile and Vietnam. They figure that one disappearance in the novel is a CIA cover-up (46n), and another is staged in order to allow a character to go underground (168). With tears in eyes and Kleenex in hands, the narrators jointly sigh, "If we could only know one way or the other" (257) what happens to people who vanish. Conspiracy theory needs missing bodies as a proof that conspiracies exist. Missing characters generate a set of interlocking tales about the meaning of invisibility itself. The invisibility of the disappeared characters is the narrative excuse for arguing that invisible machinations regulate American lives. Just as the missing characters are presumed to exist somewhere as bodies (whether dead or alive), so too hidden patterns in American politics can be detected in and through random events. A missing body is a proof, albeit an absent or negative proof, that plots exist. Conspiracy, like a missing body, cannot be seen; nonetheless, it exerts power. Disappearances are therefore crucial to Fenn and Sue's paranoid speculations about Company activities. As an analogy for, and exemplar of, behind-the-scenes manipulation, a missing body has greater authority than a visible body.

Inspiring speculation, disappearance is a trope of romance rather than a trope of realism. In *Sabbatical,* romance allows freehanded distribution of surprises, ghostly interventions, reunions, sudden resolutions, miracles, and marvels. Fenn and Sue glimpse a legendary monster, Chessie, during a placid afternoon sail on the Chesapeake (341–43). Sea monsters belong in fabulistic, not realistic, narratives. Romance allows wide latitude for inventing hypotheses about mysterious occurrences, such as the "vanishment" (167) of characters. In his preface to *The House of the Seven Gables,* Nathaniel Hawthorne claims that romance "may swerve aside from the truth" (3) in order to abide by the logic of the work of art rather than the laws of reality. The principle of deviation in romance applies to *Sabbatical* in that political meaning can only be understood by swerving from the truth. Americans understand secrets that circulate within and about the republic by fabricating stories based on possibility instead of probability. For this reason, conspiracy theories and plausibly outrageous news items are preferable to accurate information. By indirection, politicians' directions will be found out. Conspiracy theories resemble novels insofar as both rely on a performance of ideology, on fictive setups and sensational explanations of news events. Accordingly, Paisley's death, shrouded in mystery, intimates CIA interference. But the cultural logic of espionage does not end there. Exploiting the American tendency for romantic conjecture, the CIA allegedly plays on citizens' desire for signs of conspiracy. The Pentagon generates Cold War "huggermugger" (4). Specifically, agents leak confusing information about which spies sold what secrets to whom and for how much. Uncertain what they should believe, Fenn and Sue, with post-Watergate touchiness, assert that "the fingerprint business and the Company cremation and the break-ins and such [events related to Paisley's death] are all more or less routine muck-ups, contradictions, blunders, checkouts, and cover-ups for his secret contract work, unrelated to his death" (110). Fenn and Sue treat disappearance and subsequent death as personal matters, whereas conspiracy manifests itself in confused public acts. Even "muck-ups" are part of a CIA "business" that gives the overt impression of disorder to hide a detailed plan. A blunder is not just a blunder, but a clue to the plot that governs Paisley's life and death.

Disappearance is always a political event in *Sabbatical*. The narrative contradicts Fenn and Sue's blasé assumption that disappearance is only personal. The narrators frequently talk about the "desaparecidos" (148, 285) in Latin American countries. To disappear somebody, especially in 1970s and 1980s parlance, means to kill an undesirable agent who knows too much or a group of people who oppose dictators. In *Salvador,* Joan Didion's 1983 investigation into Latin American massacres, she notes that "disappear" is both an intransitive and a transitive verb in Spanish: "this flexibility has been adopted by those speaking English in El Salvador, as in *John Sullivan was disappeared from the Sheraton; the government disappeared the students,* there being no equivalent situation, and so no equivalent word, in English-speaking cultures" (57). Barth uses the verb "disappear" transitively in *Sabbatical*. When Manfred, a CIA agent with intimate knowledge of foreign affairs, disappears without rhyme or reason into the waters of Chesapeake Bay, Fenn accuses the Company of having "disappeared him" (308). Gus, Manfred's son, disappears in Chile, "where he had gone in 1973 to help oppose the CIA's successful efforts to 'destabilize' the socialist government of the late President Salvador Allende Gossens" (33n). The disappearance of the father in domestic waters of the United States squares the disappearance of the son on international territory. Manfred, father of Gus, works to promote American interests abroad but dies in home waters; Gus, son of Manfred, works to restrict American political influence to domestic manifest destiny but dies abroad. These double disappearances imply that domestic and foreign policy cannot be separated. Having fit together random incidents, whether personal, national, or international, the narrators conclude, with a wide-eyed glance at conspiracy theories, that "the world *is* a seamless web" (214). Fenn and Sue reiterate an ideology of connectedness. A design governs seemingly random events. Nothing is coincidental. Disappearances conform to CIA-generated plots, just as Fenn and Sue have always suspected. The tendency to romanticize disappearances in *Sabbatical* could be construed as a neutralization of all political positions and policies, whether they originate in leftist liberal protests against CIA interference in foreign countries or whether they legitimate the so-called struggle for democracy in distant nations. Disappearances register protests against CIA activities as well as support for CIA activities. Not attributable to one side or another, disappearances allow political ambiguity to remain in play.

In all, three male characters disappear in *Sabbatical:* Paisley, Manfred, and Gus. (A Soviet defector named Captain Shadrin disappears "while walking through a public square in Vienna" [46n], in plain view of the CIA offices, but Shadrin is incidental, not central, to the narrative.) The narrators blur together the three disappearances. Manfred's disappearance is called "a spooky instant replay of our friend John Arthur Paisley's" (112–13). Only Paisley comes back, and then only as a corpse. Manfred does return as a ghost in a dream to discuss what happened in his dying moments; ghosts, however, "are prone to ambiguity" (256) in their narration of the facts. Neither living nor dead, the disappeared character is a specter. As we have seen in *Under Western Eyes,* ghosts bespeak political contradictions without resolving them. The ghost of Manfred has an axe to grind: he is a CIA operative and consummate manipulator whose nickname is the Prince of Darkness. Ghostly Manfred returns a second time to explain how he died trying to rescue his missing son from a Chilean prison (327–28). These messages from beyond the grave, while expository, do not resolve the meaning of his disappearance. They merely compound interpretations. The body of Manfred—probably picked by crabs in Chesapeake Bay—is never recovered. The real fate of Gus, Manfred, and Paisley remains undisclosed in *Sabbatical.*[2] In any representational medium, disappearance should be construed as a metonym, not a synonym, for death.

Although it often suggests felony and murder, disappearance contains the possibility of a return, coded, in *Sabbatical,* as an "irrelevant miracle" (349). Many things return in this narrative, notably a *boina* (a Spanish beret) lost three times and three times recovered—once from a ravine in Spain and twice from the waters of the Chesapeake. Fenn and Sue close the loop of their travels by sailing back to Chesapeake Bay after a nine-month sabbatical cruise in the Caribbean. Return distinguishes literary romance from other genres: the return of Imogen to her father's court in Shakespeare's *Cymbeline,* or the coming back to life of Hermione in *A Winter's Tale,* or the recovery of Paisley's body, or the return of Fenn's beret. Romance is constructed around a possible unlikelihood, such as the return of a person or object against all odds. Aristotle, as we have already seen, declares in *Poetics* that "the poet should prefer probable impossibilities to improbable possibilities" (64). Aristotle means that representation should abide by logical rules even when those rules violate possibility, rather than venture into improbability. Unable to make sense of mysterious events, Fenn and Sue, thinking explicitly about Aristotle's dictum, drink a toast to "impermissible coincidence, implausible possibility" (350). In Barth's novel *The Tidewater Tales*, a sequel of sorts to *Sabbatical*, the joint narrators Peter Sagamore and Katherine Sherritt jeer at Aristotle's idea of "Improbable Coincidence" (161), which they apply with grandiosity to the "grossly improbable coincidence of life itself" (164). Barth constantly refers to Aristotle's observations on plot in *Poetics*. In *Sabbatical*, Aristotle is invoked as an authority on orality, writtenness, coincidence, pace, and culpability (12, 120, 232). In his essays, Barth quotes Aristotle to the effect that history deals with what was, whereas literature deals with "what might have been" (*Further Fridays* 108). For Barth, fiction veers towards the unrealized aspects of reality. It expresses a sequence of events that might have, could have, maybe ought to have happened. Stories express possibility. In short, Barth's fiction dwells at the romance end of the literary spectrum. For Aristotle, the recovery of a missing body might be an improbable possibility or an unlikely coincidence.

Riffing on Aristotelian categories, Barth makes recovery of missing bodies an unlikely narrative event, as when Manfred returns as a ghost. But the return of the lifeless body is not itself a solution. When Paisley's body is pulled from the Chesapeake, it generates further mystery. With a lesion on its neck and a bullet wound behind its ear, Paisley's cadaver is a glyph of intentions; it represents the end of an improbable possibility that could also be called, following Aristotle, an impossible probability. In short, a returned body belongs to the genre of romance, not realism.

ROMANCE

Romance contains elements of wish fulfillment, as Northrop Frye argues (186). Wish fulfillment might take the form of a return (a possibility that defies likelihood) or a coincidence (a piling up of unlikelihoods). A surprising return or a fluky coincidence expresses a desire for miracles. In *Sabbatical*, returns and coincidences are possibilities drawn out in order to enhance the effects of the marvelous, specifically the magical return of missing characters. Hence the coincidental disappearance of both Manfred and Gus *might* conclude with their live return, not the discovery of their corpses, even though, within the narrative of *Sabbatical,* their bodies are never found. In this regard, the narrative is suspended, not fulfilled. The bodies remain absent. By contrast, the recovery of Paisley's body confirms crucial differences between disappearance and death. Despite his return, Paisley's story remains "rich in discrepancies, unresolved mysteries, and loose ends" (112–13)—a puzzle that defies decipherment. The missing body of the male spy encodes the possible resurrection of strife; Manfred, his whereabouts undetected, may return with his cloak-and-dagger CIA plots in the same way that Jack Lovett, the mysterious agent in Joan Didion's 1986 novel *Democracy,* pops up unannounced in Hawaii, New York, or Saigon, carries phony business cards, and does things "devoid of ethical content" (219). Or like Herr Dollmann in Erskine Childers's *The Riddle of the Sands*—a conspirator planning an invasion of England who escapes capture by slipping overboard into the shallow waters off the Frisian Islands—the spy may return if he is only missing and not yet dead. Until the body is recovered, political conspiracy remains alive. Disappearance is therefore useful in a plot as a potential, if unactualized, threat. Whereas the romance genre permits the invention of impossible probabilities, romance in *Sabbatical* specifically reconfigures the espionage motif of disappearances as the political uncanny. What happens during the interim of the disappearance is not death but narrative, a story inaccessible to representation, a story in search of a mode of expression.

The subtitle of *Sabbatical* is "A Romance." To cast *Sabbatical* as a romance is to conceive of political representation as possibility rather than fact or event. Conversely, *The Tidewater Tales: A Novel,* despite being a companion piece to *Sabbatical,* defies romance. The narrators of *The Tidewater Tales* live within "everyday realism" (22), notwithstanding narrative dips into the marvelous (surprise storms, late-life pregnancy, coincidental meetings with family members, and whatnot). "This isn't fiction," contend Katherine and Peter; "it's the world we really live in" (276). A hair must be split here. Both *Sabbatical* and *Tidewater Tales* deal with shady CIA operations in the Chesapeake basin, with emphasis placed on prevarication in the former and verification in the latter. While decrying political writing, Barth pens a pair of novels about CIA capers. Barth exploits romance conventions in *Sabbatical* and novel conventions in *Tidewater Tales* in order to define American political consciousness in two ways: the potential and the actual. In his essay "The Literature of Replenishment," Barth declares that "a gifted writer is likely to rise above what he takes to be his aesthetic principles, not to mention what *others* take to be his aesthetic principles" (*Friday Book* 200). Barth specifies that modes and literary schools never account for all the facets of an author's oeuvre. By the same token, Barth uses literature as a modality of speculation on reality and politics by tangentially, not centrally, representing espionage activities. As his subtitles indicate, Barth asserts difference in political values in these two works of fiction. According to Barth, *Sabbatical* is "about love and spies and sailing on Chesapeake Bay and deciding not to have children at this late hour of the world" (*Friday Book* 239). *The Tidewater Tales* is about love and spies and sailing on Chesapeake Bay and deciding to have children in 1980. In *The Tidewater Tales*, Pete and Kate recover a lost beret (144), look for Chessie the legendary monster in Chesapeake Bay (366–67, 637), and discuss the death of John Arthur Paisley (239–92), much as Fenn and Sue do in *Sabbatical*. Indeed, Katherine and Peter are responsible for finding Paisley's body—quite by accident—while out sailing (239). They are, they claim, an "unpolitical couple" (238), yet they conclude that God is either a postmodernist or a CIA spook (368). If God is a CIA spook, he is the ultimate conspirator. To believe in such machinations is to be political, if only as a maladroit puppet manipulated by sneaks.

The Tidewater Tales: A Novel, despite its maze of fabulous tales, belongs to a category of realist analysis in that it criticizes conventional representations of espionage. In John Buchan's thrillers, Richard Hannay can singlehandedly uncover conspiracies. In *Tidewater Tales*, conspiracies are too comprehensive, too multifarious, to be grasped from a single point of view. The threat of global catastrophe is palpable in the narrative. Katherine and Peter wallow in doomsday gloom. While sailing around Chesapeake Bay, they remain preeminently conscious of the military infrastructure in the vicinity: rocket testing centers; navy and air force installations; surface weapons design facilities; bombing targets; ordnance stations; CIA, DIA, and NRO headquarters. They are also conscious of the congressional or presidential authority to mobilize "THE FOURSCORE PENTAGON FACILITIES ON CHESAPEAKE BAY ALONE AND ALL RELATED FORCES AND WITH THOSE FORCES DESTROY ALL HUMAN TOGETHER WITH MOST NONHUMAN LIFE ON EARTH" (73). The end of the world is nigh, according to Katherine and Peter.

As a version of protest against militarism, Katherine and Peter despise the "glamorization of espionage and counterespionage" (241), don't read le Carré novels (266) or any spy novels for that matter (406), and dismiss "cloak-and-dagger groupies, the thrillerinos" (356) who indulge in conspiracy theories and espionage fantasies. Notwithstanding their scorn of the marvelous and coincidental in spy narratives, Katherine and Peter decide that the "extraordinary coincidences in our story maybe weren't so coincidental after all" (439). In order to make sense of the political ambiguities and inexplicable contradictions that unfold in the Maryland tidal basin, Peter, a novelist, invents a "literal marvel" (572) in a narrative about spies; he requires, in short, a soupçon of romance because reality itself won't suffice to convey the complexity of the political situation as he sees it.[3]

Peter needs romance because the genre addresses reality nonmimetically. Romance is an exaggeration of some aspects of reality, an intermingling of psychological desire and circumstantial necessity. In *Sabbatical*, Fenn has deep-throatish insider's information about the CIA. He worked for the agency, as did his twin brother. Almost all of the principal characters in *Sabbatical* serve at one time or another as agents, informers, editors, or trainers for the CIA. Sue's mother Carmen is rumored to be on the Company payroll (281). Her Romanian boyfriend Dumitru and her Vietnamese employee Eastwood Ho have both received money from the CIA for tip-offs (275). Fenn's ex-wife Marsha has moved up through the ranks of the agency unbeknownst to pissed-off Fenn; "you're a fucking spy these days," he yells at her (300). Sue and her sister Miriam have indirect contact with the CIA through members of their family. Factual understanding of the agency's goings-on does not diminish the ambiguity of those procedures. Fenn does not possess all details about the Company just because he was formerly employed there. Wish fulfillment and personal ethics modify factual knowledge. Moreover, fact seldom inhibits speculation in the American espionage tradition. A sabbatical releases Fenn and Sue from obligations, obligations to their jobs as well as their usual ways of thinking. While sailing, they literally stay away from terra firma. Just as Henry James metaphorizes romance as a "balloon" (xvii) that sways above the earth, Barth allegorizes romance as a yacht that stays constantly in motion. Because it deals with impossible probabilities and hypothetical circumstances, romance is the most common narrative container for American political representation. Nina Baym thinks that "perhaps the single most powerful theoretical concept in modern American literary history and criticism has been that of the 'romance' as a distinct and defining American form" (426). In *Sabbatical,* that defining American form opens up the possibility of understanding political processes by hypothetical, rather than realistic, rendering.

American writers typically represent espionage narratives as romance to insert distance between individuals and ideologies. National activities cannot be represented directly, only by a distance from those activities. American political romances differ from British or Irish thrillers in two important ways. First, American romance emphasizes carnal passion; American romance usually means a nexus of subterfuge and sex. In films that depict White House antics or shady senatorial maneuvers, such as *Dave, The Seduction of Joe Tynan, Primary Colors,* and *The Manchurian Candidate,* love crosses the lives of presidents, lobbyists, and Washington insiders. Private motives defeat the best intentions of elected representatives. In a film such as *True Lies,* the spy's marriage is strengthened when his wife, formerly a bespectacled librarian, joins the ranks of spies and husband and wife can perform undercover work together. Ideological conviction buttresses romance just as romance buttresses ideological conviction. In *Sabbatical,* Fenn and Sue devote themselves to sexual pleasure as much as they devote themselves to speculation on CIA activities. Sensual romance, rather than alienation technique or grimly deterministic realism, shapes the American political imaginary. Second, romance, as opposed to realism or naturalism, allows fiction writers to imagine what might have been rather than what is. Hence political representation does not approach truth through facts, but through conjecture. American writers adopt the generic materials of romance, including disappearance and return, in order to speculate on political processes that would otherwise remain mysterious.

In the preface to *The House of the Seven Gables,* a document that establishes parameters for the representation of American romance, Hawthorne distinguishes romances from novels. Romance, he claims, spices narratives with marvelous occurrences. The marvelous is a "flavor," not the "substance" of story (Hawthorne 3). Fenn and Sue aim for the "Literally Marvelous" (135) in their yarn. "Reality is wonderful," Fenn declares, "but realism is a fucking bore" (136). In the footsteps of Hawthorne, Henry James, in his preface to the New York edition of *The American,* searches for the attribute that defines "romance" as distinct from "realism." Realism involves those mysteries that ultimately yield to knowledge by dint of perseverance or by accidental discovery. Romance, James confesses, depends on "the things that can reach us only through the beautiful circuit and subterfuge of our thought and our desire" (xvi). According to James, realism concerns "things we cannot possibly *not* know," whereas romance concerns things that "we never *can* directly know" (xvi). Romance bespeaks what we know but choose to conceal. Romance is sustained illusion that operates within the knowledge of its illusoriness. We can apply this understanding to American representations of conspiracy. Only by casting political events as romance will truth about the mechanisms of power be discovered. When the conventions of spy fiction cross with the conventions of romance, the "subterfuge" of desire becomes the desire to suspend the political content of espionage battles, or it becomes the desire to sustain the illusion of choice when no choice is really possible. Therefore, in *Sabbatical*, wonder has to be superadded to realism in order to arrive at an understanding of political events.

Barth's smarty-pants protagonists in *Sabbatical* dismiss the gross conventions of "paperback gothic with a Hollywood tie-in" (133). The idea of writing "another CIA novel" giving "tsk-tsk exposés of the Agency" is similarly set aside (144). The spy novel per se gets trashed by Fenn. "The public seems not to tire of spy novels," his literary agent advises him (276). "Never mind the public, says Fenn; *I'm* tired of spy novels" (276). Fenn and Sue reject other modalities of representation as well: "We don't want some tacky roman à clef or half-assed autobiographical romance" (356). They adhere to "antisupernaturalism" (255) even though Susan descends genealogically from Edgar Allan Poe, supernaturalist par excellence, about whom she writes academic articles. The narrators reject romance and espionage tropes even though the novel insistently applies them. Even a smattering of knowledge about John Barth—his love of sailing, his marriage to a former student (*Further Fridays* 3–21)—allows one to read *Sabbatical* autobiographically. It is obviously a roman à clef and a parody of spy thrillers. Fenn and Sue, it appears, do not understand the aesthetic principles that inform their imagination for conspiracy or their propensity to see the political as irredeemably personal.

This repudiation of espionage, romance, and supernatural aesthetics leaves us, the patronized and manipulated "reader," written into this novel as inarticulate interlocutor, in a state of paranoid suspicion. "What the reader doesn't know yet would fill a book," taunt Fenn and Sue (73). While the narrators skeptically repudiate mysterious disappearances, resounding gun shots on deserted islands, wondrous sea monsters, dangerous storms, evil twins, and miraculous returns, the novel uses all of these tricks to the hilt to misinform readers. This manipulation, a refusal to condone or to verify CIA connections, creates readerly incredulity. "Suppose you and I reacted with as much incredulity as the reader," Fenn says to Susan, "Wouldn't you cover our tracks?" (135). Since reactions of readers come precoded as "incredulity," we have little place to turn for reliable information. Fed disinformation through footnotes and "irreality" (135), the reader can only suspect conspiracies directed against him or her by know-it-all narrators. The footnotes leak a certain quantity of information. As timed and timely leaks, the footnotes may contain disinformation. Books about the CIA mentioned as references may not actually exist. The doubting reader ought to determine whether Philip Agee's *Inside the Company: CIA Diary* and Victor Marchetti and John D. Marks's *The CIA and the Cult of Intelligence* actually exist (they do), since they are cited beside F. S. K. Turner's *KUDOVE* (which does not exist) in adjacent references (50n). For all the reader knows, articles cited in the text that supposedly correspond to articles in the *Baltimore Sun* (86–105) might have been invented by Barth as another layer of pastiche in this multimedia, multidiscursive text. (The *Sun* articles were *not* fabricated by Barth, just cut-and-pasted. I double-checked.)[4]

Subject to doubt about his or her capabilities as an interpreter, the reader is cajoled, lectured, gulled by the narrators. The reader is interpellated into a political network where knowledge will never be equal to the demands made by Fenn and Sue. *Sabbatical* elaborates a system of coding and "supercoding" (105n) that makes CIA business uncrackable without insider information delivered by Fenn and others. By the same token, the reader is given "a spot of briefing as needed" (85), a sort of novelistic scrum that may or may not satisfy the need to know. The reader is presumed to be an interested party in the American political process, a watcher, perhaps, of the evening news, a journalist or politician badly in need of information, yet the information that the reader receives is partly intended to misinform. Whatever the identity of the reader, he or she is presumed to be hanging on the narrators' tale, trying to figure out the political position of various characters, trying to grasp the plot. Which may not be the case. Playing with the reader's credulity, Barth (as well as Fenn and Sue) inculcates paranoia in the reader who doesn't know enough, who remains ignorant, who needs briefings, who will never know enough as long as the narrators withhold information. Not given all the goods, the reader has to assert the right to fabricate stories. In this sense, Barth creates an allegory about the dissemination of truth and falsehood as intentional activities that create American political identity. That identity is a mixture of truth and lies. *Sabbatical* duplicates this swirl of information and disinformation in the guise of a romance. In this sense, through the circuits of subterfuge and deception, *Sabbatical* mimetically approximates political processes: huggermugger, diffusion of news, mediatization, espionage.

In his definition of romance, Henry James acknowledges that the genre involves physical dangers. He cites "pistols and knives" among possible threats in romantic fiction (James xvi) yet leaves aside hermeneutic pitfalls posed to readers. Danger itself does not define romance, although the feeling of being compassed round by danger is a manifestation of readerly paranoia. Paranoia is often, though not exclusively, a political effect, a keen sense that personal destinies are controlled by forces outside and beyond individual understanding. Richard Hofstadter says that the central image of the American paranoid style is "a vast and sinister conspiracy, a gigantic and yet subtle *machinery* of influence set in motion to undermine and destroy a way of life" (29). Substantiated with copious footnotes, *Sabbatical* manifests paranoia. Hofstadter argues that "heavily documented tracts" (32) attest to a paranoid fixation on detail. Hofstadter adds that "apocalyptic" ruminations (30) and the tendency to see "a vast and sinister conspiracy . . . set in motion to undermine and *destroy* a way of life" (29) also contribute to the paranoid style. Whereas most accounts of postmodern paranoia emphasize the suspicion of an "invisible design *in* the visible" (Bersani, "Pynchon" 102), Hofstadter emphasizes that paranoia produces a *style*. "Overheated, oversuspicious, overaggressive, grandiose, and apocalyptic in expression," the political paranoid believes that his nation, his culture, or his way of life is threatened—not just his fate is at stake, but the fate of millions (Hofstadter 4). The paranoid style, I venture, allows investigation into implausible possibilities through coincidence and romance. The paranoid style is an indeterminate one and, perhaps because of its indeterminacy, it could be salutary to interpretations of the American political process.

Paranoia suggests that political subjectivity is predicated on not being in full possession of oneself. The paranoid political subject has already, in part, vacated his body. He has already begun to disappear.

MAPS

In 1851, novelist Elizabeth Gaskell published an essay called "Disappearances" in *Household Words*, the magazine edited by Charles Dickens. Falling into a reverie after reading Dickens's essays on the London Detective Police, Gaskell conjures up cases in which people disappear and return, either dead or alive, as well as disappearances that do not conclude with recovery of the missing person. Gaskell argues that realist narrative conventions forbid characters from disappearing without a trace. Narrative discloses secrets; it does not preserve them. Plots do not end with disappearances; rather, a narrative concludes once the disappeared person has been tracked down or accounted for. In realism, a body cannot go missing permanently. This was not always the case, Gaskell claims. In the eighteenth century, justice was perpetrated by individuals on other individuals and this sent the guilty into hiding. Gaskell recalls romancers like William Godwin and Mary Shelley whose antagonists in *Caleb Williams* and *Frankenstein* enact roles as pursuer and prey. By contrast, nineteenth-century society is comprehensively organized. Justice is a social not an individual matter. Whereas in *Caleb Williams* a wronged protagonist chases his opponent and discovers his hiding places,

> in 1851, the offended master would set the Detective Police to work; there would be no doubt as to their success; the only question would be as to the time that would elapse before the hiding-place could be detected, and that could not be a question long. It is no longer a struggle between man and man, but between a vast organised machinery, and a weak, solitary individual; we have no hopes, no fears—only certainty. But if the materials of pursuit and evasion, as long as the chase is confined to England, are taken away from the store-house of the romancer, at any rate we can no more be haunted by the idea of the possibility of mysterious disappearances; and any one who has associated much with those who were alive at the end of the last century, can testify that there was some reason for such fears. (Gaskell 247)

The possibility of escape or indefinite concealment no longer exists within realist narrative because England is securely policed. England has no hiding places. The fears of the last century have dissipated with the advent of a policing network. Vengeance, once a personal matter, becomes the goal of social mechanisms. Sinners and criminals are crushed by the collective apparatus of a disciplinary system.

Narrative, as a discourse contiguous with criminology, equally forbids deviance. Gaskell means that narrative structures, like police techniques, aim at rational representation. The organized machinery of detection, whether finger-printing, criminology, or policemen on patrol, rules out such irrational events as escape or disappearance. As plots wind up, characters are handed rewards or punishment. Like the thief who disappears in *Silas Marner,* the criminal body will be dredged from a pond and theft will be explained as part and parcel of a mysterious disappearance. Disappearance is ultimately not irrational. Proper narrative sequencing will expose its mysteries. Although I could invoke here Foucault's insight that the human body "is caught up in a system of constraints and privations, obligations and prohibitions" (*Discipline and Punish* 11), Gaskell more sensibly suggests that missing bodies point to inconsistencies in disciplinary logic. Disappearances—like school girls gone missing in *The Picnic at Hanging Rock* or an Italian woman's inexplicable disappearance after arguing with her boyfriend in Michelangelo Antonioni's *L'avventura*—defy the comprehensiveness and precision of a disciplinary machine that posits a map for every square inch of space. Missing bodies therefore stand for the unrepresentable within narrative, whether that unrepresentability concerns nefarious political plots, criminality, or espionage itself.

Disappearances signal an abrupt transition from one identity to another —like defectors or witnesses who, after delivering sensitive information, receive new identities and settle in new cities. Narratively, a disappearance permits reflection, reformation, or transformation for the person who has vanished. The moment of vanishing defines a newly invented self. Vanishing signals a break in consciousness. *Once a citizen, I am now a renegade; once visible, I am now invisible.* Sometimes the break in consciousness occurs as a conversion from one ideological position to another, from waking to dreaming, or from material to metaphysical being. The disappeared tend to go elemental; they hide in earth, water, air. Like Harry Lime, those who choose to disappear may move underground, into the sewers of

Vienna, where they scurry invisibly in darkness. Such zones have no, or few, maps. Lakes and tunnels remain relatively uncharted or, at the very least, maps of those locales remain imprecise. In Lewis Carroll's novel, Alice vanishes down a rabbit hole and emerges in Wonderland. The narrative tracks her adventures when she steps outside the bounds of rational control. More ominously, Stephen Blackpool leaves a mining town under a cloud in Dickens's *Hard Times* and disappears. He is later discovered, dead, down an abandoned mineshaft. At the end of Walter Scott's *The Bride of Lammermoor,* Lord Ravenswood sinks into quicksand leaving only "a large sable feather" (333) detached from his hat waving in the breeze at the spot where he sank. In most cases, the disappeared body returns. Ravenswood is an exception. Interred in quicksand, he is literally swallowed up by the landscape. In contrast to the examples of Alice, Blackpool, and Ravenswood, who all disappear into the earth, spies drown. In *Sabbatical,* both Paisley and Manfred go into the watery brink. Death by drowning suggests amnesiac oblivion. Drowning erases plots, pasts, and identities. The body, decomposing underwater, eventually leaves no traces. A trace in this context invariably means a clue, an index or synecdoche of the body itself that would permit some reasonable interpretation of motive. The disappearance thus becomes a complete absorption into the environment. The body, not absent, merely grows invisible as it dissolves into elementary particles.

As Gaskell implies, the body in hiding—whether lost in water or earth —has to be somewhere. For this reason, in spy narratives, knowledge is emblematically represented in maps. Maps render spatially what is cognitively possible. Pinned to the office wall, stuck with flags to indicate the location of agents working in the field, the map is so routinely and ubiquitously present in spy fiction that it passes unnoticed. Towards the end of Joseph Conrad's *Under Western Eyes,* Natalia Victorovna and the Professor of Languages look for Razumov in a hotel occupied by anarchists plotting upheaval in Baltic countries. The Professor describes the space in which he finds the revolutionaries: "The room, quite a large one, but with a low ceiling, was scantily furnished, and an electric bulb with a porcelain shade pulled low down over a big table (with a very large map spread on it) left its distant parts in a dim, artificial twilight" (327). The over-lit map looms out of the otherwise dark room, yet the Professor mentions it parenthetically, as if its importance were incidental to the revolutionaries' plotting. Stunted Julius Laspara hunches over the map to study, presumably, national frontiers and points of vulnerability. The Professor recognizes by the "shape of the blue part representing the water, that it was a map of the Baltic provinces" (329). The political importance of space in *Under Western Eyes*, or other espionage narratives, derives from the possibility of locating any person within the grid of longitude and latitude laid out by a map. If the surface of the earth has been completely mapped, then disappearance is logically impossible.

Maps in espionage narrative represent potential territorial conflict that erupts at borders. Maps, demarcating edges, are found everywhere in works by Le Queux, Buchan, and Childers in order to suggest the fraying of the empire, the ease with which the United Kingdom could be invaded (Trotter xiv). Spy narratives invoke maps to show global reach: a bird's-eye view or the flight path of intercontinental ballistic missiles. Everything is within range. Everything that had been invisible becomes visible. By extension, the map as espionage commonplace stands for fantasies of domination, invasion, allegiance, penetration, subterfuge. In *The Thirty-Nine Steps*, Richard Hannay figures out the mystery of tide-lines while sitting in an admiralty room "lined with books and maps" (94). In *Democracy*, Americans preparing to leave Saigon in 1975 requisition a wall map of the city on which they intend to make "a population density plot" (197) using colored push pins. With its Vermeer-ish suggestibility, the map on the office wall or boardroom table does not just display points of entry, but, more often, demonstrates targets and trouble spots in global conflict. Pinpricks of light tracing Russia-bound bombers light up the gigantic map of the world that dominates the war room in *Dr. Strangelove*. Also in a comic vein, a map porcupined with flags denoting fallen agents hangs on the wall in the film version of *Casino Royale*. During World War II, a naval officer in Robert Harris's novel *Enigma* follows British convoys on an "Atlantic chart" with a pointer to indicate perils at sea (81). The map encloses dangers within representation. The map evokes what, in a geopolitical context, would otherwise remain unrepresentable: frontiers and friction. Whereas the impulse to map in other narratives encourages limitation—here the world ends, here is where the treasure is located, here is Robinson Crusoe's island at the mouth of the Orinoco—, maps in spy novels posit not just the edges between land and sea, nation and nation, property and property, but also where human bodies are located within that space as flags or comet trails of light.

A map idealizes space in the sense that no human beings exist within the two-dimensional image of space. Maps in spy fiction imply potential routes through space. At the opening of Erskine Childers's *The Riddle of the Sands,* several maps, using different scales and levels of detail, indicate the relative position of the Frisian Islands to England. These maps frame the tale by setting the boundaries for action. More tellingly, a hand-drawn map interrupts the narrative to show the layout of Dollmann's base camp and Carruthers's progress, on foot, in heavy fog, through that danger zone (Childers 189). When words fail, a map pinpoints Carruthers's movements. Lost in fog, Carruthers has no idea where he is, but the map traces his route as if he were not and never had been disoriented. The map therefore poses an interpretive challenge. How does the reader scan the space and its implicit political antagonisms? The map can only show by implication the antipathy between Carruthers and Dollmann; narrative makes explicit that antipathy. Whereas most maps omit human presence, Carruthers's map records a body in motion. Cartography shows traces of human movement, which is to say, the contradiction between a visible and invisible body.

The Riddle of the Sands is set amidst shoals and sandbars. Like Childers, John Barth is a connoisseur of lowlands, swamps, bogs, and shores—land formations that are mapped only with difficulty because they shift. Barth's fiction returns again and again to settings in and around tidewater flats, traditional places of deceit and treachery (Doody 320). The action in Barth's novel *LETTERS* arises out of an "ordurous swamp" (5), where Marshyhope State University is located. "Salty Marsha," epistolizes one character in *LETTERS,* "you shall not fuck me over over!" (429). Barth's historical novel *The Sot-Weed Factor* concerns tobacco and treacherous Maryland politics in the seventeenth and eighteenth centuries, with references to explorers who come across "stagnant waters . . . beclowded with meskitoes" (368). Barth consistently links the tidewater marshes of the Chesapeake with deception. In *Sabbatical,* he yokes environmental deception with CIA subterfuges. Puns on Fenn (fen) and Marsha (marsh) are self-evident. Because filthy and unfirm, swamps metaphorize political allegiances.

In *Sabbatical,* as Sue and Fenn enter Chesapeake Bay during a sudden summer storm, they lose nautical chart number 12221, which covers the section of the bay through which they are sailing. The chart blows overboard. Losing their map, Sue and Fenn float in familiar but fathomless waters. At sea, they don't know where all the shoals and anchorages are. They steer according to memory and landmarks. Maps "validate rational observation and predictability" (Fogel and Slethaug 186). Although maps stand for the world, they should not be mistaken for the world. Miniaturized models of reality, maps orient through images and names, rather than narrative and events. The lost map reveals Sue and Fenn's dependence on representations, their desire for predictability in the face of disorientation. Yet Fenn and Sue are better off without a chart, since they navigate un-certain circumstances in and around the waters of the Chesapeake without prior expectations. Mapless, the Seckler-Turners resist rationality in favor of stories. They fabricate plausible explanations for strange noises at night, impolite behavior on the part of a cutter crew, the sound of a gun firing. By losing their chart, they arrive at Key Island, which shows up on no satellite photos or regular maps of the Chesapeake (312). They stumble across a political contradiction. Uncharted, Key Island, although "key," points to a conflict within U.S. political discourse between the necessity for self-surveillant espionage teams and the invasion of privacy and the curbing of civil liberties wrought by spies working for the FBI or CIA. Be-cause the lost Chart 12221 does not register Key Island, we can conclude that a two-dimensional representational medium does not correspond to three-dimensional reality. The CIA compound does not show up on any maps. Reality exceeds representation to such an extent that it cannot be diagrammed. Espionage activities so far exceed the imagination that they can only be described as a blind-spot in reality. Although Fenn decries realism, he does not, baby-and-bathwater style, decry reality: "Reality is wonderful; reality is dreadful; reality is what it is" (136). The map falsifies reality, but it is also indispensable for coping with reality. In this case, rep-resentation facilitates understanding of the ambiguities that underlie American domestic and international politics. The map provides a way of shrinking and therefore mastering the mess called reality. Representations allow abstract answers to real problems, just as romance remains connected to reality but departs from it.

In both *Sabbatical* and *Tidewater Tales,* Barth creates couples who have tepid political convictions. Navigating without a map, Sue and Fenn are confronted with their fears of the known. Specifically, they voice dismay about CIA activities, then decide that the best way to negotiate their objec-tions is to write a romance about yachting and espionage. "Manfred used to talk about operating on history instead of being operated on by it," Fenn says: "My private wish, as you know, was to neutralize him, if not convert him. What happened was more the opposite" (45). Manfred converts Fenn into a CIA agent on the grounds that clandestine activities will allow him to influence the course of history, perhaps for the better. Having resigned from that job, then having written an exposé of clandestine plots, Fenn seems to reject surreptitious actions. By the same token, he gives up any claims of operating on history in a direct way. Yet history returns in the form of repeated or recycled stories. Although the rehearsal of stories may indicate an "inescapable complicity" (C. Harris 429) in cultural represen-tations, repetition also manifests political trauma that Fenn and Sue articu-late as romance in *Sabbatical*. What they have not assimilated comes back to haunt them. A former spy, Fenn cannot resolve his contradictory im-pulses towards conservative solidarity with gung-ho, go-it-alone individu-alism. In a narrative that makes a great to-do about the freedom of choice, Fenn and Sue are frequently paralyzed by the need to decide. Fenn even proposes that they make no choice at all and let the tides of history wash them hither and thither.

The self-reflexivity of *Sabbatical*—the narrative includes lengthy digres-sions on the mechanics of storytelling and point of view—possibly opens up a vista into the American political imaginary, namely, that Barth "pre-sents a vigorous defense of human will and fiction over the forces of his-tory" (Elliott 210). Barth's archness and preciosity of style, coupled with Fenn and Sue's denunciations of spy fiction conventions, obscure the poli-tics of *Sabbatical*. Critics agree that the novel has "no predominant genre" (Slethaug 654), and that Fenn and Sue, faced by political quandaries, "finally just accept their privilege" and devote themselves to "indulgence and indolence" (Matthews 54). E. P. Walkiewicz views the novel as a holiday or "respite" (140) from Barth's serious output. Most critics read Barth's fiction for its formal high jinks at the expense of reading its political sub-texts, even though Barth is demonstrably preoccupied with the War of 1812, Maryland political history, CIA subterfuge, assassinations at home and abroad, industrial negligence, and international news events. The story that Fenn and Sue tell emerges as a romance because that form allows a tiny measure of distance from the representational confines of espionage thrillers, autobiography, realist novels, epics, and other kinds of narrative. In that distance, the reader glimpses the ideological constructs that coalesce in the doctrines of choice and freedom, as they apply to American political culture. Navigating without a map, Fenn and Sue attempt to articulate a politics of responsiveness, if not responsibility, that takes into account preexistent representations—of history, of spies, of disappearances—by which politics are made and lived.

FORT-DA AND THE PRAXIS OF INVISIBILITY

A coda. Throughout *Sabbatical,* Fenn and Sue brood on death. Sue has an abortion. Fenn suffers a heart attack. Paisley drowns or is shot. The CIA sophisticate Dugald Taylor succumbs to an aneurysm. Sue contemplates suicide. Balefully, Sue acknowledges that, in time, everyone is bound "to disappear without a trace!" (226).

Disappearance provokes specific psychological reactions. Rather than resolving the mystery of identity—what drives anyone to run away?—unexplained disappearances register the trauma of abandonment that afflicts those who have been left behind. Every disappearance of someone else rehearses our own inevitable demise. One day while sailing alone, Fenn jumps overboard to shove his boat off a sandbar. He succeeds, a little too well. As the boat glides away from him, he realizes that he's stuck to his knees in riverbed muck: "his dead body might well have stayed put despite the gases of decomposition and gone undiscovered for a long time, perhaps forever" (246). Had he not worked himself free of the mud, Fenn would have vanished, leaving behind only the free-roaming boat as evidence of his death. The floating object would be the signifier of disappearance, as it is for Paisley and Manfred.

In his analysis of the *fort-da* game played by his grandson, Freud concludes that an infant's tossing away of a toy and retrieving it again functions as a trial run for being abandoned by the mother. Freud interprets the game as "the child's great cultural achievement—the instinctual renunciation (that is, the renunciation of instinctual satisfaction) which he had made in allowing his mother to go away without protesting" (*Beyond the Pleasure Principle* 15). The child masters and mutes his anxiety about the mother's disappearance by playing with a toy tied to a string. In *Sabbatical,* Susan comes close to recounting Freud's theory: "Babies, she reminds herself, normally learn before age one that a parent who disappears from view will return, almost certainly" (134). Parents always come back. It is their fate. But that interpretation misses another way of understanding the *fort-da* game. Neither Freud nor Sue gives enough credence to the child's desire to disappear, either as an enactment of death, or as a punishment of the parent, or as the literalization of invisibility. The parent leaves the child alone. In effect, the parent makes the child disappear from optical range. Therefore, the child punishes the parent for inducing a sense of invisibility in him. Instead of worrying about whether a mother or father will return, the infant, in playing *fort-da* with a toy, rehearses his own disappearance. Knowing that the parent will return, since that's what parents invariably do, the child schemes to abandon the surveillant parent. *I will disappear. No one will find me. I will become someone who does not belong to any parents.* As in hide-and-seek or other children's games involving invisibility, *fort-da* exercises the possibility that the child is already missing. Disappearing would extend perceived invisibility into fact. The child would inhabit the position of *that-which-is-already-inanimate or that-which-cannot-be-seen-because-it-does-not-exist.* By situating himself as an invisible figure, every child practices to be a spy, haunter of shadows, hoarder of secrets. Exposed to the treachery of the parent, the child masters a fundamental trait of the spy: to be detached about commitments.

Fictionally, disappearance may have nothing to do with motive, identity, or intrigue. It expresses instead lack in those who are abandoned—parents, lovers, siblings. It magnifies the anxieties of those who think that they are all too visible and who are themselves not capable of vanishing into thin air.

CHAPTER TEN

Democracy

THE DEATH OF A SPY

REMEMBER THIS

Whereas John Barth offers a mystified version of early 1980s American foreign policy cast as a romance about missing spies, Joan Didion demystifies 1980s American foreign policy by critiquing political representation. Covering Cold War politics between 1952 and 1975, Didion's novel *Democracy* investigates American influence in Pacific Rim countries through the figure of Jack Lovett, a government agent who knows about "the diversion of technology to unfriendly" nations (37), who knows how to run " 'a little coup somewhere' " (34). "Exactly what Jack Lovett did was tacitly understood by most people who knew him," writes Didion, "but not discussed" (40). Lovett's first wife identifies him as an " 'army officer' " (38). His second wife guesses that he works as an " 'aircraft executive' " (39). According to Jack's business cards, "he was a consultant in international development" (39). He picks up tips and interprets information. He understands the difference between politicians in Washington and agents in the field, between policy and implementation. He understands the difference between media events and events that occur before they reach the media. In *Democracy*, the secret agent defines political identity according to romance and symbolic action.

Democracy is about details that may or may not cohere into a meaningful pattern. Didion presents these details out of temporal sequence. Let me establish, as Didion might say, some characters and events. Jack Lovett dies on August 19, 1975, while swimming laps in the fifty-meter pool at the Hotel Borobudur in Jakarta. Inez Victor administers CPR for twenty minutes to no avail. Inez smuggles Jack's corpse out of Indonesia and buries him in the graveyard at Schofield Barracks near Honolulu on August 21, 1975, which might be one day after his death, not two, since Hawaii is on the other side of the international date line from Jakarta.

Inez Victor tells Joan Didion this story in December 1975 in Kuala Lumpur. Didion worked with Inez at *Vogue* in 1960 in New York. In 1955, age twenty, Inez married Harry Victor, who becomes a congressman, a senator, and a contender for the Democratic presidential nomination in 1972. Harry Victor loses his bid for the nomination.

After twenty years of marriage, Inez leaves her husband on Easter weekend in 1975 and flies with Jack Lovett to Hong Kong. She has known Lovett since January 1, 1952, Inez's seventeenth birthday. For twenty years, off and on, here and there, Inez and Jack have an affair. As a gesture of loyalty to Inez, Lovett leaves Hong Kong to find her daughter Jessie, who, having run away *to* Vietnam in the spring of 1975 while every other American is running away *from* Vietnam, serves drinks and fries at the Legion Club outside Saigon, which is where, by accident, Jack finds her.

The American Embassy closed in Saigon on April 29–30, 1975, the last in a series of evacuations explicitly recalled in *Democracy* (Ching 184). Sometime in early December 1975, Inez calls Joan Didion in Los Angeles, out of the blue, wondering when Didion will be in Kuala Lumpur. Inez is working with refugees in Malaysia. She wants to talk because "Jack Lovett's name was just beginning to leak out of the various investigations into arms and currency and technology dealings on the part of certain former or perhaps even current overt and covert agents of the United States government" (217). Didion suspects that Inez acts for Jack, that Inez will use her to leak information to the news services about his shady enterprises. The U.S. Congress has subpoenaed Jack to answer questions about why he was in Phnom Penh after the embassy closed. He has "reportedly made some elusive deals with the failed third force" (219). Lovett's name is linked to narcotics deals. He has possible "affiliations with interlocking transport and air courier companies devoid of real assets" (218). One of his courier companies is responsible for delivering guns to a London arms dealer. Jack is buried in Honolulu by the time these allegations surface.

In this novel laden with inference, the reader should understand that the subpoena has been instigated—although no proof of this exists—by Harry Victor. Or the subpoena might have been cooked up by Billy Dillon, Harry Victor's spinmeister. In any event, the subpoena appears to be a tactic of retaliation against Inez for walking out on Harry Victor and a way of distancing himself from the embarrassing end of the war in Vietnam.

Although it contains an undercover agent, *Democracy* reverses many conventions of spy fiction. Whereas male agents usually take charge of events in order to shape history, Didion focuses on women caught in historical turmoil.[1] Whereas athletic feats stimulate thrills in other intrigue narratives, *Democracy* is about fatigue and bewilderment. Whereas most spy thrillers demonstrate that technology serves ideology, *Democracy* represents technology as merchandise. Guns and landmines are the byproduct of ideology, not a proof of ideological worth. No matter what injuries they inflict, guns do not validate truth. Whereas many spy novels extol loyalty to the state, *Democracy* suggests that the most resonant loyalty may be to another human being. Whereas other American spy narratives use romance as a mystification of political actions, *Democracy* treats romance as a complication of political representation.

Romance, as I have claimed, is the dominant mode for political representation in American literature. Romance in *Democracy* differs from romance in *Sabbatical* in that Didion concentrates on the role that women play in the political process. Didion, who uses her own name as the "author" (16) in *Democracy* (the biographical fallacy being passé), shares a close bond with Inez. Together, these characters represent public and reportorial professions for women. They create and disseminate news. Didion invokes these public functions to deconstruct images of politicians as family men or simple, honest folk. Diametrically opposed to media manipulations, the romance between Jack Lovett and Inez Victor never appears in the news. Genuine romance happens off the screen or to the side of public events. Jack and Inez share traits of nonspecificity: "They were equally evanescent, in some way emotionally invisible; unattached, wary to the point of opacity, and finally elusive. They seemed not to belong anywhere at all, except, oddly, together" (84). The core of their romance is a lack of attachment, an invisibility that keeps them outside public scrutiny. Circumspect, they are both given to "emotional solitude" and "secretiveness" (85). Sharing a propensity for being alone, they are, paradoxically, suited to one another.

Jack and Inez are never photographed together, nor do news stories link Jack's name with Inez's. In contrast to their tact, Harry Victor travels with his mistress Frances Landau. Although Frances does not appear in front-page photographs with Harry, her Russian wolfhound shows up in one Victor family snapshot as a trace of Frances's infiltration into the Victors' marriage (50). In contradistinction to *Sabbatical* and to many narratives that cross CIA activities with a love story, romance in *Democracy* confounds representation. Jack and Inez build a romance around chance encounters and constant movement. "'Pretty goddam romantic'" (87) is how Jack characterizes his preoccupation with Inez after he first meets her. Romance, in Jack's imagination, is iconic. He pictures Inez bending her head to listen to him: "In this picture the two of them were in fact the only people on earth" (87), as if everyone else has been annihilated in a nuclear blast. Jack's gruffness—"pretty goddam romantic"—suits his instinct for catastrophe. His involvement with various narratives of disaster qualifies his image of being with Inez. Jack runs guns and supplies unspecified aid to developing nations. In 1952 and 1953, he watches nuclear bombs detonate on a South Pacific atoll, in the Aleutians, and in Nevada. His fantasy of being, with Inez, the last couple on earth is romance in extremis, a last lunge at loyalty and solidarity. Jack's refrain, "'Oh shit, Inez . . . Harry Victor's wife'" (15, 44, 107, 187), understates the degree to which a romance with Inez compromises Jack's undercover integrity. He cannot have an affair with one of the most prominent political wives in America and retain his clandestine identity.

Conflicting impulses to promote or suppress romance run throughout *Democracy*. Whereas Jack abides by a romantic ethos of do-the-dirty-work-and-win-the-girl, Inez distrusts romantic gestures because she associates them with her mother. Carol Christian behaves like "a schoolgirl of romantic tendency" (24) who believes in "happy endings" (23). Beholden to fairytales, Carol describes her marriage to Paul Christian as "her own romance" (23). She tries to inculcate an ideology of romance in her daughters. Didion skeptically mentions that "the daughters in romantic stories always remember their mothers dancing, or about to leave for the dance" (21), like Cinderella. The mother is inherently romantic because she dances, because she abandons her daughters. The absent mother is an idealized mother. After Carol flees to the mainland, her daughter Janet collects lipstick-stained cigarette butts that may or may not have been her mother's. By idolizing her mother, Janet sentimentalizes her, whereas Inez resists the maternal legacy of romance. Despite Inez's leeriness about romance, Didion construes the liaison between Jack and Inez as a romance. Didion self-consciously critiques the tendency to cast American political fables as romances while recognizing that almost no other mode exists to convey the American political imaginary. Notwithstanding Didion's doubtful view of romance, she hopes that Jessie Victor will write a novel that begins with the line, *"Imagine my mother dancing"* (233), a line that Didion herself rejects as too romantic to open her own narrative (21). In any event, Jessie is writing a "historical romance" (233), not an autobiographical narrative disguised as fiction.

Didion, as a character in and the narrator of *Democracy,* intimates that the romance between Inez and Jack cannot be represented adequately "since the heart of narrative is a certain calculated ellipsis" (162). The romantic attraction between this couple is a donnée beyond logical understanding. Official romance abides between Inez and her husband. When the band segues into the Rogers and Hart song "Isn't It Romantic" (42) during a reception on the rooftop of the St. Regis Hotel in Manhattan, the tune belies the unromantic cast of Inez's marriage to Harry. Far from being a homebody, Inez is the *icon* of a wife who enhances Harry Victor's public credibility. At the St. Regis, Inez dances and utters the word "marvelous" (42). She hands over a glass of champagne. The handing over of the glass of champagne works like a deniability clause in the Victors' marriage. Although Inez does not have a drinking problem, Harry routinely accuses her of drinking too much. This accusation allows him, should the eventuality arise, to impute alcoholism to Inez as a reason to leave her. In the meantime, the marriage is staged as a cozy romance for the sake of the media. Harry calculates every action, including his marriage to Inez, according to "practical factors" (91). Like all of Harry's public appearances, the St. Regis party conforms outwardly to a discourse of romance without being innately romantic at all.

Music provides a series of intertexts in *Democracy* that subscribe to or undermine romantic penchants in characters. In the absence of verifiable intimacy, the romance between Jack and Inez is codified through musical allusions. When Jack takes Inez to an off-limits bar across from the Schofield Barracks in March 1975, the jukebox plays "Dream a Little Dream of Me" by the Mamas and the Papas (45, 187). The song suggests that romance lives by principles of illusion. The imperative lyrics—"dream a little dream of me"—dictate that you should invest yourself in a *dream* about me as opposed to investing yourself in me as a flesh-and-blood *person.* At her daughter Janet's wedding, Carol Christian sings *"I should worry, I should care . . . , I should marry a millionaire"* (153–54). Feckless Carol remains committed to possibilities such as marrying a millionaire, even after she has married into the well-to-do Christian family and abandoned that life for fun and frivolity in San Francisco nightclubs. The romantic illusion need not end just because it has come to fruition. Romance is eternal possibility, not achievement. Jack alludes to the Gershwin song "I Got Plenty of Nothing" as an expression of his allegiance to Inez (105). Didion casually refers to the song "As Time Goes By," made famous in *Casablanca,* but she changes one crucial verb tense in the lyrics from the present to the past: "the sentimental things of life as time went by" (21). She also fudges the "sentimental things" of life, which, in Herman Hupfeld's song, are "fundamental things": "You must remember this, / A kiss is still a kiss, a sigh is just a sigh. / The fundamental things apply, / As time goes by." Fundamental things could be sentimental things. Indeed, they fuse in *Democracy.* After Jack's death, Inez devotes herself to working with refugees. Acting from sentiment and conviction, she renounces her life as media icon and wife of Harry Victor to help save people's lives. Taken together, songs comment on the illusoriness of romance in American life. Romance is plenty of nothing and a fundamental thing. Maybe it's romantic, and maybe it's not.

Each of these songs evokes a memory. *Democracy* turns again and again to the pitfalls of memory as an element in romance. Inez complains that the major cost of public life is memory. Over time, she loses "certain details" (50). So does everyone in the long run. Inez's sister Janet phones to ask if she recalls trivial details from their childhood: "Do you remember, Janet always asked on these calls" (152). Inez lies about the past. She does remember but pretends not to. Inez, upon meeting Jack for the second time, gives no "indication that she remembered him" (88). The problematic of remembrance extends to the reader, who is recruited into the narrative. From time to time, Didion alerts the reader about what to remember. First glimpses of characters and first meetings "are meant to be remembered later" (32), she declaims, with a slight edge of menace. The nonlinear, nonchronological organization of the novel poses particular challenges to the reader's powers of recall: "perhaps you would even have remembered" the news item about Inez leaving Honolulu with Jack "from the stories that appeared in the newspapers and on television when Jack Lovett's operation was falling apart" (160). If you do not remember, reader, you were not following the important story, which is not the one shouted from the front page, but the less noticeable story that appears in a couple of column inches somewhere in the thick of the front section. No one, Didion concedes, has perfect recall. Didion herself comments that the news clip of Inez dancing "temporarily obliterated my actual memory of Inez" (219). Television footage displaces personal recollection. Worse, the repeated media images and stories solidify into ideology. We might call this the Zapruder effect. A loop of footage endlessly televised, analyzed frame by frame, never yields definitive meaning. By virtue of repetition and close scrutiny, the image is immortalized as an icon. The icon, as a consequence of its abiding presence in the public imagination, shrinks events into one definitive image. The icon overwhelms personal memory.

The preoccupation with memory in *Democracy* is an extension of Didion's earlier works. In *Run River*, Didion's first novel, the characters "seemed afflicted with memory" (230). Lily wonders, *"Was there ever in anyone's life span a point free in time, devoid of memory"* (*Run River* 31). Narrative and history begin "in what we remember," Didion claims in *Slouching Towards Bethlehem* (173). Nonetheless, she acknowledges in the essay "On Keeping a Notebook" that her old scribblers contain references to encounters, bars, schedules, and waiting rooms of which she has no conscious recollection. In *A Book of Common Prayer,* the narrator reports that "Someone had shuffled [Charlotte's] memory" (156), for she has lost details about her travels and her past. Boca Grande, the Latin American country where *A Book of Common Prayer* takes place, restages military coups every so often, yet remains a country devoid of " 'history' " (14), which is to say, devoid of collective memory. In *Democracy,* public life deprives Inez of memory. The things she does remember constitute her identity and, potentially, her personal happiness.[2] Although she rarely speaks about them, she cherishes moments with Jack Lovett and what he says to her. Her romance with Jack is a way of holding onto the past. Romance arises from the perpetual tug-of-war between remembering and forgetting. If, as Didion suggests in her essays and novels, we forget more than we remember, in *Democracy,* romance serves as an explanatory structure for otherwise inexplicable actions. Romance does not by any means fill in all the gaps of a given story. Romance is an alibi for behavior, an alibi that the narrator, Joan Didion, self-consciously elaborates out of the details and photographs and reminiscences that she has to work with.

Democracy speculates on the explicability of character and action, especially when characters suppress memory. Character cannot exist without memory. What Inez and Janet remember defines each of them individually. In lieu of having personal memories, Harry Victor repeats phrases from Auden (83) and invokes Jefferson as an all-purpose conversation-stopper (57). Character exists as a tissue of quotations or recorded images that individuals invest with meaning. Character forms around unconscious behaviors that emerge through repetition, such as Harry's knee-jerk references to Jefferson whenever he is stumped for something to say. Character arises out of specific contexts. That does not mean that character is spontaneously generated in unusual situations. Paradigms of behavior exist to control crises. In this sense, the characters in Democracy abide by predetermined roles. Jack sees Harry Victor as a politician, therefore a "'radio actor,'" therefore "'a civilian'" (103). Harry, complying with Jack's assessment, treats actions as scripted opportunities for photographs and press conferences.

Didion's 1996 novel, The Last Thing He Wanted, reenacts the problem of character within a political context. Like Democracy, it is narrated by an investigative journalist suspicious of prepackaged stories. In The Last Thing He Wanted, a U.S. government operative named Treat Morrison crosses paths with a former socialite and journalist named Elena, who has been caught in a gun-running mission. Elena travels on a false passport. She intuits, but cannot figure out, the plots that have been woven around her. She doesn't know what kind of cargo she is moving on behalf of her father. She doesn't know for whom the cargo is destined. Treat, like Jack, is a careful listener who "had built an entire career on remembering the details that might turn out to be wild cards, using them, playing them, sensing the opening and pressing the advantage" (Last Thing 155). The two novels vary narrative outcomes according to gender roles. Whereas Inez works with refugees in Kuala Lumpur and Jack dies of what appears to be a heart attack at the end of Democracy, Treat gets wounded and Elena dies in a deliberate ambush at the end of The Last Thing He Wanted. Treat and Elena have a romantic connection based on a "remote" (145) quality, "a core dislocation in the personality" (154), which resembles the elusiveness shared by Inez and Jack. A government inquiry describes Elena as an assassin. The inquiry leaks disinformation about her activities while building deniability clauses into statements: *"Reports that the suspected assassin had been supplying arms and other aid to the Sandinista government in Nicaragua remain unconfirmed"* (*Last Thing* 220). To raise the insinuation, but not to confirm it, is to create a climate of doubt. The narrator corroborates a different version of Elena's death. She is killed by an assassin with a ponytail who stands atop a grassy knoll. Treat is wounded, presumably by the same gunman, as spurious proof of Elena's murderous intentions. In brief, Elena is framed for the attack on Treat.

The Last Thing He Wanted indicts U.S. support for the Nicaraguan Contras in the early 1980s. The CIA, which ran the Contras, issued "a fairly sinister manual to its Nicaraguan clients, extolling the virtues of assassination" (Berman 62). For all its investigation into the obscurities of arms deals and shifting alliances in Nicaragua, *The Last Thing He Wanted* documents the point where "romance and reality collide and the outcome is loss" (Weir 95). As in *Democracy,* tenacious romanticism motivates action in *The Last Thing He Wanted*. Reviewers of the novel cast Treat as a "romantic lead" (Hardwick 7) or a "romantic hero" (Weir 96), and Treat and Elena as "another doomed romantic couple" (Wood 10). The narrator of *The Last Thing He Wanted* concurs: "This is a romance after all. // One more romance" (209). Romantic attachment is the narrator's invention. The narrator *wants* Treat and Elena to be "together all their lives" (*Last Thing* 227). According to the narrative, they know each other for a total of a few days. During a fact-finding interview, the narrator insinuates that Treat protects Elena because he is romantically invested in her: "I suggested that he had done it for her" (*Last Thing* 223). Treat neither confirms nor denies the charge. The narrator's expectations of romance collide with Treat's patriotic duty. If this is a romance, it is not the sentimental and passionate kind that figures in some spy thrillers, such as Robert Ludlum's *The Bourne Identity: agent-gets-girl-as-byproduct-of-his-coolness-and-talents-for-survival*. Rather, Elena scrambles around as an unofficial agent and Treat operates as a smooth undercover dealer. They resemble each other in their fundamental dislocation from normal life. Restlessness and a heightened awareness of clandestine affairs unite them.

RESTLESS VOYAGERS

Travel is a form of détente, a hiatus in thinking and feeling. Travel allows passengers to suspend commitments. In transit, passengers are neither here nor there. Airborne, they give themselves over to anonymous pilots. They move without being responsible for their movements. Like omniscient narrators or aerialists, they glide over the earth without having to touch down.

Didion's characters are machines of perpetual motion. Travel soothes them. Women in particular flee. Allaying their grief or anxiety, they drive randomly or they catch planes. Maria in *Play It As It Lays* "aimlessly" (129) cruises the freeways of Los Angeles, in part to assuage feelings of sorrow about her institutionalized daughter. Sometimes movement allows people to reinvent themselves elsewhere. "People were missing. Children were missing. Parents were missing," Didion writes about late 1960s American culture (*Slouching* 75). Missing person reports get filed by people who then move on and leave no forwarding address. Charlotte in *A Book of Common Prayer* haunts airports. Elena flies ceaselessly from airport to airport in *The Last Thing He Wanted,* landing in Chicago, Los Angeles, Miami, Costa Rica, and an unnamed Caribbean island. Didion herself, in the role of campaign reporter in 1988, goes to Newark airport to pick up a flight to California, shimmies under a hangar door, discovers she is not cleared to board the press plane, waits disconsolately on the tarmac with her bags, and ends up alone, out of place, on an all-but-empty aircraft, guessing along with the pilot how many people will eventually board the flight. "None of this seemed promising," concludes Didion (*Political Fictions* 6). The scene is more or less reprised by Elena, as a reporter on an election campaign for the *Washington Post,* in *The Last Thing He Wanted* (20–24).

In *Democracy,* travel offers escape and connection. Inez flies to Honolulu holding Billy Dillon's hand for the whole trip. Inez boards a 3:45 a.m. flight east from Honolulu to Hong Kong with Jack Lovett—"dawn all the way" (188). Inez thinks about flying to Michigan. Inez recalls moments of happiness in Chicago, Paris, wherever. Inez travels for herself, for her husband. The action of the novel culminates in Inez's island-hopping journey from Jakarta to Honolulu with Jack's body. Travel from island to island stitches together disparate places. The islands, like the discrete images that Didion treats as the foundation for narrative, may or may not bear a relation to each other. Travel reveals potential similarities and coincidences, at the same time as it creates the illusion of escape. Yet Inez's trip to Kuala Lumpur can be construed as "not merely one more stage in the constant shuttling" (Stout 221) undertaken by characters in *Democracy,* but as a commitment to doing something practical. Her work with refugees falls into the category of useful deeds perpetrated for the public good—an international constituency in this instance—and it calms Inez's restlessness. Unlike her mother who migrates to San Francisco in order to have fun in nightclubs, Inez converts restlessness into a mission.

Writing about voyages, Didion emphasizes finality rather than reunion. Travel curtails contacts and context. The mothers who run away in Didion's novels try not to look back. They voyage to provisional destinations, then move on. As travelers, given over to an ethos of "ethereal mobility" (Hardwick 4), they abandon relationships. Jack Lovett would call this hardhearted leave-taking *"un regard d'adieu"* (14), or a "last look through more than one door" (15). *Democracy* makes goodbyes a severance of affection, not a sentimental lingering. The *regard d'adieu* presupposes that the goodbye was inevitable. With similar French flair, former Vietnamese officials taunt Americans for their dwindling presence in Saigon: *"en un mot* bye-bye" (207). Inez travels to cut herself off from her family. Whereas sailing in the Chesapeake embodies the possibility of return in *Sabbatical,* in Didion's novels airplane travel embodies the opportunity of never looking back and certainly never going back. *Democracy* ends with a gesture of repudiation. Didion has thought about returning to Kuala Lumpur, but "so far," she reports, "I have not been back" (234).

Restlessness substitutes for psychological agitation. In the American idiom, restlessness signifies the quixotic pursuit of cures and success. Jessie moves to Seattle for treatment of her heroin addiction, then moves further west, as it were, by fleeing to Saigon. Harry Victor's campaigns take place in the air as much as they take place in stump speeches on the ground. Travel conveys a sense of the total connectedness of American political life. Mobility itself creates the illusion of concern: if he is in Ann Arbor, the politician must care about education; if he talks nightly to advisors in Cambridge and Palo Alto, he must be in touch. The counter-example is equally true. Paul Christian, Inez's father, travels in order to escape. A playboy, he migrates from place to place without any sense of purpose. He plays backgammon with John Houston in Cuernavaca or nonchalantly steps off an elevator in San Francisco. Travel signifies in

Didion's narratives the impulse to romance, insofar as romance means the pursuit of one's illusions.

Travel causes people to disappear. Such disappearances have political utility, as in the case of secret agent Jack Lovett, who is always en route. The first time Didion meets Jack Lovett, he has "'just got off a plane'" (33). In fact, Jack is more often in the air than on the ground. Jack frequents transit lounges. He feels most comfortable "in the presence of strangers" (35). He is at ease "on airplanes" (35). He has, moreover, a mysterious degree of "access to airplanes" (31). On trips of eight or twenty-two hours, he picks up information that is, as he views it, "an end in itself" (31). Travel for Jack is an opportunity for coincidental meetings, the accumulation of fragments and details that he arranges into patterns. Whereas travel for Harry Victor is intended as a form of ubiquity, travel for Jack establishes coherence. Travel makes Harry Victor visible, but travel renders Jack Lovett invisible.

ICONS

Didion constantly accounts for the role of the media in the dissemination of political perceptions and ideas. Traveling in El Salvador as a reporter in 1982, she records that the pervasive terror in that country proved to her that fear initiates political action. Didion emphasizes "the sensation of having been in a single instant demoralized, undone, humiliated by fear" (*Salvador* 21). Terror remains "untranslatable" (*Salvador* 103). The remoteness of human rights and democratic process in El Salvador is almost "hallucinatory" (*Salvador* 38). In this report on a state embroiled in conflict, Didion construes politics as a sequence of actions, transactions, promises, compromises, treacheries, hostilities, surprises, interventions, and conversations. The investigating journalist sifts through conflicting evidence and narrates ambiguity. The first person sums up the difficult burden of bearing witness to atrocities. Similarly, in *Miami,* an analysis of Cuban exiles in Florida, Didion documents internecine Cuban skirmishes, which are at odds with the Anglo tendency to think all Cubans want the same thing. Assassinations, riots, and bombings accumulate in Miami as evidence of widespread miscommunication. Individuals use media to their advantage: "The actions of individuals are seen to affect events directly. Revolutions and counter-revolutions are framed in the private sector, and the state security apparatus exists exclusively to be enlisted by one or another player" (*Miami* 13).

In *Salvador,* Didion skewers Assistant Secretary of State Thomas Enders for extolling the difficulties in "'nascent democratic institutions'" (90). The phrase has a whiff of the Truman Doctrine about it, specifically of Truman's pledge to assist free peoples who resist subjugation anywhere in the world. Truman, having established the Central Intelligence Group in 1946, created its successor, the CIA, in 1947. In *Democracy,* Harry Victor's name evokes Harry Truman's, just as his speeches about burgeoning democracies faintly echo Truman's. Harry Victor tells a press conference that rioting in Surabaya reflects "the normal turbulence of a nascent democracy" (99). Riots have no causal connection to democracy. Harry tells another press conference that a grenade exploded outside the American Embassy in Jakarta in 1969 reflects "the normal turbulence of a nascent democracy" (103). In *The Last Thing He Wanted,* an irritatingly supercilious senator's aide claims that he wants "to do his humble best to level the playing field for democracy" in Latin America (176). Like a sports event, democracy will produce winners and losers, but, the aide implies, that is none of his affair so long as he goes on record as an exponent of a level playing field. Rhetoric about "nascent democracy" hardens into an ideological certainty, regardless of the bad faith exhibited by its exponents or the self-serving motives that gird up the rhetoric of assisting subjugated peoples. Harry Victor's understanding of democracy is restricted to electoral campaigns and programmed media performances. Campaign promises and prescriptive agendas may or may not conflict with what unfolds in the United States or abroad.

Lunching with the U.S. ambassador to El Salvador in 1982, Didion senses that the "American undertaking in El Salvador might turn out to be, from the right angle, in the right light, just another difficult but possible mission in another troubled but possible country" (*Salvador* 87–88). Like Candide searching out the best of all possible worlds, Didion deflates the naive adherence to the "possible" in such vexed and profoundly ambiguous situations. Amid information and disinformation, every event in El Salvador, being unverifiable, uncorroborated, or generally fluid in outline, takes on a legendary character, Didion claims. This legendary quality is also played up by the American presence in El Salvador, insofar as that country is just "another" troubled place that requires American aid. While Didion does not resolve any of the ambiguities implicit in the Americans' meddling in El Salvador, she realizes that the Salvadoran factions play off the American desire for "symbolic action" (65) by pretending to accept reforms and candidates and processes while going about their own campaigns and skirmishes and antagonisms. By clinging to rhetoric, Americans are snookered: "That we had been drawn, both by a misapprehension of the local rhetoric and by the manipulation of our own rhetorical weaknesses, into a game we did not understand, a play of power in a political tropic alien to us, seemed apparent, and yet there we remained" (*Salvador* 96). Stalemate occurs because symbolic action influences real action. Rhetoric about nascent democracies supplants fostering nascent democracies. Sports metaphors produce a false image of Latin America, in which winners and losers, fair play and foul, do not adequately account for the maelstrom of political complexities.

Most criticism of television and newspaper media concentrates on audiences and journalists. Didion, by comparison, begins her analysis of the media with grave suspicions about rhetorical grandiosity in American politics, especially narratives that come precoded. Sound-bites infect journalists' rhetoric. Because she so insistently criticizes the media, Didion hardly belongs "among the most fundamentally conservative writers in America" (Mallon 31). Nor is she someone whose "storytelling simplifies the complex" (Reinert 122). Nor does she publicly aver that "American democracy has become irredeemable" (Tager 183). Joseph Epstein claims that Didion does not fit easily into any political box: "she doesn't much like what has happened in America. Yet she doesn't much like it anywhere else either" (67). A card-carrying Democrat, Didion disagrees with American domestic and foreign policy. More significantly, she analyzes those policies as they filter through the media. As a journalist, Didion presents stories that contain randomness and disquiet. She distrusts journalists who overlook the "contradictions inherent in reporting that which occurs only in order to be reported" (*Political Fictions* 30).

Journalists, in order to tell a story, create characters, settings, and dramatic interludes. They kowtow to "the symbolic marketplace in which the narrative [is] not only written but immediately, efficiently, entirely, consumed" by a population that understands the contours of the story and its players (*Political Fictions* 50). Journalists pretend to deliver the unvarnished story. Politicians pretend to speak in the best interests of the nation, with unanimity of thought and feeling. "The furies and yearnings of the nation were necessarily indivisible from the furies and yearnings of its political class" (*Political Fictions* 327), Didion ironically comments about the aftermath of the Bill Clinton–Monica Lewinsky set-to and its perceived effects on Al Gore's presidential aspirations in the election campaign of 2000. Didion means that the nation cared far less about Clinton's affairs than journalists or Republican politicians did. Whatever apparent differences underscore the political classes and the chattering classes, they both presume to represent popular opinion. In doing so, politicians and journalists rehearse an old Democrat story line: a personal foible undoes the president. Didion suggests that this story line arises from a collusion between journalists who unreflectively report the news that politicians manufacture in order to be reported. In *Democracy,* Didion demonstrates how this mechanism works. Billy Dillon and Harry Victor speak in ready-made sentences in rooms set up beforehand for press conferences. Harry's political discourse ventures nothing new. He intones the familiar motifs of nascent democracies and liberalism and integration without caring overmuch about the implications of such words. Harry plays on the familiar icons of American political culture without throwing anything visionary into the mix. *Democracy* thereby impugns the icon-manufacturing tendencies within American journalism and politics.

In *Political Fictions,* Didion scorns Michael Dukakis for repeatedly staging baseball-toss scenarios on airport runways during the 1988 election campaign. The event was inserted so often into Dukakis's itinerary that it became known "among television crews as a 'tarmac arrival with ball tossing'" (*Political Fictions* 34). Dukakis's plane touches down. Someone hands him a baseball. He throws the ball as if a game of catch were the most natural thing in the world for a presidential aspirant to do on an apron at an airport. The ball toss is pure theater: forty journalists stand to the side watching as Dukakis goes through the motions of throwing a ball. In this sense, American election campaigns, like American political activities generally, take place in a world remote from the daily lives of Americans, even as those campaigns pretend to connect with average Americans and their wishes through semiotics of sportiness and casualness. Reporting the event at all may indicate some degree of journalistic gullibility. Nevertheless, journalists, even if they are being manipulated, are obliged to record what is said and done: "it's part of their age-old duty to be used" by politicians and spin doctors (Lelyveld 10).

Enriched with meaning, mediatized, scripted, the ball toss is made into an iconic moment. Similarly, in *Democracy,* meaning is interpolated into the image of Inez dancing on the rooftop of the St. Regis Hotel in New York. The clip is gussied up with falsehoods about Inez's drinking too much and the fiction of her blissful marriage. The event, broadcast repeatedly, becomes overdetermined, stagy, decontextualized. The party is, in any case, "nominally private but heavily covered by the press" (42). Seeing Inez dancing creates the illusion among viewers that they know her. Iconic moments concentrate fantasies of attachment that are necessarily coherent within specific gender codes. (Women remember their mothers dancing. Men remember mushroom clouds over the Aleutians.) Yet romantic images do not survive outside a system of iconic representations that endlessly reiterate meaning. The film clip of Inez dancing on the rooftop of the St. Regis substitutes in public consciousness for Inez herself. Even Didion as the narrator in *Democracy* begins to see Inez according to the clip, not as she knows her personally. When Inez's sister Janet is shot, the murder is sent over the wires in a skewed, off-topic fashion, as a problem confronting Harry Victor. "VICTOR FAMILY TOUCHED BY ISLAND TRAGEDY" (29), reads the caption in the *New York Times* over a photo of Paul Christian, barefoot, handcuffed, his arms raised theatrically over his head in a crucifixion pose. (After all, he is a "Christian.") The photo has only a tangential connection to Janet. In other words, Paul Christian's murder of his daughter is tragic because the act is absorbed into an iconic representation. Janet disappears into the symbolic image of a prominent family that is not hers.

As Didion says in an essay on Ronald Reagan's presidency, the media crave "character clarity" (*Political Fictions* 117). Iconic representation defies individuality. Images turn into a slide show called history. But those images, in the first instance, are theatrical. In *Democracy,* Billy Dillon coaches Inez in her performance as a presidential hopeful's wife the way a tennis coach trains a player (52). He prepares her answers for interviewers' questions. He advises her on how to speak and how to walk. He creates her as an icon for media consumption that conforms to the unspecified but intuited desires of the American population. The icon separates truth from expectation. The icon condenses meanings, none of them stable or simple, although the icon gives the appearance of stability and simplicity. For this reason, Inez goes on record as saying that the greatest cost of public life is memory. She is, like Jackie Kennedy or Joan Didion herself, an icon who belongs to the public, not a private person. Like any icon, she is "lodged in our systems of thought and reference, as if she were a concept, a numeral, a virtue, or a universal tendency" (Koestenbaum 4). Her love affair with Jack Lovett is the one relationship in *Democracy* that exists beyond public knowledge and consumption.

An icon is a visual representation, a mythic shard. As an image of a mythic person or event, an icon exists in sacred time, above decay and death. (JFK in a Dallas motorcade—Jackie in a pink Chanel suit—: a permanence around this image.) Hence the image of Inez dancing, a version of the imaginary mother dancing, is fed over the networks as the quintessence of Inez Victor. The dancing woman who whispers "marvelous" stands for an abstract notion of *politician's wife,* or *New York socialite.* The representation fossilizes. At once overdetermined and empty, the icon requires interpretation or no interpretation at all. The icon is an abridgement, a shorthand for a host of stories that cannot be spoken unless the icon facilitates their telling. In the icon, complex public personae and institutions can be reduced to initials: US, JFK, LAX, NATO, DC, AID, USIS, CIA. Likewise "democracy" as a political idea becomes a repository of various meanings, many of them too abstruse to be deciphered. *Democracy,* the novel, is filled with acronyms, which are black holes of condensed significance: "DAO" (213), "UPI" (41), "M-16s, AK-47s, FN-FALs" (37), "CODEL" (92), "C-141" (212), "Air Cav" (204). Jack Lovett speaks in a language taut with coded references. He omits connecting syntax:

> Fixed-wing phase.
> Tiger Ops.
> Black flights.
> Extraction.
> Assets.
> AID was without assets.
> USIA was without assets. (195)

This imploded language suggests that language has a tendency to drift towards nonreferentiality. Icons exist as codes, though codes with unclear messages. Ambiguity within the codes of the icon allows readers of the icon to find similarities between signs and reality. The icon demonstrates resemblances, but "similarity is such a capacious relationship that almost anything can be assimilated into it" (Mitchell 56). The icon asserts a symbolic unity among diverse and externally unconnected facts and situations. Meaning lies in the patterns extrapolated from details.

Throughout her journalism and novels published after 1980, Didion sustains a critique of the iconic habits of American politics, especially the habit of creating false icons—Dukakis throwing a baseball, helicopters lifting off the embassy roof in Saigon, Harry Victor sitting around in shirt-sleeves reiterating that he is in *"'awe'"* (62) of young, energetic Americans.[3] These packaged, reiterated moments follow scripts. The icon is motivated by the appearance of naturalness. Billy Dillon creates representations of Harry and Inez that show them in the best possible light as President and First Lady. The icon, as artifice, effaces history. The icon creates a false sense of history as that which is already determined, that which is already scripted, or that which is already enacted. The icon permits no alternative versions of history. As such, the icon is rigidly antidemocratic. All the same, icons are aspects of ourselves, or of culture, that we want to recognize but cannot entirely assimilate into a personal modus operandi. *(Every American-born citizen could be president; but I could never be president because I do not possess the* je ne sais quoi *that creates the aura of iconicity.)* The icon materializes those aspects of ourselves that we cannot otherwise imagine. In this sense, the icon—I am speaking here of political person-alities as they are manufactured by the media in conjunction with the consensual process of voting—lives in us as much as we live in the icon. The icon challenges categories of representation insofar as we live in and through iconic representations (elected officials) and the iconic represen-tation depends on us (the electorate) for its verifiability and authenticity.

Because icons are antidemocratic, Didion includes herself as a char-acter within *Democracy* and invokes readers as participants who need to decipher the codes of American politics. "Call me the author," writes Didion (16). Echoing the opening of *Moby-Dick,* the statement implies an epic grandeur to the process of defining democracy in the United States in the 1980s. Using the imperative, Didion commands the reader to perform specific chores. The reader is deliberately stranded without the guidance of the author, even though the author is as much at sea as the reader amidst meanings and events in this book. Didion issues a "narrative alert" (164), as if the reader were lacking in vigilance. She goads the reader. "You tell me" (188) what Inez's running away means, she charges. The reader needs to develop a memory. Yours may be awfully short. The reader should avoid being lulled by repeated phrases and images, even those images and phrases that Didion uses in *Democracy*. Instead of relying on the author's careful explanation of connections and meanings, Didion requires participatory readership, an analogue for participatory democracy: "The boundaries between narratives of personal policy and national policy are in fact hard to maintain, because if our history contains both the 'free world' and the communist world, it also contains the readers who consumed this narrative, making them participants in the historical performance by virtue of the fact that they had consumed it" (Nadel 289). If you read *Democracy* to confirm your convictions, to abide by contracts and obligations normally played out in realist fiction, you are letting down your side in the participatory dialogue. You treat representations as truth, when they should be treated as representations. If you cannot evaluate for yourself what Inez's dancing on the St. Regis rooftop means, or what Harry Victor's sound-bites signify, then reading *Democracy* is going to be a frustrating experience.[4] For this reason, the inclusion of Joan Didion as a character in the narrative is indispensable to her political point. Policies may be mandated by wonks in Washington and Langley, Virginia, but policy decisions have local and personal consequences.[5] The individual has to figure out what the benefits and demerits are of any system of governance. One at a time, and over time, individuals negotiate their relations to the republic. In a National Public Radio interview in 1977, Didion stated, "My adult life has been a succession of expectations, misperceptions. I dealt only with an idea I had of the world, not with the world as it was. The reality *does* intervene eventually. I think my early novels were ways of dealing with the revelation that experience is largely meaningless" (Stamberg 27). If her early novels considered the nature of postmodern meaninglessness, Didion's later novels, including *Democracy* and *The Last Thing He Wanted*, recruit the reader into the process of discerning meaning, whatever it may be, without resorting to prefabricated icons.

Throughout *Democracy*, references to newspapers and magazines proliferate. Inez and Didion work at *Vogue* (55). Dwight Christian cribs quotable tidbits from *Forbes* magazine (27). Victor and Inez appear, photographed, in *Life*, *W*, and *Vogue* (49). *Newsday* and *People* print gossip about the Victors (65). A news junkie, Didion, following events in Vietnam in the spring of 1975, buys morning editions of "the San Francisco *Chronicle*, the Los Angeles *Times*, and the New York *Times*. Every afternoon I got the same dispatches, under new headlines and with updated leads, in the San Francisco *Examiner,* the Oakland *Tribune,* and the Berkeley *Gazette*" (73). She notices discrepancies in reports. Newspapers in Jakarta in 1969 leak disinformation along with rumors and stories (98). Paul Christian bizarrely demands the "'retraction'" (135) of a photograph in the *Honolulu Advertiser,* as if images were slanderous and could be deleted from public memory. As Paul's demand makes clear, the media cannot reverse information; they only convert it into disinformation or unsubstantiated stories. Inez reads about her family in the *South China Morning Post, International Herald-Tribune, Time,* and *Newsweek.* Similarly, Didion keeps abreast of Inez's personal life by reading about her in newspapers and magazines. The sheer quantity of news and newspapers in *Democracy* raises the ante on information. Does a novel, as kin to other print media, convey disinformation? Moreover, Didion implies, news exists in order to stoke the desire for news, regardless of its factual content. Jack Lovett, trying to convey how dangerous the situation is for Congressman Harry Victor and his family in Jakarta in 1969, separates reality from news: "'You don't actually see what's happening in front of you. You don't see it unless you read it. You have to read it in the New York *Times,* then you start talking about it. Give a speech. Call for an investigation'" (100). Lovett distinguishes between representations and reality. Reality exists only insofar as newspapers create that reality. More damning still, Lovett suggests that journalistic representations already exist at a remove from reality, and they exist in order to cater to the iconic expectations of readers, including Harry Victor.

Democracy, replete with photos, begins with a photograph of sorts. Jack Lovett explains that he witnessed nuclear bomb tests on South Pacific atolls in 1952 and 1953, tests meant to demonstrate the efficacy of American technologies of destruction. The tests were designed to be photographed. Jack refers to them as "shots": "None of the observers would fly down until the technical guys had the shot set up, that's all I was, an observer. Along for the ride. There for the show" (12). The relative absence of grammatical subjects in Jack's sentences makes him melt away from scenes of disaster or involvement. No personal pronouns mark his presence, not even off the record. He remains an observer, a nonparticipant, treating nuclear destruction euphemistically as a "show." He jokes that one test fizzled, yet "the Los Alamos photographers started snapping away at that Livermore tower—still standing" (13). Such shots, diffused through the usual channels, prove American nuclear capacity more effectively than detonation of the bomb itself. In the essay "Pacific Distances," Didion encapsulates the dawn of the atomic age, and the rhetoric of progress and new tomorrows that such a "dawn" implies, in a snapshot taken during the 1950s of a very young Livermore scientist on a beach while he worked on tests of "atmospheric nuclear weapons in the Pacific" (*After Henry* 125). History distills into a series of photographs. The meaning they possess must be deduced by inferential clues. Similarly, although Jack Lovett appears in no photographs, his role is crucial in the making of history.

For this reason, the death of the U.S. government spy may seem like the realization of his already secretive nature, the disappearance into an obscurity of his own making. Jack's death fulfills a paradigm of espionage invisibility. The CIA spy, as an iconic figure, represents not just covert intelligence operations. He also represents a set of inexpressible psychological meanings that converge on his invisibility. Romance figures among those meanings. Jack blows his cover as an agent when he flees to Hong Kong with Inez. A decision taken for personal reasons makes him more visible to the media than all the decisions that he has taken over the years under the closest security. The death of Jack Lovett four months after he elopes with Inez suggests that happiness and romance are ultimately intolerable for a spy within the American writer's political imagination. *Democracy* intimates that a spy has no business having a love life, unless it occurs once his spying days have ended. Public duty and personal gratification occupy incompatible zones of experience. The spy dies in the attempt to cross the no-man's-land between those two zones. Romance, either in the sense of carnal union or in the sense of hypothesizing alternatives to reality, is forbidden. In this regard, Didion critiques romance as a political modality. American political representation, she suggests, is too indebted to the making of images rather than dealing with things as they are, is too enamoured of symbolic action rather than action itself, is too smitten with icons generated by the media and spy thrillers rather than devoted to the evaluation of other kinds of representation that might better articulate the political process in the United States.

In most narratives of intrigue dealing with CIA operations, the spy expresses conflicting allegiances by going undercover yet remaining loyal to the state apparatus that employs him. The spy performs ideology without believing in what he does. The spy expresses ambiguity of motive, identity, and action. Avoiding thrills while including a CIA agent in the narrative, *Democracy* shows how global politics might be represented outside the conventions established by Buchan, Conrad, and le Carré. The death of Jack Lovett—for all his butch James Bond-style name—signifies the end of a certain kind of political representation that relies on thrills and chases.

CHAPTER ELEVEN

Conclusion

LITTLE ROOMS

SPIES ARE ICONS of political identity in the twentieth century, especially the ethical dimensions of identity that pertain to just conduct in hazardous circumstances. Recruited into missions that he may not approve of fully, the spy keeps his commitments fluid. Although party affiliation and life-long loyalty to specific ideologies—communism, republican democracy, czarist police states, parliamentary monarchy—may be possible, the spy demonstrates that such commitments conceal conflicts between character and action. The spy affirms allegiances impermanently in order to preserve the right to doubt the wisdom of official decisions. Moreover, while he represents a particular nation or political party, the spy modifies his convictions with private motives and emotions, including love, anger, and fear. "The need for amusement, the fear of boredom," is how Victor Maskell explains the hidden springs of spying in *The Untouchable* (23). As *Under Western Eyes, The Spy Who Came in From the Cold, The Bourne Identity,* and other narratives indicate, the reasons for spying are multiple, and some-times retaliatory. Where justice has not been enacted by due process, at least in the minds of Razumov, Leamas, or Jason Bourne, administering justice becomes a personal matter. Razumov violently beats the carriage driver Ziemianitch with a pitchfork, then betrays Haldin to the police. Lea-mas reads about his so-called crimes in the English newspapers, a bit of disinformation authenticating his defection that Control never mentioned to him beforehand. Perilously situated with respect to the law, as a renegade or as a wronged person who has lost recourse to institutional forms of justice, the spy takes the law into his own hands. The private motives for exacting justice do not diminish the ethical consequences that a spy's actions have for others, especially as they bear on harm, security, and the common good.

The spy's identity, always a political identity within an allegory of intrigue, is emblematic of an individual's position with respect to the law and the state. By virtue of his presence in a narrative, the spy evokes the shadowy underpinnings—secret committees and covert plots—that keep the state functioning. Trading in secrets, professional spies exist because statehood itself is defined by secrecy and access to information. Inveterate dissimulators, spies circulate undetected through the body politic. The spy keeps close his affiliations and therefore embodies unavowed policies, alliances, deals, and information within the state. Jeopardized by threats of injury or death, the spy carries out his mission under ambiguous conditions: should the agent risk bodily safety or his life for a particular country? Cut off from his operators, the spy enforces the laws, policies, and ambitions of the state at a distance, as does Leamas in East Germany or Razumov in Geneva. Of course the spy may have his moments of revolt and anguish, yet he also knows that state power exists in and through his deeds. Narratives of intrigue therefore question the duties and rights of citizenship in terms of dissenting from and, contrarily, serving the state. As such, espionage plots figure issues of justice and obligation, not in order to let readers abstract themselves from those obligations, but to allow readers to evaluate the ways in which secrets and authority are transmitted by every individual within a polity.

By awakening an ethical dimension in representation, the spy enlists the judiciousness of the reader. The reader evaluates the meaning and fairness of actions taken within a narrative according to the specifics of each case. Because they so pointedly include an ideological dimension, espionage narratives, perhaps more so than other genres, enable speculation on the nature of commitment. Readers negotiate their position within ideology by interpreting the behaviors and actions of spies. As decoders, readers are recruited into narrative. In certain instances, the reader may be implicated through an act of hailing, such as Didion uses in *Democracy* in order to prod the reader into assuming responsibility for democratic debate and thoughtfulness amidst divergent reports and disinformation. Erskine Childers presents himself as the editor of *The Riddle of the Sands*, the first reader of documents, memos, and diaries that Carruthers gives him. Childers's stated goal in this novel is "to reach everyone" (260), by which he means, as he clarifies in the preface, "every thoughtful citizen," who, after careful scrutiny of the evidence, will establish, with others, "a community sanely conscious of its powers, limitations, and duties" (2). Childers views reading as a decipherment of duty, in which individuals perform as thoughtful citizens. Other narratives call upon readers less directly, as when the Professor of Languages reads Razumov's diary and interjects himself into the story of Razumov's spy mission, or as when Calloway creates a dossier on Harry Lime that Rollo Martins contributes to and, in effect, closes. As readerly presences within the plot, both the Professor and Calloway interpret data. They therefore substitute for the reader, who equally must make sense of achronological jumps, bias, and disinformation. Narratives of intrigue do not resolve ideological conflicts —who is right or wrong—but provide models for thinking about the laws that control narrative, the laws that narrative perpetuates, and the ways that such laws are communicated to a reader who is called upon to make judgments about justness and ideology.

Novels of intrigue supplement notions of statehood advanced by Althusser, Rawls, Elster, Mouffe, and other political theorists. Novels do not substitute for history or political theory. They do, however, offer ways to think about violence, conformity, and duty. After a fashion, political concepts enable novelistic interpretation. A theory of overlapping consensus or democratic reasonableness tempered by personal interest requires proofs, and fiction is one way of delivering hypothetical proofs. Althusser's notion of state apparatuses can be applied as a paradigm for readerly recruitment in spy fiction, a hailing that occurs via thrilling chases and encrypted meanings. Technique in narratives of intrigue, whether an interpellative hailing of "you" the reader, or a first-person police dossier, or a journalistic report, situates questions in specific contexts and circumstances—not real, not even necessarily realist, but representations that describe problems of agency, consensus, and citizenship.

In narratives of intrigue, recruitment demonstrates the disposition of characters towards ideology. Whereas most political and literary critical considerations of Althusser's idea of interpellation—when a policeman hails a person in the street—emphasize guilt and shrinking before the state, espionage narratives give more complicated accounts of recruitment. Some spies are recruited for personal or psychological reasons, such as Razumov's consciousness of his illegitimacy, or Leamas's desire to retire on a secure pension, or Victor Maskell's need for intellectual and sexual stimulation. Others are recruited because of prior military experience, such as Jack Lovett possesses, or because of financial necessity, such as Fenn Turner faces as a young man. Recruitment in espionage narratives does not presuppose guilt alone as a determining factor. Rather, recruitment appeals to an individual's desire to serve the state, not to swerve from its power. Althusser's exemplum of interpellation skews the notion of ideology towards its manifestations in the police or other state apparatuses.

The state, however, is not always present so concretely. For instance, when a burglar enters your home in the dead of night and you awake to find him at your bedside or riffling through your belongings, you may wish, fervently in fact, that authorities of some sort were present at that moment. But the diverse appointees of state power—policemen, sheriffs, peacekeepers—are nowhere to be seen. You may cringe under the covers fearfully or you may spring bravely from your bed to confront the burglar. In either action, you take a position with respect to the law and its powers. At this moment, the power of justice is vested in you. You can chase the thief from your house, subdue him while you call the police, or let him go. You can yell for help, a verbal conjuring of state power or other citizens that directly complements, in mirror fashion, Althusser's example of a policeman hailing a person in the street. That call for help continues to sound over time and to unite individuals in solidarity with state control. Althusser's model of interpellation should not be taken so literally as to exclude instances in which the hailed citizen arrogates power to himself or solicits help. In a more expansive interpretation of interpellation, the citizen need not cravenly shrink before ideology, as if that were the only means of being interpellated. Instead, the citizen understands that he takes multiple positions with respect to ideology according to his perceived interests at different moments in time. Sometimes the citizen will be cast as an enforcer of ideology and state power, even if that citizen styles himself as disaffected with civil authority. Certain positions situate the citizen as an arbiter of justice. To be recruited in narratives of intrigue means, on occasion, to take on the guise of power with the guise of ideology.

Recruitment in spy narratives happens in multiple ways. Indeed, historical forces couple with psychological imperatives to create the conditions for drawing individuals into spy plots. Recruitment during the Cold War in the United States, for example, carries with it a semiotics of duplicity in which, typically, the recruit has no conscious knowledge of being a double agent. In the 1953 film *Pickup on South Street,* a woman, acting as a go-between for communists, carries a microfilm in her bag on a crowded New York subway. A pickpocket, not knowing what he is stealing, lifts the microfilm from her purse. The microfilm contains a chemical formula, a coded message that the layperson cannot understand but that could prove key in the technological struggles of the Cold War. Two policemen witness the theft on the subway because they are trying to locate members of the communist cell by tailing the woman. Both the woman and the pickpocket are recruited into a political plot without specific cognizance of that plot. The woman does not know that a gang of communist infiltrators use her as a messenger, nor does she know that the police are following her. Out of vestigial love for her communist ex-boyfriend, whom she does not recognize as a traitor let alone an agent for inimical forces, the woman carries sensitive information between him and his cronies. Characteristic of women within narratives of intrigue, the template for whom is Stella in *The Heat of the Day,* the go-between in *Pickup on South Street* is recruited because of her emotional attachments. In any event, her ex-boyfriend may have loved her *only* so that he could use her as a messenger —an emotional doublecross with a political edge.

Similarly, the thief does not initially understand the extent of the plot that ripples out from picking the woman's purse on the subway. He remains innocent of ideology. Nevertheless, the isolated incident has broad implications for national security. The pickpocket learns the value of the microfilm from the police, then tries to sell the film back to the communists at an inflated price. Thinking that he can appeal to patriotism, a policeman tells the thief that, unless he cooperates with the investigation by returning the microfilm, he will "be as guilty as the traitors who gave Stalin the A-bomb." The film plays on shifting degrees of culpability and innocence. As one policeman claims, there is "a big difference between a traitor and a pickpocket." The difference depends on the magnitude of the crime. A thief harms people by stealing their belongings, whereas a traitor theoretically harms an entire nation. In *Pickup on South Street,* the pickpocket catches the communists red-handed. He sees the microfilm being turned over in the public toilets at a subway station. By virtue of his previous convictions for larceny, the pickpocket is recruited to act in the national interest, though that recruitment occurs because the thief decides, *of his own accord,* to cooperate with the law. He sees advantages in working on behalf of the police, who ultimately clear his criminal record. In fact, his skills as a thief help him lift a gun out of the communist's pocket. This prudent action prevents further bloodshed; the communist has already fatally shot an informer, injured his former girlfriend, and killed a policeman. Being a thief does not bring any discredit to the pickpocket's identity as an American. Small-time criminality serves the larger interests of the United States even if the thief has no intention of acting patriotically. Of his own volition, the pickpocket administers justice, which puts him, for a change, at rights with the law.

Tension in *Pickup on South Street* hinges on the moments when individuals decide to act from personal or civic interest. A money-hungry stool pigeon refuses to give information to the communist agent even when he throws crumpled bills at her. As she says, she does not "like commies." Although *Pickup on South Street* clearly delineates between bad Americans (who act as communist agents) and good Americans (who are unwittingly run by communists or who refuse to give in to communists), that delineation depends on the judgment of characters to side with the law, to allow themselves to be recruited to act for the law, or to go outside the law when required in order to catch communist outlaws. Regardless of which ethical stance characters take, that stance always relates to legality. Characters perceive themselves as helping legal processes by selling information only to the authorities or by acting as couriers for the police. By doing so, they transmit justice.

The Cold War scene of recruitment, in which American citizens do not realize they are acting for the communist enemy, plays out slightly differently in the 1962 movie *The Manchurian Candidate,* starring Frank Sinatra as Ben Marco, a U.S. Army officer. During a mission in Korea, Captain Marco is abducted, flown by communists to Manchuria, and brainwashed, as are other members of his patrol. Back in the United States with a promotion and disabled by recurring nightmares, Major Marco takes sick leave. On the train from Washington, D.C., to New York City, he meets Eugénie Rose Cheyney, played by Janet Leigh. Shot in close quarters between two carriages of the train, a scene of mutual interrogation unfolds between Ben and Eugénie, who goes by the nickname "Rosie." The conversation leapfrogs from topic to topic in non sequiturs, which may or may not have coded meaning. Rosie—perfectly coiffed, impeccably made up, composed, smoking—could be an agent sent to assign Ben to a nefarious mission. Out of the blue, Ben asks Rosie, "Are you Arabic?" Answering negatively, she asks him in turn if he is Arabic. When he says no, she replies, "Let me put it another way: are you married?" "Arabic" momentarily means "married" in her lingo. At the same time as the conversation is a romantic pickup between a strikingly beautiful woman and a startlingly handsome serviceman on a train, Ben and Rosie speak in code that may, in the political context of the narrative, have another, more sinister meaning.

Although Rosie finds Ben attractive and shows great determination in cruising him, her conversational gambits give every appearance of doubleness. Rosie triggers unconscious recollections in Ben by pressing random information upon him and asking him to memorize it:

> ROSIE: I live at 53, West 54th Street, Apartment 3B. Can you remember that?
>
> BEN *(in a hushed voice, after a pause):* Yes.
>
> ROSIE *(with quiet insinuation):* Eldorado 59970. Can you remember that?
>
> BEN *(after a pause):* Yes.
>
> ROSIE *(brightly):* Are you stationed in New York, or is "stationed" the right word?
>
> BEN *(after a pause):* I'm not exactly stationed in New York. I was *(pause)* stationed in Washington, but *(pause)* I got sick and now I'm on leave and *(pause)* I'm going to spend it in New York.
>
> ROSIE: Eldorado 59970.

Unprompted, as if relaying urgent secrets, she repeats her telephone number: "Eldorado 59970." In response to this unsolicited information, Ben closes his eyes and tightens his lips in a grimace. The scene is acted *as if* it were an espionage recruitment. Her insistence that he remember makes her seem to be transmitting sensitive material.[1] Trafficking in ambiguity, Rosie, who is not Chinese (just as she is not Arabic), claims to have been "one of the original Chinese workmen who laid the track" through Delaware. Her allusion to Chinese workmen activates suspicions against her, since the brainwasher in *The Manchurian Candidate,* a psychiatrist who works at the Pavlov Institute in Moscow, is Chinese. Linked to communism via her identification as Chinese, Rosie positions herself, unconsciously and consciously, as the enigmatic other to Major Marco.

During the conversation between Ben and Rosie on the train, he refuses to look at her or casts only fleeting glances in her direction. Her body is of little interest to him, though his body is carefully scrutinized by Rosie. The scene is shot in alternating close-ups of Ben and Rosie; seldom do they share the same frame, and when they do, a train window separates them. Ben intones answers in a faraway voice. He constantly changes the subject of the conversation to protect his privacy, or more specifically, the nature of his suffering. Evidently ill, and ill at ease, Ben sweats profusely throughout this scene. Beads of perspiration appear on his upper lip and forehead. Rosie conspicuously does not sweat. Sweat, restricted to Ben, signifies some interior fever that comes out on his face —the illness of having been indoctrinated to support a communist plot without his consent. His body betrays the pressure of ideological doubleness. Coincidentally, in *Pickup on South Street,* the communist traitor sweats buckets. Perspiration in these two films is a symptom of nonconformity in the Cold War, the uncontainable leakage of fluids from the American male body. Brainwashed in Manchuria, Ben suffers from conflicting allegiances. The duplicities of citizenship materialize in the brainwashed agent's body as sweat. Generally speaking, the spy's body, whether straight or queer, athletic or lame, spectral or full-blooded, is a site where fears and ambiguities work themselves out.

The pseudorecruitment scene between Rosie and Ben takes place between two carriages of a train, in a private gap within a public place. Topological constraints often define the spy's activities. The spatial coordinates of espionage narratives, manifest in walls, sewers, maps, bunkers, and frontiers, figure the spy's adaptability. The spaces of spy fiction may be spaces of surveillance, such as the watchtowers that stand over the checkpoint in Berlin in *The Spy Who Came in From the Cold,* or the parks and vestibules in which the Professor in *Under Western Eyes* observes the comings and goings of Razumov. Other spaces, such as underground bunkers and networks of sewers, conceal the spy's movements. Occasionally walls constrain the spy, imprison him rather than hide him. Living between visibility and invisibility, the spy tries to take up no space at all. The spy's complex psychology attests to deep-seated fantasies of death and disappearance—the desire for spacelessness. "Survival means you learn how to narrow the space you take up," Don DeLillo writes in *Mao II* (145). As representational containers for character, spaces provide refuges for hidden identities and secrets. The smaller the space, the less likely secrets and hidden selves will be discovered. If DeLillo is right, the narrower the space, the greater your chance of surviving. Needless to say, the representation of character demands the representation of space of some kind. Unable to disappear, the spy retreats to a tiny or invisible room.

In DeLillo's 1988 novel *Libra,* CIA agent Win Everett is pensioned off and sent to teach at Texas Women's University, where he lurks in the "gloom of the basement nook" (178) that he calls his office. *Libra,* as an interpretation of the assassination of JFK, offers the theory that "men in small rooms" (41) create conspiracies and manufacture history. Some of the small rooms in this novel are offices, prison cells, darkrooms, and safe houses. Some rooms hang "above the world" (221). Some have their own "time zone[s]" (42). Physical dimensions alone do not determine space; space relies on human perception and the activities conducted within the little room. The "little room" that Lee Harvey Oswald calls his study is "like an airtight compartment, part of the building but also separate from it" (276). Oswald occupies a series of little rooms with his mother and his wife, even though he prefers to keep his private spaces to himself, as hidey-holes or zones of cogitation. His desire to be sequestered becomes a character trait. As a child at his aunt's, "he hid in the back room reading funnybooks while his cousins fought and played" (305). In the marines, he is tossed into a cell for breaching regulations: "The brig was invented just for him. It was just another name for the stunted rooms where he'd spent his life" (100). Within these little rooms, momentous plans may be hatched. Oswald tries to "feel history in the cell" (100), as if small spaces compact time and make it more dense. The little room serves as a spatial depiction of the secret self, a place of strictest privacy. A world within a world, the little room need not be exposed to the light of day. Every character in *Libra* occupies a private room, including the researcher Nicholas Branch who builds an office to house all the data he has collected about the assassination of JFK. Win Everett visits his wine cellar to be alone. His wife Mary Frances Everett never answers the phone and more or less stops leaving her house. Their daughter Suzanne Everett sits in her bedroom and decides on "a safer hiding place" for her totemic "Little Figures" (365); she settles on a narrow ledge behind a dresser, against a wall, a tiny crevice that only her hand can reach. "A cell is the basic state, the crude truth of the world" (418), thinks Oswald. The cell isolates by keeping one person in and everyone else out. The little room allows fantasies to be born and thrive because they are not contested and cannot be disproved. The little room represents hypothetical individualism untouched by contradictory opinions. Assassins scheme in little rooms. Researchers theorize. Children daydream. Readers shut out the world in order to understand it better.

Although Lee Harvey Oswald is not a spy, he is implicated in a conspiracy generated by disaffected ex-CIA agents. In *Libra*, DeLillo innovates on literary representation as a form of legal representation. The novel neither gives voice to the president nor directly depicts him. In this regard, DeLillo defies the iconic tendencies in American fiction. He effectively shifts emphasis away from the indeterminacy of an iconic event and towards the principles that underlie justice. DeLillo also stretches out the recruitment of Lee Harvey Oswald so that no single moment or gesture can be called the point at which he is absorbed into ideology. Oswald happens to be in several wrong places at several wrong times, and to possess a profile that the conspirators can exploit. They fabricate their agent out of hints and traces. In this sense, *Libra* perpetuates the American tradition of representing individuals as *unwitting* agents, as exemplified in both *Pickup on South Street* and *The Manchurian Candidate*. Those who assassinate the president or pass microfilm over to communists do not understand the rationale for their actions. Their innocence or guilt is not straightforward.

As we have seen in novels such as *The Bourne Identity, Under Western Eyes,* and *The Spy Who Came in From the Cold,* violence constitutes subjectivity to some degree, and that violence bespeaks the dangers attendant on the individual's accommodation to ideology. In *Libra*, Oswald is regularly assaulted by schoolmates, fellow marines, and policemen. His life is a series of scuffles. As a schoolboy, his mouth is bloody from fighting (32). In the Marines, he slops a drink on a sergeant and they skirmish (97). A guard beats Oswald (104–5). He gets mixed up in a shoving match on the street and cannot account for how it started (321). He has another dustup over leaflets (326). He fights a cop (409–10). Any interaction is a pretext for Oswald to fight. He has a talent for provoking others to rage. In part, physical violence produces him as a subject. Imagining that he is a "zero in the system" (151, 357), he fights in order to make himself visible. Oswald externalizes his desire for and his repulsion towards the invisibility of his ideological commitments, a phenomenon that he characterizes as "faceless-ness" (108). Experts barrage Oswald with tests of various kinds—report cards, polygraphs, psychometric analyses—that measure his capacities without ever solving the enigma of his identity. Consular dossiers and court-martial transcripts attest to his status as legal subject. He can be measured and judged, but he remains, to a significant extent, invisible.

In *Libra,* justice of a sort is administered by individuals on other indi-viduals, whether through approved means such as the police or through unofficial channels such as a brawl in the streets. Oswald draws people into fistfights because of an aggravated persecution complex. Oswald's mother, by contrast, assumes that justice is a lonely affair. Marguerite rou-tinely imagines herself in soliloquy, before the television, as if she were a defendant at a trial. In her head, she addresses a "judge" (10, 242–44), whom she calls "your honor" (48–49, 448–56). Marguerite's sense of legal entitlement to speak before the bench creates a "prosecutorial" or "justificatory" form, in the sense that Marguerite, arguing in the first per-son, expects, even hopes, to be arraigned in court to explain herself. She has rights. She *will* bear witness. She *will* answer to the law. She *will* re-fute allegations of being a bad mother. "I have information pertinent to the case," she pleas (449–50). In court, truth will come to light. The invisible parts of identity, those that have been hidden away in little rooms, will be exposed as right and just. She habitually invents her monologues to the judge in the presence of a television (35, 48, 242). On television, the law as a spectacle, manifest in innumerable courtroom dramas and legal cases, answers a cultural need for alibis and defenses, not to mention sentences and punishments. Marguerite imagines that television can filter her story and prove her right to a wide audience. By the same token, tele-vision, as Marguerite claims, fells her son: "TV gave the cue and Lee was shot" (450). Marguerite's and her son's identities are extensions of the law as it filters through the cathode tubes of the television. Television is the forum in which Lee's guilt is debated. Television recruits Marguerite and stirs her to self-justification.

Marguerite watches television in her living room. She bears witness to herself, for herself. A defector in a small, subsidized Moscow apartment, dyslexic Lee Harvey Oswald pens his "Historic Diary" (149). He bears witness to the position of the individual in history by writing out his tribulations. The person in a little room—Razumov in his apartment, Rollo Martins in the dark with a parrot, Stella in her blacked-out London flat, Leamas in an unlit cell in East Germany, Maskell in his study, Fenn and Sue in the cabin of their boat, Didion at her desk—is a person confronted by the question of political identity. Inside the room, that person registers an opinion that may or may not dissent from ideology. Little rooms accommodate espionage and counterespionage plots that leak into the world beyond. Analogous to the interdependent scenes that make up a plot, little rooms are spaces where individuals determine their commitments, then justify them through words and actions. Even when alone in a little room, everyone is politically determined. Alone in little rooms, ordinary individuals work out the ways that the state converts them into its plenipotentiaries, its delegates, its agents, its spies.

NOTES

1. At an early stage of planning, I thought I might include a chapter on Canadian espionage fiction. Mordecai Richler's novel *A Choice of Enemies* spoofs McCarthy's witch-hunts in America. Norman in Richler's novel writes "thrillers and the occasional film script" (4). George Bowering's novel *Harry's Fragments* deconstructs the thriller. Examples of Canadian thrillers, however, are not legion. Margaret Atwood intimates in a prose piece called "Happy Endings" that Canadians cannot write credible spy plots. To avoid bourgeois plots of happiness and infidelity, Atwood advises, start with a couple of characters named John and Mary: "make John a revolutionary and Mary a counterespionage agent and see how far that gets you. Remember, this is Canada" (40). Historically, if not novelistically, Canada is important for an international espionage incident that instigated hostilities between Russia and the West. In September 1945, a Russian cipher clerk named Igor Gouzenko defected in Ottawa with documents proving that Russians had spied on their allies during the war (Whitaker and Marcuse 28–42). The defection set off an international scandal (Bothwell 13–16). Gouzenko, after defecting, became an author and won a 1954 Governor-General's Award—Canada's highest literary prize at the time—for his novel *The Fall of a Titan*. To protect his identity, he appeared in public with a white bag over his head, most famously on the current affairs show *Front Page Challenge* (Whitaker and Marcuse xxvi; Hannant 19–23). Gouzenko's getup made creepiness an attribute of the defector's insubstantial shadow life. Anonymous in his balaclava, Gouzenko lived out the split between his old identity as a Russian and his new identity as a defector (Jonas 25–27).

2. Bond's sexuality has inspired much thoughtful commentary. From an anthropological perspective, Lee Drummond interprets Bond movies as quintessentially American, not British at all. Invoking the specter of conspiracy theory, Drummond claims that Bond represents the "concept-myth of America itself" in which "discrete, bounded societies, groups, or situations" can be infiltrated by "the clever agent" (168). Kingsley Amis unapologetically coddles heterosexist Bond. "Whatever Bond's personal ideology about women, he treats them badly in practice," writes Amis, then adds, speaking in the oblivious male plural, "Any number of us, however, could afford to take a couple of leaves out of Bond's book" (50, 52–53). Amis excuses Bond's sadism as *"enjoyment"* (150). Using Lacanian and cultural theory, Tony Bennett and Janet Woollacott spot Bond as an agent of playboy patriarchy. Free of marriage and fidelity, Bond puts "girls" who err from the sexual order back in their place. This indicates the liberty of Bond's "girls": "Released from the constraints of social inhibition and from the hypocrisy of the double-standard, the only (!) restriction placed on the Bond girl—the model, once finely tuned, of a free and independent sexuality—is that she should submit to the regime of the phallus in the ordering of her desires" (Bennett and Woollacott 118). Christine Bold, summing up these arguments, claims that the resistant female reader "can destabilize the hierarchy of gender and race on which the Bond institution rests, interpreting textual fissures as faultlines in the construction of patriarchal nationhood" (325). I agree, though one need not be a female reader to identify Bond's nervous heterosexuality. For instance, in *Casino Royale,* the first Bond novel that Ian Fleming published, Bond fears impotence. After being tortured by the villain Le Chiffre, who paddles Bond's genitals with a carpet-beater, Bond, transferring his feelings of humiliation onto someone else, expresses a desire to "spank" (174) his female coworker and love interest Vesper Lynd, just as he has been beaten. In *Casino Royale,* he typically sleeps with his hand on his gun as if to empower himself (13). Never once in the novel, however, does he shoot his gun, though he is the object of several attacks and assassination attempts. He frustrates a henchman who sticks his rubber-tipped cane "right into the cleft between [Bond's] two buttocks" (87). Bond has already fantasized what this henchman would look like naked, which may account for Bond's pushing himself back onto the henchman's cane, which happens to be a gun in disguise. Bond's masculinity relies on codes of homosociality, especially those that liken villain to spy in motivation and demeanor. I discuss Bond further in my chapter on *The Untouchable.* Throughout this book, I opt for masculine pronouns when I refer to spies on the grounds that fictional spies are more often male than female. For this reason, narratives of intrigue permit investigation into some forms of twentieth-century masculinity.

3. This detail in the film is not included in Ludlum's novel, which is the basis for two film treatments. *The Bourne Identity* was a 200-minute, two-part, made-for-television movie in 1988. The 2002 version, directed by Doug

Liman, shortens the script and includes a hair-raising car chase along the Seine in Paris—against the flow of traffic. I do not wish to comment extensively on the film versions of spy scenarios, although I am fully aware that Graham Greene wrote the novella *The Third Man* expressly as a predecessor for the film script, that Deighton's, Ludlum's, and le Carré's novels have been rewritten for the screen, and that thrillers constitute a cinematic category. Cinema allows a wider range of *scopic* information than novels do: angle, shot, countershot, shadow, light, montage, crosscutting, detail, frame, distance, motion, visual inference. A study of surveillance and scopophilia implicit in spy films would be a worthy undertaking, but that is not the study I offer here.

4. The historical studies of espionage being vast, I can name only a few books that complement my literary analysis. Norman Polmar and Thomas B. Allen's *Spy Book: The Encyclopedia of Espionage* lists terms, dates, agencies, and events. Walter Laqueur's *A World of Secrets: The Uses and Limits of Intelligence* covers the meaning and strategic uses of intelligence gathering. Bernard Porter's *Plots and Paranoia: A History of Political Espionage in Britain, 1790–1988* and Richard J. Aldrich's edited book *Espionage, Security and Intelligence in Britain 1945–1970* are helpful introductions to British security. Reg Whitaker and Gary Marcuse's *Cold War Canada: The Making of a National Insecurity State, 1945–1957* supplements J. L. Granatstein and David Stafford's *Spy Wars: Espionage and Canada From Gouzenko to Glasnost*. Among shelves of material about American spying, Allen Dulles's *The Craft of Intelligence* stands out, because the former director of the CIA has a personal investment in explaining Cold War policies. Ralph de Toledano's *Spies, Dupes and Diplomats*, Clive Ray's *Secrets, Spies and Scholars*, Nigel West's *Seven Spies Who Changed the World*, Phillip Knightley's *The Second Oldest Profession*, and Jeffrey Richelson's *A Century of Spies: Intelligence in the Twentieth Century* provide information about diplomacy, technology, universities, and other matters pertinent to a historical and social analysis of espionage. Biographies of specific spies (Mata Hari, Kim Philby, "Intrepid"), as well as histories of specific spy rings or clandestine agencies (the Cambridge Spies, the KGB, the Profumo Affair), run to hundreds of volumes.

CHAPTER 2. THRILLS

1. I do not believe, as do most philosophers who discuss fear, that "real life emotion" is different from "art emotion" (Feagin 491). Kendall Walton argues that "works of art generate make-believe truths" (12). Walton, in a Platonic haze, distinguishes fear from quasi-fear brought about by looking at representations. Walton's theory does not account for the ideological consequences of so-called make-believe truths. Just because a "truth" is made up does not preclude belief in that "truth." Alex Neill modifies Walton's argument to claim that the experience of representation—reactions of horror and alarm— "do not require an explanation in terms of making-believe, any more than

they do in terms of belief proper" (55). None of these philosophers considers the political import of fear, which may be instilled either by gun-toting policemen or by action thrillers.

CHAPTER 3. CODES

1. Many spy novels include the calculation of odds, which should be taken as the introduction of calculable probabilities and hazards into the sequence that forms a plot. Hannay in *The Thirty-Nine Steps* inveterately calculates his odds of surviving, as when he luckily finds lentonite in a room where he is imprisoned and blows a hole in the wall, or as when he drives a stolen car through a hedge and over a cliff but is saved by a hawthorn branch that catches him and breaks his fall. The principle of calculating odds holds true in Ian Fleming's *Casino Royale*, in which the chief antagonism occurs at a baccarat table where, against all odds, Bond wins a jackpot. Luck in these novels helps spies defy the odds. Luck is an incalculable factor that is nevertheless factored into any good spy's plans as a variable that may assist or impede a mission. This contrast of luck and odds is meant therefore as a contrast between irrationality and rationality, although the two are fused together in the improbabilities and coincidences that characterize espionage narratives. Rollo Martins arrives haphazardly in Vienna on the day of Lime's burial in *The Third Man;* a SMERSH agent appears fortuitously and kills Le Chiffre while Bond is being tortured in *Casino Royale*.

2. Georges Ifrah's *The Universal History of Numbers* is one of several entertaining accounts of the evolution of number systems. Charles Seife's *Zero: The Biography of a Dangerous Idea* recounts the evolution of the idea of a void in mathematics.

3. Mathematicians have invaded postmodern drama and film. An infant math wizard appears in Tom Stoppard's play *Arcadia*. Hugh Whitemore's play *Breaking the Code* concerns Alan Turing's cracking of the Enigma code. David Auburn's drama *Proof*, an investigation of the border between genius and madness, features two mathematicians, a father and daughter. The film *A Beautiful Mind* lionizes math savant and Nobel-laureate John Nash. Mathematical ability defies class and education in the movie *Good Will Hunting;* Will Hunting, played by Matt Damon, is a janitor who solves complex mathematical problems left on the blackboard at MIT. An autistic boy with a preternatural mathematical intelligence narrates Mark Haddon's novel *The Curious Incident of the Dog in the Night-Time*. This concentration on mathematicians suggests a cultural preoccupation with inexplicable genius and numerical representation—a potential transcendence through numbers alone. I discuss mathematicians further in my chapter on *The Untouchable*.

CHAPTER 4. GHOSTS

1. Raymond Williams calls *Under Western Eyes* Conrad's "gesture" (149) at the English novel without elaborating the specific valence of gestural repetition in the novel.

2. Conrad was named after the hero of Mickiewicz's poem, *Konrad Wallenrod*. Joseph Conrad's father, a translator and Polish nationalist, highly revered Mickiewicz. It is therefore possible that he was thinking of Konrad in *Fore-father's Eve* as well as Konrad Wallenrod when he named his son. For direct allusions to *Forefather's Eve* in *Under Western Eyes*, see Gustav Morf (193) and Addison Bross (68–71).

3. St. Cyril created the Cyrillic alphabet. Although the name "Razumov" is linked to the Russian word for "reason," his given names equally identify him with the Russian church and state. David R. Smith speculates further on Razumov's name (44–45).

CHAPTER 5. SEWERS

1. Without accounting for the political content of the novel, Seymour Chatman finds the narrative of *The Third Man* flawed because Calloway filters the tale: "Much of the moral disequilibrium achieved in the film is disallowed in the novel by making Calloway narrator" (191). He comments too liberally and too leisurely on details that have no place in a police file, according to Chatman. Chatman judges the text according to realist standards of consistency and credibility without considering that the thriller has other generic goals. By comparison, film critics tend to disparage the limitations of the novel without appreciating narrative technique and textual richness. Glenn Man complains that "the final effect of the novel is that of a mere thriller, while the final effect of the film is that of an existential thriller," whatever "a mere thriller" may be (171). Ulrike Schwab, a naive interpreter of cultural artifacts, seeks Cold War "facts" and "reality" (3) about Vienna in the film and is rather disappointed to learn that cinema distorts reality. William F. Van Wert denigrates the novel and lauds the film, because the former relies on nineteenth-century narrative structures and the latter portrays "multiple perspectives," repetition of time, and "the controlled eccentricity of the camera eye" (341); such analysis tendentiously extols one medium at the expense of another. Connecting the novel to Greene's other works of the 1930s and 1940s, Norman Macleod, in a more reasonable critique, finds elements of "parody" or "self-parody" in the novel (231).

2. In "Some Reflections on the Ego," Jacques Lacan discusses the fantasy of the "body in bits and pieces," a fantasy that results from the incongruity between the subject who posits unity in self-image and the failure of that idealized image (13). Lacan further claims that an image is "essentially dismemberable from its body" (*Seminar I* 148). Of course cinematic cropping and camera tilt affect Greene's depictions of bodies. Greene was an avid movie-watcher and learned techniques of narrative from cinematic montage.

3. Harry's double death recalls Christ's return to life after his crucifixion. Commentary on Greene's Catholic novels is voluminous. David Lodge interprets Catholicism in Greene's oeuvre as "a system of concepts, a source of situation, and a reservoir of symbols with which he can order and dramatize certain intuitions about the nature of human experience" (6). Harry Lime

is a Catholic, though the detail appears as incidental, not central, to his character.

4. Greene's attitudes towards capitalism come down to specific transactions and valuations in the text. Martins receives so much money for doing nothing that he quips, "Come to Vienna to make money" (34). In a sinister vein, Lime values people at "twenty thousand pounds" tax free (104). The concluding paragraph of the novel ironically refers to Martins's expense claims (119).

5. For this and other ideas about subterranean spaces, I am indebted to David Pike, whose talk on "Modernist Space" at the Modern Studies Association Conference (October 9, 1999) provided invaluable direction. For motifs of descent in modernist literature, see Pike's *Passage Through Hell*.

6. Historical fiction published since 1990 has taken a different tack on shit, effluvium, sewers, and disgust. Typically, bodily waste gets associated with the past. In David Liss's *A Conspiracy of Paper,* a desperado leads a constable through an alley moist with "piles of excrement and pools of piss" (291) in eighteenth-century London. The "contents of the nightpots of a hundred and twenty thousand men and women" bob in the canals of seventeenth-century Amsterdam in Liz Moggach's *Tulip Fever* (81). A prostitute in Sheri Holman's neo-Victorian fantasia *The Dress Lodger* services clients along the sludgy banks of a river where "dead-fish sewer stink rises in the fog" (13). A doctor in Keith Oatley's *A Natural History,* a novel about nineteenth-century English medicine, warns that drinking water contaminated "by way of drains and sewage" (281) spreads cholera. In all of these cases, filth, sewage, and garbage recall the remoter past. From this we can conclude that contemporary writers are fascinated by, if more fastidious about, hygiene than early twentieth-century writers, with the exception of scatological novelists, such as Martin Amis and Irvine Welsh, who take pleasure in the "MacFlecknoe" or "Yahoo" tradition of English writing. For an elaboration of scatology in contemporary novels, see my article, "Historical Fiction" (11–14). An excremental turn in cultural criticism happened in the 1990s, mostly via an adaptation of theories by Mary Douglas, Julia Kristeva, Mikhail Bakhtin, and Sigmund Freud. Discussing disgust within Freudian dream theory, Bert States concludes that excrement is not only material but "uncanny as well, except that familiarity and cultural effort—survival itself—keep it well out of sight and mind, until our dreams give it this dark rebirth" (188). For a detailed discussion of cloacal enigmas, see Dominique Laporte's *History of Shit*. Ralph Lewin jauntily discusses sewage in terms of indoor plumbing and flushing in *Merde* (66–70). More useful in its theoretical and applied thoroughness, an issue of the journal *Genre: Forms of Discourse and Culture* 27.4 (winter 1994), edited by Richard A. Barney and Grant Holly, covers filth and its cultural meanings from Rochester and Pope through to DeQuincey and T. E. Lawrence. Barney, in his introduction to this special issue, argues that the political and cultural meanings of filth tend to get absorbed into symbolic systems, rather than practical ones: "Freud sanitized filth by mythologizing it, consigning filth to the realm of the Symbolic. Foucault tried to disguise his fascination with

filth by treating it in the history of hygiene" (277). Thomas DiPiero argues that filth "*has no meaning*, but it demarcates social zones that produce meaning. In the process, it produces the ideological limit of outrage, transgression, resistance, and/or subversion" (298). Such an insight allows us to see that the sewers in *The Third Man* embody the undefined parts of political experience at the start of the Cold War, the inability to absorb the detritus of the political past in Vienna specifically and Europe largely, and the complicated commitments, deferred, denied, shoved underground that the sewers *mean*.

CHAPTER 6. COLLABORATIONS

1. This story, published in a collection called *London Calling*, edited by Storm Jameson, was explicitly designed to develop fellow-feeling between American and English Allies. The collection describes, for the most part, London in the Blitz and includes contributions by Rebecca West, Cecil Day Lewis, and T. S. Eliot, among many others.

2. All the men in the novel resemble each other, in name if not in deed. Robert Kelway shares a first name with Robert Harrison. Colonel Pole accidentally calls Roderick "Robert" (82). Louie names her illegitimate child Thomas Victor in an unconscious tribute to Stella's husband (329).

3. For samples of Mosley's objectives, speeches, and programs, go to www .oswaldmosley.com. Mosley's internment lasted until 1943. Thereafter, he wrote his autobiography and promoted right-wing ideologies about labor, nationalism, and immigration through the Union Movement, which was organized in 1948.

4. Sartre's works appeared very quickly in English translation after their French publication. Bowen mentions Sartre explicitly in her 1956 BBC broadcast on "Truth and Fiction" (*Afterthought* 118).

CHAPTER 7. WALLS

1. Jens Fiedler in *The Spy Who Came in From the Cold* is definitely Jewish and Liz may be Jewish. Leamas guesses that Liz is Jewish (30), but she remembers going to church for "mid-week evensong" (159). Regardless of her ambiguous religious affiliations, Liz, a patently stupid character, unravels Leamas's alibi. Fiedler, too assiduous in his prosecution of Mundt, dies for his fidelity to communism. The representation of Jews in spy fiction requires a full analysis. Buchan's anti-Semitism, for instance, has been discussed by Mordecai Richler in "James Bond Unmasked" (352–54). Yet a more complete roster of Jewish characters would include Myatt in Graham Greene's *Stamboul Train*, Serge Frankel in Len Deighton's *Yesterday's Spy*—"only Jews could be trusted not to turn you over to the Fascists" (34)—Joseph and the Israeli cohort in *The Little Drummer Girl*, Nick in *The Untouchable*, among others. Jewish characters in spy narratives harbor secret, communist connections, which makes them noncapitalist villains. Especially in pre–World War II narratives, Jews' patriotic allegiances are thought to be suspect. Hence migrant Jews stand in for border-crossing spies. To reverse the trope, we

might say that all spies are always already Jewish in the sense of having multiple perspectives on identity, allegiance, and commitment.

2. Although I do not think *The Naive and Sentimental Lover* a terribly good novel
—a rich businessman's midlife crisis sprawls over 462 pages—and although
it is not a spy novel, I think that it should be read not, as its title suggests, as
a version of Schiller's theories of poetry but as a rewriting of Goethe's *Faust*.
Mephistophelian Shamus tempts Cassidy with love, regained youth, sensual-
ity. In the manner of Satan, Shamus often appears in bursts of flame or peculiar getups. His wife Helen, modeled after the vision of Helen in Marlowe's
Doctor Faustus, is first seen darting naked through a fire-lit room. The hallucinatory aspects of *The Naive and Sentimental Lover* suggest that Cassidy has
made a Faustian pact. With reference to Shamus and Helen, Cassidy thinks,
"They never existed. // I dreamed them. // To nothing" (353).

3. For an exception, see Andrew Rutherford's chapter on "The Spy as Hero:
Le Carré and the Cold War" in his book *The Literature of War: Five Studies in
Heroic Virtue*. This piece, recuperated for the cause of making le Carré sui
generis, appears also in Harold Bloom's edited collection *John le Carré* (13–
26). For a partial review of the critical literature on le Carré, see Jack Cohn's
review essay, "The Watch on John le Carré" (323–37).

4. Recent studies of allegory proclaim their indebtedness to Walter Benjamin
(Teskey 12–14; Madsen 124–26; P. Smith 105–7). Timothy Bahti (220–25)
gives an expert reading of Benjamin, Baudelaire, and allegories of emptiness
that tangentially apply to my reading of allegories of death. Yet no convincing
study of twentieth-century allegories exists. In American fiction, allegory
quickly slips into conspiracy theory. In theoretical studies, the word "allegory" automatically triggers associations with Paul DeMan's and Jacques
Derrida's deconstructionist allegories of reading.

CHAPTER 8. LEAKS

1. In *The Novel and the Police*, D. A. Miller comments that this exchange epitomizes "the regular fate of the lesbian in male representations: who defiantly
bides her time with women until the inevitable and irrevocable heterosexual
initiation that she, unlike everyone else, may not have known that she always
wanted" (182). In the case of Fleming's James Bond novels, and in the specific case of Pussy Galore's conversion to heterosexuality, women voice the
consequences but not the components of masculinity, because masculinity
remains opaque to men. Bond neither speaks his mind about pleasure
nor reveals the secrets of his libertine successes. In this sense, the gay spy
expresses what the straight spy represses: pleasure.

2. The correspondences between fact and fiction in *The Untouchable* have been
teased out by Joseph McMinn (143). Further untangling of historical fact
from Banville's fiction would merely state the obvious. Blunt did publish
monographs on Poussin. He directed the Courtauld Institute and was Keeper
of the Queen's Pictures. Significantly, Banville makes Maskell Irish and gives
him a mentally handicapped brother named Freddie. These details do not

correspond to facts in Blunt's biography. Sources for Blunt's life are too copious to list here in their entirety but include Goronwy Rees's *A Chapter of Accidents*, George Steiner's "The Cleric of Treason," John Costello's *The Mask of Treachery*, Peter Wright's *Spycatcher*, Barrie Penrose and Simon Freeman's *Conspiracy of Silence: The Secret Life of Anthony Blunt*. Banville derives all manner of curious detail from these sources, some of which he mentions at the end of *The Untouchable* in his acknowledgments. Miranda Carter's *Anthony Blunt: His Lives* provides an impressive docket of information on Blunt; having been published in 2002, however, Carter's biography does not contribute to Banville's novel. Banville freely gambols over the line between fact and fiction. Indeed, Banville's earlier novels are cited by Linda Hutcheon as examples of "historiographic metafictions" (186), especially *Doctor Copernicus* and *Kepler*. In a related interpolation into history, Nigel West's 1989 novel *The Blue List* recasts Kim Philby, Blunt's fellow Cambridge spy, as a triple agent.

3. I will not fuss about distinctions between such terms as "homosexual," "gay," and "queer" here, because others have done that fussing for me and have done it much better than I could ever do. Eve Kosofsky Sedgwick in *Epistemology of the Closet* points out the "official, not to say diagnostic" resonances of the term "homosexual," as opposed to the liberatory post-Stonewall term "gay" adopted by "a large number of people to whom it refers" (16). Allan Bérubé slyly implies that "gay" and "normal" have a "bottom/top" nuance during World War II. Misguided psychiatrists charged with evaluating gay men assumed that the homosexual, unlike "normal" men, "did not sexually penetrate his partners. They [psychiatrists] assumed that homosexuals were active partners in oral sex or passive partners in anal sex—or in the soldier slang of the day, that all queers were cocksuckers or got fucked" (Bérubé 160). Such distinctions allow for lots of queer shenanigans within the category of "normalcy." Sedgwick in *Tendencies* gives one definition of "queer" that stymies the identification of homosexuality with sex. "Queer" refers to "the open mesh of possibilities, gaps, overlaps, dissonances and resonance, lapses and excesses of meaning when the constituent elements of anyone's gender, of anyone's sexuality aren't made (or *can't be* made) to signify monolithically" (8). Once, during a job interview at a university that will remain nameless, I was commanded to declare my queerly theoretical allegiances. An inhospitable faculty member, thinking herself suave, asked me, "If you are a queer critic, what kind of queer critic are you?" I resisted this question, which I considered dopey. She wanted me to "signify monolithically," as Sedgwick would have it. I did not get the job.

4. *A word on form:* The decision to write this chapter using asterisks separating paragraphs, with clever titles lending counterpoint, at first arose as what seemed a means to clarify my thoughts and to introduce *leakiness* into formal presentation. The cheek of doing so was augmented when, dredging up remote remembrances of Kurt Vonnegut's *Breakfast of Champions*, I realized what connotations an asterisk might have for the reader of cult classics favored by the high school set. But this format, as I subsequently realized,

is so much a *gay stylistic* that I see it everywhere—: in Roland Barthes's *The Pleasure of the Text*, in D. A. Miller's *On Broadway*, in Lawrence Kramer's *After the Lovedeath*, in Wayne Koestenbaum's *The Queen's Throat*—, all of which I have read with admiration but repressed, if only temporarily, during my own bid for stylistic originality. Forensically I wish to draw attention to Banville's own asterisk-punctuated narratives. If somewhat less constellated than my own galaxy of star-studded text, *Kepler* and *Doctor Copernicus* have their fair share of transition-hullooing asterisks.

5. Andrew Hodges recounts details of Turing's life in *Alan Turing: The Enigma*. See also http://www.turing.org.uk/turing/ for online information based on Hodges's biography. In a dramatic evocation of Turing's life and death, Hugh Whitemore's play *Breaking the Code* connects mathematics and sexuality. In a speech relevant to *The Untouchable*, and, in fact, relevant to codification in espionage narratives generally, Turing says, "Even in mathematics there's no infallible rule for proving what is right and what is wrong. Each problem— each decision—requires fresh ideas, fresh thought. And if that's the case in mathematics—the most reliable body of knowledge that mankind has created—surely it might also apply in other, less certain, areas" (Whitemore 83–84).

6. Auden is a tutelary deity in *The Untouchable*. Maskell alludes to him several times (6, 57). He passingly cites Auden's poem "Our hunting fathers" (103), which Benjamin Britten set to music. Banville is an allusive writer. T. S. Eliot shows up in *The Untouchable* (76). When Victor thinks of a "vast, far, dark, deserted plain" (274), he evokes Matthew Arnold's "Dover Beach" with its "darkling plain." Blake, about whom Anthony Blunt published a monograph in 1959 called *The Art of William Blake*, appears throughout Banville's novel (78, 262, 289, 332). In an echo of the "wild surmise" of Cortez's men in Keats's "On First Looking into Chapman's Homer," a seagull studies Nick, Boy, Baby, and Victor with "cold surmise" (43).

CHAPTER 9. DISAPPEARANCES

1. Narratives of disappearance are a staple of mainstream and tabloid journalism, which does not decrease the toll of disappearances. For example, on September 30, 2000, Kris Howard, a twenty-year-old student at the University of Winnipeg, left a group of friends at a pub to get some air. He never came back. In the lingo of the *Globe & Mail*, which fleetingly covered the story, he disappeared "without a trace" (Moncrieff 17). A kayaker found his body floating in the Red River about a month later (Mullens 19). Similarly, on May 1, 2001, Chandra Levy, having just finished a six-month internship in Washington, vanished without leaving any indication of her whereabouts. Set to return to California, her home state, Levy left neatly packed suitcases in her apartment. According to early newspaper reports of the case, there was "no evidence of foul play in her unexplained disappearance" (Koring 12). The remains of Levy's body were discovered more than a year later, on May 22, 2002, in Rock Creek Park. She was murdered. The Internet, space

of notional invisibility, not surprisingly has innumerable sites devoted to disappearances. The United Nations, most Western nations, the FBI, many U.S. states, and the Salvation Army maintain sites for missing people. My concern is principally with the political implications of disappearance. The UN gives a fact sheet on enforced disappearances at http://www.unhchr.ch/html/menu6/2/fs6.htm.

2. It needs must be said that the disappearances in *Sabbatical* are more or less clarified in *Tidewater Tales:* "Father and son really did die" (644). Manfred Turner (under the alias Frederick Mansfield Talbott) commits suicide by attaching eighty pounds of lead to his body and falling into the sea; with weights already attached, he slips, hits his head, and falls unconscious, an unforeseen misstep that prevents him from feeling any pain while drowning. His son was tortured to death in Chile (*Tidewater Tales* 645). Disappearance, as usual, turns out to be a metaphor for death, not a metonymy. Nevertheless, the explanation of the disappearances in *Tidewater Tales* does not alter the semiotics of disappearance within *Sabbatical,* a novel that, for its brevity and relative lack of interpolated intertextual puffery, is superior to its sequel.

3. Barth recycles. And how. *Tidewater Tales* reprises *Sabbatical* in its entirety. Correspondences between the two books are self-evident. Peter, a novelist, decides to write a novel about CIA activities after meeting Fred Talbott (aka Fenwick Turner). In *Sabbatical,* Fenn writes an exposé of CIA clandestine operations called KUDOVE (27n, 50n); in *Tidewater Tales,* Fred writes an exposé of the CIA clandestine operations called KUBARK (256). At the end of *Tidewater Tales,* Peter gives the reader to understand that he authored *Sabbatical.* As an ecological question, recycling is foregrounded in *Sabbatical.* Manfred's body enters the food chain, or so we are led to believe (340). Susan Seckler writes her Ph.D. dissertation on "Ecology and Ecological Literature" (46). Recycling has more *recherché* manifestations. A sophomoric play called "SEX EDUCATION: Play" in *Tidewater Tales* is a reprise of a sophomoric short story called "Night-Sea Journey" in *Lost in the Funhouse* (3–13). At great cost to readers' concentration, the narrators in *Tidewater Tales* retell large portions of *The Odyssey, Don Quixote,* and *Arabian Nights.* Variations and prolongations alter these tales, Barth implies. He further implies that originality is not all that it is cracked up to be. Barth's later fictions, such as *Once Upon a Time,* lengthily discuss the making and the meaning of his earlier works.

4. Of course, copy and leads vary with different editions of the newspaper over the day, which means that a definitive text cannot always be located for particular articles. But the front-page story from the *Baltimore Sun* for October 5, 1978, concerning Paisley's death, is accurately quoted in *Sabbatical* (86–87). Stephen LaBash, assistant director and head of reference, Langsdale Library, University of Baltimore, kindly tracked down *Baltimore Sun* articles for me.

CHAPTER 10. DEMOCRACY

1. Didion's representation of gender is complex. Didion excoriates 1970s feminism in the essay "The Women's Movement": "To those of us who remain

committed mainly to the exploration of moral distinctions and ambiguities, the feminist analysis may have seemed a particularly narrow and cracked determinism" (*The White Album* 113). Didion implies that women's political identity should not be based exclusively on spurious class solidarity among women—"I am woman hear me roar," as Helen Reddy sang in the 1970s. Male critics viciously attack Didion's political representations. George Yúdice makes the ludicrous suggestion that Didion, when she visited El Salvador in 1982, should have set up "interviews with mass organizations of peasants, workers, students, and women or a visit to the guerrilla zones of control" (225). Yúdice seems not to understand that the country was in disarray at that time and that neither workers nor students nor women were organized. Female critics, I find, give far more intelligent readings of Didion's fiction by paying attention to her heroines and the bonds they forge with other characters. Katherine Usher Henderson comments that "the affair between Inez and Jack is one of the most heroic and moving sexual and emotional relationships of contemporary American fiction" (77).

2. Happiness in *Democracy* deserves a full investigation. Because happiness is embedded in the Declaration of Independence, it is a political variable. Inez's "'quite palpable unhappiness'" (58) in *Democracy*, together with her recollections of happy moments, defies the pursuit of happiness, because happiness, in keeping with the backward-looking tendency of romance, may be located exclusively in the inaccessible past.

3. Didion frequently asserts the imagistic origins of her fiction. In the essay "Why I Write," she states, "I write entirely to find out what I'm thinking, what I'm looking at, what I see and what it means. . . . *What is going on in these pictures in my mind*" (6). In "Making Up Stories," Didion adds that the writer, beginning with the raw material of images, makes "the world hang meaningfully together, [makes] all the images coherent" (244).

4. Reviews of *Democracy* in 1984 single out Didion's narrative intrusions as errors of judgment. Joseph Epstein thinks the novel would be better without Didion's presence (67). Mary McCarthy, baffled by Didion's merging of fiction and fact, wonders in a review of *Democracy*, "What is a live fact—Joan Didion —doing in a work of fiction? She must be a decoy set there to lure us into believing that Inez Victor is real in some ghostly-goblin manner, as real anyway as the author herself is" (18). Both Epstein and McCarthy fail to see the aesthetic and political subtleties of Didion's narrative gambit.

5. The title *Democracy* alludes to Henry Adams's novel *Democracy*, set principally in Washington. At Berkeley Didion teaches examples of Adams's prose to unveil political attitudes, as she explains in *Democracy* (71).

CHAPTER 11. CONCLUSION

1. The screenplay of *The Manchurian Candidate* quite faithfully follows Richard Condon's novel. Minor deviations, however, do occur. In the novel, Major Marco sweats "continuously" (164), but he also weeps. He thinks about Muslim women, which explains why he asks Rosie if she is Arabic (Condon 165–

66). The strangeness of the scene in the film depends on its relation to the semiotics of recruitment, which is not the case in the novel. For this reason, I have transcribed the dialogue from the film version.

Abelove, Henry, Michèle Aina Barale, and David M. Halperin, eds. *The Lesbian and Gay Studies Reader*. New York: Routledge, 1993.

Abraham, Nicholas. "Notes on the Phantom." 1975. Trans. Nicholas Rand. In *The Trials of Psychoanalysis*, ed. Françoise Meltzer. Chicago: University of Chicago Press, 1988.

Acton, Harold. *More Memoirs of an Aesthete*. London: Methuen, 1970.

Adams, Hazard, ed. *Critical Theory Since Plato*. Rev. ed. Orlando: Harcourt Brace Jovanovich, 1992.

Adorno, Theodor. *Aesthetic Theory*, trans. C. Lenhardt, ed. Gretel Adorno and Rolf Tiedemann. 1970. London: Routledge & Kegan Paul, 1984.

———. "Commitment." In *The Essential Frankfurt Reader*, ed. Andrew Arato and Eike Gebhardt. New York: Continuum, 1988.

———. *Minima Moralia: Reflections from Damaged Life*, trans. E. F. N. Jephcott. London: Verso, 1974.

———. *Prisms*, trans. Samuel Weber and Shierry Weber. Cambridge: MIT Press, 1992.

Aldrich, Richard J. *Espionage, Security and Intelligence in Britain 1945–1970*. Manchester, U.K.: Manchester University Press, 1998.

Allain, Marie-Françoise, ed. *The Other Man: Conversations with Graham Greene*, trans. Guido Waldman. New York: Simon and Schuster, 1983.

Althusser, Louis. *Lenin and Philosophy and Other Essays*, trans. Ben Brewster. New York: Monthly Review Press, 1971.

Ambler, Eric. *A Coffin for Dimitrios* (published in England as *A Mask for Dimitrios*). 1939. New York: Alfred A. Knopf, 1945.

Amis, Kingsley. *The James Bond Dossier*. London: Jonathan Cape, 1965.

Anderson, Dana. "Sign, Space, and Story: Roller Coasters and the Evolution of a Thrill." *Journal of Popular Culture* 33.2 (fall 1999): 1–22.

Aristotle. *Poetics*. Adams 49–66.

Aronoff, Myron. *The Spy Novels of John le Carré: Balancing Ethics and Politics.* New York: St. Martin's Press, 1999.

Ash, Timothy Garton. "The Real le Carré." *New Yorker* 75.3 (March 15, 1999): 36–45.

Atwood, Margaret. *Murder in the Dark*. Toronto: Coach House Press, 1983.

Auden, W. H. *Selected Poems,* ed. Edward Mendelsohn. New York: Vintage, 1979.

Bahti, Timothy. *Allegories of History: Literary Historiography after Hegel*. Baltimore: Johns Hopkins University Press, 1992.

Baldridge, Cates. *Graham Greene's Fictions: The Virtues of Extremity*. Columbia: University of Missouri Press, 2000.

Banville, John. *Athena*. New York: Alfred A. Knopf, 1995.

———. *Eclipse*. London: Picador, 2000.

———. *Ghosts*. 1993. London: Minerva, 1994.

———. *Kepler*. 1981. London: Picador, 1999.

———. *Mefisto*. 1986. London: Minerva, 1993.

———. *The Untouchable*. 1997. New York: Vintage, 1998.

Barley, Tony. *Taking Sides: The Fiction of John le Carré*. Milton Keynes, Eng.: Open University Press, 1986.

Barney, Richard A. "Filthy Thoughts, or, Cultural Criticism and the Ordure of Things: Introduction." *Genre: Forms of Discourse and Culture* 27.4 (winter 1994): 275–93.

Barth, John. *The Friday Book: Essays and Other Nonfiction*. New York: G. P. Putnam's Sons, 1984.

———. *Further Fridays: Essays, Lectures, and Other Nonfiction 1984–94*. Boston: Little, Brown, 1995.

———. *LETTERS*. New York: G. P. Putnam's Sons, 1979.

———. *Lost in the Funhouse*. 1968. New York: Anchor Books, 1988.

———. *Sabbatical: A Romance*. 1982. Normal, Ill.: Dalkey Archive Press, 1996.

———. *The Sot-Weed Factor*. Garden City, N.Y.: Doubleday, 1967.

———. *The Tidewater Tales: A Novel*. New York: G. P. Putnam's Sons, 1987.

Barthes, Roland. *Camera Lucida: Reflections on Photography,* trans. Richard Howard. New York: Hill & Wang, 1981.

———. *S/Z,* trans. Richard Miller. New York: Hill & Wang, 1974.

Baym, Nina. "Concepts of the Romance in Hawthorne's America." *Nineteenth-Century Fiction* 38.4 (1984): 426–43.

Beckett, Samuel. *Endgame*. New York: Grove Press, 1958.

Beene, LynnDianne. *John le Carré*. New York: Twayne, 1992.

Beevor, Antony, and Artemis Cooper. *Paris After the Liberation, 1944–1949*. New York: Doubleday, 1994.

Benjamin, Walter. *Illuminations,* ed. Hannah Arendt, trans. Harry Zohn. New York: Schocken Books, 1969.

————. *The Origins of German Tragic Drama,* trans. John Osborne. London: New Left Books, 1977.

Bennett, Andrew, and Nicholas Royle. *Elizabeth Bowen and the Dissolution of the Novel: Still Lives.* New York: St. Martin's Press, 1995.

Bennett, Tony, and Janet Woollacott. *Bond and Beyond: The Political Career of a Popular Hero.* London: Macmillan, 1987.

Berman, Paul. "In Search of Ben Linder's Killers." *New Yorker* 72.28 (Sept. 23, 1996): 58–81.

Bersani, Leo. *Homos.* Cambridge: Harvard University Press, 1995.

————. "Pynchon, Paranoia, and Literature." *Representations* 25 (winter 1989): 99–118.

Bérubé, Allan. *Coming Out Under Fire: The History of Gay Men and Women in World War Two.* New York: Free Press, 1990.

Bishop, John. *Joyce's Book of the Dark: Finnegans Wake.* Madison: University of Wisconsin Press, 1986.

Blaise, Clark. *Lunar Attractions.* Garden City, N.Y.: Doubleday, 1979.

Bloom, Clive, ed. *Spy Thrillers: From Buchan to le Carré.* London: Macmillan, 1990.

Bloom, Harold, ed. *Elizabeth Bowen: Modern Critical Views.* New York: Chelsea House, 1987.

————. *John le Carré.* New York: Chelsea House, 1987.

Bloomfield, Morton W., ed. *Allegory, Myth, and Symbol.* Cambridge: Harvard University Press, 1981.

Blumenthal, Sidney. "The Cold War and the Closet." *New Yorker* 73.4 (March 17, 1997): 112–17.

Bold, Christine. "'Under the Very Skirts of Britannia': Re-reading Women in the James Bond Novels." *Queen's Quarterly* 100.2 (summer 1993): 311–27.

Bothwell, Robert. *The Big Chill: Canada and the Cold War.* Toronto: Irwin, 1998.

Bowen, Elizabeth. *Afterthought: Pieces About Writing.* London: Longmans, Green, 1962.

————. *Bowen's Court.* London: Longmans, Green, 1942.

————. *The Collected Stories of Elizabeth Bowen,* intro. Angus Wilson. New York: Ecco Press, 1981.

————. *The Death of the Heart.* 1938. London: Penguin, 1966.

————. *Eva Trout.* 1969. London: Random House, 1999.

————. *The Heat of the Day.* 1949. New York: Penguin, 1976.

————. *The Last September.* 1929. Harmondsworth, U.K.: Penguin, 1982.

————. *The Little Girls.* New York: Alfred A. Knopf, 1964.

————. *The Mulberry Tree: Writings of Elizabeth Bowen,* ed. Hermione Lee. New York: Harcourt Brace Jovanovich, 1986.

————. *Pictures and Conversations,* intro. Spencer Curtis Brown. New York: Alfred A. Knopf, 1975.

————. *To the North.* 1932. London: Penguin, 1986.

————. *A World of Love.* 1955. London: Penguin, 1983.

Bowering, George. *Harry's Fragments: A Novel of International Puzzlement.* Toronto: Coach House Press, 1990.

Boyle, Andrew. *The Climate of Treason: Five Who Spied for Russia.* London: Hutchinson, 1979.

Bronfen, Elisabeth. *The Knotted Subject: Hysteria and Its Discontents.* Princeton: Princeton University Press, 1998.

Brooks, Peter. *Body Work: Object of Desire in Modern Narrative.* Cambridge: Harvard University Press, 1993.

Bross, Addison. "The January Rising and Its Aftermath: The Missing Theme in Conrad's Political Consciousness." In *Conrad and Poland*, ed. Alex S. Kurczaba. Boulder: East European Monographs, 1996. 61–87.

Buchan, John. *Greenmantle*, ed. and intro. Kate Macdonald. 1916. Oxford: Oxford University Press, 1993.

———. *Mr. Standfast.* 1919. Oxford: Oxford University Press, 1993.

———. *The Thirty-Nine Steps*, ed. and intro. Christopher Harvie. 1915. Oxford: Oxford University Press, 1993.

Burke, Edmund. *A Philosophical Inquiry into the Origin of Our Ideas of the Sublime and the Beautiful.* Adams 298–306.

Butler, Judith. *Excitable Speech: A Politics of the Performative.* New York: Routledge, 1997.

———. *Gender Trouble: Feminism and the Subversion of Identity.* 1990. New York and London: Routledge, 1999.

Camus, Albert. *The Plague*, trans. Stuart Gilbert. 1947. Harmondsworth, U.K.: Penguin, 1960.

Carpenter, Lynette. "I Never Knew the Old Vienna": Cold War Politics and *The Third Man*." *Film Criticism* 11.1–2 (1987): 56–65.

Carson, Anne. *Plainwater: Essays and Poetry.* New York: Alfred A. Knopf, 1995.

Caruth, Cathy. *Unclaimed Experience: Trauma, Narrative, and History.* Baltimore: Johns Hopkins University Press, 1996.

Caruth, Cathy, ed. *Trauma: Explorations in Memory.* Baltimore: Johns Hopkins University Press, 1995.

Casablanca. Dir. Michael Curtiz. Perf. Humphrey Bogart, Ingrid Berman, Paul Henreid, Claude Rains. Warner Brothers, 1942.

Caserio, Robert. "The Heat of the Day: Modernism and Narrative in Paul de Man and Elizabeth Bowen." *Modern Language Quarterly* 54:2 (June 1993): 263–84.

Cawelti, John G. *Adventure, Mystery, and Romance: Formula Stories as Art and Popular Culture.* Chicago: University of Chicago Press, 1976.

Cawelti, John, and Bruce Rosenberg. *The Spy Story.* Chicago: University of Chicago Press, 1987.

Cecil, Robert. "The Cambridge Comintern," In *The Missing Dimension: Governments and Intelligence Communities in the Twentieth Century*, ed. Christopher Andrew and David Dilks. Urbana: University of Illinois Press, 1984. 169–98.

Channon, Sir Henry. *'Chips': The Diaries of Sir Henry Channon*, ed. Robert Rhodes James. 1967. London: Orion/Phoenix, 1996.

Chatman, Seymour. "Who Is the Best Narrator? The Case of *The Third Man*." *Style* 23.2 (1989): 183–96.

Childers, Erskine. *The Riddle of the Sands*, ed. and intro. David Trotter. 1903. Oxford: Oxford University Press, 1998.

Ching, Stuart. "'A Hard Story to Tell': The Vietnam War in Joan Didion's *Democracy*." In *Fourteen Landing Zones: Approaches to Vietnam War Literature*, ed. Philip K. Jason. Iowa City: University of Iowa Press, 1991. 180–88.

Cline, Ray S. *Secrets, Spies, and Scholars: Blueprint of the Essential CIA*. Washington, D.C.: Acropolis Books, 1976.

Cobbs, John L. *Understanding John le Carré*. Columbia: University of South Carolina Press, 1998.

Cohn, Jack R. "The Watch on John le Carré." *Studies in the Novel* 20.3 (fall 1988): 323–37.

Condon, Richard. *The Manchurian Candidate*, intro. Louis Menand. 1959. New York: Four Walls Eight Windows, 2003.

The Conformist. Dir. Bernardo Bertolucci. Perf. Jean-Louis Trintignant, Stefania Sandrelli, Dominique Sanda. Malofilm Group, 1971.

Conrad, Joseph. *Heart of Darkness*, ed. Ross C. Murfin. 1899. New York: Bedford, 1996.

———. *Joseph Conrad's Letters to R. B. Cunninghame Graham*, ed. Cedric Watts. Cambridge: Cambridge University Press, 1969.

———. *The Mirror of the Sea and A Personal Record*, intro. Zdzisław Najder. 1906/1912. Oxford: Oxford University Press, 1988.

———. *Nostromo*. 1904. Harmondsworth, U.K.: Penguin, 1983.

———. *Notes on Life and Letters*. London: Dent, 1921.

———. *The Secret Agent*, ed. Martin Seymour-Smith. 1907. London: Penguin, 1984.

———. "The Secret Sharer." In *'Twixt Land and Sea*. 1912. London: Penguin, 1988.

———. *A Set of Six*. 1908. London: Dent, 1923.

———. *Under Western Eyes*, ed. and intro. Jeremy Hawthorn. 1911. Oxford: Oxford University Press, 1983.

Corber, Robert J. *Homosexuality in Cold War America: Resistance and the Crisis of Masculinity*. Durham: Duke University Press, 1997.

Costello, John. *Mask of Treachery*. London: Collins, 1988.

Costiglione, Frank. "'Unceasing Pressure for Penetration': Gender, Pathology, and Emotion in George Kennan's Formation of the Cold War." *The Journal of American History* 83.4 (March 1997): 1309–39.

Craig, Patricia. *Elizabeth Bowen*. Harmondsworth, U.K.: Penguin, 1986.

Davenport-Hines, Richard. *Auden*. London: Heinemann, 1995.

De Certeau, Michel. *The Practice of Everyday Life*, trans. Steven Rendall. Berkeley: University of California Press, 1984.

Deighton, Len. *Yesterday's Spy*. 1975. St. Alban's: Granada, 1976.

DeLillo, Don. *Libra*. New York: Viking, 1988.

———. *Mao II*. New York: Viking, 1991.

————. *Players.* 1977. New York: Viking, 1984.

DeMan, Paul. *Allegories of Reading: Figural Language in Rousseau, Nietzsche, Rilke, and Proust.* New Haven: Yale University Press, 1979.

D'Emilio, John. "The Homosexual Menace: The Politics of Sexuality in Cold War America." Peiss and Simmons 226–40.

————. *Sexual Politics, Sexual Communities: The Making of a Homosexual Minority in the United States 1940–1970.* 2nd ed. Chicago: University of Chicago Press, 1998.

Denning, Michael. *Cover Stories: Narrative and Ideology in the British Spy Thriller.* London: Routledge & Kegan Paul, 1987.

Derrida, Jacques. *Specters of Marx,* trans. Peggy Kamuf, intro. Bernd Magnus and Stephen Cullenberg. New York: Routledge, 1994.

Des Cars, Jean, and Pierre Pinon. *Paris—Haussmann.* Paris: Picard, 1991.

Diamond, Elin. "The Shudder of Catharsis in Twentieth-Century Performance." Parker and Sedgwick 152–72.

DiBattista, Maria. "The Spy's Body: *The Heat of the Day.*" Paper presented at Narrative Conference, April 9, 2000, Atlanta, Georgia.

Dickens, Charles. *Oliver Twist,* ed. Kathleen Tillotson. Oxford: Oxford University Press, 1999.

————. *Our Mutual Friend,* ed. Stephen Gill. New York: Penguin, 1971.

Didion, Joan. *After Henry.* Toronto: Stoddart, 1992.

————. *A Book of Common Prayer.* New York: Simon and Schuster, 1977.

————. *Democracy.* 1984. New York: Vintage, 1995.

————. *The Last Thing He Wanted.* New York: Alfred A. Knopf, 1996.

————. "Making Up Stories." Martin 231–44.

————. *Miami.* New York: Simon and Schuster, 1987.

————. *Play It As It Lays.* 1970. New York: Noonday Press, 1990.

————. *Political Fictions.* New York: Alfred A. Knopf, 2001.

————. *Run River.* 1963. New York: Pocket Books, 1978.

————. *Salvador.* Toronto: Lester & Orpen Dennys, 1983.

————. *Slouching Towards Bethlehem,* intro. Elizabeth Hardwick. 1968. New York: Modern Library, 2000.

————. *The White Album.* New York: Simon and Schuster, 1979.

————. "Why I Write." Friedman 5–10.

Diemart, Brian. *Graham Greene's Thrillers and the 1930s.* Montreal and Kingston: McGill–Queen's University Press, 1996.

DiPiero, Thomas. "Shit Happens: Rabelais, Sade, and the Politics of Popular Fiction." *Genre: Forms of Discourse and Culture* 27.4 (winter 1994): 295–314.

Donald, James. "The City, The Cinema: Modern Spaces." Jenks 77–95.

Doody, Margaret Anne. *The True Story of the Novel.* New Brunswick: Rutgers University Press, 1996.

Dr. Strangelove; or How I Learned to Stop Worrying and Love the Bomb. Dir. Stanley Kubrick. Screenplay by Terry Southern, Stanley Kubrick, Peter George. Perf. Peter Sellers, George C. Scott, Sterling Hayden, Slim Pickens. Hawk Films, 1964.

Drummond, Lee. *American Dreamtime: A Cultural Analysis of Popular Movies, and Their Implications for a Science of Humanity*. Lanham, Md.: Rowman & Littlefield, 1996.

Eagleton, Terry. *Marxism and Literary Criticism*. London: Methuen, 1976.

Easthope, Anthony. *Poetry as Discourse*. London: Methuen, 1983.

Eco, Umberto. *The Role of the Reader: Explorations in the Semiotics of Texts*. Bloomington: Indiana University Press, 1979.

Edelman, Lee. "Tea Rooms and Sympathy, or, the Epistemology of the Water Closet." Abelove, Barale and Halperin 553–74.

Eliot, Thomas Stearns. *The Complete Poems and Plays of T. S. Eliot*. London: Faber, 1969.

Elkins, James. *The Object Stares Back: On the Nature of Seeing*. New York: Harvest/Harcourt Brace, 1996.

Elliott, Emory. "History and Will in *Dog Soldiers*, *Sabbatical*, and *The Color Purple*." *Arizona Quarterly* 43.3 (autumn 1987): 197–217.

Elster, Jon. *Making Sense of Marx: Studies in Marxism and Social Theory*. Cambridge: Cambridge University Press, 1985.

———. *Political Psychology*. Cambridge: Cambridge University Press, 1993.

Epstein, Joseph. "The Sunshine Girls." *Commentary* 77.6 (June 1984): 62–67.

Erikson, Kai. "Notes on Trauma and Community." Caruth, ed., *Trauma: Explorations in Memory*, 183–99.

Evans, Peter W. "*The Third Man* (1949): Constructions of the Self." *Forum for Modern Language Studies* 31.1 (1995): 37–48.

Feagin, Susan L. "Imagining Emotions and Appreciating Art." *Canadian Journal of Philosophy* 18.3 (September 1988): 485–500.

Felman, Shoshana, and Dori Laub. *Testimony: Crises of Witnessing in Literature, Psychoanalysis, and History*. New York and London: Routledge, 1992.

Fisk, Robert. *In Time of War: Ireland, Ulster and the Price of Neutrality, 1939–45*. London: André Deutsch, 1983.

Flanner, Janet. *Paris Journal, 1944–1955*. New York: Harcourt Brace Jovanovich, 1988.

Fleishman, Avrom. *Conrad's Politics: Community and Anarchy in the Fiction of Joseph Conrad*. Baltimore: Johns Hopkins University Press, 1967.

Fleming, Ian. *Casino Royale*. 1953. London: Hodder and Stoughton, 1988.

———. *Goldfinger. James Bond Quintet*. London: Jonathan Cape, 1993.

———. *The Man With The Golden Gun*. 1965. London: Hodder and Stoughton, 1989.

———. *Octopussy and The Living Daylights*. 1966. London: Hodder and Stoughton, 1989.

———. *On Her Majesty's Secret Service*. 1963. London: Hodder and Stoughton, 1989.

———. *You Only Live Twice*. New York: New American Library, 1964.

Fogel, Aaron. *Coercion to Speak: Conrad's Poetics of Dialogue*. Cambridge: Harvard University Press, 1985.

Fogel, Stan, and Gordon Slethaug. *Understanding John Barth*. Columbia: University of South Carolina Press, 1990.

Foran, Charles. "A Dazzling, Brilliant Eclipse" Rev. of *Eclipse*, by John Banville. *Globe & Mail* (Toronto). Nov. 11, 2000, national ed., D21.

Forster, E. M. *Two Cheers for Democracy*. New York: Harcourt Brace Jovanovich, 1951.

Ford, Andrew. "Katharsis: The Ancient Problem." Parker and Sedgwick 109–32.

Forsyth, Frederick. *The Day of the Jackal*. 1971. Toronto: Bantam/Corgi, 1990.

Foucault, Michel. *Discipline and Punish: The Birth of the Prison*, trans. Alan Sheridan. 1975. New York: Vintage, 1979.

———. *The History of Sexuality: An Introduction*, trans. Robert Hurley. New York: Vintage, 1980.

Freese, Peter, ed. *Germany and German Thought in American Literature and Cultural Criticism*. Essen: Die Blaue Eule, 1990.

French, David. "Spy Fever in Britain 1900–1915." *Historical Journal* 21 (1978): 355–70.

Freud, Sigmund. *The Standard Edition of the Complete Psychological Works of Sigmund Freud*. 24 vols. Trans. and ed. James Strachey, with Anna Freud, Alix Strachey and Alan Tyson. London: Hogarth Press, 1955–73.

———. *Beyond the Pleasure Principle*. Standard Edition. Vol. 18, 3–64.

———. *From the History of an Infantile Neurosis*. Standard Edition. Vol. 17, 1–123.

———. *Introductory Lectures on Psycho-Analysis: Part III*. Standard Edition. Vol. 16.

———. *Three Essays on the Theory of Sexuality*. Standard Edition. Vol. 7, 122–244.

———. "The Uncanny." *Standard Edition*. Vol. 17, 217–56.

Friedman, Ellen G., ed. *Joan Didion: Essays & Conversations*. Princeton: Ontario Review Press, 1984.

Frye, Northrop. *The Anatomy of Criticism: Four Essays*. Princeton: Princeton University Press, 1957.

Fussell, Paul. *The Great War and Modern Memory*. London: Oxford University Press, 1975.

Gardner, John. "The Espionage Novel." *Whodunit? A Guide to Crime, Suspense and Spy Fiction*, ed. H. J. R. Keating. New York: Van Nostrand Reinhold, 1982.

Gaskell, Elizabeth. "Disappearances." *Household Words*. 1851. 246–51. [Also available online at http://www.lang.nagoya-u.ac.jp/~matsuoka/EG-Disappearances.html]

Get Smart. Perf. Don Adams, Barbara Feldon, Edward C. Platt, Robert Karavelas. NBC/CBS. 1965–70.

Gide, André. *Journals of André Gide, 1939–1949*. Vol. 4. Trans. and intro. Justin O'Brien. New York: Alfred A. Knopf, 1951.

Glendinning, Victoria. *Elizabeth Bowen: Portrait of a Writer*. 1977. Harmondsworth, U.K.: Penguin, 1985.

GoGwilt, Christopher. *The Invention of the West: Joseph Conrad and the Double-Mapping of Europe and Empire*. Stanford: Stanford University Press, 1995.

Goode, Erica. "The Making of a Spy." *New York Times*. Feb. 25, 2001, national ed., sec. 4: 1, 3.

Goodwin, Sarah Webster, and Elisabeth Bronfen. "Introduction." In *Death and Representation,* ed. Goodwin and Bronfen. Baltimore: Johns Hopkins University Press, 1993.

Green, Henry. *Back.* 1946. London: Harvill Press, 1999.

Greene, Graham. *Brighton Rock.* 1938. London: Penguin, 1970.

———. *Collected Essays.* New York: Viking Press, 1969.

———. *Collected Short Stories.* London: Penguin, 1986.

———. *The Confidential Agent.* 1939. Harmondsworth, U.K.: Penguin, 1963.

———. *Doctor Fischer of Geneva or the Bomb Party.* London: Bodley Head, 1980.

———. *The End of the Affair.* 1951. London: Penguin, 1975.

———. *A Gun For Sale.* 1936. London: Penguin, 1973.

———. *The Heart of the Matter.* 1948. London: Penguin, 1971.

———. *The Human Factor.* New York: Simon and Schuster, 1978.

———. *Journey Without Maps.* 1936. London: Penguin, 1983.

———. *The Ministry of Fear.* 1943. London: Penguin, 1974.

———. *The Power and the Glory.* 1940. London: Penguin, 1971.

———. *A Sort of Life.* New York: Simon and Schuster, 1971.

———. *Stamboul Train.* 1932. London: Penguin, 1975.

———. *The Third Man and The Fallen Idol.* 1950. London: Penguin, 1971.

———. *Ways of Escape.* Toronto: Lester & Orpen Dennys, 1980.

———. *A World of My Own: A Dream Diary.* New York: Penguin, 1992.

Halperin, John. *Eminent Georgians: The Lives of King George V, Elizabeth Bowen, St. John Philby, and Nancy Astor.* New York: St. Martin's Press, 1995.

Hannant, Laurence. "The Man With a Bag on His Head: Igor Gouzenko and Canada's Cold War." *The Beaver* 75.5 (Oct./Nov. 1995): 19–23.

Hantke, Steffan. "'God Save Us From Bourgeois Adventure': The Figure of the Terrorist in Contemporary American Conspiracy Fiction." *Studies in the Novel* 28.2 (summer 1996): 219–43.

Hardwick, Elizabeth. "In the Wasteland." Rev. of *The Last Thing He Wanted,* by Joan Didion. *New York Review of Books* 43.17 (Oct. 31, 1996): 4, 6–7.

Harris, Charles B. "The Age of the World View: The Critique of Realism in John Barth's *Sabbatical*." Freese 407–32.

Harris, Robert. *Enigma.* 1995. London: Arrow Books, 1996.

Hawthorne, Nathaniel. *The House of the Seven Gables,* intro. Mary Oliver. New York: Modern Library, 2001.

Hay, Eloise Knapp. *The Political Novels of Joseph Conrad.* Chicago: University of Chicago Press, 1963.

Henderson, Katherine Usher. "The Bond Between Narrator and Heroine in *Democracy*." Pearlman 69–86.

Hepburn, Allan. "The Historical Novel." *Literary Review of Canada* 8.10 (winter 2000/2001): 11–14.

Hiley, Nicholas. "Decoding German Spies: British Spy Fiction, 1908–18." Wark, *Intelligence and National Security* 55–79.

Hiroshima Mon Amour. Dir. Alain Resnais. Screenplay Marguerite Duras. Perf. Emmanuelle Riva, Eiji Okada. Janus/Pathé, 1959.

Hodges, Andrew. *Alan Turing: The Enigma.* New York: Simon and Schuster, 1983.

Hofstadter, Richard. *The Paranoid Style in American Politics and Other Essays.* 1964. New York: Vintage Books, 1967.

Holman, Sheri. *The Dress Lodger.* New York: Atlantic Monthly Press, 2000.

Holt, Hazel. *A Lot To Ask: A Life of Barbara Pym.* London: Macmillan, 1990.

Homer. *The Iliad,* trans. Richmond Lattimore. Chicago: University of Chicago Press, 1951.

Hoskins, Robert. *Graham Greene: An Approach to the Novels.* New York: Garland, 1999.

Hupfeld, Herman. "As Time Goes By." Lyrics and Music. Warner Brothers, 1931.

Hutcheon, Linda. *A Poetics of Postmodernism.* New York and London: Routledge, 1988.

Hyde, Anthony. *The Red Fox.* Toronto: Penguin, 1985.

Hynes, Samuel. *The Edwardian Turn of Mind.* Princeton: Princeton University Press, 1968.

Hynes, Samuel, ed. *Graham Greene: A Collection of Critical Essays.* Englewood Cliffs, N.J.: Prentice-Hall, 1973.

Ifrah, Georges. *The Universal History of Numbers: From Prehistory to the Invention of the Computer,* trans. David Bellos, E. F. Harding, Sophie Wood, Ian Monk. 1994. London: Harvill Press, 1998.

Imhof, Rüdiger. "An Interview with John Banville." *Irish University Review: A Journal of Irish Studies* 11.1 (spring 1981): 5–12.

Iser, Wolfgang. "Do I Write For an Audience?" *PMLA* 115.3 (May 2000): 310–13.

Jackson, Tony E. "Science, Art, and the Shipwreck of Knowledge: The Novels of John Banville." *Contemporary Literature* 38.3 (fall 1997): 510–33.

Jackson, Tony. "Postmodernism, Narrative, and the Cold War Sense of an Ending." *Narrative* 8.3 (October 2000): 324–38.

James, Henry. *The American.* New York Edition. Vol. 2. 1907. Fairfield, N.J.: Augustus M. Kelley, 1976.

Jameson, Fredric. *The Political Unconscious: Narrative as Socially Symbolic Act.* Ithaca: Cornell University Press, 1981.

———. *Postmodernism, or, the Cultural Logic of Late Capitalism.* Durham: Duke University Press, 1991.

Jameson, Storm, ed. *London Calling.* New York: Harper and Brothers, 1942.

Jenks, Chris, ed. *Visual Culture.* New York: Routledge, 1995.

La Jetée. Dir. Chris Marker. Perf. Davos Hanich, Hélène Chatelain, Jacques Ledoux. Argos Films, 1963.

Jonas, George. "The Family Who Came in from the Cold." *Saturday Night* (December 1995): 25–27.

Jonson, Ben. *Ben Jonson's Plays and Masks,* ed. Robert M. Adams. New York: Norton, 1979.

Jordan, Heather Bryant. *How Will the Heart Endure: Elizabeth Bowen and the Landscape of War.* Ann Arbor: University of Michigan Press, 1992.

Joyce, James. *Finnegans Wake.* 1939. New York: Viking, 1976.

———. *Ulysses,* ed. Hans Walter Gabler with Wolfhard Steppe and Claus Melchior. 1922. New York: Vintage, 1986.

Kavanaugh, James H. "Ideology." Lentricchia and McLaughlin 306–20.

Kennan, George F. *American Diplomacy, 1900–1950.* Chicago: University of Chicago Press, 1951.

Kermode, Frank. "Secrets and Narrative Sequence." *Critical Inquiry* 7.1 (1980): 83–101.

Koch, Stephen. "Bloomsbury and Espionage." *Partisan Review* 61.1 (1994): 23–45.

Koestenbaum, Wayne. *Jackie Under My Skin: Interpreting an Icon.* 1995. New York: Plume, 1996.

Korda, Michael. "The Third Man." *New Yorker* (March 25, 1995): 45–51.

Koring, Paul. "Speculation Grows over Absent Intern." *Globe & Mail* (Toronto). May 19, 2001, final metro ed., A12.

Kristeva, Julia. *Powers of Horror: An Essay on Abjection,* trans. Leon S. Roudiez. 1980. New York: Columbia University Press, 1982.

Lacan, Jacques. *The Four Fundamental Concepts of Psycho-Analysis,* ed. Jacques-Alain Miller, trans. Alan Sheridan. New York: Norton, 1978.

———. *The Seminar of Jacques Lacan, Book I: Freud's Papers on Technique, 1953–54,* trans. John Forrester. Cambridge: Cambridge University Press, 1988.

———. "Some Reflections on the Ego." *International Journal of Pscyhoanalysis* 34 (1953): 11–17.

The Lady Vanishes. Dir. Alfred Hitchcock. Perf. Margaret Lockwood, Michael Redgrave, Paul Lukas, Dame May Whitty. Allied Artists, 1938.

Laporte, Dominique. *History of Shit,* trans. Nadia Benabid and Rodolphe el-Khoury. Cambridge: MIT Press, 2000.

Larkin, Phillip. *Collected Poems,* ed. and intro. Anthony Thwaite. London: Faber, 1988.

Lassner, Phyllis. *British Women Writers of World War II: Battlegrounds of Their Own.* London: Macmillan, 1998.

———. *Elizabeth Bowen.* London: Macmillan, 1990.

Le Carré, John. *Call for the Dead.* In *The Le Carré Omnibus.* London: Victor Gollancz, 1964.

———. "Introduction." Page, Leitch and Knightley 9–24.

———. "Le Carré: The Dishonorable Spy." *Harper's* 273.1639 (Dec. 1986): 17–19.

———. *The Little Drummer Girl.* 1983. New York: Bantam, 1984.

———. *The Looking Glass War.* 1965. Toronto: Penguin, 1992.

———. *A Murder of Quality.* In *The Le Carré Omnibus.* London: Victor Gollancz, 1964.

———. *The Naive and Sentimental Lover.* 1971. Toronto: Penguin, 1990.

———. *A Perfect Spy.* 1986. Toronto: Penguin, 1987.

———. *A Small Town in Germany.* 1968. Toronto: Penguin, 1992.

———. *Smiley's People.* 1980. Toronto: Penguin, 1992.

———. "Spying . . . the Passion of My Time." *Queen's Quarterly* 100.2 (summer 1993): 269–72. (Reprint, in slightly altered form, of "Tinpots, Saviors, Lawyers, Spies.")

———. *The Spy Who Came in From the Cold*. 1963. Toronto: Penguin, 1989.

———. *Tinker Tailor Soldier Spy*. 1974. Toronto: Penguin, 1989.

———. "Tinpots, Saviors, Lawyers, Spies." *New York Times*. May 4, 1993, late ed., A25.

———. "To Russia, with Greetings." *Encounter* 26 (May 1966): 3–6.

———. "Why I Came In From the Cold." *New York Times*. Sept. 29, 1989, late ed., A35.

Lee, Hermione. *Elizabeth Bowen*. Rev. ed. London: Random House, 1999.

Le Fanu, Sheridan. *Uncle Silas*, ed. W. J. McCormack. 1864. Oxford: Oxford University Press, 1981.

Lelyveld, Joseph. "Another Country." Rev. of *Political Fictions*. *New York Review of Books* 48.20 (Dec. 20, 2001): 8–12.

Lentricchia, Frank, and Thomas McLaughlin, eds. *Critical Terms for Literary Study*. 2nd ed. Chicago: University of Chicago Press, 1995.

Lessing, Doris. *The Good Terrorist*. 1986. London: Flamingo, 1993.

Lewin, Ralph. *Merde: Excursions in Scientific, Cultural, and Sociohistorical Coprology*. New York: Random House, 1999.

Lewis, Peter. *John le Carré*. New York: Frederick Ungar, 1985.

Liss, David. *A Conspiracy of Paper*. New York: Random House, 2000.

Litvak, Joseph. *Strange Gourmets: Sophistication, Theory, and the Novel*. Durham: Duke University Press, 1997.

Lodge, David. *Graham Greene*. Columbia Essays on Modern Writers 17. New York: Columbia University Press, 1966.

Lord, James. *Six Exceptional Women: Further Memoirs*. New York: Farrar Straus and Giroux, 1994.

Lowell, Robert. *Selected Poems*. New York: Farrar Straus and Giroux, 1977.

Lowenthal, Leo. *Literature, Popular Culture, and Society*. Palo Alto: Pacific Books, 1961.

Ludlum, Robert. *The Bourne Identity*. 1980. New York and Toronto: Bantam, 2001.

Lukács, Georg. *The Theory of the Novel*, trans. Anna Bostock. London: Merlin Press, 1963.

Macherey, Pierre. *A Theory of Literary Production*, trans. Geoffrey Wall. London and New York: Routledge, 1978.

Macleod, Norman. "'This strange, rather sad story': The Reflexive Design of Graham Greene's *The Third Man*." *Dalhousie Review* 63.2 (1983): 217–41.

Madsen, Deborah L. *Rereading Allegory: A Narrative Approach to Genre*. New York: St. Martin's Press, 1994.

Mageean, Michael. "*The Secret Agent*'s (T)extimacies." *Seeing Double: Revisioning Edwardian and Modern Literature*, ed. Carola M. Kaplan and Anne B. Simpson. London: Macmillan, 1996

Mallon, Thomas. *In Fact: Essays on Writers and Writing*. New York: Pantheon, 2001.

Man, Glenn K. S. "*The Third Man*: Pulp Fiction and Art Film." *Literature-Film Quarterly* 21.3 (1993): 171–77.

The Manchurian Candidate. Dir. John Frankenheimer. Screenplay by George
　　Axelrod, based on a novel by Richard Condon. Perf. Frank Sinatra, Laurence
　　Harvey, Janet Leigh, Angela Lansbury. United Artists, 1962.

Marker, Chris. *La Jetée: Ciné-Roman.* New York: Zone Books, 1992.

Martin, Robert A., ed. *The Writer's Craft: Hopwood Lectures, 1965–81.* Ann Arbor:
　　University of Michigan Press, 1982.

Marx, Karl, and Friedrich Engels. *The Communist Manifesto,* intro. Eric
　　Hobsbawn. London: Verso, 1998.

———. *The German Ideology.* Amherst, N.Y.: Prometheus Books, 1998.

Marx, Karl. *The Eighteenth Brumaire of Louis-Napoleon.* 1852. New York:
　　International Publishers, 1963.

Massumi, Brian. "Preface." In *The Politics of Everyday Fear,* ed. Brian Massumi.
　　Minneapolis: University of Minnesota Press, 1993. vii–x.

The Matrix. Dir. and screenplay by Andy and Larry Wachowski. Perf. Keanu
　　Reeves, Lawrence Fishburne, Carrie-Anne Moss. Warner Brothers, 1999.

Matthews, John T. "Intertextual Frameworks: The Ideology of Parody in John
　　Barth." O'Donnell and Davis, 35–57.

Maugham, Somerset. *Ashenden, or the British Agent.* London: Heinemann, 1928.

McCarthy, Mary. "Love and Death in the Pacific." Rev. of *Democracy,* by Joan
　　Didion. *New York Times Book Review* (April 22, 1984): 1, 18–19.

McEwan, Ian. *The Innocent.* New York: Doubleday, 1990.

McMinn, Joseph. *The Supreme Fictions of John Banville.* Manchester, U.K.:
　　Manchester University Press, 1999.

Meerloo, Joost A. M. *Patterns of Panic.* New York: International Universities Press,
　　1950.

Meltzer, Françoise. "Unconscious." Lentricchia and McLaughlin 147–62.

Mickiewicz, Adam. *Forefather's Eve Part III,* trans. and ed. George Rapall Noyes,
　　rev. by Harold B. Segel. Ithaca: Cornell University Press, 1977.

Miller, William Ian. *The Anatomy of Disgust.* Cambridge: Harvard University
　　Press, 1997.

Miller, D. A. *Narrative and Its Discontents: Problems of Closure in the Traditional
　　Novel.* Princeton: Princeton University Press, 1981.

———. *The Novel and the Police.* Berkeley: University of California Press, 1988.

Miller, J. Hillis. "The Two Allegories." Bloomfield 355–70.

Mitchell, W. J. T. *Iconology: Image, Text, Ideology.* Chicago: University of Chicago
　　Press, 1986.

Moggach, Liz. *Tulip Fever.* London: William Heinemann, 1999.

Monaghan, David. *The Novels of John le Carré: The Art of Survival.* Oxford: Basil
　　Blackwell, 1985.

Moncrieff, Holli. "Student Vanishes Without a Trace." *Globe & Mail* (Toronto).
　　Oct. 14, 2000, national ed., A17.

Moravia, Alberto. *The Conformist,* trans. Tami Calliope. 1951. Royalton, Vt.:
　　Steerforth Press, 1999.

Morf, Gustav. *The Polish Shades and Ghosts of Joseph Conrad.* New York: Astra
　　Books, 1976.

Moretti, Franco. *Signs Taken For Wonders: Essays in the Sociology of Literary Forms,* trans. Susan Fischer, David Forgacs, David Miller. London: Verso, 1983.

Mosley, Oswald. "Objectives." "Union Movement, 1948–1984." July 21, 2001. Online essays posted by Friends of Oswald Mosley. <http://www.oswaldmosley.com/um/um.html>

Mouffe, Chantal. "What Ethics for Democracy?" In *The Turn to Ethics,* ed. Marjorie Garber, Beatrice Hannssen, Rebecca L. Walkowitz. New York and London: Routledge, 2000. 85–94.

Mullens, Anne. "Cheers to Tears: A Cautionary Tale of Wasted Youth." *University Affairs* 42.3 (March 2001): 19–21, 29.

Murphy, Lawrence R. "The House on Pacific Street: Homosexuality, Intrigue, and Politics During World War II." *Journal of Homosexuality* 12.1 (fall 1985): 27–49.

Nadel, Alan. *Containment Culture: American Narratives, Postmodernism, and the Atomic Age.* Durham: Duke University Press, 1995.

Najder, Zdislaw. *Joseph Conrad: A Chronicle,* trans. Halina Carroll-Najder. New Brunswick: Rutgers University Press, 1983.

Neill, Alex. "Fear, Fiction and Make-Believe." *Journal of Aesthetics and Art Criticism* 49.1 (winter 1991): 48–56.

North by Northwest. Dir. Alfred Hitchcock. Perf. Cary Grant, Eva Maria Saint, James Mason. MGM, 1951.

Notorious. Dir. Alfred Hitchcock. Screenplay. Ben Hecht. Perf. Ingrid Bergman, Cary Grant, Claude Rains. RKO Radio Picture, 1946.

No Way Out. Dir. Roger Donaldson. Perf. Kevin Costner, Sean Young, Gene Hackman. Orion Pictures, 1987.

O'Donnell, Patrick, and Robert Con Davis, ed. *Intertextuality and Contemporary American Fiction.* Baltimore: Johns Hopkins University Press, 1989.

Oatley, Keith. *A Natural History.* Toronto: Penguin, 1998.

Orwell, George. *Nineteen Eighty-Four.* 1948. New York: Harcourt Brace Jovanovich, 1983.

———. *The Road to Wigan Pier.* 1937. London: Penguin, 1989.

———. *The War Commentaries,* ed. W. J. West. Harmondsworth, U.K.: Penguin, 1985.

Page, Bruce, David Leitch, and Phillip Knightley. *Philby: The Spy Who Betrayed a Generation.* London: André Deutsch, 1968.

Parker, Andrew, and Eve Kosofsky Sedgwick, eds. *Performativity and Performance.* New York and London: Routledge, 1995.

Patton, Cindy. "To Die For." In *Novel-Gazing: Queer Readings in Fiction,* ed. Eve Sedgwick. Durham: Duke University Press, 1997. 330–52.

Pearlman, Mickey, ed. *American Women Writing Fiction.* Lexington: University Press of Kentucky, 1989.

Peiss, Kathy, and Christina Simmons, eds. *Passion and Power: Sexuality in History.* Philadelphia: Temple University Press, 1989.

Penrose, Barrie, and Simon Freeman. *Conspiracy of Silence: The Secret Life of Anthony Blunt.* London: Grafton Books, 1986.

Phillips, Adam. *Terrors and Experts.* Cambridge: Harvard University Press, 1995.

Pickup on South Street. Dir. and screenplay by Samuel Fuller. Perf. Richard Widmark, Jean Peters, Thelma Ritter. Twentieth Century Fox, 1953.

Piette, Adam. *Imagination at War: British Fiction and Poetry, 1939–1945.* London: Papermac, 1995.

Pike, David. "Modernist Space." Paper presented at Modern Studies Association Conference. Oct. 9, 1999. State College, Pa.

———. *Passage Through Hell: Modernist Descents, Medieval Underworlds.* Ithaca: Cornell University Press, 1997.

Plato. *The Republic.* Adams 18–38.

Polmar, Noman, and Thomas B. Allen. *The Encyclopedia of Espionage.* New York: Random House, 1997.

Powell, Anthony. *Casanova's Chinese Restaurant.* 1960. London: Fontana, 1970.

Pym, Barbara. *A Glass of Blessings.* London: Jonathan Cape, 1958.

Quilligan, Maureen. *The Language of Allegory: Defining the Genre.* Ithaca: Cornell University Press, 1979.

Rashkin, Esther. *Family Secrets and the Psychoanalysis of Narrative.* Princeton: Princeton University Press, 1992.

Rawls, John. *Collected Papers,* ed. Samuel Freeman. Cambridge: Harvard University Press, 1999.

Reid, Donald. *Paris Sewers and Sewermen: Realities and Representations.* Cambridge: Harvard University Press, 1991.

Reinert, Thomas. "Joan Didion and Political Irony." *Raritan* 15.3 (winter 1996): 122–36.

Richler, Mordecai. *A Choice of Enemies.* 1957. N.p.: Quartet/Paperjacks, 1973.

———. "James Bond Unmasked." Rosenberg and Manning 341–55.

Rosenberg, Bernard, and David Manning, eds. *Mass Culture Revisited.* New York: Van Nostrand Reinhold, 1971.

Ross, Andrew. *No Respect: Intellectuals and Popular Culture.* New York: Routledge, 1989.

———. "Master of the Secret World." Interview with John le Carré. Oct. 21, 1996. Http://salon.com/weekly/lecarre961021.html.

Rowling, J. K. *Harry Potter and the Goblet of Fire.* Vancouver: Raincoast Books, 2000.

———. *Harry Potter and the Prisoner of Azkaban.* Vancouver: Raincoast Books, 1999.

Rutherford, Andrew. *The Literature of War: Five Studies in Heroic Virtue.* New York: Barnes & Noble, 1978.

Sartre, Jean-Paul. *Anti-Semite and Jew,* trans. George J. Becker. New York: Shocken Books, 1948.

———. *Being and Nothingness,* trans. and intro. Hazel Barnes. New York: Washington Square Books, 1956.

———. *Huis Clos/Les Mouches.* 1947. Paris: Folio, 1980.

———. *Le Mur.* Paris: Gallimard, 1958.

———. *Situations 3.* Paris: Gallimard, 1949.

Sauerberg, Lars Ole. *Secret Agents in Fiction: Ian Fleming, John le Carré and Len Deighton*. London: Macmillan, 1984.

Saussure, Ferdinand de. *Course in General Linguistics*, ed. Charles Bally, Albert Sechehaye, and Albert Riedlinger, trans. and intro. Wade Baskin. New York: McGraw-Hill, 1966.

Schwab, Ulrike. "Authenticity and Ethics in the Film *The Third Man*." *Literature-Film Quarterly* 28:1 (2000): 2–6.

Schwarz, Daniel. *Rereading Conrad*. Columbia: University of Missouri Press, 2001.

Scott, Walter. *The Bride of Lammermoor*. 1819. London: Dent, 1983.

Sedgwick, Eve Kosofsky. *Between Men: English Literature and Male Homosocial Desire*. New York: Columbia University Press, 1985.

———. *Epistemology of the Closet*. Berkeley: University of California Press, 1990.

———. *Tendencies*. Durham: Duke University Press, 1993.

Seife, Charles. *Zero: The Biography of a Dangerous Idea*. New York: Penguin, 2000.

Sharrock, Roger. *Saints, Sinners and Comedians: The Novels of Graham Greene*. Notre Dame: University of Notre Dame Press, 1984.

Shelden, Michael. *Graham Greene: The Man Within*. London: Heinemann, 1994.

Sheridan, Alan. *André Gide: A Life in the Present*. Cambridge: Harvard University Press, 1999.

Sherry, Norman. *The Life of Graham Greene. Volume 1: 1904–1939*. New York: Viking, 1989.

Silver, Brenda. "Woman as Agent: The Case of le Carré's *The Little Drummer Girl*." *Contemporary Literature* 28.1 (1987): 14–40.

Sinfield, Alan. *Literature, Politics and Culture in Postwar Britain*. Oxford: Basil Blackwell, 1989.

Singh, Simon. *The Code Book: The Evolution of Secrecy from Mary Queen of Scots to Quantum Cryptography*. New York: Doubleday, 1999.

Six Million Dollar Man. Perf. Lee Majors, Richard Anderson. ABC, 1974–78.

Slethaug, Gordon. "Floating Signifiers in John Barth's *Sabbatical*." *Modern Fiction Studies* 33.4 (winter 1987): 647–55.

Smith, David R. "The Hidden Narrative: The K in Conrad." In *Joseph Conrad's 'Under Western Eyes': Beginnings, Revisions, Final Forms*, ed. David R. Smith. Hamden, Conn.: Archon Books, 1991. 39–81.

Smith, Paul. "The Will to Allegory in Postmodernism." *Dalhousie Review* 62.1 (1982): 105–22.

Smith, Stevie. *Novel On Yellow Paper, or Work it Out For Yourself*. London: Jonathan Cape, 1936.

Sommer, Fred. "Anthony Blunt and Guy Burgess, Gay Spies." *Journal of Homosexuality* 29.4 (winter 1995): 273–93.

Sorrow and the Pity. Dir. Marcel Ophuls. Image Entertainment, 1971.

Spender, Stephen. *The Thirties and After*. London: Macmillan, 1978.

Stafford, David. "John Buchan's Tales of Espionage: A Popular Archive of British History." *Canadian Journal of History* 18.1 (April 1983): 1–21.

———. "Spies and Gentlemen: The Birth of the British Spy Novel, 1893–1914." *Victorian Studies* 24.4 (summer 1981): 489–509.

———. *The Silent Game: The Real World of Imaginary Spies.* Toronto: University of Toronto Press, 1988.

Stallybrass, Peter, and Allon White. *The Politics and Poetics of Transgression.* Ithaca: Cornell University Press, 1986.

Stamberg, Susan. "Cautionary Tales." Interview with Joan Didion. National Public Radio, April 4, 1977. Friedman 22–28.

States, Bert O. "Dirty Dreams." *Salmagundi* 126/127 (2000): 173–88.

Steiner, George. *George Steiner: A Reader.* New York: Oxford University Press, 1984.

Stevenson, Randall. *The British Novel Since the Thirties: An Introduction.* Athens: University of Georgia Press, 1986.

Stevenson, Robert Louis. *Treasure Island,* ed. Emma Letley. 1883. Oxford: Oxford University Press, 1985.

Stewart, Garrett. *Death Sentences: Styles of Dying in British Fiction.* Cambridge: Harvard University Press, 1984.

Stout, Janis P. *Through the Window, Out the Door: Women's Narratives of Departure, from Austin and Cather to Tyler, Morrison, and Didion.* Tuscaloosa: University of Alabama Press, 1998.

Swift, Jonathan. *Journal to Stella.* Vol. 1. Ed. Harold Williams. Oxford: Oxford University Press, 1948.

Szittya, Penn R. "Metafiction: The Double Narration in *Under Western Eyes.*" *ELH* 48.4 (winter 1981): 817–40.

Tager, Michael. "The Political Vision of Joan Didion's *Democracy.*" *Critique* 31.3 (spring 1990): 173–84.

Terminator. Dir. James Cameron. Perf. Arnold Schwarzenegger, Michael Biehn, Linda Hamilton. HBO/Orion Pictures, 1984.

Terminator 2: Judgment Day. Dir. James Cameron. Perf. Arnold Schwarzenegger, Linda Hamilton, Edward Furlong. TriStar Pictures, 1991.

Teskey, Gordon. *Allegory and Violence.* Ithaca: Cornell University Press, 1996.

39 Steps. Dir. Alfred Hitchcock. Perf. Robert Donat, Madeleine Carroll, Peggy Ashcroft. Gaumont-British Pictures, 1935.

Thomas, Brian. *An Underground Fate: The Idiom of Romance in the Later Novels of Graham Greene.* Athens: University of Georgia Press, 1988.

Three Days of the Condor. Dir. Stanley Pollock. Perf. Robert Redford, Faye Dunaway, Cliff Robertson, Max von Sydow. Adapted from James Grady, *Six Days of the Condor.* Paramount Pictures, 1975.

Tompkins, Jane P. "Introduction." *Reader-Response Criticism: From Formalism to Post-Structuralism,* ed. Jane P. Tompkins. Baltimore: Johns Hopkins University Press, 1980.

Trotter, David. "Introduction." *The Riddle of the Sands* by Erskine Childers. 1903. Oxford: Oxford University Press, 1998.

———. "The Politics of Adventure in the Early British Spy Novel." Wark, *Spy Fiction, Spy Films and Real Intelligence* 30–54.

True Lies. Dir. James Cameron. Perf. Arnold Schwarzenegger, Jamie Lee Curtis. Twentieth Century Fox, 1994.

Uris, Leon. *Mila 18.* New York: Doubleday, 1961.

Van Wert, William F. "Narrative Structure in *The Third Man.*" *Literature-Film Quarterly* 2 (1974): 341–46.

Vidal, Gore. *Palimpsest: A Memoir.* New York: Random House, 1995.

Walkiewicz, E. P. *John Barth.* Boston: Twayne Publishers, 1986.

Walton, Kendall L. "Fearing Fictions." *Journal of Philosophy* 75.1 (Jan. 1978): 5–27.

Wark, Wesley K., ed. *Intelligence and National Security. Special Issue on Espionage: Past, Present, Future?* 8.3 (July 1993). London: Frank Cass, 1993.

———. *Spy Fiction, Spy Films and Real Intelligence.* London: Frank Cass, 1991.

Watson, Barbara Bellow. "Variations on an Enigma: Elizabeth Bowen's War Novel." Bloom 81–101.

Weir, John. "American Passions." Rev. of *The Last Thing He Wanted,* by Joan Didion. *New Yorker* (Sept. 16, 1996): 95–96.

West, W. J. *The Quest for Graham Greene.* London: Weidenfeld & Nicolson, 1997.

West, Rebecca. *The Meaning of Treason.* New York: Viking, 1947.

Whitaker, Reg, and Gary Marcuse. *Cold War Canada: The Making of a National Insecurity State, 1945–1957.* Toronto: University of Toronto Press, 1994.

White, Andrea. *Joseph Conrad and the Adventure Tradition: Constructing and Deconstructing the Imperial Subject.* Cambridge: Cambridge University Press, 1993.

Whitemore, Hugh. *Breaking the Code.* New York: Samuel French, 1987.

Wilde, Oscar. *Complete Works,* intro. Vyvyan Holland. New York: Perennial, 1989.

Williams, Raymond. *The English Novel: From Dickens to Lawence.* 1975. London: Hogarth Press, 1984.

Wilson, Angus. *Anglo-Saxon Attitudes.* 1956. London: Penguin, 1958.

Wolfe, Peter. *Corridors of Deceit: The World of John le Carré.* Bowling Green: Bowling Green State University Popular Press, 1987.

Wood, Michael. "The American Way of Walking Out." Rev. of *The Last Thing He Wanted,* by Joan Didion. *New York Times Book Review.* (Sept. 8, 1996), 10.

Woolf, Virginia. *Between the Acts.* 1941. New York: Harcourt Brace Jovanovich, 1969.

———. *The Diary of Virginia Woolf 1936–1941.* Vol. 5. Ed. Anne Olivier Bell and Andrew McNeillie. San Diego and New York: Harvest/Harcourt Brace Jovanovich, 1984.

———. *The Essays of Virginia Woolf, 1991–1924.* Vol. 3. Ed. Andrew McNeillie. New York: Harcourt Brace Jovanovich, 1988.

———. "London in War." Monk's House Papers A 20:5, University of Sussex Library.

Wright, Peter. *Spycatcher: The Candid Autobiography of a Senior Intelligence Officer.* Toronto: Stoddart, 1987.

Wyatt-Brown, Anne M. *Barbara Pym: A Critical Biography.* Columbia: University of Missouri Press, 1992.

Yeats, William Butler. *Collected Poems.* London: Macmillan, 1982.

Yúdice, George. "Marginality and the Ethics of Survival." *Universal Abandon? The Politics of Postmodernism*, ed. Andrew Ross. Minneapolis: University of Minnesota Press, 1988. 214–36.

Žižek, Slavoj. *The Plague of Fantasies.* London: Verso, 1997.

Zwerdling, Alex. *Orwell and the Left.* New Haven: Yale University Press, 1974.

INDEX

academics, 13, 57–58, 72, 219, 222, 224–26

accents, 12–13, 31, 72, 95, 144

acting, xiv, 22–23, 39, 68, 77, 94, 106, 115–16, 136, 152, 178, 202–03, 214–18, 223

action, 22, 71–73, 85, 98, 112–16, 134–35, 157–62, 215–18, 232, 276

Acton, Harold, 196

airplanes, 16–17, 263–65, 270

allegory, 25, 51, 132, 166–67, 179–86, 219, 296

Althusser, Louis, 21, 31, 88, 278–79

American Psychiatric Association, 187

Amery, John, 159

anger, 8–9, 99, 182–84

Angry Young Men, 182

anti-Semitism, 52, 111, 159–60, 167, 295–96

apocalypse, 128–29, 180, 239–40, 244, 257

Aristotle, 45, 67–68, 158, 159, 161, 237

Arletty, 141

Ashenden (Somerset Maugham), 67–68, 188

assassination, 3–4, 6, 9, 22, 85–87, 99, 251, 262, 265, 284–85

Auden, W. H., 137, 205–07, 209, 216, 261, 298

The Avengers, xiv, 129

Baltimore Sun, 243, 299

Batman and Robin, 129

Berlin Wall, xv, 18, 166, 169, 170, 174, 177–78, 180, 183–86, 204

betrayal, 73, 78, 85–88, 93, 100, 107–08, 121, 137, 139–43, 171, 203–04, 222–25

The Big Lift, 122

blackmail, 193, 206

Blake, William, 227, 298

Bletchley Park, 49, 58, 73, 195

Blitz, 122, 127, 140, 146–47, 154–57, 175, 218

Blunt, Anthony, 191, 196–97, 224, 296–97, 298

bodies, 8–10, 11–17, 28–29, 32–33, 36, 46–47, 94, 97, 118–19, 126, 181, 232, 247, 283, 293

Bond, James. *See* James Bond

boredom, 20–31, 155, 206–07, 276

Bourne Identity (Robert Ludlum), 3–10, 12, 15–19, 262, 276, 285, 290–91

Brecht, Bertolt, 46